MARTINI

A~Z

of
Fencing

E.D.Morton

With a Foreword by Nick Halsted,
President of the A.F.A.

Macdonald
Queen Anne Press

© Antler Books Ltd
First published in Great Britain by
Queen Anne Press
a division of Macdonald & Co
(Publishers) Ltd
Greater London House,
London NW1 7QX

Produced by John Stidolph
Editor Nicki Harris
Assistant Editor Peter Fitzmaurice
Designed by Peter Hedges

British Library Cataloguing in Publication Data

Morton, E.D.
    Martini A-Z of Fencing.
    1. Fencing—Dictionaries
    I. Title
    796.8'6'0321   GV1143.2

ISBN 0–356–154394

Typesetting and origination by Falcon Graphic Art Ltd
Jacket origination by BBE Colour Ltd
Printed by Purnell Book Production Ltd

Foreword

Fencing is a unique and fascinating sport. It is practised today by supreme athletes whose swift, intricate movements with their foils, épées and sabres are single-mindedly aimed at penetrating the defences of the opponent whilst protecting their own targets. Valid touches are recorded audibly and visibly on sophisticated electrical apparatus. As a modern sport, it is one of the most complete, demanding both physical and mental agility combined with the mastery of tactics and guile.

The richness of its history is without equal. Dating back at least to the civilisation of ancient Egypt, fencing has enjoyed a long but chequered career in the Old World. It has been associated with such pursuits as duelling, prize-fighting and military training and has attracted the interest of all classes of person ranging from the common pugilist to royalty itself.

This book, unique in its field, encapsulates the variety and history of the sport. Monarchs and statesmen vie for space in its pages with Elizabethan brawlers; Shakespeare and Ben Johnson rank alongside gold and silver medallists; trial by combat, transvestism, the *stramonzello* and the 'feinthore', all have a place. It is with pleasure that I commend this A-Z of Fencing, not just to fencers and historians, but to all those intrigued by the glamour and excitement of the sport.

Nick Halsted.
President, Amateur Fencing Association

Picture Credits

Preface

*M*y original intention was to compile an extended glossary, incorporating as many as possible of the technical terms of the three great historical schools of swordsmanship; Italian, Spanish and French. I decided further to include brief notes on famous masters of the past and at least a few on the distinguished fencers of this century. From this it was but a step to the legendary swordsmen of fiction and those more generalised entries on historical institutions and personages which I hope may be of some interest apart from their links with fencing and swordsmanship.

Little reference is made to the Middle Ages, it being thought best to make the starting-point the sixteenth century, when the first generation of masters appeared professing to analyse and teach the art of swordsmanship on an allegedly scientific basis. A few exceptions from an earlier period owe their inclusion either to their particular interest or the likelihood of references to them being found in general or historical reading.

I am well aware that some of the inclusions, not less than the topics or personalities omitted, will appear to be arbitrary; to that charge I can but plead the vagaries of personal taste and the difficulty, in some cases, of obtaining the necessary information. It must further be emphasised that this work was never intended to be an exhaustive directory of internationals, or a comprehensive list of championship winners, which may temper the indignation of those who do not find the name of their favourite fencing master or youthful hero. It is to be doubted if any book on fencing could be truly encyclopaedic; considerations of time alone would prove to be an insuperable obstacle, while the exigencies of publication precluded any further additions after the date of penning this apologia.

E.D. Morton

Acknowledgements: I must express my grateful thanks to all who have provided me with information, readily answered my queries, or loaned illustrations for copying, in particular, Mr M. Fare, editor of *The Sword*, who also gave much useful and patient advice, while Mr N. Halsted, president of the A.F.A., most kindly consented to write a foreword. Others who readily assisted were Mr P. Jacobs, the international fencer, Signor Mangiarotti, the famous Italian swordsman, Mr Raymond Paul of Léon Paul Equipment Co., Mr J. Arlett of the Wilkinson Sword Company, Professor R. Goodall, Professor Moldovanyi, and Mr E. Kelman, B.A.F. Ladies supplying information and reminiscences are Mesdames Joan Pienne, Hilary Philbin and Marjorie Jacques, while the ladies of the Chorleywood library, in particular Miss Edith Beech, were tireless in unearthing books.

I am also much in the debt of my old master, Professor A.T. Simmonds, with whom I had discussions on some of the technical points which can only be described as animated and which were finally settled by means of practical demonstration and experiment with a pair of rulers or pencils. Nor would this section be complete without mention of my typist-in-chief, Mrs R. Puliston, and her accurate and quite beautiful work.

Above all, I must pay tribute to Martini and Rossi and their representative, Mr D. Rutherford. Their encouragement of sport in general and fencing in particular is well known and without their invaluable support this volume might never have appeared before the public.

A.F.A. (See Amateur Fencing Association.)

Abduction, (U.S.). A movement of the sword-arm away from the central line of the body.

Académie d'Armes Internationale. The world governing body of professional fencing.

Academy. The term generally used for an association of fencing masters; there may or may not be a material head quarters. The objects of such academies are usually to assert minimum qualifications for new entrants, to examine and confer grades of proficiency on their members and in general to safeguard the interests and to maintain the standards of all those concerned with the teaching of fencing. Some of the more famous academies are listed below.

Academy of Arms, Paris. Its full title was the *Compagnie des Maîtres en fait d'Armes des Académies du Roi en la Ville et Faubourg de Paris.* Originally formed in the reign of Charles IX (1560–74), it was officially recognised and patronised by Henry III, Henry IV, and Louis XIII. Subsequently, Louis XIV granted the association its coat of arms and conferred patents of nobility on six prominent masters nominated by their colleagues, vacancies caused by death to be filled by the next most senior member.

Membership of the academy was only granted after six years training under a recognised master of that body, and a creditable display in bouts with at least three existing members. The teaching of fencing throughout the kingdom was a monopoly confined to those who had trained under some master of the academy.

The long and distinguished history of the corporation ended with its

Camillo Agrippa, 1553.

dissolution during the ill-starred and destructive revolution of 1789.

Academy, Brussels. The association of fencing masters of the Netherlands during the sixteenth and seventeenth centuries, when this area of Europe was included in the Spanish Empire. Regular fencing competitions were held at which aspiring masters had to perform creditably before being authorised to teach.

Academy of Fencing, British. A statute of Edward I in 1285 actually forbade the teaching of fencing within the City of London, presumably from fear of the brawls and disorder that might result; it was not until 1540 that a Corporation of Masters of the Science of Defence was established under the patronage of Henry VIII. It was granted a coat of arms (*Gules*, a sword *pendant argent*) and the valuable privilege of enjoying the sole right of teaching throughout His Majesty's domains. Any unauthorised master presuming to give instruction was liable to a

term of imprisonment.

The monopoly lapsed with Henry VIII's death, but seems to have been renewed under James I, only to lapse again with the passing of the Monopolies Act of 1624. The reputation of masters and professors declined disastrously during the Restoration period, when many of those laying claim to their titles were little more than professional show-men, deficient in knowledge and skill, and indulging in public exhibitions and challenge matches of a crude and often brutal character. Although they were not lacking masters in this country in the eighteenth and nineteenth century, the general decline of fencing in that era was signalised by the virtual absence of any governing body, whether for professional teachers or anybody else.

However, in 1931 Professor Felix Gravé took the lead in the establishment of the British Academy of Fencing Masters. The organisation languished during the Second World War, but was revived under its present title in 1949 at the instigation of Mr C.-L. de Beaumont and Professor Roger Crosnier. The first president was Professor Léon Bertrand.

Academy of Strasboug. The famous fortress town and episcopal see of Strasbourg was annexed by the French in 1681, which marked the peak of Louis XIV's policy of territorial aggrandisement. The fencing establishment, which had been in the hands of the Marxbruder (q.v.), was re-named the Academy of Strasbourg, and reorganised on French lines, French influence being then at its height in swordsmanship, as in every other branch of human activity.

Academy of Toulouse. The Academy of Languedoc, the leading association in the south of France under the *Ancien Régime*, was better known by this name. The celebrated Labat family was long connected with it.

Acceleration. The tendency in modern foil fencing is to close the distance by means of a rapid advance, accompanied by sundry beats and pressures on the opponent's blade. These preparations are most effective if the footwork is steadily accelerated, starting with a smooth, insidious motion and ending with an increasingly rapid series of steps and *balestras*.

Acfield, D.L. An international sabreur, Cambridge cricket blue and fencing half-blue, he won the British Sabre Championships in four successive years (1969–72). It is quite possible that his record might have been even more impressive, had he not decided to concentrate on cricket as Essex's off-spin bowler; to the end of 1983 he had taken 830 wickets in first-class cricket at an average of 27.52. With the bat, he enjoyed less success, his average remaining in single figures. In this era of intense specialisation it is accepted that it is no longer possible to maintain the highest standard at more than one game; nevertheless, it is matter for surprise that there is no previous parallel for Acfield's dual success, considering that cricket and fencing, above all other activities, combine the most complex and subtle technique with the widest historical and literary associations.

Acquired Parry. The circular or counter parry.

Acrobatic Lunge. The unarmed hand is placed on the ground, supporting the body, while the rear foot is slid back as far as possible. (Cp. Passata Sotto.)

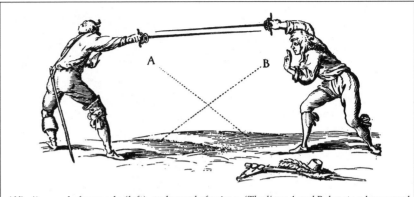

Alfieri's guard of seconde *(left), and guard of* prime. *(The lines A and B denote a low guard similar to that of modern* seconde.*)*

Actor's Parry. The parry of *seconde.* Executed with an exaggeratedly wide sweeping action, somewhat reminiscent of the old universal parry (q.v.), it is much favoured by the protagonists in stage and screen duels, because of its spectacular appearance.

Advanced Coach. The grade in the Amateur Fencing Association's scale of coaching awards which is of higher status than that of coach (formerly leader). A taxing examination in all three weapons must be passed, the equivalent of the provost's examination in the British Academy; successful candidates may, if they so desire, join the professional body with provost rank without undergoing any further test.

Affondo, (It.). The lunge.

After-Cut. Beke and Polgar's terms for the riposte.

Agente, (It.). On the attack.

Agrippa, Camillo. A famous Milanese master of the sixteenth century, best known for having stressed the value of the thrust as opposed to the cut, and simplifying the bewildering number of guards advocated by the different masters. He recommended the use of only four guards, which correspond roughly to our *prime, seconde, tierce,* and a low *quarte.*

Aids. The second, third and fourth fingers of the sword-hand. They assist or aid the thumb and forefingers (the manipulators) and are also known as the 'last fingers'.

Al Distacco. An offensive action executed without contact with the opponent's blade.

Alfieri, Francesco. A seventeenth-century master of the Academy of Padua who modelled himself on Capo Ferro. Author of *La Scherma* (1640), he also produced work on the pike and the two-handed sword (1653).

Alfred Hutton Memorial Challenge Cup. It was presented in 1913 by Mr A. Miller-Hallett for an international Ladies' Individual Foil Competition. Having disappeared during the Second World War, the cup was replaced in 1946 by the C.-L. de Beaumont Cup.

All-England Fencing Club. The club was founded in 1933 with the object of improving overall fencing standards by means of practices, demonstrations, matches, and by providing judges for competitions at clubs, schools and universities throughout the country. Membership was at first limited to male internationals, but ladies were admitted in 1937.

Amateur Fencers League. The controlling body of fencing in the United States, founded in 1891.

Amateur Fencing Association. The widespread growth of enthusiasm for all forms of sport led the Amateur Gymnastic Association to establish a Fencing Branch Committee in 1895. The first set of rules was adopted in 1896 and at the same time the association changed its name to the Amateur Gymnastic and Fencing Association. In 1902 the fencing element separated from the parent body and established the Amateur Fencing Association. After many years of occupying the premises off Hanover Square, subterranean, but full of character, the association moved to the new de Beaumont Centre at West Kensington, spacious indeed, but strangely bleak and anonymous.

Amateur Gymnastic Association. The parent body of the Amateur Fencing Association, founded in London, in 1888. A fencing branch committee was formed in 1895 and in the following year the association's name was changed to the Amateur Gymnastic and Fencing Association. The fencing members, however, increasingly dissatisfied with the conduct of their affairs and the organisation of the association, resolved upon secession and in 1902 founded the present Amateur Fencing Association.

The first A.F.A. foil championship. Montgomerie is for once defeated by Evan James (illustration by F.H. Townsend).

Amateur-Professors Competitions. These are organised for each of the three weapons by the Foil, Sabre and Epée Clubs, respectively, in conjunction with the British Academy of Fencing; amateurs and professionals alike taking part.

Amberg, M.J. The leading British sabreur in the middle and late fifties. Sabre Champion in 1957-8-9, he was runner-up in 1953 and 1963. He won the Corble Cup in 1953 and 1958 and the Cole Cup in 1954, besides being twice runner-up for both these trophies.

Anderson, Professor R.J.G. He started his fencing as an amateur while serving with the Royal Marines, reaching the rank of Colour Sergeant before quitting the service. He won the Corble Cup (sabre) in 1951-2-3, represented England in the Empire Games of 1950, and Great Britain at the World Championships of 1950 and 1953 and the Olympics of 1948 and 1952. However, it was as a professional that he became most widely known, first as an assistant to Professor Roger Crosnier, the first national coach, and then as Crosnier's successor in that position. He was instrumental in introducing the group system of training and coaching devised by his former master to innumerable fencers throughout the length and breadth of the country. He also saw fit to amend and modify it from time to time, seeking to render it more flexible and more closely adjusted to the individual fencer's capacity. No doubt these were valuable developments in a scheme intended to impart as much instruction as possible to students limited in time and further handicapped by a shortage of qualified masters. He was himself a spectacular sabreur and has delighted many an audience with his skill in exhibition bouts, film duels and television programmes.

Andrieux, Chevalier d'. One of the most insatiable of duellists in that hey-day of duelling, the reign of Louis XIII. He was supposed to have despatched seventy-two men.

Anelace. A very broad dagger, generally less than two feet long.

Angelo, House of. A celebrated family of fencing masters, originating in Italy in the eighteenth century and removing, via Paris, to this country where they opened the London salle which, during the Victorian era, developed into an English institution.

The founder of the dynasty, Domenico Angelo Malevolti Tremamondo, who was also an expert rider on the 'high horse' found in the *Manège Royale* at Versailles and the Spanish Riding School in Vienna, adopted

A bout at Angelo's: Henry Angelo attacks while his father, Domenico, (holding foils) watches with a critical eye (illustration by Rowlandson).

the simple name Angelo on arrival in this country. After proving his ability in a match with one Dr Keyes, an Irish physician, he established his salle in Carlisle Street (1763). The same year, he published his monumental work, the *Ecole des Armes*, for long regarded as the ultimate authority on fencing and enjoying such high esteem that it was reproduced verbatim under the heading *Escrime* in the French *Encylopédie*, greatly to the disgust of the masters and pundits of the *Académie du Roi*, who felt themselves seriously slighted. Angelo was also appointed fencing master to the sons of the Prince of Wales and was reported to have made £4,000 a year by teaching fencing alone, apart from whatever he earned by his riding lessons. He eventually relinquished the academy to his son Harry, finding sufficient occupation in the direction of the fencing at Eton, where his son had been at school.

His daughter Sophia was a dame, and the famous house over which she had presided still bears the family name in testimony to the long connection.

The second Angelo transferred the academy to the Opera House in the Haymarket, the scene of many well-publicised bouts between the leading English masters and their counter-parts from abroad. When this building was destroyed by fire in 1789, the establishment moved again, this time to Old Bond Street. During the long wars against the French revolutionaries and Bonaparte, the light cavalry played an important part; Angelo devised a system of swordsmanship based on the curved cavalry sabre originally associated especially with the Hungarian hussars, but copied by most of the Western nations. His scheme was officially adopted by the British Army and to further his own connection with a City Volunteer

regiment, he transferred his own activities to an address in the City, leaving the Bond Street premises in the hands of his second son, Henry.

The latter, the third Angelo, was in due course succeeded by his own son, Henry Charles. Upon his death, the academy, by now in St James's Street, was continued by William McTurk, who had been his chief assistant. It flourished there until the very end of Victoria's reign when trouble arose over the renewal of the lease and the famous establishment ceased to exist.

Angelo, William Henry was the youngest son of Harry Angelo. (See above.) After abandoning his own unsuccessful salle at Oxford, he became manager of the St James's Street establishment, where he was known as 'Old William'. According to Aylward, an injury obliged him to fence with his foil strapped to his hand, in the Italian fashion.

Angolazione, (It.). Angulation.

Angulation. To hit the opponent with the weapon held at an angle to one's sword-arm, instead of in direct prolongation of it. Such angulation of a point attack can be upwards, downwards, or lateral and is effected by means of a 'breaking of the wrist' and naturally makes it more difficult for the defender to form an effective parry. Even if some blade contact is made, the attacking point will still often arrive on target. Angulation is very frequently employed when attacking the wrist at épée.

Anneau. A ring placed in front of the *quillons* (q.v.) to protect the forefinger, following the old custom of passing it over the *quillons* in order to exert better control of the weapon.

Annelets. La Tousche's term for the *pas d'âne* rings.

Anspach, M. Paul. A distinguished Belgian fencer who was Epée Champion at the 1912 Olympics. At Geneva in 1931, he fenced a number of bouts with the epée against Mr C.-L. de Beaumont, to test the new electrical judging apparatus, and won by the narrowest of victories. During the Second World war he manfully resisted all attempts by the Nazis to dissolve the F.I.E., of which he was then president, and replace it by a European federation in conformity with Hitler's 'New Order', even though his defiance resulted in a term of imprisonment. Possibly his greatest claim to fame, however, is his collaboration in 1914 with the Marquis de Chasseloup-Laubat in the formulation of what was virtually the definitive code of rules for foil competitions, which, slightly amended and expanded in various particulars, is still in force today.

Appel. The striking of the ground with the leading foot, during, or immediately before, the execution of an attack. That this should in any way unsettle or discompose the opponent seems a fond hope, but it has the two great advantages of ensuring that the weight is not thrown on the front foot too early and that the extension of the sword-arm is fully completed before the front leg is advanced in the lunge. (A double stamp of the foot is a double *appel*.)

According to Egerton Castle, the *appel* was in nineteenth-century England termed an attack, presumably because it almost invariably accompanied an offensive action. A highly characteristic action of the Italian school (antique and modern), it was often accompanied by a loud shout.

Appuntata. The name applied by the Italians to a *remise*; or, by an extreme refinement of analysis, a stop-hit or stop-cut against the riposte. Barbasetti avers that the *appuntata* should be accompanied by a tap of the leading foot.

Aramis. One of the Three Musketeers in the celebrated romance by Dumas.

Arches or Archetti, (It.). Two thin metal bars which curve upwards from opposite edges of the guard to join the cross-bar of the Italian foil.

Arm Judges. The use of the unarmed hand and arm for defensive purposes has always been prohibited; latterly, the rule in question has been strengthened. A practice had grown up of letting the unarmed hand dangle inelegantly over parts of the target area; even though the opposing blade is not thereby intercepted, this habit at foil is now forbidden. To lighten the responsibility of the president, judges are appointed from quarter-finals onwards, at World Championships, one at each end, to advise him when the offence occurs. They may be demanded at any time. Arm judges are also employed at épée to check any attempt to parry with the unarmed hand; as is also the case at foil. It goes without saying that a hit scored in the course of such malpractice is immediately annulled, with appropriate penalties. To ensure perfect impartiality, arm judges are required to exchange positions halfway through each bout.

Army Fencing Union. It was formed in 1919 and is the governing body for fencing throughout the Army.

Arrebatar, (Span.). To cut with the whole arm, from the shoulder.

D'Artagnan. The hero of Dumas' celebrated romance *The Three Musketeers*. That the traditions and stories of the French swordsmen of the seventeenth century were by no means exaggerated is proved by the fact that the character was based on an historical personage, one Charles de Baatz, who served in the King's Musketeers, became General of Brigade and eventually fell at the siege of Maestricht (1673). A later work, the *Mémoires de M d'Artagnan* by de Sandras, was used by Dumas and his collaborator as the basis of the novel.

The fictional character and his historical counterpart both hailed from Gascony, that legendary birth place of braggarts and swashbucklers. Anecdotes about them, ever more outrageous, multiplied over the years. 'At our place, we use our Marshal's batons to kindle the kitchen fire.' 'The Louvre? It compares not unfavourably with our stables at home', and so on. What prevented such sallies from degenerating into mere presumption was a devoted readiness – even eagerness – to accept the consequences of such impudence at the point of the sword. By all accounts, the later historical novelists in no way exaggerated the readiness of the seventeenth-century French gentleman to indulge, for the merest trifles, in desperate life-and-death duels.

Ascendente, (It.). An attack delivered upwards.

Assalto, (It.). An attack.

Assault. Another word for a bout between two fencers; usually an informal one, the hits not being officially counted.

Assault Point. The deciding point when the scores are equal. (See La Belle.)

Assaut de Gala. An exhibition bout at some festivity or social function.

Athos. Another leading character in *The Three Musketeers*.

Attack. The rules state that at foil and sabre the fencer whose arm is first extended with the point or edge in line threatening his opponent's target, has the priority to attack. It is this convention which enables the president, in the event of both fencers receiving hits simultaneously, or more or less simultaneously, to identify the attacker and award the hit against his opponent. (See Conventions.)

Attack into the Attack. Is to attack the opponent as he himself is attacking, though it is very far from constituting a genuine counter-attack, a period of fencing time not being gained, nor is the opposing blade necessarily deflected as with a time-hit. The action is sometimes the last resort of fencers who doubt their ability to parry and riposte effectively, or who are confronted by one of those clumsy 'rushers' who are always at such close quarters that anything like a recognisable phrase is virtually impossible.

The attack into the attack is generally executed with a straight-thrust, with occasionally some attempt at opposition of blades; much more rarely, it incorporates some variety of *prise-de-fer*, probably a *croisé* into *octave*; in any event, it creates great problems for the president, as it follows the initial attack almost immediately.

Attack of Authority. (See Attack with Opposition.)

Attack with Opposition. Must be carefully distinguished from the foregoing. To attack with opposition is to maintain a strong controlled contact with the opponent's blade which may deflect it out of line.

Auxiliary Parry of high octave *(from Hutton).*

Attack on the Preparation. This is to attack the opponent during his preparation of attack, whether the latter be executed with footwork, bladework, or both. To be valid at foil and sabre, the attack on the preparation must gain a period of fencing time over the opponent's attack. The principle and practice of such attacks is really identical with the counter-offensive action. Strictly speaking, however, the latter or counter-attack (e.g., the stop-hit) is delivered from the on-guard position, while the attack on the preparation involves a lunge. It is to be noted that Barbasetti advocates execution with a lunge.

It does not require a very profound knowledge of fencing to perceive that the most frequent and most successful form of attack on the preparation is against the opponent's step forward, especially if he omits to accompany the latter with some action of his blade.

Attack on the Recovery. Having parried the opponent's attack, it is sometimes rewarding to delay the riposte and to wait until he has almost completed his recovery to the on-guard position. The moment when his leading foot is about to be grounded is the time when his concentration is most likely to waver, or a careless movement may inadvertently expose some part of his target. At such a juncture, a vigorous attack, driven well home, may catch him unawares. Exactly when such an action ceases to be a delayed riposte with a lunge and constitutes a fresh attack is a nicely-balanced question to be decided by the president.

Attack in Time or in Tempo. An attack delivered when the opponent is preoccupied with some feint or preparatory movement and therefore not ready to parry instantly.

Attacks. Composed, Composite, Compound, Direct, Double, Indirect, Progressive, Renewals of, Simple, Simultaneous, Varieties of. See appropriate sections.

Attacks on the Blade. There are three main varieties of the attack on the blade, all designed to prepare an attack proper, which can profit from either the opponent's blade reaction, or lack of it:

1) The beat. Executed by bringing the blade smartly into contact with the opponent's, the blades generally meeting about half-way up.

2) The pressure. A preparation very popular at one time, but whose utility has now been much reduced by the advent of the electric foil and the tendency to fence with absence of blade. By the exertion of subtle pressures of varying strength on the opposing blade, using a combination of wrist and finger play, the adversary's reaction could be sensed and timed to a nicety. The *sentiment du fer* really came into its own, and on the return of the pressure, a disengagement could often be executed

with an excellent change of success.

3) The *froissement*. A very strong sharp grazing of the opponent's blade, by means of a movement forwards and downwards and a simultaneous flexing of the wrist. The action should be distinctly audible. This preparation is almost always followed by a straight-thrust, since the intention is quite definitely to displace the adversary's blade from its existing position.

In addition to the above, certain Hungarian authorities include in attacks on the blade, the bind and the *filo*. (See *Prises-de-Fer*.)

Attacks by Interception. (See Attacks in Opposition and Time-hit, Offensive.)

Attacks in Opposition. An attack launched at the outset of the opponent's offensive action, which must necessarily involve the deflection and domination of his blade, generally by means of a *prise-de-fer* executed as a time-hit. The terminology is that of Professor Crosnier. (See Time-hit, Offensive.)

Attaco Responsivo, (It.). A counter-attack.

Attention, Position of. The initial position taken prior to the salute facing the opponent, heels together and feet at right angles. The weapon is usually held point downwards, just clear of the floor, to the front and slightly to the right of the leading foot.

Auxiliary Parries. Hutton regards the main sabre parries as *tierce* and *quarte*, protecting respectively the right and left sides of the body. In addition, he enumerates six auxiliary parries: high *octave* and *seconde*, high, central and low *prime* and St George (*quinte*). He advocates their

use only against ripostes and counter-ripostes when the hand cannot readily return to *tierce* or *quarte*. High *octave* sounds a most awkward, even contorted position, with the hilt on a level with the head and the last fingers relaxed to allow the blade to drop forward as near vertically as possible, with the edge turned to the right front.

Avancés. The *avancés* are the advanced parts of the target, e.g. the leading leg and sword-arm.

Avantage. The slight curve in the blade (both in the modern fencing weapon and the small-sword) which allows of its correct 'arching' in the classically executed hit.

Awards. The A.F.A. recognises three standards, bronze, silver and gold. Awards are made by a qualified master after a practical and theoretical examination. Metal and cloth badges in the three colours, depicting the appropriate weapon (either foil, épée or sabre) are available to successful candidates. Recently the B.A.F. introduced a similar 'Five Star' scheme, consisting of as many grades, the badges in this case inscribed with the number of stars and the Tudor roses of the Academy.

Axis or Line of Attack. This is an imaginary line down the centre of the *piste*, parallel to it and corresponding to the general direction in which each fencer will deliver his attacks.

Aylward, J.D. who died in 1966 was the author of three books, *The Small-Sword in England*, *The House of Angelo, a Dynasty of Swordsmen* and *The English Master of Arms*, all notable for much absorbing and curious scholarship nicely flavoured with an urbane irony. Mr Aylward himself

possessed, it is said, a superb library of fencing books. Apart from this, his own career as a fencer was remarkable. Initially self-taught as a boy of twelve, from some manual he had picked up, he was obliged to desist in his twenties for business reasons, but actually resumed fencing at Salle Zaaloff at the age of seventy and received his last lesson when over ninety.

Back-Edge. The back-edge of a cutting weapon is the edge of the blade nearest the swordsman, when he faces his opponent with his weapon directed towards the latter and held in the normal position. In a modern fencing sabre only the top third of the back-edge nearest the point is edged, or theoretically edged, and therefore cuts delivered with any other part of the back-edge are invalid.

Backsword. 1) The weapon used in a species of sword-play popular in the eighteenth century, especially amongst those whose social position hardly admitted of their wearing and using the small-sword. Public contests were frequently staged by professionals for money stakes. The weapon was very similar to a claymore, basket-hilted, the right edge only sharpened and the point rounded, not sharp. A graphic account of such a contest and the slashes which the competitors sustained, is given by Steele in 1712 in *The Spectator* (No 436). In the second half of the century, the popularity of the sport declined and was largely replaced by prize-fighting with the fists. Backswordsmanship lived on, however, in the slightly different form of singlestick (q.v.).

2) A seventeenth-century cavalry broadsword, with single or basket guard. The blade was flat, broad and

single-edged, which distinguished it from the more common two-edged cavalry broadsword.

Backward Lunge. An old fencing and duelling trick when the measure between the opponent has been greatly reduced and the weapons are very strongly engaged near the guards; by extending the rear leg backwards and lowering the left arm, the lunge position is assumed and room is made for a disengagement or other offensive action. Szabo regards the practice as obsolete, but there would seem to be a strong case for teaching it as a means of extricating oneself from the close-quarter fencing so often imposed by the modern opponent.

Bacon, Francis, Baron Verulam and Viscount St Alban's. Lord Chancellor of James I in 1618, courtier, philosopher, essayist and scientist, and by some still reputed to be the real author of Shakespeare's plays. He was, like many legal men, strongly against duelling and threatened to prosecute not merely the principals and seconds, even if they met overseas, but all who gave or accepted a challenge, whether or not they actually appeared on the ground.

Balestra. A short jump forward, used as a preparation of attack (q.v.). The toes of the front foot are raised, the leading heel is cleared of the ground and the sole meets the floor with a considerable stamp some eighteen inches or two feet further forward. Simultaneously, the rear foot, just clear of the ground, is brought forward a corresponding distance. It is important to keep the legs bent throughout, for if the knees should be straightened, it is impossible to follow the *balestra* with an immediate lunge. Similarly, it is essential that on the completion of the action,

An example of a true Basket-Hilt.

the weight should still be distributed equally between both feet; should the centre of gravity have been allowed to come too far forward, with the rear foot already leaving the ground, the attack will inevitably lose half its drive and penetration. (See also False Balestra.)

Balogh, Bela. A famous Hungarian sabre master who toured Europe in the 1950s, giving demonstrations with his equally famous pupil, Mikla Bela. They fought spectacular exhibition bouts to a musical accompaniment.

Barbasetti, Luigi. He was the pupil of the great Italian master Radaelli. In 1894 he went to Vienna to take charge of the Austro-Hungarian Central Fencing School. Favouring the Italian sabre style, i.e., the delivery of cuts from the elbow by the use of the forearm, his system replaced that of Keresztessy, who had preferred the wrist-cut.

In *The Art of the Foil*, a work of considerable scholarship and imagination, apart from its practical

value, Barbasetti expounds, with total dedication and conviction, and no little relish, the technique of the neo-Italian school; that is, the classical French school adapted and modified to suit the Italian genius. Nothing is too subtle; the most complex examples of *contretemps* are for him not only feasible, but in themselves admirable as exemplifying the ultimate development of the art.

Barrage. A method of classifying competitors in order of merit when their placings in a pool are absolutely equal, not just on victories gained, but even after the complex procedure enjoined by Article 521 has been applied. For promotion from one pool to another, those concerned must fight a 'barrage' round. In the highly unlikely event of the issue still being undecided even after the Indices (q.v.) have been taken into consideration, a further barrage must be fought. In a final pool, the first place only is decided, if necessary, by a barrage. Only in the Olympic Games, where the second and third places must be established for the award of medals, will there be further barrages for these positions.

Basic Position. In Hungarian theory, it is similar to the position of attention (q.v.). The heels are touching each other, the feet are at right angles, the leading foot pointing ahead, and the trunk half-turned towards the fencer's front. In England it is usually the normal on-guard position.

Basket-Hilt. The triangular-shaped guard, entirely covering the hand, either solid or formed of interlaced metal strips, and associated particularly with the military sword. The guard of the modern sabre, albeit perfectly smooth and unpierced, is derived from this type. The singlestick and backsword of the eighteenth and nineteenth centuries had guards of this sort actually made from wickerwork, so that in these cases the name was really justified.

Bastard. A short, thick sword, in use in the sixteenth century. It was not considered proper for duelling and a second raised strong objection to its use by the Baron des Guerres in his duel with the Lord of Fendilles, but he was over-ruled. According to J.D. Aylward, the name applied also to the 'hand-and-a-half' sword.

Battavile. A feint to distract the opponent's attention while his weapon is seized; a curious term found only in an anonymous M.S. mentioned in Aylward's *The English Master of Arms.* (See also Feinthore, Gazee, Traverse, Vouclousant.)

Battement. The beat.

Battery. The somewhat grandiloquent term used by Sir John Hope for beating with the *foible* of the weapon upon the adversary's *foible*; whereas, in his terminology, the beat proper was executed with *forte* against *foible*.

Battle-Axe Grip. A term contemptuously applied to a grip where the thumb does not lie flat along the foil handle, but where the latter runs more or less diagonally across the palm, with the fingers wrapped round it as would be the case in gripping an axe handle.

Battre de Main. To parry with the hand.

Battuta, (It.). The beat.

Battute. According to Herman Freiherr von Friesen in his notes to *Hamlet* (Works of William Shakespeare,

Baptiste Bertrand (portrait by François Burnary).

ed. Irving and Marshall), this was a very strong downward beat on the opponent's blade, preparatory to disarming him. The rest of the note, dealing with the exchange of rapiers in the Hamlet-Laertes duel (Act V Sc. ii) is totally obscure and the commentator at one stage seems to be uncertain whether he is referring to the rapiers themselves or the daggers which are wielded in the left hand. The good Teuton admits that he is 'depending on the memory of his schooldays' which, if the passage in question is any guide, had served him none too well.

Bavette. (See Bib.)

Bavin. An ashstick, apparently used as a singlestick in some Elizabethan fencing schools.

Beat. A preparation of attack (q.v.). As the name suggests, the execu-

tant's blade is brought smartly into contact with that of his opponent, thus knocking it aside. There are several varieties of the beat:

1) Answering beat. (See Return Beat.)

2) Change beat. To pass the blade under the opponent's blade and deliver the beat in the opposite line. (*Over* the blade in the low line.)

3) Circular beat. The term applied by the Hungarian Master Imre Vass to a change beat; the distinction he makes is that the change beat proper must start from an actual engagement of the blades.

4) Counter-beat. A term used for the return beat. Barbasetti, on the other hand, says it is a change beat.

5) Direct or Simple beat. A beat delivered without any change in the relative position of the blades.

6) Double beat. Two beats delivered in quick succession on the same side of the opponent's blade.

7) Double change beat. A change beat having been executed, the blade is again brought underneath the opponent's (over in the low line) and a second beat is delivered from the original side.

8) False beat. A beat employed as a feint (Hutton), probably with the object of deceiving the return beat with a disengagement or parrying and riposting if the opponent counter-attacks.

9) Reconnaissance beat. Usually delivered with the *foible* of the weapon, in order to keep at a safer distance, the intention is simply to observe the opponent's reactions, or lack of them. Then, subsequently, another beat followed by the appropriate form of attack will be executed. All this, needless to say, rests on the somewhat optimistic assumption that the opponent will react in identical fashion on the second occasion.

10) Return beat. A beat executed in immediate reply to the opponent's

beat. It may be in the form of a change beat. At foil and sabre, the priority of attack, lost when the opponent made his beat, is thus regained.

11) Reverse beat. (See Change Beat.) At sabre, a beat with the back-edge.

12) Semi-circular beat. Vass's term for a beat executed in a low line by a blade travelling diagonally across the target, or vice versa.

Beat Parry. This form of parry deflects the opponent's blade by administering to it a sharp beat, as opposed to the whole arm, hand and blade moving across to close completely the threatened line. The beat parry is not infrequently used by the épéeist, who desires to parry *quarte* without exposing the outer arm by adopting the full *quarte* position and so employs this method, which allows him to keep his sword-hand well out to the right.

Beaumont, C.- L. de. The celebrated international fencer, British captain before the Second World War, Cambridge half-blue and sometime president of the Amateur Fencing Association, after whom the present A.F.A. headquarters at West Kensington, the de Beaumont Centre, are named. Charles de Beaumont represented his country at épée and sabre, but his greatest enthusiasm was for the former weapon, with which he achieved most success. He was British Épée Champion in 1936-7-8 and again in 1953. He was runner-up in 1947 and third in 1935 and 1948. He was Miller-Hallett winner on six occasions (1930-31-32, 1934-5, 1938) and second in 1929 and 1936. It was he who brought Professor Crosnier to this country in the late forties and was instrumental in pressing the latter's National Training Scheme and, indeed, the needs and potentialities of fencing as a whole, on the Central

Sir Richard Burton as maître d'armes (portrait by Letchford, 1882).

Council for Physical Education. Charles de Beaumont devoted himself wholeheartedly to the development and popularisation of fencing and for years never failed to attend the last day of the coaches' examinations held under the auspices of the A.F.A.

Beehive. The name given to the earlier form of head attached to the electric foil; it was cone shaped, tapering to a point. It was banned on safety grounds, being replaced by the present cylindrically-shaped head.

Beke, Z. This Hungarian master will always be associated with his colleague, J. Polgar, with whom he collaborated in compiling the *Methodology of Sabre Fencing* (1963), a massively analytical work which contains some 1500 exercises and the

corresponding corrections of their common faults – a feature unusual at that time. The two of them developed, systematised and codified the classic Hungarian wrist-finger technique which had carried all before it when it was first exhibited at the London Olympics of 1908. It is generally agreed that the *Methodology* did for Hungarian sabre what Crosnier's equally famous work did for the foil; if proof were needed, Dr Geno Fuchs, Dr Sandor Posta, Odon Tersztyanski, Gyorgy Piller, Endre Kabos, Aladar Gerevitch, Pal Kovacs, Rudolf Karpati, who were all World Champions, were also one and all the products and ornaments of the system.

Bela, Mikla. (See Balogh.)

Bell. A name for the guard of the épée; derived not only from its shape, but possibly from the quite musical note often emitted when it is struck by the opponent's point.

Belle, La. The deciding hit in a bout when the fencers' scores are level.

Benefit of Clergy was the medieval system whereby clergy, or clerks (i.e. those who could read) were tried on secular charges in the Church Courts where the penalties, if imposed at all, were either trivial or of an entirely spiritual nature. The worst that could happen was that the offender could be unfrocked; after that, as a layman, he was of course liable to answer for any subsequent offences in the ordinary courts. He was accordingly virtually guaranteed one crime with complete immunity. Obviously, all this led to the most scandalous abuses and malpractices. Matters were exacerbated by the rapid spread of literacy far beyond the ranks of genuine clerics; worse still, the test of literacy was always the same – to read the first verse of the fifty-first Psalm, so many a brazen rogue who could not tell A from B managed to learn it by heart, solemnly rattling it off while he quite possibly held the book upside down.

Henry II attempted to amend the system by demanding, in the Constitutions of Clarendon (1164), that clerks found guilty in the Church Courts should be handed over to the King's Courts for condign punishment. Thomas Becket, Archbishop of Canterbury, refused to agree and this was one of the causes of the celebrated quarrel between them, culminating in the Archbishop's murder by four of the King's knights.

Henry VIII made great inroads on the powers of the ecclesiastical courts, but by a statute of Edward VI it was enacted that Benefit of Clergy could be claimed once in cases of homicide; peers could claim even if illiterate, although, of course, even in Tudor times, few if any were. Those escaping justice were branded on the thumb to prevent them 'pleading their clergy' on a second occasion, though it would appear that by the eighteenth century, if not well before, this was either omitted altogether or was purely symbolic, with a cold iron. It was this statute which enabled many a duellist of a more recent era to evade sentencing, for although Benefit of Clergy was steadily limited and qualified over the centuries, it was not formally abolished in its entirety until as late as 1827, while the special privilege for peers remained in existence, at least in theory, until 1841.

Bergerac, Cyrano de. The eponymous hero of the nineteenth-century playwright Emile Rostand's drama. One of Louis XIII's Musketeers, he exhibited every trait of recklessness, 16

swagger and superbly irrational sense of honour, which in the seventeenth century characterised the poor but proud Gascon gentleman from whom the corps was largely recruited. In addition, he was a gentleman of the keenest sensibility and most cultivated intellect, able to compose an extempore sonnet metrically corresponding to the rhythm of the thrusts and parries he was exchanging in a duel to which his brilliant swordsmanship could bring but one end.

However, as if the gods will allow no man to advance too far, one hideous disfigurement blighted these intellectual and athletic gifts – a nose of such grotesque proportions that the sight of it aroused either revulsion or ridicule in the onlooker. Hence arose his reputation for endless duelling – those who discreetly averted their gaze, no less than those who stared with horrified fascination, were alike alleged to have insulted him.

He was credited with numerous heroic exploits in the Low Countries during the Thirty Years War against Spain, not the least being the nightly passage of the encircling enemy lines at the siege of Arras, for the purpose of maintaining an unbroken series of letters to his mistress who, however, eventually retired to a convent. The lovers were only re-united on the occasion of Cyrano's last visit, when he was already mortally wounded; and this encounter forms the moving climax to the final act of Rostand's play.

As with d'Artagnan, the character was based on a real personage. The historical Cyrano was likewise a man of letters as well as a soldier and swordsman, his best known work being *Comic Histories of the States and Empires of the Moon* (1656).

Bersaglio, (It.). An opening.

Bertrand, Baptiste was not related to the 'Napoleon of the Foil'. Visiting

The attacker (left) clearly has his opponent baffled with this Broken Time Attack.

London in 1856, it was he who was the founder of the great Salle Bertrand which functioned successively in Golden Square, Warwick Street and finally Tenterden Street. He was renowned as the leading arranger of stage fights for the London theatre and was justly regarded as without equal in this branch of the art. His masterpiece was the famous duel between Henry Irving and Squire Bancroft in *The Dead Heart* produced at the Lyceum in 1889. A pioneer in the popularisation of fencing for ladies, he was entrusted with the instruction of the daughters of Edward VII.

Bertrand, Felix. The son of Baptiste, he took over the salle on his father's death in 1898 in conjunction with his sister Hélène; a lady fencing master was a rarity indeed in those days.

Bertrand, François-Joseph. He flourished in France under the Second Empire and was perhaps no unworthy representative of that colourful, if slightly garish, epoch. Said to have been undefeated in professional encounters, he was highly original, not to say eccentric in his teaching methods, which may possibly have been the reason for his sobriquet 'the Napoleon of the Foil'. He is also alleged to have reduced the number of parries to four – *quarte, tierce, seconde* and *septime*; but similar simplification had been undertaken long before by such masters as Besnard and Labat and, as far back as the sixteenth century, Giganti had attempted to standardise and reduce the bewildering variety of guards and parries. So Bertrand's reputation for striking originality does not seem to rest on very strong ground here. Perhaps more important is his alleged popularisation of the parry *de tac* – the light, detached parry followed instantly by the lightning riposte, in contrast to the somewhat formal and stately riposte with a lunge pre-

viously favoured. He was also a great believer in the stop-hit and time-hit, previously frowned upon. Furthermore, he strongly encouraged mobility on the *piste*, especially a rapid retreat if pressed hard; even as late as 1950, some very old, ultra-traditional masters concentrated almost exclusively on the blade rather than footwork. Bertrand did much to restore the popularity and prestige of fencing in an age when the pistol had largely replaced the sword in the affair of honour and in both France and England a new, influential middle class had arisen with no inherited tradition or love of the sword behind them.

Bertrand, Professor Léon. 'Punch' Bertrand was the member of the famous family best remembered by the generation of fencers who are already leaving middle age behind them. He became the senior master in charge of Salle Bertrand on the death of his father, Felix, in 1930, his elder brother, Philippe, having been killed in the First World War. He presided over the remarkable run of success enjoyed by the members of the salle, especially the lady members in the inter-war years. That was the golden era, 'when the worlds of fashion and talent met' on the *piste* at Bertrand's. 'Punch' himself used generally to spend his vacations in Italy, indulging his unslakable thirst for the theory and practice of fencing. As he himself phrased it: 'Glorious days – fencing, fencing, fencing.'

In 1939, the Professor re-joined the R.A.F. and reached the rank of Flight-Lieutenant. On the return of peace, the salle was unable to resume activities in its historic premises and after a brief period of sharing the Tenterden Street building with the London Fencing Club, was tragically wound up. However,

A latterday Boar's Thrust by Pierre Harper against Grimmet.

'Punch', who became the first president of the British Academy of Fencing when it was re-formed in 1949, continued to teach at the L.F.C. until shortly before his death in 1980 – an unmistakable figure, with an air and idiosyncrasies that set him apart. He was never averse to instilling feelings of guilt or embarrassment in a clumsy or inattentive pupil, often to the secret amusement of the bystanders, if not the victim.

Bertrand Riposte or tac-au-tac. Named after François-Joseph Bertrand, it was the detached or 'tac' parry and immediate direct riposte.

Besnard, Charles. One of the celebrated French seventeenth-century masters who did so much to refine, classify and systematise swordplay. Basically, he reduced the number of his guard positions and their corresponding parries to four; two high and two low. This led him to enumerate four engagements and as a logical consequence, four straight-thrusts and four engagements. The introduction of the practice of formally saluting one's opponent before a bout (the *révérence*) is attributed to this master.

Beuvron, Marquis de. (See Montmorency.)

Bib. The stout cloth protection, attached to the bottom of the mask and protecting the fencer's neck. At foil, it must not extend more than two centimetres below the collar of the jacket, and in any case not below the line of the collar-bone.

Bilbao. The town in Spain famed for the excellence of its sword-blades, which rivalled those of Toledo.

Bill of Challenge. The formal announcement that, on a stated day,

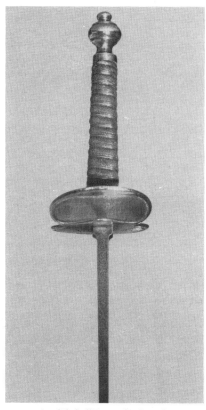

A solid shell Butterfly Guard.

a provost was ready to submit to his master's examination in the several weapons required by the Corporation of Masters of Defence in the sixteenth and seventeenth centuries; the candidate had the choice of four out of a number of weapons and these included, besides the traditional long-sword, backsword, sword and buckler and a pole weapon, the modern rapier and dagger.

Bind. 1) To force the opponent's blade diagonally across the target from high to low line, or vice versa. (See Prises-de-Fer.)
2) In Hungarian parlance, the bind

is a generic term used to describe virtually any type of blade contact or engagement.
3) Barbasetti defines it as controlling the opponent's blade, *forte* to *foible* and diverting it to another line.

Bind-Thrust. In Hungarian theory, it seems that the two blades remain in contact from the moment they are bound to the conclusion of the thrust.

Blackstone, Sir William. Educated at Charterhouse, Pembroke College, Oxford, the Middle Temple, elected Fellow of All Souls 1744, Doctor of Civil Law 1750; the measured stages of his academic progress sound with soothing familiarity on the ear. He entered the House of Commons in 1761, became solicitor-general to Queen Charlotte two years later and was elevated to the Bench of the Court of Common Pleas in 1770. His legal career was distinguished, but his real fame rests above all on his *Commentaries on the Laws of England.* Blackstone was one of those great eighteenth-century lawyers whose vast learning and professional integrity were at once the buttress and the glory of the independent judiciary and balanced constitution for which England was then envied and admired. Like that other great opponent of despotism and protagonist of the Common Law, Sir Edward Coke, he declared fencing to be against the law. Neither he nor anyone else ever made the slightest attempt to enforce this opinion, which apparently derived from the ancient common law contention that the tournament of the Middle Ages was illegal.

Blackwell, Henry. His *English Fencing Master*, published in 1705, evidently owed a good deal to Sir William Hope's *Scots Fencing Master.* Nevertheless, it contains a good deal of sound advice, though Blackwell advocates rolling the rear foot forward in the lunge, so that the ankle touches the ground. This, condemned by practically all other masters, ancient and modern, was alleged to prevent slipping. His general sentiments are praiseworthy in the extreme – fencing, he says, is 'the only proper qualification for constituting a Man a Gentleman'. In 1730 he published a sequel. *The Gentleman's Tutor for the Small-Sword* was accompanied by an extraordinary set of plates, bearing little relevance either to the text or the theory of eighteenth-century small-sword play, but apparently owing more to the crude and opportunistic tricks of the Italian school of 150 years previously. No doubt some of these illustrations fulfilled Blackwell's promise of adorning his treatise with 'several curious postures' (perhaps slightly reminiscent of Lewis Carrol's Anglo-Saxon attitudes) which, in any case, can hardly have been stranger than those with which the twentieth-century master is habitually confronted.

Blade. The blade is subdivided into several parts. Theoretically, in all weapons it is divided about halfway up, the thinner part near the point being known as the *foible* (seventeenth-century French for weak) and the broader part nearer the guard being designated as the *forte* (strong). On entering the guard, the blade narrows very abruptly into what is termed the 'tang' – little more than a rod which is inserted into and through the inside of the handle and secured by the locking nut inside the pommel at the top end. The points of the three weapons, however, differ considerably.

1a) Non-electric foil. The so-called point is actually a tiny flat cap which

La Botte de Nuit (from Ficher).

is further protected by a plastic button.

1b) Electric foil. The point is replaced by a spring-head in the form of a small cylinder which, when depressed, enables an electrical contact to be made, and when fully wired up by means of a flex plugged to the inside of the weapon's guard and leading to the fencer's sleeve and out of the back of his jacket, causes the recording apparatus to register a hit.

2) The sabre point has no button, but is 'rebated' i.e., folded back on itself so that the actual hitting area of the point is a minute rectangle.

3) The épée point is constructed on a similar basis to that of the electric foil. Non-electric épées are rarely seen nowadays.

There are right-handed and left-handed blades for all weapons, angulated at the junction of tang and *forte*, so that in all cases the point is directed slightly inwards. The blades of all three weapons are sufficiently flexible to arch in the shape of a shallow rainbow when the point fixes on the target. Foil blades of the earlier part of this century were much lighter and softer than those in general use today, especially those

wired for use with the electrical foil.

Blade, Absence of. When the blades are not engaged (touching each other) then fencing proceeds with what is called 'absence of blade'. The era of the electric foil produced almost a revolution in tactics, one aspect of which was a much longer fencing measure. Hence, fencing with absence of blade is today the normal option for most fencers.

Blade, Attacks on the. (See Attacks on the Blade.)

Blade, The Maraging is a strengthened and improved blade alleged to last at least twice as long as current types, besides retaining its spring better and being less likely to break in vigorous close-quarter fencing. A further development by the Leon Paul Company ('Paul steel') allows the balance and weight to be adjusted to each fencer's needs.

Blade, Taking of the. (See *Prise-de-Fer*.)

Blount, Edward. A late Elizabethan master who seems to have anticipated George Silver in his assertion of the superiority of the traditional English broadsword over the Italian rapier.

Boar's Thrust. An attack devised by McBane in the late seventeenth century. The sword-hand was suddenly dropped to knee level, then the thrust was jabbed upwards. McBane observed, with disarming casualness, that he only used it 'when he had a mind to kill'.

Board. Another term for the *piste*. At competitions, presidents are frequently heard to call: 'On the board, numbers one and four; two and five, get ready' and so forth.

Bobadil, Captain. The swaggering, ranting soldier in Ben Jonson's *Every Man in his Own Humour*. This type of braggart, a stock figure in Elizabethan comedy, owes his ultimate origin to the similar characters in the plays of Menander and Terence. Prolific of blood-curdling threats and the most exaggerated and melodramatic invective, he is invariably exposed at the crisis, as the most pitiful of cowards; and Bobadil is no exception to this rule. (Cp. Ancient Pistol in Shakespeare's *Henry IV* and *Henry V*.) The Captain claimed to be an expert fencer and condescended to give a lesson to Master Mathew, the 'Town Gull', interlacing his instructions with all the fashionable jargon about *passados*, *stoccatas* and the like, (Act I, Sc.iv). Subsequently, (Act IV, Sc.v) he asserted his ability to train twenty gentlemen to such a pitch of perfection in swordsmanship that they would be able to put to flight an army of 40,000.

Body Feints. (See Feints.)

Body-Wire. Part of the equipment used in conjunction with the electrical recording apparatus. Plugged into the inside of the guard of the weapon, it runs up the fencer's sleeve, and emerges under the back of his jacket, where it is connected to the other wire which coils and uncoils from a spring-loaded spool and from there leads to the recording apparatus itself.

Boitelle, Roland was well to the fore as a fencer, reaching the finals of the French Sabre Championship on three occasions and captaining the French foil team for over twenty years (1955-76). He also had fifteen years' experience as an international president, but it was as an administrator that he made his greatest

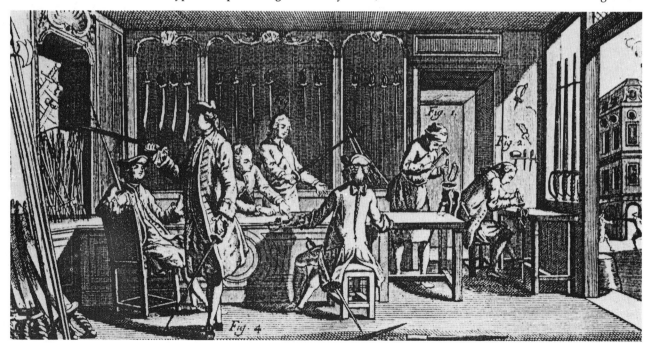

Testing a Blade (from Diderot).

mark. For thirty-five years he was a member of the committee of the Fédération Française d'Escrime and subsequently became its general secretary and then its president from 1981 to 1985. Finally, in the latter year, his services received their highest recognition when he was appointed president of the Fédération Internationale d'Escrime, in which position he still finds time to appear as a welcome guest at important competitions abroad.

Bonetti, Rocco. An Italian master, one of several who introduced the new school of rapier-play to England in the course of the sixteenth century. In consequence, he was permanently at odds with the corporation of Masters of Defence. They desired either to force him to join their company, or to discredit him by proving his incompetence. Therefore, they issued persistent challenges to exhibit his skill or betray his lack of it, which Rocco as persistently ignored. Finally he was worsted in a brawl with one Austin Bagger, a champion of the nationalist, anti-Italian faction, who bearded him in his own house; though we are informed that Rocco faced his enemy's traditional sword and buckler not, as might have been expected, with the Italian rapier, but a great two-handed sword.

Rocco's salle – which he termed his 'college', deeming the word 'school' to be beneath his dignity – was in London and George Silver (q.v.) says he charged his pupils anything from £20 to £100, though we are not told how many lessons they might expect in return. Rocco, as he was most commonly known, is supposed to have been the original of Ben Jonson's Captain Bobadil.

Borsody. An early twentieth-century Hungarian master. With the re-nowned Italian, Santelli, he revolutionised sabre technique, introducing and popularising the modern light fencing weapon, with rules and conventions similar to those of foil.

Botta, (It.). An attack.

Botta Dritta, (It.). The straight-thrust.

Botta Lunga, (It.). Capo Ferro's term for the lunge.

Botta Segrete, (It.). In the Italian schools of the sixteenth century, most masters professed to know of some secret attack, against which there was no defence. They were generally prepared to reveal its details to some favoured pupil – if the remuneration was generous enough. It is needless to add that no such attack exists, or can exist.

Botta In Tempo, (It.). (See Attack in Time.)

Botte. An attack.

Botte de Nuit. The *passata sotto*.

Botte du Paysan. A crude attack involving the use of both hands and a stabbing action akin to a bayonet thrust. Obviously quite impermissible in fencing or a formal duel, it was regarded, in the seventeenth century, as a possibility in an unregulated brawl. (See La Tousche.)

Botte Secrete. The secret attack. (See Botta Segreta.)

Bottone, (It.). The button.

Boulanger, General Georges. After wide service overseas and in the Franco-Prussian war, he helped in the suppression of the revolutionary Paris Commune in 1871, becoming minister of war in 1886, in which post he was able to improve service conditions. An extensive speaking tour won him wide acclaim and the handsome demagogue, wearing his *képi* at a rakish angle, soon became the figure-head and focal point of every militarist, patriotic, authoritarian or religious faction openly or secretly aiming at the discredit or overthrow of the Third Republic.

So far as he was associated with any distinct policy at all, it was the recovery of the lost provinces of Alsace and Lorraine; a project dear to the hearts of Paul Déroulède's League of Patriots and others planning a war of revenge against the new German Empire. The climax of the hysteria he engendered came when, having already been elected to the Chamber of Deputies in 1886, he demanded a revision of the constitution and fresh elections, in the course of which he was simultaneously elected in three *Départements* and in the municipal elections in Paris triumphed in every *arrondisement* except one. His tide was at the flood; the packed masses of his exultant supporters thronged the boulevards, urging him to put all to the hazard with a *coup d'état*; but the General, with that indecisiveness which ever characterised him, preferred to spend the evening quietly with his mistress. The delay was fatal; the government was given valuable time and some of the dissidents were appeased, but Boulanger's parliamentary immunity was withdrawn and his prosecution was soon in hand. Boulanger did not call their bluff; he absconded to Brussels and was tried and condemned for treason *in absentia*. Once before, his spell had nearly been broken when he had been run through the neck in a duel with the aged lawyer, Floquet, and the absurd excuse had been made that 'the General was not used to sword-play'. Now the bubble was entirely burst by his own vacillation and irresolution and he stood exposed as a theatrical posturer. In 1891, his mistress, the Vicomtesse de Bonnemain, died and Boulanger, an exhibitionist to the last, shot himself at the side of her grave.

Bourne, E.O. bounded into prominence in 1965 when, still at Brentwood, he came second to J. Pelling in the Epée Championship. Thereafter, he never looked back and was always to the forefront, winning the championship in 1966, and following that with two hat-tricks, from 1972 to 1974 and again from 1976 to 1978. He came second in 1967, 1971 and 1973. He won the Miller-Hallett trophy four times (1968, 1974, 1975 and 1977) and was second on the same number of occasions (1971, 1972, 1975 and 1978). He won the Epée Club Cup in 1975 and 1976, and was second in 1977 and 1978. He was no mean foilist and achieved second place in the British Championship of 1974.

Bout. An encounter between two fencers when the hits are counted as part of an official competition or match.

Bouts, Duration of. The duration of a bout varies according to the number of hits required for victory. The period at all weapons is five minutes for four hits, six minutes for five, eight minutes for eight and ten minutes for ten. Five minutes is allowed for an épée bout of one hit. In all cases, competitors are warned when one minute only of the fencing time remains.

Should time expire without one fencer obtaining the maximum, he who is in the lead is declared the winner, the remaining hits he requires for the full number being added to both scores. If the scores are level, a deciding hit is fenced for without limit of time. As double hits can be scored at épée, both competitors can receive the maximum number of hits simultaneously. If this occurs before time has expired, they must continue to fence until the time limit, in the hope that by then one has taken the lead. If this is still not the case, a double defeat is recorded. Only in direct elimination (the knock-out system) must the fight go on until a decision is reached.

Just as with the number of hits, the duration of bouts has been altered repeatedly over the years. In the 1895 Foil Championship, bouts in the preliminary rounds lasted three minutes, in the semi-finals and final, five minutes. In the original rules (1896) of the Amateur Gymnastic and Fencing Association, as it was then styled, eight minutes is prescribed for a bout, the winner simply being he who had scored more hits when time was called. In the Foil Championship of 1895, the times were the same as ten years previously, but points were awarded for the quality of the fencing; we are not told on what basis.

When the first British épée team went abroad to compete for the International Cup at the Palais Royal in Paris, two minutes' rest was allowed after five minutes' fighting; if, after twenty minutes, no hit had been scored, a double defeat resulted. In the early years of this century, it was customary in the national championship for there to be two periods of five minutes' play, with an interval of a minute; but at the championship of 1913, it was stipulated that there should be a simple time-limit of ten minutes for bouts in the preliminary rounds, and no less than fifteen for those in the semi-finals and final. It must be remembered that in those days bouts at épée were still for one hit only – which tells us as much about the caution as the skill of those concerned.

In the first Ladies' Foil Championship to be held in this country (1907), the time limit for a bout was as little as four minutes. Then, for many years, ladies fenced for a maximum period of five minutes only (for the first to score four hits) and have only recently been put on the same footing as men, namely, the conditions given in the first paragraph.

Julio Martinez Castello, writing in 1933, when resident and teaching in the U.S., rather surprisingly gives the times as fifteen minutes for the best of nine hits at foil and sabre, and ten minutes for the best of five (three hits) at épée. He also refers to not one, but two warnings, given respectively at two minutes and one minute before the expiration of time.

Bow. The knuckleguard, so-called because of its shape.

Box. A slang term for the electrical recording apparatus. (See Recording Apparatus.)

Box, Defensive. The imaginary rectangle defining the limits of the sabre target. The horizontal sides pass respectively through the top of the head and the folds in the breeches at the junction of the thighs and torso, when the fencer bends his knees in the on-guard position. The vertical sides include not merely the trunk, but both arms.

Brantome, Pierre de Bourdeilles, Seigneur de (1540-1614). A French soldier and courtier who saw service against the Huguenots and Turks and held various court appointments to the last Valois kings, as well as to Mary, Queen of Scots. In retirement, he wrote his *Mémoires* containing much fascinating and at times scandalous detail of the eminent personages he had met; he likewise faithfully recorded several of the spectacular duels of the period, including that between de Jarnac and La Chasteignerai.

Braquemar. A term somewhat loosely applied to many different types of sword; the essential feature was a broad blade. Possibly the word was derived from the Walloon *braquet*. (See Malchus.)

Brassard. An armlet, usually bearing the insignia of the fencer's club. In 1947, British fencers in foreign events of importance, but slightly below full international standard, were permitted to wear a brassard consisting of a shield bearing the Union Jack, backed by crossed swords and the words 'Amateur Fencing Association' below.

Break the Game. To parry a feint.

Breaking the Attack. An attack on the blade (e.g. a beat) delivered on the adversary's blade as he feints and lifts the leading foot for an advance.

Brissac, Duc de. As officer commanding the King's Regiment in France in the eighteenth century, he terminated duelling among his officers by insisting that all duels should be to the death, even if this necessitated repeated encounters. In at least one case, this threat was rigidly enforced.

British Empire Fencing Federation. The federation was founded in 1950, when the Empire Games, held that year in New Zealand, were the first to include fencing. Its declared object was 'the co-ordination of fencing in the British Empire and Commonwealth' and the general support of

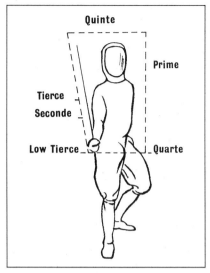

The Defensive Box.

fencing at future Empire Games.

Broadsword. The traditional English edged weapon, essentially designed for cutting and much extolled by George Silver (q.v.) and other conservatives, but in the course of the sixteenth century it was superseded by the infinitely more deadly rapier. However, it was still used by the professional prize-fighters right into the eighteenth century, largely because the wounds, as opposed to those inflicted by a thrusting weapon, were very rarely fatal. Silver described it as 'manly and traditionally English', but it was never regarded as the 'gentleman's weapon'.

Various types of broadsword have always been popular for military use, as the original rapier was too long and awkward to handle in close-quarter fighting. During the English Civil War, the name was bestowed on the basket-hilted, straight cavalry sword issued to the troopers of the New Model Army.

Brochiero, (It.). A variety of buckler.

Broken Guard. At sabre, an attacking blade making contact with the opponent's guard, before reaching the target is said to have 'broken the guard', and no hit is scored (see Cooky). If on the other hand, the attacking blade meets the two above surfaces simultaneously, the hit is valid.

Broken Time is the separation of two movements normally forming a continuous whole by means of a deliberate and unexpected pause; this tending to provoke a mistimed or even superfluous action on the part of the opponent. For example, the sword-arm may be extended as if for a straight-thrust, then abruptly retracted; the defender parries instinctively but to no purpose and so at best leaves one line open; more typically, having failed to find the blade, he parries and moves his weapon irresolutely here and there, thus opening much of his target to the real attack. Again, the defender may be conditioned into taking successive parries by repeated one-two attacks; if the attacker pauses on the feint, the defender may mechanically execute both parries, thus leaving himself open for the feint to be developed into a leisurely simple attack. We have spoken here of the attacker, but of course, similar tactics can be applied with the riposte.

Brook, Roger was the hero of a cycle by Dennis Wheatley, covering the years 1784 to 1815. He was entrusted with a series of secret diplomatic missions to several of the European Courts, including Versailles, where he gained the patronage and confidence of Marie Antoinette. He seems to have possessed all the qualities required by the foremost secret agents, for he was a consummate liar

23

fully prepared to undertake missions for others besides the Prime Minister, William Pitt the Younger. He served and betrayed one French government after another and had no scruples in eliminating, by direct or indirect means, anyone who was an obstacle to his public or private designs. His sexual appetite was evidently insatiable and relegates him to the role of the James Bond of the eighteenth century.

This charming character, for whom we are apparently expected to feel unqualified admiration, was at least an excellent swordsman, fearing neither numbers nor reputation. At Sherborne, his Housemaster, 'Old Toby', described him as 'quite a dangerous antagonist with the foils'. Later he took lessons from M St Paul of the Musketeers at his salle in Rennes; afterwards he practised rapier and sabre with Chenou, an ex-sergeant of the Breton Dragoons and the Marquis de Rochambeau's huntsman, 'in the tennis court next to the stables'. In consequence, Brook was himself able to give lessons to his friend, M de la Tour d'Auvergne.

Having fallen desperately in love with Athenais de Rochambeau, he provoked an encounter with her fiancé, the Comte de Caylus, a desperate affair in the forest, described with dramatic vigour rather than any real attempt at technical analysis. Finally, Brook was victorious when he executed a low time-thrust (an *imbroccata*?) on de Caylus' downward-thrust as the latter came charging in to close quarters – a highly hazardous venture. The thrust of de Caylus 'passed harmlessly over his shoulder' but any moderately experienced fencer would incline to the opinion that the young man, to say the least, was extremely lucky.

At Le Havre, the villainous Chevalier de Roubec accused Brook of failing to pay his share of the expenses in a local brothel. De Roubec was taller and stronger than Brook, but the latter had the longer sword. Suddenly closing, Brook locked the blades near the guards and with a deft twist disarmed his adversary; these measures are always successful in fiction, but the idea is authentic enough. Brook had been taught the trick by his fencing master at Sherborne and virtually all masters in that era taught these methods of disarmament for use in just such a crisis as this. It worked again with

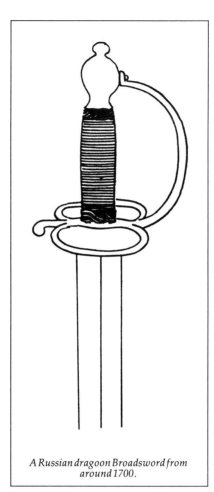

A Russian dragoon Broadsword from around 1700.

the Marquis de Rochambeau. Brook slithered the blades together until he was able to disarm his enemy with a violent twist. It is wonderful how, when these elaborate manoeuvres are going on, the victim never seems to take any counter-action.

Returning to England on leave, Brook fought a duel with one Gunston, a Captain of Dragoons, over a young lady to whom both were paying attentions. The rules against duelling in the British Army being extremely strict, the affair had to be conducted with buttoned foils under cover of a fencing tournament. Brook, with the advantage of his French experience behind him, first toyed with his adversary to entertain the audience, then proceeded to 'whip him round the yard'. Years afterwards, the two met again in a bloody and unscientific mounted encounter on the fringes of the field of Waterloo.

Long before 1815, Brook was recognised as 'one of the finest swordsmen in Europe'. During the French occupation of Venice, he faked a kidnap attempt on General Bonaparte in furtherance of his schemes. In the course of this enterprise, he fought off four assailants simultaneously, using a heavy cutting sword, a double-edged army weapon, against light rapiers. Not surprisingly, he was wounded in several places, but was ultimately able to escape by making free use of a cloak and his feet – in the latter case, literally.

Bruniges, R. exemplified the modern trend towards youthfulness in athletic pastimes when in one and the same year (1976), he combined second place in the British Foil Championship with an outstanding triumph in the World Under-Twenty Youth. Championship at the same weapon. In 1974, 1976, and again in

1980, he was second in the Coronation Cup. Very much a fencer of the modern school, he cultivated a variety of spectacular strokes, notably a riposte delivered over his shoulder with his back turned. Less effective as an épéeist, he nevertheless took third place in the British Championship of 1974.

Buck, Timothy was an eighteenth-century prize-fighter immortalised in number 436 of *The Spectator* by Steele, who described his gladiatorial bout with James Miller in 1712 at the Bear-Garden, Hockley-in-the-Hole, a favourite place for such exhibitions. Miller, a regular soldier, was subsequently commissioned; Buck remained the archetypal professional. Steel describes him as 'calm' and 'exhibiting a perfect composure' as indeed befitted the 'Pillar of the Art' and a 'most solid Master'.

Buckingham, George Villiers, Second Duke of. Son of the first Duke who was James I's favourite, he was one of the leading figures in the tortuous politics at the dissolute court of the Restoration. He was a prominent member of the little group known as the 'wits', which included John Wilmot, Earl of Rochester, the Earl of Mulgrave and Sir Charles Sedley, all notorious for their debaucheries, affectations and cynical insolence. They were all, nevertheless, men of excellent parts and in some cases, outstandingly brilliant intellect. Although Buckingham is best remembered for the merciless caricature in Dryden's political satire *Absalom and Achitophel*, he was really unfortunate to be permanently saddled with an undeserved reputation for folly, as he was the author of at least one work of lasting value, the play entitled *The Rehearsal*, a rollicking comedy which can still entertain and formed the

basis of Sheridan's *The Critic*.

Brought up with Charles II in the latter's boyhood, he accompanied him abroad during his exile, but nevertheless returned to England before the end of the Cromwellian regime. He became a member of that seventeenth-century council of ministers known as the Cabal, a sort of early version of the Cabinet; but his intrigues were so numerous and he was so evidently untrustworthy that the King finally dismissed him. During the struggles on the Exclusion Bill, from 1678 onwards, when an elaborate but imaginary Popish Plot was exploited as cover for the attempt to exclude the King's Catholic brother, James, Duke of York, from the succession, Buckingham threw in his lot with the Earl of Shaftesbury in opposition to the court, becoming one of the leaders of what was soon to become known as the Whig Party. Shaftesbury was disgraced and driven into exile, but Buckingham, having withdrawn into private life, continued to live unmolested when James II finally became king. Despite his irregular and voluptuous life, Buckingham, like many a Restoration courtier, was no stranger to the use of the sword. During the Civil War he was present at the storming of Lichfield Close (1643) and after the Restoration, killed the Earl of Shrewsbury in a famous duel arising from his adulterous affair with the defeated principal's Countess.

Buckler. A small round shield used in conjunction with the broadsword. With the introduction of the long rapier in the sixteenth century, however, defence was generally conducted by means of a matching dagger in the left hand, the *main-gauche*.

Buhan, J. was the brilliant French foilist who won the individual gold

medal at the London Olympics of 1948. A fencer of great versatility and keen powers of observation, he was clearly unaffected by the pressure and excitement inseparable from the climax of such an occasion; for Crosnier (see below) reports that out of sixteen of his attacks which ended successfully, no fewer than thirteen were different.

Bully's Blade. (See Tour du Bretteur.)

Burton, Sir Richard. An army officer and one of the group associated with Captain Hutton who did so much to revive and restore interest in fencing in the late nineteenth century. His ambitious but unsuccessful production was entitled *The Book of the Sword*. In a posthumous edition renamed *The Sentiment of the Sword* he is on record as saying (with relation to fencing) 'Nothing is bad if it succeeds.' Burton viewed matters from the military standpoint, still apparently regarding the sword as a serious weapon, rather than the agent used to enjoy the graceful and conventional exercise of the salles.

Butler, Miss M.M. was, for a few years, the outstanding lady fencer in the country. She won the Desprez Cup in 1928 and 1929; the Hutton Memorial Cup (now de Beaumont Cup) in 1929 and 1931, coming second in 1928 and 1930 and was the first to win a hat-trick of championships in consecutive years, 1930-31-32.

Butterfly Guard. On certain eighteenth-century small-swords the guard or shell consisted of two symmetrical parts, one either side of the blade, each broadening outwards in an ellipse; the whole thus forming a shape roughly resembling a butterfly.

Button. The general term for the globular protection covering the point of the non-electric foil and épée. In the late seventeenth century, when the foil proper appeared, the button was fashioned from leather and its resemblance to a flower bud resulted in the weapon itself being termed a *fleuret*. Later, adhesive tape was often wound round and round the point. However, for some years now plastic buttons have been in use.

Byron, Lord. The duel between William Byron, the great uncle of the poet and a Mr Chaworth, arose from a meeting of the Nottinghamshire Club held at the Star and Garter Tavern in Pall Mall in 1765. It was a most irregular affair, held precipitately in a small room lighted by only one candle, just as the other members were on the point of leaving. The result was fatal for Chaworth who, however, before dying, admitted that he had made the first pass; this, together with the fact that it was generally agreed that Chaworth had been guilty of some provocation, although it was uncertain who had actually issued the challenge, ensured that Byron was convicted in the House of Lords only of manslaughter, not murder; tantamount to an acquittal as a statute of Edward VI, which still held good, entitled a peer guilty of this offence to immediate discharge 'on payment of his fees'. (See Benefit of Clergy.)

Byron, Lord, George Gordon. Amongst his many highly-coloured poems, the most notable was probably *Childe Harold's Pilgrimage*, though *Don Juan* is almost equally famous. Byron typified to a high degree the self-conscious, theatrical despair and sense of doom-ridden destiny of the Romantic movement. He posed as a herald of democracy,

though with his aristocratic origins and tastes he would probably have felt little sympathy with the logical consequences of his radicalism. Despite suffering from the handicap of lameness from birth, he played for Harrow in the first match against Eton at Lord's in 1806, making seven and two in a match that resulted in an innings defeat. It is recorded that he took lessons in the broadsword in his rooms in the Albany – perhaps because it was the fighting weapon undergoing a resurgence of popularity as a result of the long wars against the French. With a characteristic final flourish, he joined the Greeks in their War of Independence against the Turks, and died of fever at Missolonghi (1824).

Cadence. The rhythm in which a fencer performs a series of inter-related movements, e.g, feints or successive parries.

Cadence, Change of is to alter the rhythm in the course of a series of movements. For instance, a fencer may parry an attack, and then riposte very rapidly and with no pause between the actions. If, after parrying his opponents's counter-riposte, he then delays his next (the second) counter-riposte, his adversary, having anticipated an immediate reply, may well lose confidence and in his attempts to find the blade, open one line or another to the delivery of the final and successful offensive action.

As phrases at foil are, or at any rate were, much longer and more elaborate than with the sabre, it is, generally speaking, the attack with the latter weapon which is executed with a change of cadence. Successive parries with the sabre being none too easy, owing to the large target area to be protected against attacks

from many angles, the sabreur is taught not to react to false attacks and feints, but to reserve his parry until the very last moment ('en finale'). Therefore the cadence of a compound attack with the sabre is generally long-short – a very long, deep feint to force the defender to commit himself to a parry, which is then deceived by a very fast final blade movement. A more elaborate alternative for sophisticates is a short-long-short cadence. Here the attack starts with a deliberately brief, unconvincing feint, to create the impression that his technique is poor and that his real attack is nevertheless to be delivered with the second blade action. This, it is hoped, will draw the defender's parry, which is finally deceived rapidly, in the same way as in the more usual procedure described above.

Another common way of altering the cadence at sabre, is to execute a series of false attacks or feints at normal speed, then suddenly to attack with extreme rapidity in the hope of catching the opponent unawares.

It should be clearly understood that the term 'cadence' is not synonymous with 'speed' in itself; properly interpreted, cadence is speed successfully regulated in relation to the opponent's speed.

Cadence, Imposing the. Mere speed does not necessarily and in all cases ensure the success of an attack, especially if exploited mechanically and without intelligence. For example, a very fast compound attack against an opponent very slow to parry, may entirely fail to draw any reaction, and the final action of the attack may be met by the opponent's blade which has never moved from its original position. This is known as 'parrying oneself'. In such a case, the speed should be considerably re-

Capo Ferro's lunge.

Capo Ferro's lunge in action.

duced in order to allow time to the defender to form his parry and leave a line open to the final line of the attack. In other words, the correct cadence in all such cases is a speed slightly greater than that of one's opponent. To find this speed, either by increasing or reducing it as the case may be, is called 'imposing the cadence'.

Caius, Doctor. A blustering French physician in Shakespeare's *Merry Wives of Windsor*, who challenged Sir Hugh Evans to a duel, although the latter failed to appear. The host of the Garter Inn said he had come to see Caius 'foin, to traverse, to see thee pass, thy punto, thy stock, thy reverse, thy distance, thy montant'. (Act II, Scene iii.)

Caize. A sixteenth-century master who was said to have taught de Jarnac his celebrated back-handed cut.

Cambiamento, (It.). The change of engagement.

Camineering was a corruption of the above term used by the author of *Pallas Armata*, an anonymous treatise on fencing found among the papers of a seventeenth-century Bristol merchant.

Camminando, (It.). Attacking *en marchant*, with a step forward.

Campbell-Gray, Hon. I.D. Always to be regarded as a formidable opponent in the épée competitions of the twenties and thirties, he was described by one leading authority as 'a beautiful classical fencer of the old school'. He was British Champion in 1926, 1930, 1932 and 1935 and shared the second place with Dexter and Monro in 1929.

Capa. The Cloak. (See Cloak and Sword.)

Capo Ferro. The great Italian master of the sixteenth century, credited with the invention of the lunge as a more effective means of attacking the opponent than the pass, or extension of the rear foot beyond the leading foot. In fact, it seems quite possible that he was anticipated in this by his contemporary Giganti, but, nevertheless, it is with this seminal development, the starting point of all modern fencing, that Capo's name is indissolubly associated.

It will be of hardly less interest to the modern generation of fencers than to their immediate predecessors who practised innumerable varieties of compound attacks, to learn that Capo Ferro was strongly against the use of feints, on the grounds that if within distance they were dangerous, if out of distance, futile; advice which, in view of the modern tendency to retreat whenever attacked, is doubtless as pertinent today as it was then.

Capstan Rivet. A small rivet sometimes found on top of the pommel.

Carr, John Dickson. A famous detective story writer, born in the United States in 1906, but resident most of his life in Britain, the setting of the great majority of his books. His first novel, *It Walks by Night*, by reason of its melodramatic characterisation, its macabre situations, its vivid descriptions and its gleeful suggestions of the supernatural, created something of a sensation when it was published in 1931. One scene is laid in a Parisian salle d'armes, the proprietor of which, one Maître Terlin, kept his pupils at the *tirer au mur* for eighteen months 'before allowing them to try the simplest parry in *tierce'*. Mr Carr had evidently been something of a fencer himself, though the use of the term *tierce* betrays his vintage.

One of Mr Carr's most celebrated works and certainly by far his most scholarly, revealing a surprising familiarity with seventeenth-century *minutiae*, was *The Devil in Velvet*. The hero, Professor Fenn, a Cambridge don obsessed with the seventeenth century, sold his soul to the devil in order to return to his favourite period where, as one Sir Nicholas Fenton, a cavalier courtier, he became involved in the tangled politics of the Restoration. He remained fully conscious of his former identity and established a reputation as a veritable wizard of swordsmanship, since, as a skilled twentieth-century fencer, he was naturally familiar with a considerable variety of strokes which in 1675 had not yet been invented. This highly attractive notion must, regrettably, be classed as artistic licence, as against a fighting adversary armed with the relatively heavy transition rapier and bent on taking time on any unguarded feint or opening, the delicacies of foil play in the nineteenth and twentieth century must have proved not merely futile, but perilous in the extreme.

Carranza, Jeronimo de. A Spanish master of the late sixteenth century, well known as one of the originators of that fantastic and elaborate school of swordsmanship based on the irrelevant mathematical principles of arcs, tangents and related angles, a comprehensive knowledge of which, it was claimed, must infallibly lead to victory. He was well known in seventeenth-century England and there are several contemporary literary allusions to him.

Carte. Another form of *quarte*, the

Case of Rapiers (from Marozzo).

fourth position and parry.

Cartoccio, (It.). The *passata sotto*.

Case of Rapiers. Twin rapiers, generally carried in the same sheath, for those swordsmen who favoured double rapier-play, one weapon in each hand.

Castello, Julio Martinez. The distinguished master of the *Sala de Armes* of Carbonal in Spain, who followed many personal triumphs in Europe with widespread success in the United States where he resided for many years. He coached the American Olympic team in 1924 and taught at many of the leading clubs and universities in both North and South America. He was the author of *The Theory and Practice of Fencing*, a profusely illustrated work, which aroused considerable interest when it was published in 1933.

Castiglione, Baldassare. A distinguished courtier and diplomat of the early sixteenth century who enjoyed the favour of the Dukes of Mantua and Urbino, but after being sent as the latter's ambassador to Pope Leo X, became a record keeper in the Papal Curia, and was subsequently appointed Papal Nuncio to Charles I of Spain (Charles V of the Holy Roman Empire). His book *Il Cortegiano* (The Courtier) is generally supposed to express the Renaissance ideal of the cultivated gentleman, well-read, accomplished, informed on politics and displaying in all situations an easy goodbreeding. It is the more surprising, therefore, to find that in a passage on fencing he is an advocate of the crude practice of using wrestling grips to supplement the action of the sword.

Castle, Egerton. A nineteenth-century fencer and writer who compiled, in his *Schools and Masters of Fence*, what was, and probably still is, the definitive history of fencing and sword-play in Europe from the sixteenth century onwards. The work also contains a comprehensive bibliography. Castle's great contribution was to show how the scientific school of French small-sword play, on which modern foil fencing is still very largely based, replaced its erroneous predecessors in Italy and Spain.

Cavatione or Cavazione, (It.). The disengagement.

Cavazione Angolata, (It.). The cut-over.

Cavazione Circolata, (It.). The counter-disengage.

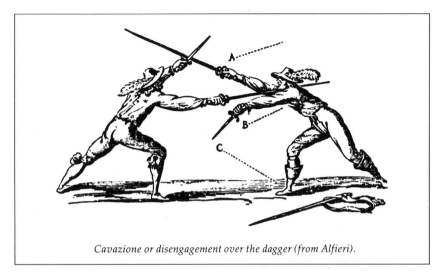

Cavazione or disengagement over the dagger (from Alfieri).

Cavazione in Tempo, (It.). A stop-hit by disengagement.

Cavens, F. A Belgian master resident in the United States, whose fame rested less on his contribution as an orthodox instructor than on his ability and ingenuity in staging many of the celebrated screen duels of the golden age of Hollywood, notably those in *The Mark of Zorro* and *Don Juan*.

Ceding Parry. One method of defence when one's blade is trapped by the opponent's *prise-de-fer*. Broadly speaking, contact of the blades is maintained, while at the same time the elbow is bent and the executant's blade is allowed to pivot over that of his opponent, until it terminates in the covered position required, e.g., when the opponent has taken one's blade into *octave*, the defender, following the above method 'cedes' into *quarte*. When the blade is trapped in *septime, tierce* is the position eventually reached. In both cases, the point is elevated rather more than is usual. Much more rarely used are the ceding parries of *prime* and

seconde, but these would be at least theoretically appropriate when the blade is held in *sixte* and *quarte* respectively. The other sort of parry used against the *prise-de-fer* is the parry with opposition (q.v.) in the same line.

Cedute, (It.). A ceding parry.

Central Guard. A faulty defensive position; the hand and blade being placed equidistantly between the *sixte* and *quarte* positions, the fencer is thus open to attack in either. It may, of course, be assumed deliberately, for tactical reasons, to invite the opponent's attack. (See Invitation.)

Cercle. The somewhat misleading term used in the late seventeenth century for the parry starting in the high line and ending in *septime*, which the moderns describe as half-circle, half-circular or semi-circular.

Cercle les Ongles en Dessous. Girard's term for the parry of *seconde*, i.e., 'nails underneath' or hand pronated.

Cercle les Ongles en Dessus. Girard's term for the parry of *septime*, i.e., 'nails on top' or hand supinated.

Cervantes, Saavreda Miguel de. His life reads like one of the picaresque novels so popular in seventeenth-century Spain. Starting as a soldier, Cervantes served in Italy, then a Spanish sphere of influence, and was then present at the spectacular and decisive naval victory over the Turks at Lepanto (1570). Captured by pirates, he was enslaved for five years in Algiers and despite three attempts to escape was not ransomed until 1580. Back in Spain, he endeavoured to fulfil his literary ambitions and the remainder of his lifetime was divided between recurrent spells in gaol and the composition of sundry pieces, none attracting much attention until the appearance of the immortal *Don Quixote* in 1605 which brought him instant fame.

Like any Spaniard of the period, Cervantes' imagination was captivated by ornate and ostentatious sword-play and he informs us that contemporary experts were in the habit of advertising their superiority by making an opponent 'kiss the button', i.e., placing a hit upon his mouth. By the eighteenth century such habits were, of course, regarded as uncouth and the arrival of a hit anywhere but on the breast was supposed to be followed by an immediate apology.

Chalais, Adrien Blaise de Talleyrand, Prince de. A rival of M de La Frette for the affections of some lady, the two finally fell foul of each other at a ball in 1662, and according to some accounts, so far forgot themselves as to lay hands on each other. Despite the strict injunctions of Louis XIV, who forbade any meeting

30

Egerton Castle, a cartoon by Spy in Vanity Fair.

on pain of death, there was an encounter next morning in a secluded spot of the *Faubourg St Germain*, each principal being accompanied by three seconds. The Marquis d'Antin, one of the Prince's seconds, was killed, and all the other combatants were wounded. They all managed to escape abroad, however, and were sentenced by the *Parlement* of Paris in their absence.

As a matter of interest, La Frette's father had been wounded in an encounter with the celebrated Comte de Bouteville (see Montmorency) who had eventually been executed in the previous reign for persistent duelling.

Change Beat. The blade is passed beneath that of the opponent and the beat is delivered on the side opposite to that of the original engagement. Should the action be executed in the low line, the executant's blade must, of course, go over that of his opponent. (See Preparations of Attack.)

Change Bind. In Vass's terminology, to change the engagement of the blades to the opposite side, contact being briefly broken.

Change of Engagement. To engage the opponent's blade in the line opposite to the original engagement, by passing either over or under his blade. (See Preparations of Attack.)

Change Parry. The name given by some foreign authorities to the circular parry.

Change-Thrust. The name given by Imre Vass, the Hungarian master, to a disengagement, following an initial engagement by the adversary.

Changement. The change of engagement.

Chapman, George. He is said to have been one of the few who kept English fencing afloat during its decline in the early nineteenth century. After early and apparently disappointing experience of Angelo's, he and some kindred spirits founded the London Fencing Club in Piccadilly in 1848. At Baptiste Bertrand's instigation, he published *Foil Practice* in 1861. Its most interesting feature, stressed by Aylward, is that he advocated that the initial stages of instruction should be in defence, not attack, contrary to almost all masters and systems both then and now.

Charles IX, King of Franch, 1560-74. The second and the most degenerate of the sons of the notorious Catherine de Medici, he had the misfortune to rule over a nation riven by the civil wars between Catholics and Huguenots. His physical and mental defects caused him to alternate between apathetic and irresponsible indifference and feverish assumptions of usually ill-judged initiative. In one such spell he was persuaded to give his assent to the Massacre of St Bartholomew (1572), though Catherine, who instigated it, was far from being the monster that popular legend has made of her. For political reasons generally inclined to a policy of balance, her one great principle being the maintenance of the Crown's independent authority and the continuation of the dynasty, it has been argued that she made the fatal decision in the belief that the Huguenots had become so strong that it was essential, temporarily at any rate, to co-operate with their opponents. As for her wretched son, he was subsequently tormented by remorse and, it is said, haunted to his dying day by appalling nightmares of corpses and blood.

In attendance at Charles IX's court were the well-known masters, Pompée and Silvie, the latter of whom was celebrated for having taught the Duke of Anjou, later Henry III (q.v.); and the King also issued an edict in 1564, authorising such duels as he himself approved.

Charles X, King of France, 1824-30. The grandson of Louis XV and younger brother of Louis XVI and Louis XVIII, he was created Comte d'Artois as a child and in his youth achieved some notoriety for the same sort of wildness and debauchery popularly attributed to our own Henry V at the same age. When his mistress was grossly insulted by the Duchess de Bourbon, apparently out of jealousy, at a ball in 1778, he so far forgot himself as actually to lay

George Chapman (illustration at the London Fencing Club).

hands on her, albeit without inflicting anything in the nature of an injury. Nevertheless, it was generally felt that it was incumbent on the Duke to demand satisfaction and equally, that the Count must waive his status as a Child of France, although, at the last minute, attempts were made to call a halt to the whole matter. However, it was allowed to proceed, but after two or three lunges and parries, the seconds, wrongly supposing the Duke to be wounded, tried to interfere. D'Artois offered to continue as long as the Duke wished, the latter being the offended party, but instead he gracefully expressed his thanks for the honour conferred upon him, and a touching reconciliation was effected, followed by a re-

turn of the whole party to the Palais Bourbon where, a handsome apology having been made to the Duchess, sweetness and light once again prevailed.

Subsequently, d'Artois put these escapades behind him and took seriously to politics, opposing the early stages of the Revolution so strongly that the King (Louis XVI) felt constrained to send him into exile. After the Bourbon restoration in 1815, he led the 'Ultras' as the extreme monarchists were called, and on succeeding to the throne in 1820, he restored lands to the *emigré* nobles, relied heavily on the Church and adopted repressive measures to deal with unrest. The old tag about the Bourbons 'forgetting nothing and learning nothing' applied to him only too well. On the outbreak of a second revolution in 1830, he suddenly found his position untenable, abdicated, and sought refuge, first in England and later Italy, where he died six years later.

Chasse-Coquin. A stiff, heavy foil; according to George Roland, the early nineteenth-century master, monstrosities of this sort were used by heavy-handed, ignorant, or badly taught fencers who relied on mere strength and aggression.

Chasseloup-Laubat, Marquis de. The French nobleman who, with the assistance of M Paul Anspach, in 1914 codified the rules of foil fencing and produced what was virtually their definitive version. Formally adopted the same year by a committee of the F.I.E. under the presidency of General Ettore of the Italian Fencing Federation, they were translated from the French and, extended and modernised, are presently to be found in the A.F.A.'s *Rules for Competitions*.

Cheese. An Elizabethan blusterer, one of those traditionalists insanely jealous and resentful of the Italian masters then touring and teaching in England. Forcing a quarrel on one of them, Jeronimo, he ran him fatally through the body. It is not known if he subsequently faced an indictment.

Cherbury, Lord Herbert of. A man endowed with all the arts and graces of civilisation, brother of the famous devotional poet George Herbert, he was himself the distinguished author of a number of works, philosophical, devotional and historical and a soldier and diplomat for good measure. He indulged, besides, a pronounced taste for fencing and duelling. He received lessons from a number of different masters, but preferred the French school. Writing in 1620, he advises the swordsman to 'keep his eye on the opponent's point' and declares that no-one who has learned the art properly incurs the slightest risk so long as he does not misapply the correct theory and technique. Unfortunately, he does not explain how such errors are to be avoided; but his principles were evidently vindicated when he triumphantly repelled a gang of ruffians set on him in Whitehall by a cuckolded husband.

Choice Reaction occurs when in the course of a lesson the master gives the pupil the choice of alternative actions, only one of which, however, is appropriate. He may execute two different forms of attack, the pupil having to select the correct defence or counter-attack in each case; or he may instruct the pupil to renew his attack in different ways following the master's parry and his subsequent varied actions. Again, the pupil can be informed that he will be faced with a choice half-way through a phrase, the particular stage being sometimes revealed and sometimes remaining undisclosed. The number of choices can be increased from two to three (see Multiple Choice Reaction) or even more in the case of an advanced pupil who is meeting the challenge with assurance and precision. Some masters, however, have been known to harbour reservations, and voice doubts of the entire procedure on the grounds that it tends to undermine confidence and impair technique.

Christian IV, King of Denmark 1588-1648. A strong and popular, but by no means successful monarch who attempted to emancipate the peasants and who intervened on the Protestant side in the Thirty Years War, only to suffer a disastrous defeat by Tilly at Lutter (1626). He waged two wars against Sweden, the second of which was equally unfortunate and only terminated by the Treaty of Bromsebro (1645), involving considerable losses of territory. He was keenly interested in nautical matters, founding the Danish Navy and promoting attempts to discover the North West Passage. He was equally devoted to the science of arms and swordsmanship and it was in his reign that the great Fabris was invited to the Danish Court where he published his famous treatise.

Churchill, The Rt. Hon. Sir Winston Leonard Spencer, K.G., O.M., C.H., M.P. Winston, as he was most generally and affectionately known, must have achieved greatness in any age and any sphere. A brilliant journalist and commentator, with an unrivalled command of language and a style that was unmistakable, he was a considerable minor painter and in his own right, a leading historian. His biography of his great ancestor, the first Duke of Marlborough, was, at any rate until quite recently, regarded as almost the definitive work on the subject. His histories of the two World Wars are too well known to need much mention here; his *River War*, on the late nineteenth-century campaign in Egypt and the Sudan, during which he himself took part in the famous charge of the 21st Lancers, was a brilliant and arresting account of what was to be almost the last of Britain's 'Boy's Own Paper' wars, with all the traditional trappings of colonial troops, sun-helmets, camels and Gatling guns. Only his *History of the English-Speaking Peoples*, written during his declining years, seemed devoid of originality, and lacking in the usual force and effect.

Many have questioned his greatness, exaggerated his failings, or condemned his alleged relish for warfare; but then many have questioned the greatness of Shakespeare and railed at him for not reflecting their own opinions. The undistinguished carper is usually remembered solely by the lofty target at which he aimed.

After all, it is in a series of cameos that we remember Churchill: the subaltern in the blue and gold of the 4th Hussars, the top-hatted home secretary in the siege of Sidney Street, the Fusilier officer in the trenches of the First World War, clad in a long raincoat and for some unexplained reason, a Belgian Army helmet, the bricklayer at Chartwell in an enormously high-crowned bowler, then posing on the steps of the Admiralty in 1939; and so to the immortal rhetoric of the Battle of Britain speeches and that unforgettable night of 1945, when the familiar stocky figure with the white-spotted dark bow tie stood on the balcony at Buckingham Palace, next to the Royal Family, brandishing the inevitable cigar and giving his victory sign in reply to the crowds roaring their acclaim of the last great triumph of the Empire.

As a boy, Churchill experienced the utmost difficulty in passing into Harrow. He himself relates that all he could do in the written examination was to inscribe the figure 'one' in the margin, and after a prolonged interval for meditation, to place a pair of brackets round it. On this insubstantial evidence of scholarship, he was, nevertheless, admitted to the school by the judicious decision of the Head Master, Dr Welldon. Once there, he evinced a characteristic inclination to occupy the centre of the stage. In his first summer term, he distinguished himself by shoving Leo Amery, later to be a Cabinet colleague, into 'Ducker', the school swimming pool; this was the more unfortunate, as Amery was not only head of the school, but occupied half-a-dozen other positions of eminence, athletic and otherwise. Nor did Churchill mend matters by explaining that his mistake arose from Amery's diminutive size. Later a visiting fencing master was given a demonstration in Speech Room when he called for a volunteer to participate in an apple-on-the-head experiment in the style of William Tell. We are told that for a few moments there was an uneasy pause; not from any motive of self-preservation, but from considerations of precedence. 'The Head of the School looked in mute enquiry towards the Captain of Cricket'; the latter raised his eyebrows in the direction of the rackets pair; and so on. 'Suddenly there was a commotion up at the end where the lower-boys sit' and the youthful Churchill burst into sight and onto the platform where the apple was duly and neatly skewered from his head without so much as disturbing his parting. In 1892, the year Churchill won

Practising on the Mysterious Circle (from Thibaust).

the Public Schools Foil Championship, the proceedings were diversified by an exhibition bout between him and Instructor Dearnly of the Life Guards, sometime army champion. The future prime minister won a convincing victory, earning high praise for his skill, though the newspaper reporter had to admit that the soldier was at a considerable disadvantage, fencing in his ordinary clothes and shoes on a slippery floor.

It would seem that Winston took no further active part in fencing in later life; his favourite recreation in the Army was polo; but in 1953 all fencers experienced much pleasure and satisfaction when he accepted the Honorary Presidency of the Amateur Fencing Association.

Circle. (See Cercle.)

Circle, The Mysterious. The geometrical basis of all footwork and dis-

tance in the seventeenth-century Spanish school. According to Thibaust, its diameter was the length of an average man from the soles of his feet to his finger-tips extended at arm's length above his head. (See Spanish School and Thibaust.)

Circolazione, (It.). 1) A circular parry, or circular action described with one's point round the opponent's weapon.

2) Barbasetti treats such actions more specifically as the second (counter-disengaging) action of a *doublé*. He goes so far as to distinguish these actions according to the line in which they are executed. The deception of a counter of *quarte* is the circular outward feint; of a counter of *tierce*, the circular inward feint; of a counter of *seconde*, the circular upward feint, and of the counter of *quinte* (that is to say his own definition of *quinte*, really a high *quarte*) the circular downward feint.

Circolazione E Finta, (It.). Barbasetti's term for the *doublé*.

Circular Beat. (See Beat.)

Circular Bind. A bind (in the Hungarian sense of an engagement, probably with some opposition) following an initial circular movement by the executant round his adversary's blade. It seems almost indistinguishable from the change bind (q.v.).

Circular Double Feint Attacks. The name given by Vass to such compound attacks as the feint straight-thrust, counter-disengage twice, or the feint disengagement, counter disengage twice (*triplé*). Again, his definition – at least in translation – seems likely to cause confusion.

Circular Feint. (See Circolazione.)

Circular Parry. So-called because the point of the weapon describes a circle. The action and technique are very similar to a change of engagement; the defender's point is dropped under the attacking blade, then lifted, and by means of the 'principle of defence' (opposition of *forte* to *foible*) the opponent's weapon is deflected outside the target area. The defender's blade thus finishes in the position whence it started, having roughly described a circle – clockwise in *sixte*, anti-clockwise in *quarte*. The parry is performed with the fingers, not the wrist, and it is most important to keep the hand in one place. There is a tendency to raise it in *sixte*, and in *quarte* to make the circle with the hand and not the point. The former error sometimes results in a failure to catch the opponent's blade, besides militating against an accurate riposte. In the latter case, the line is temporarily opened to the attack.

In the low line, everything is reversed. The defending blade is carried over the attacking blade and the movement, in *septime* is clockwise, in *octave*, anti-clockwise.

Some confusion has arisen from the fact that a synonym for this parry is the counter-parry, i.e., it counters the circular or partly circular action of a disengagement.

Circular Single Feint Attacks. The name given by Vass to such compound attacks as the feint straight-thrust, counter-disengage, or the feint disengage, counter-disengage (the *doublé*). The term seems slightly misleading since it is not the feint in such cases which is the circular blade action, but the concluding movement of the attack which deceives the opponent's attempt to change the line of his parry.

Circular Transfer, (Hung.). The *enveloppement*.

Civil Salute. (See Salute.)

Classified are those lady fencers included in an annually prepared list of approximately one hundred, based on the results of home competitions during the previous season. It is divided into three categories, A, B, and C, and each individual's category admits or precludes her entry to the most important events.

Claybeg. The original name for what is now known as the 'claymore' (q.v.). The claybeg was much smaller than the claymore proper, which was a two-handed weapon.

Claymore. The Highland broadsword, the long straight blade alone often reaching forty-two inches in length. The weapon was generally distinguished by a rather elaborate and quite unmistakable basket-hilt.

Cloak and Sword. In the sixteenth century, the rapier was too long and heavy to allow of defensive actions being performed with it at all readily. Generally, parries were executed by the dagger (*main-gauche*) in the left hand, but as an alternative the cloak could be employed for protection, and was regarded as important enough to warrant serious discussion in the contemporary manuals of instruction. It was supposed to be wound twice round the unarmed forearm and a part was left dangling loose, which was capable not only of entangling the point in a thrust, but also of stopping cuts, provided, of course, that the swordsman's leg was kept out of the way, for there must be no resistance behind it.

Close Quarters. Fencing may continue at close quarters when the normal fencing distance has been reduced, either accidentally or by design. Formally it was much deprecated, as leading to confused, unsystematic actions which it was impossible for the jury to follow; it has now become an integral feature of fencing with the electric apparatus and has resulted in much body movement and displacement of the target, as well as highly angulated thrusts directed at unusual parts of the target, such as the shoulder and the back.

Clover, The Four-Leaf. An elementary training exercise in point control and finger-play. By the correct use of manipulators and aids, the point must describe in the air the outline of a four-leaf clover, conjoined in the centre like the four leaves of the plant. (See Training of Eight Leaves.)

Coaches' Club. The association of those who have qualified as coaches, by passing the Coaches' or Adv-

The Cloak used for offence as well as defence (from Alfieri).

anced Coaches' Examinations of the Amateur Fencing Association.

Cob's Traverse. A derisive name for a side-step, a step backwards in preference to parrying, or even incontinent flight; this last being the resort of one cob, a notorious Elizabethan brawler whenever he discovered that his adversary was likely to give as good as he received.

Coccia, (It.). The guard of the weapon.

Codolo, (It.). The tang of the blade.

Cohen, R.A. One of the leading British sabreurs of the seventies and early eighties. He was the winner of

the Championship in 1974 and 1980 and runner-up in 1973, 1975, 1976 and 1978.

Colichemarde. A peculiar variation of the small-sword which appeared in the early eighteenth century. The top third of the blade next to the hilt was much thicker than usual; below this, it narrowed very abruptly to the usual inconsiderable width. This odd construction was supposed to increase its strength; while its triangular section, hollowed on the three sides, rendered it very light in the point. It was said to have been devised by Count John Charles von Konigsmark (q.v.) and is allegedly a corruption of his name.

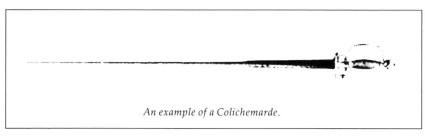

An example of a Colichemarde.

Collecting Parry. The circular or counter parry.

Colman, Ronald. Not only one of the best-looking, but the most debonair of the great Hollywood actors of his day. He had seen service on the Western Front with the London Scottish, by coincidence the regiment in which Basil Rathbone served. His style and delivery were unique – the whimsical sideglance, the nonchalant irony, the hint of disillusioned wisdom were alike unmistakable and inimitable. He was a gentleman, both on and off the screen. The part of Sydney Carton in *A Tale of Two Cities* fitted him like a glove and he played Rudolf Rassendyl in what most critics regard as the definitive version of *The Prisoner of Zenda*. Few will forget his duel with Count Rupert (Fairbanks junior) and their ironically sinister repartees as their shadows darted and leaped on the gloomy castle walls; although one rather prolonged phrase of repeated *redoublements* from *seconde* to *tierce*, effective as it may have been on the sound-track, was not in itself too impressive to the initiated.

Colours. In 1905, English internationals were awarded a white cap with a red Tudor Rose worked on the peak; but exactly when, if ever, this headgear was actually worn, is hard to say. In 1906, not only the cap, but the Union Jack armlet were made compulsory for international teams; recommended, were a ribbon for straw hats and two coats, a white blazer with the Tudor Rose on the pocket and a most curious garment – a long, double-breasted coat of blue flannel, similarly adorned. Precisely when the latter was supposed to be worn remains a mystery. Members of the A.F.A. were entitled to the last two articles of attire without the breast pocket insignia. Further developments followed in due course. In 1922 lady internationals were granted a badge consisting of a Tudor Rose and sword, while from 1932 fencers participating in the Anglo-Scottish match, which has never been regarded as being of full international status, wore an English Rose embroidered on a brassard of white silk. Then in 1951, by which time the Quadrangular Contest had replaced the Anglo-Scottish, England teams wore the St George's Cross instead of the English Rose. In 1947, fencers in certain overseas events of importance, but below full international level, were distinguishable by an armlet of crossed swords and a shield bearing the Union Jack over all, with the words 'Amateur Fencing Association' beneath.

Colpo d'Arresto and Colpo di Tempo, (It.). The stop-hit and time-hit respectively. Léon Bertrand speaking for the Italian school, claims that the meaning of the terms should be reversed. The time-hit deflects the opponent's attack while simultaneously hitting him, thus 'stopping' the blade; while the stop-hit must arrive ahead of the opponent's attack, thus gaining 'time'.

Combined Feints are feints of different types of simple attack which deceive successive combinations of the various parries.

Combined Services Fencing Association was founded in 1936; its post-war revival was largely due to Colonel G. Gelder. Not only has the association given valuable support to fencing in general as well as in the services; its members have provided the extremely efficient scorers and time-keepers at the Martini Epée Competition, the World Youth Championships and other events.

36

Coming to the Close. Getting within distance and seizing the opponent's blade (Angelo).

Commanding. Hope's term for seizing the opponent's blade.

Commanding the Sword. A phrase used by the Scottish master, Sir John Hope, for seizing the adversary's weapon with the unarmed hand; a surprise action recommended by masters for use in a free-for-all as late as the early eighteenth century.

Compagnie des Maîtres en Fait d'Armes. (See Academy of Arms, Paris.)

Compases, (Span.). The different lengths of the several steps or *pasadas*.

Compass, Thrusting within, (arch.). To thrust with the blade in a straight line with the arm.

Compelling Distance. A distance between master and pupil somewhat less than is customary, advocated by Szabo for teaching the rudiments.

Compelling Positions and Tasks. Szabo's term for the practice of regulating or limiting the movements of the pupil's blade and body, by means of obstacles or barriers. For example, a fencer whose feet are not clear of the ground when performing certain actions might have some article placed in his path which must not be disturbed; or the master might use his own weapon or arm to ensure that the pupil's blade travelled to the target on the appropriate line and at the correct height.

Composed Attack. An attack composed of one or more feints; the same as a compound attack.

Composed Riposte. A compound riposte.

Composite Attack or Riposte. Other terms for the compound attack and compound riposte.

Compound Attack. A compound attack is composed of more than one blade action and incorporates one or more feints. The conception is this: a feint attack is made to draw the defender's blade towards it in an attempt to parry; the defending blade is then deceived (the *trompement*) and the real attack delivered in one of the lines left open. At one time attacks including two, or even three feints, which deceived the corresponding number of parries were fairly common; at present owing to the heavier electric foil and the tendency to fence with absence of blade, more than one feint is extremely rare. Formerly, too, in the days when the conventional foilist at all costs maintained contact with his adversary's weapon by means of constant covering actions and changes of engagement, the compound attack was often launched *au pied ferme*, i.e., the feint was delivered from the on-guard position and the real attack not executed until it was seen what sort of parry the defender decided to make. Then the appropriate *trompement* could be executed.

More recently, the progressive compound attack became fashionable, that is to say, the feint and the final action of the attack were combined into one smooth continuous movement during the course of the lunge itself. Obviously, this demanded expert judgement of distance and considerable skill in finger-play – the defender's parry having to be rounded at comparatively close quarters – and suffered from the further disadvantage that as there was no pause

Corps-à-Corps. Berger and Damotte, 1904. Damotte finds an answer to the flèche (from F.H. Townsend).

Feint of cut-over, the simple parry being deceived by a disengagement into the low line. In practice, the two blade actions were, in this case, often combined into one.

5) Counter-disengagement disengage. On the opponent's attempt to change the line of his engagement, his circular blade action was deceived by a feint of the counter-disengagement. If he then attempted a simple parry, this was in turn deceived by an ordinary disengagement. This attack was often called the 'one-two on the change'.

6) Counter-disengagement twice. If the feint of counter-disengagement was met by a counter (circular) parry, the latter had to be deceived by another counter-disengagement.

7) *Coulé-dégagé.* A feint of the *coulé*, followed by a disengagement. A most effective attack when the feint was delivered with real conviction into a slightly opened *sixte* engagement. The opponent tended to cover instinctively, exaggeratedly and with some contraction of the sword-arm, so that the attacking point, with good timing, swung under his blade and with no further obstacle to circumvent, was on his target almost before he realised what had happened.

It will be observed, that all the above examples, which do not pretend to be exhaustive, and indeed all compound attacks, are merely composed of various permutations and combinations of the four simple attacks (straight-thrust, disengagement, cut-over and counter-disengagement). For instance, a variation of the one-two, often employed when fencing with absence of blade, is the feint of straight-thrust disengagement. This general principle, however, is not always apparent to novices until it is pointed out to them. It must also be stressed that the nature of the second and any

at all between the attacker's blade actions, he had to anticipate the type of his opponent's parry and match his deception of it on the basis of probability alone. Hence the fencer who consistently relied on the progressive compound attack had to endure a high percentage of failures and a considerable degree of frustration when, as often happened, his opponent executed a parry different from that which had been expected.

The most common form of compound attack with the foil was, and still is, the one-two, consisting of a feint of disengagement to draw a simple parry, which is then deceived

by a second disengagement. Other common forms of compound attack were the:

1) *Doublé.* Feint of disengagement, then, if this was met by the counter (circular) parry, the latter was deceived by a counter-disengagement.

2) *Coupé-coupé* or double cut-over. In the same way as the one-two, this deceived the simple parry by a second *coupé*, or cut-over.

3) *Coupé-dégagé* or cut-over-disengagement. A feint cut-over, followed by a disengagement, which together again deceived the simple parry.

4) *Coupé-dessous* (cut-over-below).

subsequent feints and similarly the final action of the attack must perforce depend on the parry or parries executed by the defender; the counter-disengagement will only deceive a circular blade action; the cutover and disengagement will only be successful against simple parries. Hence the difficulty in making the 'progressive' attack successfully, as it is impossible to be certain in advance what the opponent's reactions will be.

The most common two-feint attacks were the one-two-three deceiving two simple parries and the *triplé* or feint of disengagement followed by a feint of the counter-disengagement and a final counter-disengagement attack. This, of course, could only prove effective against an opponent taking two counter (circular) parries in succession.

A famous compound attack, but confined largely to the fencing lesson rather than the bout, was the *doublé de doublé* – a feint of the *doublé* – followed immediately by another *doublé* in the opposite direction. Old-time masters used to derive grim pleasure from reducing their pupils to a state of frustrated confusion and nervous exhaustion by requiring them to execute several such attacks in rapid succession, starting alternately from opposite lines of engagement.

Compound attacks at sabre depend on the same basic principle, namely, the defender's parry is drawn by a feint and then deceived, though as fencing with this weapon is normally practised with absence of blade, the number of possible attacks is, in practice, somewhat more limited. The most widely used are the feint head, cut at flank and vice versa and the feint flank, cut at chest and vice versa.

At one time elaborate compound attacks at the wrist and arm were

38

rehearsed during lessons, but these seem to have gone out of fashion, for few are the sabreurs today who will stand their ground and take the parry to the feint at wrist or inner arm upon which all the subsequent actions depend; they just tend to spring back out of harm's way.

In theory, at any rate, any compound attack with the foil can be executed with the sabre, as the latter possesses a point as well as an edge. A one-two with the point would be a perfectly valid method of deceiving a simple parry; and since any attack with the sabre's point is often met by a counter (circular) parry, a feint straight-thrust, counter-disengagement, whether the latter concludes with edge or point, is an entirely practical possibility.

Owing to the greater distance between the fencers, which for tactical reasons obtains at sabre, two-feint attacks are still far more common with this weapon than is now the case at foil. Also, the bigger target area renders it far more difficult for the sabreur to recover from a parry or parries which have been deceived, in order successfully to ward off the final offensive action. The most popular and successful two-feint attacks are head-flank-head and flank-head-flank; and the other varieties and combinations should be sufficiently obvious.

It may be noted here that Castello, in his remarks on sabre fencing, classifies as 'compound' not only attacks incorporating a feint, but those preceded by an attack on the blade.

At épée, a very high percentage of all attacks are delivered at the opponent's wrist and forearm; hence the compound attacks are usually intended to deceive the three parries, *sixte*, counter-of-*sixte*, and *octave*, with which the épée fencer protects this part of his target. Bearing this in mind and allowing for the tactical

differences arising from the large épée target and the absence of formal blade engagements, compound attacks with this weapon differ little, at any rate in theory, from those at foil.

Compound Counter-Attack. A counter-attack including one or more feints.

Compound Feints. Combinations of feints.

Compound Parries. Castello's term for successive parries; not illogically, as they are the defence against compound attacks.

Compound Preparation of Attack. Two preparations of attack, performed simultaneously; as, for example, a step forward combined with some action against the opponent's blade, such as a beat.

Compound Prise-de-Fer. Two *prises-de-fer* performed successively, contact with the opponent's blade, however, being fully maintained throughout both actions.

Compound Riposte. A riposte which includes one or more feints. If executed with a lunge it is technically indistinguishable from a compound attack; if executed from the on-guard position against an opponent remaining on the lunge, or at close quarters, the feints must be delivered with a bent arm; otherwise, owing to the close proximity of the fencers, it will prove impossible to pass over or under the adversary's blade without hitting either his mask or his sword-arm, or entangling one's point in his guard. In conception, compound ripostes are exactly the same as compound attacks; they may be executed by one-two, *doublé*, and so on.

Condé, Louis-Joseph, Duc de Bourbon, Prince de. An eighteenth-century descendant of the 'Great Condé' (1621-86) who had been the hero of the Fronde and the architect of some of the greatest military successes of the reign of Louis XIV. When the Vicomte d'Agout, a guards captain, broke off his engagement on the grounds that the lady concerned had been the Prince's mistress, Condé ordered him to resign his commission. D'Agout obeyed, but high words passed between them and a meeting was arranged. Condé on this occasion displayed much of the high breeding and chivalry which characterised the *Ancien Régime* at its best; he handed his opponent a written declaration of his own responsibility in the matter and letters of recommendation to foreign courts, lest his death should oblige the other to leave the country. In the event, it was the Prince who was slightly wounded and he gave further proof of his magnanimous disposition by re-instating and even promoting d'Agout.

Confrérie Royale et Chevalière de Saint-Michel. Perhaps the most celebrated fencing club of all time, it was founded at Ghent in the early seventeenth century. Its headquarters were the old Drapers' Hall in that city. In 1603 it received the distinction of being awarded the Order of the Golden Fleece in recognition of the services of some of its members at the siege of Ostend; the only comparable honour in our own day must be the award of the G.C. to Malta. From that time onward the association became increasingly exclusive and none but royalty or members of the greatest families of the Low Countries were admitted.

Contra-Cavatione or Cavazione, (It.). The counter-disengagement.

Contra-Caveating Parade. Hope's term for the circular parry which he strongly recommends, almost to the exclusion of simple parries; but he stresses that speed is of the essence, otherwise the movement will prove futile.

Contra-Guardia, (It.). A covered engagement of the blades; a term coined by Giganti.

Contra Postura, (It.). Against any guard or attacking position adopted by the adversary, an appropriate counter-position was, in seventeenth-century theory, always supposed to be assumed.

Contra-Tempo. 1) Counter-time or counter-tempo.
2) Capo Ferro's expression for a counter-attack in *tierce* or *quarte.*

Contraction Parry. (See Cutting the Line.)

Contrarisposta, (It.). Counter-riposte.

Contre Dégagement. The counter-disengagement; until about the mid eighteenth century, the term was also applied to the counter (circular) parry, because it was 'against' the disengagement.

Contre Parade. (See Circular and Counter Parry.)

Contre Prinse. A sixteenth-century French term for a disarmament.

Contretemps. 1) Counter-time. 'Every action made by an attacker against a stop-hit made by his opponent.' (Szabo.) (See Time and Counter-Time.)
2) In the vocabulary of Sir William Hope, the famous fencing master of the late seventeenth and early eighteenth century, it meant the double hit (*coup fourré*) caused when a fencer mistakenly attacks his opponent just as the latter has already embarked on his attack. In such a case, the culprit may be said to be attacking 'against the time' or 'against the *tempo*'; *tempo* being the delivery of an attack when the antagonist is inattentive, performing some subsidiary action, or in an unfavourable position.
3) Barbasetti's interpretation: a feint to draw the adversary's compound counter-attack (the adversary anticipating a parry and intending to deceive it); but his feint is ignored and the final action of his compound blade-work is forestalled by a stop-hit. Barbasetti blandly comments that this is 'easily seen as an action into *tempo* directed against your adversary's feint into *tempo*'.
4) In colloquial English, 'contretemps' has come to mean 'a disastrous blunder', presumably deriving from Hope's interpretation of the phrase.

Conventions are found in those sections of the rules of foil and sabre fencing which govern the priority of hits and are intended to encourage correct play and to reduce fencing phrases to recognisable and analysable movements. Briefly, in the case of a double hit, priority is given to that fencer whose arm was first straightened with blade in line and point or edge threatening the opponent's target. In the case of absolutely simultaneous attacks, or when the president is unable to decide on the initiator of the attack, no hit at all is awarded and the fencers are simply replaced on guard. Renewals of attacks, such as the *remise* and *redoublement* must arrive one movement ahead of the final movement of any riposte. Similarly, stop-hits and stop-cuts must gain a period of fencing time on the attack.

'Conventional' though such rules are, it is clear that they are based on a reality. No-one but a fool would, in the course of a duel, attempt to attack into a straight arm and threatening point without first deflecting it. Again, in actual combat, the stop-hit must arrest the attacker in his tracks; a renewed attack, to be made with impunity, must ensure that no riposte is ever delivered at all. These are the realities reflected in these apparently artificial regulations, although it must be admitted that in the very fast exchanges of foil and sabre-play, a technically legitimate *remise* or stop-hit might not really have been early enough entirely to have prevented a riposte or an attack if sharps were being used.

In épée fencing, there are no conventions at all. It is purely a matter of time as registered by the electrical recording apparatus. If both hits arrive within one twenty-fifth of a second, then hits are scored against both competitors. If more than that interval elapses, then the first alone is registered as valid. Obviously, so small a margin of time would not in practice prevent both swordsmen being killed or wounded; paradoxically, therefore, épée fencing, which originally was supposed most closely to resemble the real duel, has become in this respect quite as conventional as the other two weapons.

In fact, a genuine duel between accomplished swordsmen would be far more likely to acquire something of the character of a classic foil bout (attack, riposte, counter-riposte) than the contemporary scuffle in which mere prancers, who would be better employed in track events, are quite prepared to risk sustaining four hits (i.e., four deaths), if by reason of their mere speed and **opportunism** they retain a reasonable chance of registering five hits

on their opponents. In the event of failure, they can always blame the president; even the eastern Europeans face nothing worse than a return to the salt-mines.

Cooky. A derisive slang expression heard principally at sabre, to indicate that the cut arrived not on the target, but on the guard, or, if it did touch the arm, had been intercepted by the guard first, thus being robbed of all penetrative power and validity; a corruption of *coquille* (the guard).

Cooperman, A.R. started fencing during his national service in the R.A.F. His original weapon was foil and he was good enough to take second place in the British Championships of 1953, besides representing his country on a number of occasions with this weapon. However, it was with the sabre that he excelled; a tall left-hander, he was three times successful in the Championship (1954, 1960 and 1961), four times second (1958, 1959, 1962, 1964) and was ever-present in internationals until well into the 1960s. In 1958 he reached the semi-finals of the World Sabre Championship, the best performance ever by an Englishman at this weapon. He won the Corble Cup in 1963 and at foil and sabre together, amassed no fewer than eight Commonwealth gold medals.

Copertino, (It.). The *croisé* according to Lukovitch. The *Sports Dictionary in Seven Languages* defines it as 'a bind into *seconde*'. P.E. Nobbs (*Fencing Tactics*, 1936) took a radically different view, regarding it as a 'small feint of cut-over', the opponent's point not being cleared.

Coquille. The guard; so-called because at one period, the two parts of the guard, one on either side of the

handle, might have been thought to bear a fanciful resemblance to a sea-shell. (See Shell-Guard.)

Corble, A.H. British Sabre Champion in 1922 and 1927, he represented Great Britain on eight occasions at the Olympics and elsewhere. The Corble Cup, first contested in 1947, was named after him, but probably his chief claim to fame was his stupendous collection of weapons and fencing books. Of the latter, he was said to have amassed more than 2000.

Corps-à-Corps. The situation arising when the fencers' bodies are in contact. It is not permitted at foil and sabre; the bout must be halted and the opponents replaced on guard in their original positions. The fencer who systematically and deliberately forces a *corps-à-corps* is penalised by a penalty-hit following a warning in the same bout. *Corps-à-corps* is legitimate at épée, provided that it is not conducted with violence or brutality.

Coulé. To extend the sword-arm, the blade remaining in contact with the opponent's blade and slipping lightly along it. The action may be completed by an attack, or the *coulé* may serve as a feint to force the opponent into a hasty covering action, which may then be deceived by a disengagement. Some authorities have even been known to classify the *coulé* as an attack on the blade, though this seems to be straining the interpretation or perhaps confusing it with a light *froissement* (q.v.). Another name for the *coulé* is the *glissade*.

Counter. 1) In the sixteenth and seventeenth centuries, an attack with point or edge 'into' the opponent's attack, so that the latter was

Cups — Leon Paul International Competition. Gosbee (England) has his stop-hit parried by Esparanza (Spain).

hit while his own weapon was deflected; a parry and riposte performed, as it were, simultaneously. (See Stop-Hit with Opposition and Time-Hit.)

2) A shortened form of counter parry and counter-riposte. Thus we hear fencers and presidents referring to the 'first counter', meaning 'the first counter-riposte' and so on.

Counter-Action. The time-hit. (Barbasetti.)

Counter-Action Parry. The same thing as a contraction parry. (See Cutting the Line.)

Counter-Attack or Counter-Offensive Action. These are attacks delivered against the opponent's attack. Assuming that both hits arrive, the counter-attack, at foil and sabre, can only be valid if it gains a period of fencing time and lands on the opponent before he has initiated

the final movement of his attack. Thus if the counter-attacker registered a hit while his opponent was still executing a feint, the counter-attack would be valid, even though the original attacker's blade eventually arrived on target.

At épée, the counter-attack can only be completely successful if it arrives more than one twenty-fifth of a second ahead of the attack; otherwise, a double hit is scored. It is the electric apparatus which automatically decides this delicate timing.

The two most common forms of the counter-attack are the stop-hit and time-hit (q.v.). The latter is now generally termed the stop-hit with opposition and as it is intended to deflect the adversary's blade while simultaneously hitting him, the question of fencing time, in this case, should be immaterial. The stop-hit and stop-cut, on the other hand, must most definitely gain a period of fencing time on the attack.

Counter-Bind. The circular bind.

Counter-Change. Upon the opponent's change of engagement, instantly to perform the same action oneself, thus restoring the original relative position of the blades.

Counter-Disengagement. One of the three indirect attacks. It deceives the opponent's blade as he attempts to change the engagement. Although the technique is identical with that of the ordinary disengagement, it is the one attack in fencing which cannot be executed until the opponent makes the first move.

Counter-Guard. An additional bar or bars, on the inside of the swordsman's wrist, opposite to the knuckle-bow; generally found in rapiers dating from the sixteenth and early seventeenth centuries.

Counter-Offensive. (See Counter-Attack.)

Counter Parry. A circular parry (q.v.); a term derived from the French *contre-parade*, first appearing in the seventeenth century.

Counter-Pass. To advance or retire by means of a pass, in the opposite direction to one's opponent, so maintaining the measure.

Counter-Return. (See Counter-Riposte.)

Counter-Riposte. The next offensive action delivered by the original attacker, after he has successfully parried his opponent's riposte. It is known as the 'first counter-riposte', and may consist of any type of blade action, simple or compound, i.e., it corresponds exactly to all the possible blade actions of the simple or compound attack and the simple or compound riposte. It may be accompanied by further movements of the feet, or be delivered while still on the lunge, or during or after the recovery to guard, forward or backward. It is the sequence alone which makes a counter-riposte what it is. Exactly the same considerations apply to the second counter-riposte (the next offensive action following the successful parry by the original defender of the first counter-riposte), the third and fourth counter-ripostes and so on. It will be observed that the odd numbers in an exchange of several counter-ripostes are delivered by the original attacker; the even numbers by the original defender.

Counter-Riposte in Counter-Time. A very complicated sequence of actions analysed by Professor Crosnier and arising from the tendency of some épéeists to execute an indirect riposte against the unsuccessful attacker who is in the habit of recovering to guard with a circular or half-circular parry. Such ripostes can be outwitted by the attacker starting his parry, then executing a stop-hit or very delayed *redoublement*, according to the phrasing, against the riposter. Professor Crosnier suggests that the latter might then feint a riposte to draw the stop-hit, parry it and 'counter-riposte in counter-time'. (See Time and Counter-Time.)

It may be that there exist swordsmen capable not only of such subtle analysis, but also possessing the ability to translate it into practice at a moment's notice: we can only say, that we have never met them.

Counter-Thrust. When both antagonists were hit together.

Counter-Time. The art of drawing a stop-hit or stop-cut from one's opponent, parrying it and riposting. This

A Counter-Attack, the adversary's thrust having been parried by a dagger (from Fabris).

definition seems logical, as the fencer who takes advantage of some feint or unwary move on the part of his adversary in order to stop-hit, is said to be exploiting time. He who foresees this and turns it to his own advantage must therefore be acting against the time, in other words, counter-time. But for other interpretations, see Contretemps.

Counter-time, one example of 'second intention', is frequently employed at sabre and even more at épée, since the larger target area at these weapons and the longer fencing measure dictated thereby, which has to be closed before an attack can be made, create conditions in which counter-attacks are highly popular. The answer, in turn, is therefore counter-time, much employed by practitioners of these weapons.

Counter-Time, Defensive and Offensive. Some masters made a very subtle distinction between defensive and offensive counter-time. In the former case, the executant merely feints to draw the stop-hit, then parries and ripostes, quite possibly from the on-guard position, though this need not necessarily be the case. In the case of offensive counter-time, the fencer's intentions are from the start more definitely aggressive. He is looking all the time for the opportunity to attack, but

knowing that his opponent is in the habit of regularly stop-hitting, hesitates to do so until he has drawn the stop-hit with a feint and successfully parried it, then he can safely execute the riposte with a full-blooded lunge, or *flèche*.

Coup. The hit.

Coup d'Arrêt. A stop-hit.

Coup Cavé. An angulated hit. Hutton advocates the pronation of the hand when attacking the opponent's inside line, supination when threatening his outside line.

Coup Double. A double hit.

Coup Droit. The straight-thrust.

Coup Fourré. A simultaneous attack, resulting in both swordsmen being hit.

Coup de Jarnac. A stop-cut at the back of the thigh, which hamstrings the opponent. (See de Jarnac.)

Coup Jeté. (See Thrown Hit.)

Coup Lancé. The A.F.A. rules clearly interpret this as a hit resulting from an attack already started (*lancé*) before the president's cry of 'Halt!'. It therefore stands, but this is not the case when full-time is called or signalled before the actual arrival of the hit on target.

Coup Sec. A crisp meeting of the blades.

Coup de Temps. 1) A time-hit. 2) An attack in time.

Coup au Tranchant. A stop-cut.

Coupé or Cut-Over. One of the three indirect attacks. (See Simple Attacks.) In this case the attacking blade passes over that of the opponent and into the opposite line. The *coupé* was one of the distinguishing marks of the French, as opposed to the Italian School, although Danet advocated the restriction of its use to the riposte. Clearly, it is of especial value against the fencer who tends to drop his hand and elevate his point too much.

Coupé-Coupé, Double Cut-Over or Cut-Over Twice. A feint of the cut-over, followed by a second cut-over which carries the attack to the opponent's target. (See Compound Attacks.) This is not an attack to be used often; the withdrawal of the sword-arm for the second cut-over means that a period of fencing time is quite definitely being lost, and an opponent who is anticipating it will be able to stop-hit successfully.

Coupé Dessous. Feint of cut-over, followed by disengagement into the low line to carry the attack to the target. (See Compound Attacks.)

Coupé Sous les Armes. (See Coupé Dessous.)

Court of Appeal. A body consisting of one representative from each competing nation is established for all international competitions other

than those between two countries only. Those submitting a complaint do well not to act over-hastily, as a deposit of a hundred francs or its equivalent is required, which may be confiscated if the appeal is considered to be frivolous.

Court of Honour. In 1679, an Edict of Louis XIV prescribed the death penalty for all involved in duels, including seconds and thirds. Further, a Court of Honour, consisting of the marshals of France, was established to decide on the reparation and penalty when provocation had occurred. However, the novelty soon wore off, the King, like all contemporary monarchs, was inconsistent in his enforcement of the law and the Court of Honour faded into an obscurity which deepened under the lax regency of Philip of Orleans in the next reign; perhaps this was what had been intended all along.

Court Sword. A somewhat impracticable, indeed, almost symbolic survival or imitation of the smallsword, still worn today with official court dress.

Coustil à Croc. A single-handed short sword of the Middle Ages.

Couteau de Chasse. Literally, a hunting-knife; in fact, a short sword worn by eighteenth-century gentlemen at night or when travelling, especially in the country.

Covered. A term relating to the position of the blades when engaged; that is to say, the fencer's weapon is held in such a position that his opponent cannot hit him without first altering the relative position of the blades. (See Engagement.)

Covered Stop-Hit. The same as a time-hit (q.v.).

Covering. When the blades of the fencers are crossed (engaged), one or even both may be uncovered, i.e., vulnerable if the opponent extends his arm and attacks without having to alter the relative position of the blades (the 'straight-thrust'). However, by exerting a slight pressure on the adversary's blade, the latter may be carried across the target area and just sufficiently far outside it to render such an attack futile. This process is known as covering.

Coward Guard. A name for the hanging guard (q.v.), so-called because it was supposed to be highly effective for defence, but not allowing much scope for offensive action.

Coward's Parry. (See Ninth Parry.)

Crab. A derisive term used by masters of the peppery order for the fencer who fails to keep his heels in line and consequently advances and retires diagonally instead of in a straight line along the *piste*. Hence 'crabbing' and 'to crab'.

Craig Sword. A trophy presented by Captain A.D.E. Craig. In 1949 the All-England Fencing Club held the first competition for the Sword, 'fought under somewhat complicated and original rules'.

Croisé. To force the opponent's blade downwards while keeping it on the same side of the target. (See Prise-de-Fer.) The literal translation of *croisé* is crossed and would therefore seem to be more appropriate to the bind, with its diagonal action across the body; indeed, by certain masters in former days, the term was in fact applied to that preparation. In western Europe, however, the word is now exclusively used to describe the action whereby the opponent's blade is transported from high to

43

low line on the same side of the target, i.e., *quarte* to *septime* or *sixte* to *octave*. Possibly the use of the term is justified by the initial stages, in which the executant's blade is allowed to pivot over and across his adversary's at a slight angle, the better to gain control of it.

Quite the most difficult of the *prises-de-fer*, because of the difficulty of controlling the opposite blade while angulating the point back towards the target for the final attack, it is also the most risky, because of the likelihood of the opposing blade escaping from the contact. Very difficult indeed from *sixte* to *octave*, it is seldom used on this side except, of course, when facing a left-hander.

Nor is this vertical preparation ever used from low line to high line, owing to the dangerous lack of control of the adversary's point during the process, although, as a somewhat theoretical possibility, *octave* to *sixte* might conceivably be employed against a left-hander, terminating, presumably, with a thrust under his arm-pit.

Croisé, Time Hit by. The execution of the *croisé* against the opponent's attack, effected by the simultaneous extension of the sword-arm, forcing down of the adversary's blade, and placing of the point on target; a stroke much recommended at épée and the electric foil. (See Octave, Quarte, Septime, Croisés of.)

Cromarty-Dickson, Professor A. More than forty years ago, he was giving his immaculate foil lessons to members of the University Fencing Club in his salle up the staircase from an Oxford side-street; amongst his pupils was H.W.F. Hoskyns. All blade movements had to be minute, parries feather-light, and the rear foot had to remain absolutely flat without the slightest drag when

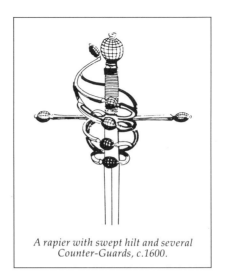

A rapier with swept hilt and several Counter-Guards, c.1600.

lunging. Mobility was not in great demand; the *flèche* was discouraged; was it an entirely false impression that épée and sabre were regarded as being of somewhat secondary importance?

Crosnier, Professor Roger. The son of Professor Léon Crosnier, who did much to popularise fencing in Scotland in the early years of this century. Roger taught at the Salle Crosnier in Edinburgh, in Dublin, in the French Army, the University of Paris and acted as Technical Adviser and Trainer to the Olympic Fencing Teams of France (1948) and Britain (1952). One of the most distinguished fencing masters of this century, he became, in 1949, the first National Coach in this country, and devised the National Coaching Scheme which could be taught to a whole class of novices by anyone who had qualified for what was then known as the A.F.A. Leaders' Certificate. Basically, all fencing actions were divided into their fundamental movements, which could be rehearsed separately, and then by a system of so-called 'progressions',

gradually joined together by reducing the number of stages from four to three, three to two and so on, until the attack, parry, etc., could finally be executed as a unity. This programme, when conducted properly, could certainly lay the foundation of a reasonably correct technique, but clearly left a good deal to be desired in the field of tactics and in the application to a competitive situation of movements only practised mechanically. However, it must be remembered that the Professor's object had been to spread a knowledge of basic foil technique as widely and quickly as possible.

The Professor's *magnum opus* was, of course, his *Fencing with the Foil*, which not only contained the scheme described above, but constituted probably the most concise, logical and comprehensive analysis of basic foil theory and technique ever compiled. The companion volumes, *Fencing with the Sabre* and *Fencing with the Epée*, though of great value to anyone seeking a coaching award, as well as any novice or intermediate fencer, did not, perhaps, emphasise quite sufficiently the need to adapt basic theory and practice to the demands of these two very different weapons.

The Professor was by no means convinced that the electric foil must inevitably lead to a drop in standards and technique, and his last work, *Fencing with the Electric Foil*, contains a number of ingenious suggestions for the successful use of the new weapon; especially may be noted the time-hit by *croisé*, following engagements in *quarte, octave* and even *septime*.

Cross. Silver's term for a parry.

Cross-Bar. The vestigial remains of the old cross-hilt, or straight *quillons*. In the Italian foil it is a thin bar set at right angles to the handle, and inside the guard, beyond which it may not project.

Cross-Blow. Saviolo's term for the *Mandritta* (q.v.).

Cross-Guard. The very simple form of guard, consisting of straight *quillons* projecting at right angles from the weapon and so forming a cross with the blade and handle.

Cross-Step. To advance or retire by crossing the legs in the manner of the old-time 'pass'.

Crossing the Line. (See Cutting the Line.)

Cuba. Under the influence of visiting Spanish masters, Cuba enjoyed a brief and startling period of supremacy in the early years of this century, due wholly to a remarkable trio; Raymond Fonst, Albertson Post and Charles Tatham. In the Olympic Games of 1904, they made a clean sweep of both foil and épée competitions; Fonst being gold medallist at both. There were no team competitions in those days, or Cuba must infallibly have won them too, and devotees of the sabre may be surprised to learn that this weapon was not included at all until the year 1908. After this spectacular and totally unheralded success, Cuba relapsed into a state of fencing obscurity from which the country has never emerged.

Cuevas, Marquis de. He was the opponent of Serge Lifar in one of the last recorded duels in France (1958), the trouble arising from some dispute over the performance of the latter's ballet *Noir et Blanc*. The really remarkable feature about this affair was its apparently well-organised publicity – not merely the meeting itself, in which Lifar was grazed on the arm – but the reconciliation and even the challenge were witnessed and photographed by the press.

Cup-Hilt. This type of guard is fashioned in the shape of a fairly shallow cup; it was common among rapiers in the sixteenth and seventeenth century and is a feature of the modern épée.

Cups. The following are the chief Challenge Cups in this country at the present time:
Baptiste Bertrand. Ladies' Junior Foil; presented by Mr A. Miller-Hallet in 1927.
De Beaumont. Presented by Mr C.-L. de Beaumont to replace the Alfred Hutton Memorial Cup (1913-1938) which was lost during the Second World War.
Cole. The R.E. Cole Memorial Cup for Amateur and Professional Sabre.
Corble. The Corble Memorial Cup for International Individual Sabre was bequeathed by Mr A.M. Corble, an Olympic Sabreur and individual Sabre Champion and first contested in 1947.
Coronation. A men's individual international foil competition. The cup was presented in 1937 by Mr F.C. Reynolds to commemorate the Coronation of George VI and is open to all foreign fencers and those British fencers who have appeared in internationals or reached the semi-finals of the open Foil Championship.
Desprez. Originally (1925) a ladies' West of England championship. Now recognised as the award for the Ladies' Individual Foil Championship.
Doyne. Presented in 1921 by the Oxford F.C. in memory of Mr R.W. Doyne, killed in the First World War, for the Men's Junior Foil Championship.

Eden. Under Twenty International Men's Foil.
Emrys Lloyd. This was originally the Doyne Cup. Now awarded at the Amateur–Professional Foil Competition.
Epée Club. The Amateur–Professional Epée Competition. Originally the Fildes Cup.
Felix. Presented by Miss G. Neligan in memory of Professors Felix Bertrand and Felix Gravé. First contested during the Second World War, it is now an invitation competition for junior lady fencers.
L.V. Fildes. Presented in 1930 by Mr Luke Fildes for the Junior Epée Championship.
Charles Gault. For the runner-up in the Graham-Bartlett Cup.
Graham-Bartlett. A cup awarded in 1939 to the school gaining the most points in the final pools of the Public Schools Championships.
Granville. A cup for teams of four, comprising a lady foilist, a man foilist, an épéeist, and a sabreur.
Horatii. See separate entry.
Magrini. Originally an individual sabre event, now the award for the Sabre Team Championship. The trophy was presented to the Sabre Club in 1913 in memory of Professor Magrini.
Martin Edmunds. The Ladies' Foil Team trophy, presented in 1909 by Mrs C.E. Martin Edmunds, Ladies' Foil Champion that year. In the first competition, it is reported that the Salle Mimiague team were so incensed by the jury's decisions that they withdrew in protest, leaving Salle Bertrand to enjoy their hollow triumph.
Miller-Hallet. An international individual épée competition of considerable prestige. The cup was presented by Mr A. Miller-Hallett and the competition, which started in 1928, was held outdoors until 1933.
Millfield. A men's and ladies' under

twenty international competition.

Nairn. Presented by Mrs C.J. Nairn in 1920, for teams of three (one at each weapon) from a select list of entrants, comprising the Services, the Sabre Club and Salle Bertrand. The competition has not taken place since 1952.

Parker. A ladies' foil competition for unclassified and category C entrants only.

Leon Paul. Replaced the Coronation Cup in 1979, the latter having been stolen.

Pearson. For the winners of the annual meeting between the B.A.F. and the A.F.A. Coaches Club.

Perigal. Ladies' Under Twenty International Foil.

Ridley Martin. The cup for the Junior Sabre Championship, presented by Lieut. Colonel A. Ridley-Martin. The first contest was in 1930. In 1937, the A.F.A. replaced the Sabre Club as the organisers.

Sporting Record. Men's Foil Team Championship; the trophy was donated by the directors of the *Sporting Record* and the event first held in 1948.

Toupie Lowther. Ladies' Foil, held annually for unclassified entrants.

Vincent Bonfil Memorial Trophy. Presented annually to the male foilist with the most successful record in all British open events.

Willoughby. The award for the Senior Schoolboys' Championship, presented in 1955 by the Misses Willoughby, in memory of Major R.P. Willoughby.

Winton. A team competition between A.F.A. sections (geographical areas) which field teams of four at Ladies' Foil, Men's Foil, Epée and Sabre. The winning team has the right to a challenge match against a London club.

Cushion or Cuscinetto, (It.). A circular piece of leather padding on the

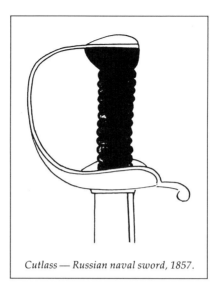

Cutlass — Russian naval sword, 1857.

inside of the guard, to prevent the fingers jarring against the metal.

Cut. A hit delivered by the edge of the sabre. Such hits may be inflicted with any part of the fore-edge, or the top third of the back-edge nearest the point.

Cut-Over. (See Coupé.)

Cut-Over Downward, The *coupé-dessous*. (Barbasetti.)

Cut-Over the Point. A circumlocutory phrase for the cut-over.

Cut-Under. The name given – originally half in jest – by some masters to the rarely used low-line attack corresponding to the cut-over. Just as the disengagement, executed in the low line, requires the blade to pass over, not under, the opponent's weapon, so the cut-over, executed from *septime* or *octave*, necessitates a smart withdrawal of the sword-arm from the elbow and the passing of the blade beneath the adversary's point. Many fencers still call this

action the cut-over, though such a description is, of course, in practice, misleading.

Cutlass. Virtually the naval equivalent of the cavalry sabre; a broad-bladed, slightly curved cutting weapon. Authorities differ on the etymology of the word; the most probable derivation appears to be from the French *coutelas*.

Cutting Edge. The modern fencing sabre is, at least partially, a two-edged weapon. The fore-edge (known to the Italians as *filo dritto*) is that edge of the blade which, when the weapon is held correctly, is naturally directed at the opponent. The back-edge (*filo falso*), like the fore-edge, is in fact blunted on the modern fencing weapon, but the third of it nearest the point is theoretically capable of dealing a cut.

Cutting the Counter Parry is when the counter (circular) parry is not properly completed, but the point cuts inwards across the last quadrant of the circle, in too much haste to close the line and complete the parry. Either the attacking blade is missed entirely, or the full opposition of *forte* to *foible* is lacking and the parry thereby rendered ineffective.

Cutting the Line. 1) Executing a circular (counter) parry in the opposite direction to what is normal, i.e., the defender's hand and blade are in *sixte*, but he executes his circular parry anti-clockwise, or vice versa if he is in *quarte*. It is most effective when taken in the *sixte* position against a left-hander who attacks on the outside of the defender's blade and can have the effect of robbing the less experienced fencer of all confidence in his attacks. Should the attack be launched on the inside of the blade, however, there are some fencers with a taste for theory and a bent for highly logical analysis who will deny that this so-called contraction parry can be performed at all; in the very nature of things, they argue, it must in practice assume the character of a rather badly executed *quarte* parry and bind.

2) A parry taken diagonally across the target from high to low line, e.g. from *sixte* to *septime*, or vice versa. The Hungarian masters term this a semi-circular parry.

Cutto. A corruption of *couteau de chasse* (q.v.).

Dagger. (See Main-Gauche.)

Damascening or Damasking. Inlaying a steel blade with patterns of gold or silver.

Damascus Blade. A watered steel blade, not really from the city of Damascus; most came from Persia.

Danet, Guillaume. A leading French master and syndic of the Paris Academy of Arms during the eighteenth century, whose chief claim to fame lay in his attempt to revise, on a more logical and systematic basis, the names of the various attacks and parries, which even today appear to be somewhat arbitrary and at that time still differed slightly between the several academies. A further refinement was a cross-analysis by which nine different positions of arm and wrist whilst delivering an attack could each be distinguished by their 'degree', i.e., the height of the hand. Danet recognised no less than five such degrees counting from above downwards, while the question of whether the hand was in pronation or supination had also to be taken into consideration. Danet distinguished between the tradi-

tional nomenclature and his own by using the terms *ancienne* and *moderne*. Thus, the traditional *prime* position he called *prime ancienne* while his re-classified *prime moderne* was the familiar quarte, since he was not the only master to regard this position as the basic on-guard position equally well adapted to attack or defence. Similarly, *tierce* became *seconde des modernes*, whilst our *seconde* was re-christened *tierce des modernes* and so forth. That he gave free reign to his genius for extreme refinements of analysis is clear from the fact that he claimed to have identified and taught no fewer than eighteen different simple parries alone.

If Danet hoped that his innovatory schemes would gain him universal gratitude and acclaim, he was grievously disappointed. His colleagues of the *Compagnie des Maîtres en fait d'Armes* rose to a man in defence of the old order and the campaign against him reached its climax with the publication of a tirade by La Boessière, who ridiculed his entire system and above all his obstinate refusal to recognise the distinction between the counter and the half-counter parry. (*Contre* and *demi-contre parade*.)

Subsequently, an influential section of the masters announced their approval of Danet's theories and although his revised terminology was never adopted, his general principles – which, indeed, were not particularly revolutionary – became the basis of foil fencing in the nineteenth and early twentieth century.

Debole, (It.). The *foible*.

Deceive. The evasion of the opponent's attempt to make contact with one's blade, either when he tries to parry, engage, or attack the blade.

Castello uses the term as a noun in place of *trompement* (q.v.).

Decisive Play. Fighting with sharps.

Defensive Position. At sabre, the guard position adopted when, for one reason or another, the fencer has committed himself to largely defensive tactics. The position generally adopted in these circumstances is virtually that of low *tierce*; the elbow very close to the right hip and the blade almost vertical. Thus the whole right-hand side of the fencer's target is protected and any attack or feint must be delivered at his head or chest. It is, of course, possible to launch an attack from the defensive position, but clearly, the blade has further to travel and the opponent has proportionately longer to see it coming.

Dégagement. The disengagement (q.v.).

Dégager. To disengage, to effect a disengagement.

Delayed Riposte. A riposte which does not follow immediately after the parry, but is delayed, either through inexperience or lack of confidence, or else deliberately for tactical reasons. The opponent, anticipating a riposte, may be discomposed by his inability to find the blade immediately, and inadvertently expose some part of his target to a delayed riposte. Moreover, a slight pause to await the opponent's reaction may provide the opportunity to deceive his covering action or change of engagement with the appropriate indirect riposte. When executed with a lunge, the delayed riposte is very difficult to distinguish from an attack; indeed, precisely when such an action ceases to be a riposte and becomes an altogether fresh attack inaugurating a new phrase is all in the mind and a matter of the president's opinion.

Déliement. Besnard's term for the disengagement.

Démarches. The name given by Sainct-Didier to the steps by which the adversaries advanced and retired.

Demi-Circle. (See Half-Circle.)

Demi-Contre. The half-counter parry, distinguished by some French masters of the eighteenth century from both the counter (circular) and simple parries. However, it was not, it seems, our half-circular or semi-circular parry, which at that time was called *septime*, or, rather misleadingly, *cercle*; but as far as can be judged, was a counter parry executed against an attack initiated from absence of blade.

Derived Attacks, (*Altachi riflessi*). Attacks whose nature is predetermined by the opponent's action.

Dérobement. The evasion of the opponent's attempt to take or attack the blade, one's own arm being extended with blade in line and point threatening the opposition target. In such a case the opponent must, of course, by the rules of foil and sabre fencing, deflect his adversary's weapon before making his attack, if he wants the priority in the event of a double hit. The idea is, that by means of the *dérobement*, the attacker's beat or *prise-de-fer* will be evaded and that he himself, continuing immediately into his attack, will run onto the point.

Désarmement. The Disarmament of one's opponent by the removal of the weapon from his grasp, by force

or leverage. A bout is stopped when a fencer loses possession of his weapon, even if he should only drop it; the competitors are then replaced on guard. A hit occurring as part of the action which causes the *désarmement* is, however, valid; on the other hand, a hit occurring afterwards is annulled.

Until well into the eighteenth century, when duels or brawls involving the use of the sword were still of common occurence, most masters gave advice on methods of disarming an enemy. These varied from seizing the opponent's blade or hilt to heavy parries, binds or other *prises-de-fer*, usually accompanied by a firm grip on some part of the other's arm or guard, so that considerable leverage could be executed.

Descendente, (It.). A cut delivered downwards.

Destreza. The traditional Spanish style of fencing, especially that of the sixteenth and seventeenth centuries, with its elaborate pseudo-philosophical sub-structure.

Destroying or Destruction Parry. The Hungarian term for the semicircular parry. Szabo, however, defines a destructive parry as one 'taken with a movement corresponding to a change'. In other words, his interpretation could include the circular parry.

Detached Parry. A parry that leaves – indeed, almost rebounds from – the opponent's blade, the moment the latter has been deflected. Very fast and light, it leaves the executant free to riposte in any line. This type of parry was more common when the non-electric foil was in general use; especially when the rules defined a parry as any contact, however light, made by the defender's blade with that of the attacker. Today, the parry with opposition (see Opposition) is more popular.

Detached Riposte. A riposte executed without blade contact, especially a direct riposte executed in this way, instead of with a light opposition, as a protection against the *remise*. A detached direct riposte is, of course, the fastest of all ripostes.

The Dagger used in defence while the sword passes over the opponent's dagger (from Capo Ferro).

Deux Temps, En. This is emphatically not the same as a two-time attack (q.v.), but signifies separate parries and ripostes, as standardised by the great French masters of the late seventeenth century. Until then, the time-hit or time-thrust (q.v.) had been the normal method of defence, especially among the Italians.

Development. The extension of the sword-arm and lunge.

Deviamento, (It.). The deflection of the opponent's blade.

Deviation. A small action of blade against blade, such as a pressure.

Dig. An angulated attack with the hand well out and the point directed inwards towards the target; at épée, such an attack directed particularly at the wrist and forearm.

Dig, Second. Might be a *redoublement* of the attack described above; more probably the wild and instinctive action of a novice whose initial attack has been parried and who lacks the experience to fall back on

defence; to that extent, therefore, a term of opprobrium.

Direct Attack. 1) An attack of one blade movement, the relative positions of the blades remaining the same throughout. There is but one direct attack, the straight-thrust; or, at sabre, a cut delivered to any part of the opponent's target without passing over or under his blade. (See Simple Attacks.)
2) Direct attack or direct decision, is, according to Barbasetti, to attack the opponent when he is entirely on the defensive.

Direct Elimination is when the loser of the bout is eliminated altogether from the competition, as in a F.A. Cup-tie, while the winner advances to face another winner. In most competitions, direct elimination, if included at all, is reserved for the closing stages, such as the final bouts of the Martini-sponsored competitions, when the number of hits is increased to ten from the normal five.

Direct Riposte. A riposte corresponding to the straight-thrust, the

only direct attack. Following a successful parry, the direct riposte takes the most direct route to the target, with no change in the relative blade positions. The term 'direct' carries no implications regarding either clock time or fencing time, and such a riposte can, in fact, be delayed. A riposte which follows the parry without any loss of time whatsoever is said to be 'immediate'.

Director. The president of the jury in the U.S.

Directoire Technique. The organising committee at international and Olympic events, consisting of six or seven members of different nationalities, one of whom must be a member of the host country. It organises the various competitions and selects the jury, the composition of which it is entitled to alter. It hears complaints against decisions of the president, imposes penalties and if necessary convenes the Court of Appeal.

Disarming. (See Désarmement.)

Disengage. 1) In the vaguest and most generalised sense, to remove the blade from contact, or an engagement, with the opponent's blade.
2) An indirect attack, executed by passing the blade under that of the opponent in the high line, over it in the low line and terminating on the side opposite to the original engagement. Nowadays to disengage is not just to free one's blade from the opponent's contact, or engagement; it is to execute this particular attack.

Disengagement Parry. The same as a change parry; what we, in what might be termed the Anglo-French school, would term a circular (counter) parry.

The Dagger used in attack while the oponent's cut is parried with the rapier (from Capo Ferro).

49

Disengagement into Tempo. Barbasetti's term for a disengagement on the opponent's attempt to attack or engage the blade.

Displacement occurs when, owing to some unorthodox or illegal body-action, the position of the normal target-area at foil or sabre is altered and replaced by an off-target part of the body; in such a case, a hit on the latter area is valid. For example, although ducking is in itself within the rules, a foilist who in so doing covers his trunk with his mask and is hit upon it, is considered to have received a valid hit.

Distance. (See Measure, The Fencing.)

Distance, Out of. A fencer is out of distance when his opponent cannot hit him by means of a lunge alone, but must employ some additional footwork, such as a preparatory step. The Hungarian master, Lukovitch, takes this a stage further – in his view, a fencer is only out of distance when his opponent cannot deliver an attack on him without preparing his lunge with at least two steps.

Distance, Sense Of. Some fencers seem to have an instinct, doubtless cultivated by assiduous practice, of instantly sensing and adopting the best possible distance in relation to their opponents, and this they maintain with the minimum of movement and effort. This sense of distance often seems to be inherent, in particular, in certain expert sabreurs, who have been known to amuse themselves and tantalise their opponents by repeatedly exposing some part of the sword-arm, only for the inevitable cut at wrist to fall fractionally short, resulting in glee on the one side and fury on the other. A foilist's sense of distance may often

50

A Disarm having parried in prime, *first position (from Angelo).*

be appreciably improved by practice with the sabre or épée, both of which require a longer fencing measure.

Distance Stealing. To take a series of varied steps forwards and backwards and so gain a favourable position for attacking one's opponent, without the latter realising that he has become vulnerable. Alternatively, the same method can be used to lure him into advancing too far, so that once again he is threatened while still unconscious of the danger.

Doigté. The manipulation of the weapon by the fingers. (See Finger-Play.)

Doppio Circulazione or Doppio Contro-Cavazione, (It.). (See Double Counter – Disengage.)

Dorset, Sir Edward Sackville, Earl of. In consequence of James I's proc-lamation against duelling in 1613, the Earl was obliged to fight Lord Bruce, with whom he had fallen out over some woman, at Bergen-op-Zoom in the Low Countries. It was an extraordinarily brutal and blood-thirsty affair, the two principals standing ankle-deep in water – they were a couple of miles outside the town – and each receiving several dangerous thrusts in various parts of the body at close quarters. Dorset only just survived, severely wounded in three places and narrowly escaped death in the end; for while his injuries were being examined, Lord Bruce's surgeon suddenly assailed him with his master's sword and was only repelled in the nick of time by his own medical adviser, correspondingly armed. Lord Bruce, wounded and from his position recumbent on the ground, indignantly ordered his employee to desist, this being in accordance with his conduct throughout, described by his enemy as 'undoubtedly noble'.

A Disarm having parried in tierce, *first position (from Angelo).*

Doublé. A compound attack. A feint of disengagement is met by a circular (counter) parry which, in turn, is deceived by a counter-disengagement. (See Compound Attack.)

Double Attack. According to Egerton Castle, attack was at one time synonomous with *appel* (q.v.). Hence a double attack was a double *appel*, two smart beats with the sole of the foot on the floor, immediately prior to the launching of the attack; it had nothing to do with the *doublé* described above, though the latter might, of course, eventually follow the *appel*.

Double Beat. Two beats delivered against the opponent's blade in quick succession. Their strength and cadence, in relation to the attack they precede, may be varied for tactical reasons.

Double Change Beat. Two change beats in succession. (See Beat.)

Double Change of Engagement. Two successive changes of engagement in rapid succession; the blade being each time passed beneath the opponent's blade (over it if in the low line) the latter is finally re-engaged in the original position.

Double Circular Feint. (See Double Counter–Disengage.)

Double Counter–Disengage. Two counter-disengagements which deceive two circular parries.

Double Cut-Over or **Coupé-Coupé.** A feint of cut-over, followed by a second cut-over which deceives the parry drawn by the feint. Sometimes termed 'cut-over twice'. (See Compound Attack.)

Double Defeat. At épée, owing to the possibility of a double hit, it can arise that both fencers simultaneously receive the maximum number of hits being fought for. In such a case,

a defeat is recorded against each competitor. A double defeat is quite impossible at foil or sabre; apart from the fact that in the case of a double hit at least one is annulled, the rules declare that in the event of the hits standing equal when the allotted period expires, a deciding hit must be fought for without limit of time.

Doublé-Dégagé. A classical two-feint compound attack; a feint of the *doublé* followed by a disengagement to deceive the final simple parry.

Doublé-de-Doublé. The feint of a *doublé*, followed by another *doublé*. (See Compound Attack.)

Double Engagement. A term very rarely met with: to engage the opposing blade, break the contact and then re-engage. Sometimes, it is true, it is used loosely for an engagement followed by a change of engagement, as well as for a double change of engagement.

Double Feint. Barbasetti's term for a pair of feints in a compound attack, e.g., the two feints of disengagement in a one-two-three.

Double Feints as Ripostes. Barbasetti's phraseology for compound ripostes.

Double Hit. When at foil and sabre, both fencers are hit within the same period of fencing time, or at épée, both hits arrive within one twenty-fifth of a second of each other, a double hit is said to result. In the first two cases, the president, if unable to assign priority to one or other of the combatants, must award no hit at all, and replace them on guard. In the latter instance, a hit is recorded against both fencers and may result in a double defeat, except, of course, in a bout by direct elimination.

Double Intention. The attacking fencer has two things in mind: he aims at scoring a hit (first intention), but at the same time is quite prepared to parry a possible counter-attack and riposte from it (his second intention).

Double Parries. Two parries one after the other, the first of which parries the attack, the second the renewal of the attack; in other words, blade contact is established twice in immediate succession and hence double parries must most emphatically be distinguished from successive parries (q.v.).

Double Preparations of Attack. Two preparations executed successively, not simultaneously. (See Preparations of Attack.)

Double Prises-De-Fer. Two *prises-de-fer* performed in succession, contact with the opponent's blade being lost and regained between the two. (See Prises-de-Fer.)

Double Thrust or Double Touch. The double hit.

Dress. The rules concerning the dress and equipment of fencers have become progressively stricter and more elaborate with the passing years. Old prints and other records show that two or three centuries ago, fencers retained much of their ordinary clothing when in action. Even *tricornes* were not discarded. At Sir William Hope's Scottish academy in about 1700, black velvet caps, white waistcoats, breeches and stockings were obligatory. In the early nineteenth century, we read of short white jackets and wire masks which, however, lacked the modern bib. By
52

Toupie Lowther in the ladies' dress of 1900.

the middle of the century, thick padded leather jackets were in common use. The rules of 1899 merely stated that jackets (it is to be observed, not necessarily breeches, stockings or shoes) must be light in colour. Very loose jackets, those of blue, black or very dark colours, or of material so shiny or so thick that hits could not properly be registered or recognised, were all barred. In the International

Cup of 1903 in Paris, épéeists were forbidden to wear breeches. Their jackets and trousers had to be white, gloves might not be stuffed and, what must be a matter of great surprise and interest to the modern fencer, ordinary boots or shoes had to be worn. The same obligation was included in the rules for the Epée Club's Open Tournament in 1904; in addition, gloves covering the sleeve (now compulsory) were prohibited. In 1914, the rules for men's competitions specified that dress should be white or 'a very light colour' throughout, excluding shoes and masks, the wire mesh and frame of the latter being then, and for many years afterwards, generally black.

The dress for ladies has varied just as much. At the Ladies' Foil Championship of 1907, several ladies wore white breeches and 'rather long' white jackets; others, black breeches or black skirts. In 1938, the F.I.E. forbade the wearing of skirts in international events, requiring 'wide' breeches 'closed below the knee'; although, in less important competitions, or for ordinary practice, white pleated and divided skirts remained a common sight until very recently.

Dritto, (It.). The fencer's right hand, or sword-arm, side.

Dritto Filo, (It.). The right edge, or fore-edge of the weapon.

Duel. The traditional single combat conducted according to the laws and regulations of honour; the challenged party, in England at any rate, having choice of weapons. It was essentially different from the 'trial by combat' (q.v.), customary in the Middle Ages in certain countries and certain classes of society as a method of settling legal disputes or accusations of criminal conduct, it being then supposed that the Almighty

Double Hit — it's to be hoped the blades are of the best quality!

would intervene to ensure that the innocent party triumphed. The duel proper, on the other hand, prevalent first in France and subsequently elsewhere, became fashionable in the reign of Francis I (1515-47), partly, no doubt, in consequence of his abortive challenge to his arch-rival of the House of Habsburg, the Holy Roman Emperor Charles V, who was far too old a political hand to be impressed by such palpably theatrical devices; these more recent affairs were designed to settle purely personal differences and to avenge personal insults.

During the reign of Henry IV of France (1589-1610), it was computed that not fewer than 4,000 valiant gentlemen lost their lives in such encounters. Under his successor, Louis XIII (1610-48, the 'Musketeers' period), duelling in France became a fashion, a madness, an obsession; for not only did fanatics, desperados, eccentrics abound, who delighted in issuing challenges on grounds less than flimsy, for taking a preferential place on the pavement, for wearing similar clothes, for wearing unfashionable clothes, for delivering an (allegedly) insulting glance, for averting the gaze entirely, but at that period the seconds also were obliged to join combat. (See Seconds and Multiple Duels.) It was with the utmost difficulty and only after several executions of noblemen and gentlemen of the highest rank, that Louis XIII and Cardinal Richelieu were able to contain the practice within some sort of bounds.

The duel was never legal in England, where the death of a duellist was categorised as murder, or at best as manslaughter, though Benefit of Clergy (q.v.) often provided the offender with an escape clause. At the turn of the eighteenth and nineteenth centuries, the pistol generally replaced the small-sword as the duelling weapon. In France, on the other hand, duelling with the épée persisted throughout the nineteenth and well into the twentieth century; at least one duel is reported to have taken place in France within the last thirty years (See Cuevas), although, latterly, the conditions enforced in these affairs were such that serious injury was highly improbable.

A highly specialised form of sabre duelling was a feature of the German Universities (q.v.) before 1914 and in the same period officers of the German Army habitually settled their differences by means of this type of duel. Duelling between officers of the British Army, on the other hand, has always been regarded as a most serious offence, punishable by a court-martial sentence of cashiering or dismissal from the service, as being altogether prejudicial to good order, discipline and a healthy regimental spirit.

Dui Tempi, (It.). To parry and riposte in two distinct actions, for long regarded as one of the hallmarks of the classical French school. The characteristic Italian practice, namely, combining parry and riposte into a single action (what is now termed a 'time-hit' or 'covered stop-hit') was called *stesso tempo*.

Duke's Walk. A favourite locality near Holyrood Palace for the meetings of duellists. It is named after James II (1685-88) who, when still Duke of York, had enjoyed a regular stroll there.

Dupont, General. An unprecedented series of duels between

53

two Napoleonic officers began when Captain Fournier, who was in disgrace for already having killed his man in an entirely frivolous duel, was barred from attending a ball on the orders of General Moreau. To Captain Dupont, as Moreau's A.D.C., was entrusted the thankless task of delivering this piece of intelligence. It afforded Fournier, who cannot at any time have been wholly in his right mind, the pretext for an apparently endless series of duels, in which first one, then the other, and sometimes both combatants were wounded. At one point they actually drew up a formal agreement binding the contracting parties to meet sword in hand whenever their duties brought them within a hundred miles of each other, the exigencies of the service being the one acceptable excuse. A temporary truce, as it were, occurred from time to time when the adversaries were unable to engage in hostilities because of inequality of rank; as soon as one or the other had been promoted, the normal state of warfare was resumed. Finally, when both were general officers, Dupont brought the prolonged vendetta to a conclusion by proposing that the enemies should exchange their swords for a pair of pistols each and stalk each other through a wood; this being agreed, he tricked Fournier into wasting both his shots by holding out, first his coat, then his hat, from behind a tree. His foe being effectively disarmed, Dupont emerged from cover and although Fournier was at his mercy, let him go in return for a promise never to molest him again.

A few years ago a film, aptly entitled *The Duellists*, and based on these astonishing events, followed the actual facts very closely.

Dusack. A weapon originating in Hungary and Bohemia and once

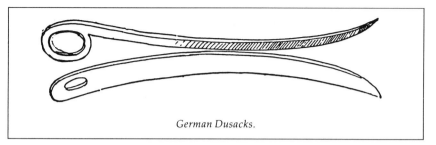
German Dusacks.

very common in Germany. It was a cutting weapon, the main part of which was fashioned as a curved blade, while its upper extremity, curving in the opposite direction, formed a loop which served as both grip and knuckle-bow. There was no formal or separate hilt at all.

Eboli, Princess d', Donna Ana de Mendoza de la Cerda. (See Ladies' Fencing.)

Ecarting. (See Quarting.)

Echappement. The backward lunge (q.v.).

Edward I, King of England 1271-1307). Renowned for his conquest of Wales and his prolonged but inconclusive campaigns against the Scots, as a result of which he became known as *Malleus Scotorum* ('Hammer of the Scots'). Also nicknamed 'Longshanks' because of his great stature, he was one of the foremost rulers and statesmen of his own or any other age and the legal and constitutional bases of modern Britain may be said to have been laid in his time. Certainly his desire to associate the towns and their citizens with the levying of taxes led directly to the development of the House of Commons. One slightly surprising statute was that of 1285 which forbade the holding of tournaments or the teaching of fencing within the

bounds of the City of London. There was, of course, more than one medieval ban on football (and in Scotland, golf) as being an activity likely to interfere with the practice of archery; but the prohibition of fencing was probably due to the suspicion that the schools encouraged brawling and duelling and were likely to attract large numbers of dissolute and lawless individuals. Certainly all kings, with the one exception of Stephen (1135-54) had always regarded the tournament with the utmost distaste as tending to private war and public disorder; even Richard I (1189-99) only licensed tournaments as a means of raising enough money for the Third Crusade. Ironically enough, Edward himself, on his way home from the Eighth Crusade, had been involved in a tournament in France resulting in such an effusion of blood that it became known as 'The Little War of Chalons'.

Edward VII, King of Great Britain 1901-1910. A great patron of sport, especially racing, and the theatre, he enjoyed the society of beautiful women and while still Prince of Wales was involved in an unsavoury gambling scandal which, although he himself emerged with totally unstained reputation, necessitated his appearance in court as a witness. Nonetheless, he discharged his duties as a constitutional monarch with the utmost tact, dignity and conscientiousness and while controversy still centres on the exact extent of his contribution to the *Entente Cordiale* with France (1904), there is no doubt that his personal charm eased the settlement of all outstanding disputes by the statesmen of the two countries which for so long had been deadly rivals.

Edward VII, himself a fencer, allowed his daughters to learn the art at the academy of Baptiste Bertrand and continued to show the greatest interest in fencing, frequently attending important matches and competitions. In 1906, he consented to become Patron of the Amateur Fencing Association, a position held by all his successors on the throne and granted British internationals the right to wear the Tudor Rose on their brassards. In the same year, he was present at the Athens Olympics and exhibited obvious delight when Britain easily defeated the German épée team, thereby emphasising not only the darkening trends and portents of the international scene, but his private sentiments, for he never was on cordial terms with the German Kaiser William II.

Effort. An attack on the blade from *foible* to *forte*.

Eight Leaves, Tracing of. Having performed the finger-play exercise known as the 'four-leaf clover' (q.v.), the difficulty can be increased by reversing the pattern and tracing the outline of the clover backwards with the point of the weapon, so describing eight leaves in all.

Eighth. Position and parry. (See Octave.)

Elbow Guard. A pad of leather or some other suitable material worn by some sabreurs as a protection against hard cuts.

D'Eon as the chevalier.

Elek, Ilona of Hungary was the outstanding Lady Foil International of her own, or, perhaps, any generation. Two others (Mayer and Hanisch) have rivalled her in winning three World Championships, which in her case were those of 1934, 1935 and 1951. In addition, however, she triumphed at two Olympics (1936 and 1948) and for good measure took a silver medal in 1952, thus clearly establishing her supremacy over the other two in this remarkable trio.

Elizabeth I, Queen of England 1558-1603, was the legitimate or illegitimate daughter of Henry VIII, according to religious persuasion or the ability to thread one's way through the labyrinth of Tudor succession statutes, altered, re-altered and repealed in turn. Like most historical figures magnified by legend, she is now estimated as far less than the super-woman venerated by our ancestors. Iconoclasm has had its way: she was a puppet manipulated by Cecil; she was wax in the hands of unworthy favourites; she was

fatally indecisive and her niggardly finance almost undid England in the war against Spain; while her once-famed Navy proved sadly ineffective when it came to grips with the Spanish Armada, which was defeated by the elements and the elements alone. But as the rhymester said:

'We still believe Elizabeth
Was England's greatest Queen.'

For that reason her entry is included on grounds that Macaulay and Newbolt would have applauded; if further justification is needed, it is her proclamation of 1579 limiting the length of rapiers to a yard and a half.

Elliptical Counter or Circular Parry. A certain amount of controversy has arisen over whether the circular parry should literally justify its name or whether it should constitute an oval, or vertical, ellipse. The protagonists of the latter method emphasise its greater ease and speed; those who support the former view, argue that if the point of the weapon describes a genuine circle covering the extremity of the target, it is far likelier to catch a wide feint or attack. Moreover, there is the danger of the elliptical parry failing to make contact with *forte* to *foible*.

Elonge. Sir William Hope's term for the lunge.

Eluding Cut or Thrust. An attack launched immediately following the avoidance of the opponent's attempt to take or attack the blade.

En Deux Temps. 'In two actions'; a phrase relating especially to the seventeenth-century French school, one of whose hallmarks was the distinct separation of parry and riposte, in contrast to the contemporary Italian school, in which the two actions were generally combined into one.

(See Time-Hit.) *En deux temps* is not quite the same thing as two-time, which today refers to a compound attack, in which there is a momentary pause, deliberate or not, between the feint and the final action.

En Finale. 'At the last moment'; a phrase generally applied to a parry deliberately executed as late as possible, which not only reduces the possibility of its being deceived by a feint, but enables the riposte to be delivered with the maximum speed and authority.

En Garde. (See On Guard.)

En Main. 'In', or 'into the line of'; e.g. *en main quarte*, in, or into the line of *quarte*.

En Marchant. Stepping forward while simultaneously straightening the sword-arm for an attack. With a simple attack, the arm is extended with blade in line and point threatening the target as the step is taken, then a lunge generally follows. In the case of compound attacks, the step is normally combined with the first feint. The frequency of this sort of attack has greatly declined in recent years, owing to the growing popularity of counter-attacks and beat-attacks into the opponent's offensive actions.

Enclosing. Sir William Hope's term for closing the distance, even to the extent of forcing a *corps-à-corps*.

Encounter. The double hit.

Engage. To establish contact with the opponent's blade.

Engagement. When the blades are in contact with each other, they are said to be 'engaged'. When the blades are thus crossed, the line of engagement

Gillray's famous engraving of d'Eon against St George at Carlton House in 1787. D'Eon attacks strongly, despite obvious handicaps, while the Prince of Wales looks on.

depends on the relative position of the blades and not on the position of one or other of the fencers' hands as it would do were there 'absence of blade'. Thus, if the blades are crossed on the outside (right) of the fencers' wrists, that engagement is in *sixte*, even though it is perfectly possible in such a case for one fencer to have his hand and blade in what would have been *quarte* had there been no engagement. Some masters try to obviate this difficulty by speaking of false *quarte*, etc. that is, a *quarte* position which is uncovered and vulnerable to a straight-thrust. The matter is often the cause of considerable perplexity in beginners, who fail to realise that when the blades are engaged, only one of the fencers at a time can be covered in the line of the engagement; although it is, of course, perfectly possible for both simultaneously to be uncovered.

Engagement, Change of. (See Change and Double Change.

Envelopment or Enveloppement. To control the extended and threatening blade of the opponent by carrying it around in a circle, thus dominating it and preparing the way for an offensive action. This preparation may be executed in *quarte* and in theory even the low-line positions; but in the two latter especially, there is a grievous danger of the opponent's blade escaping and hence the movement is normally confined to *sixte*. The size of the circle should be regulated and certainly not the great windmilling action seen in stage duels. (See Prises-de-Fer.)

Eon, Chevalier d', Charles Geneviève Louis. The Chevalier was a swordsman, adventurer and secret agent of Louis XV, heavily involved in that eccentric monarch's private and unofficial foreign policy, known as *le secret du Roi*, which at times was at variance with the official plans of his own ministers. It is certain that the Chevalier played an important part in gaining the support of the Empress Elizabeth of Russia in the Seven Years' War and is supposed to have wormed his way into her confidence by assuming female attire and passing himself off as a woman. He served on the Duc de Broglie's staff during the ensuing conflict and then after a brief spell as Minister Plenipotentiary in London during the peace negotiations flatly refused to return home or to surrender his confidential documents when a regular ambassador was appointed. It was at this time that bets were being laid all over the town as to d'Eon's true sex, but he resolutely refused to satisfy the punters' curiosity. On the accession of Louis XVI some years later (1774), a compromise was arranged, partly, perhaps, because he knew too much about the tortuous politics of the preceding reign, and he was permitted to reside in France with a generous pension on the odd condition that he should permanently adopt feminine dress. It was in this guise that 'Mademoiselle' d'Eon dined in the mess of his old regiment, the Dragoons d'Antichamp. At the onset of the French Revolution, he sought refuge in England once more, eking out a living in his straitened circumstances by giving fencing lessons and demonstrations. A friend of the Angelos, he was a member of their academy. There was at one time a well-known print by Gillray depicting him fencing at Carlton House, clad in the flowing feminine garments of the period. The Chevalier died in 1810 and although at an earlier date two witnesses had given sworn evidence that d'Eon was in fact a woman, medical experts of unimpeachable

Early Epée, c.1880.

reputation, after examining the corpse, affirmed it to be that of a perfectly normal male.

Epée. The duelling sword evolved during the nineteenth century when the small-sword had ceased to be worn. It is the same length as the foil and sabre, but the blade is much stouter than that of the foil, is triangular in section and the *forte* is fluted, i.e., grooved, to allow the blood to drain away. As the target includes the whole body, the guard is constructed in the characteristic cup shape to protect the hand and wrist. As the arm forms an advanced target, the fencing measure is much longer than that at foil – approximating in fact to the sabre measure – and the vulnerability of the sword-arm tends to restrict the positions and parries to the outside lines of *sixte* and *octave*.

Nevertheless, the basic épée technique is very similar to that of foil, only modified by the tactical considerations dictated by the longer fencing measure, the unrestricted target and the absence of conventions. One difference in the theory may be noted. Many (though not all) attacks at épée are initiated from absence of blade. Therefore, with this weapon, such examples of the compound attack as the feint straight-thrust-disengage, or the feint straight-thrust-counterdisengage are generally referred to respectively as the one-two and the *doublé*, for the sake of convenience. This is in contrast to the French foil school, according to which the one-two, *doublé* and all their subsequent variations can *only* be accepted as such if the initial feint is by a disengagement.

Originally, the idea was to reproduce as closely as possible the conditions of an actual duel (one did in fact occur in France within the last twenty-five years – see Cuevas) and consequently the first fencer to receive a hit was adjudged the loser. Subsequently the number of hits was increased, first to the best of five in 1932, finally to the best of nine in 1955, similarly to the other weapons and accordingly somewhat reducing the realism. In pursuance of the utmost verisimilitude, moreover, the majority of épée competitions took place in the open air; not until 1937 was the British Championship held indoors, at Salle Bertrand.

The épée was the first weapon to be electrified, with a spring-head in place of the *pointe d'arrêt* (triple-barbed flat head) previously used to cover the sharp point left exposed when duelling.

The rules for épée, like those of foil and sabre, were more or less definitively framed in Paris in 1914, by codifying the several existing sets of laws of such bodies as the *Académie d'Epée* and the *Société à l'Epée de Paris*.

It is at this weapon that this country has achieved its best results internationally. Quite apart from the superb individual performances of Jay and Hoskyns, the British Epée Team came second in the Olympics of 1906, 1908, 1912, and 1960 and second again in the World Championship of 1965. Apart from a brief flash of brilliance in the Sheen-Jay era, however, British foil results have hardly risen above mediocrity, while at sabre the achievement has been negligible.

Epée de Combat or Epée de Terrain. The weapon actually used in the duels of the late nineteenth and twentieth centuries. It was the pre-electric or 'steam' épée, without the button or *pointe d'arrêt* protecting the point. The latter was sharpened and dipped in disinfectant, both at the outset of the proceedings and again after any hit insufficiently serious to warrant the termination of the combat.

Epée de Passot. A straight sword of the Middle Ages.

Epée de Salle was simply the duelling weapon with a protected point, used for training and practice.

Epée Club of London was founded in 1900 by Mr C. Newton-Robinson who brought over to this country two acknowledged épée experts, Professor Spinnewyn and Mr W. Sulzbacher, to foster interest and skill in this weapon. As a result, English épée fencing flourished for a short period and a team led by Mr T.A. Cook took second place in the International Epée Competition at Paris in 1903.

Equipment, New and Improved. Certain new articles of equipment are now obligatory at all World Championships (including Youth), Olympic Games and grade A competitions. A new type of steel blade ('maraging' or 'Paul') is to be used, masks must have a mesh of stainless steel and a much tougher under-plastron (the 'Kavlar') must be worn. Moreover, stainless steel replaces silver conductors in the latest *lamé* foil overjackets.

Escrime. Fencing.

Escrime Loisir. Leisure fencing for those who wish to do it purely for amusement and relaxation, who seek to play stylishly with the blades, to experiment with archaic strokes or ingenious new tricks; for those, in short, who are too old, idle or imaginative for the repetitive grind of serious competition fencing.

Espada, (Span.). A sword; also, the épée as such.

Espadachin, (Span.). A swordsman.

Espadin, (Span.). A diminutive of *espada*; the small-sword.

Espadon, (Span.). The long-sword, replaced by the rapier.

Espadrilles. French fencing shoes.

Espée. An early French spelling of *épée*.

Esquive. A displacement of one's target.

Estafilade. A cut.

Estoc. In the Middle Ages, a long, narrow, two-handed sword, designed for use on foot. It was a thrusting weapon and usually attached to the right-hand side of the saddle. Subsequently, the word *estoc* or *estocade* became synonomous

Equipment. This shouldn't happen today. (Illustration by F. Regamey.)

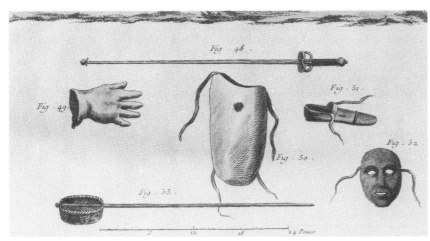

Early equipment showing fleuret, glove, plastron, shoe, singlestick and mask *(from Diderot Encyclopaedia).*

with the rapier. Sainct-Didier, in the sixteenth century, used the term *estoc* simply to mean a thrust.

Estocada, (Span.). A thrust.

Estocade. A heavy French edged sword of the late Middle Ages, superseded by the rapier.

Estocade de Passe. (See below.)

Estocade de Pied Ferme. La Tousche's extraordinary exaggeration, or perhaps even perversion, of the lunge. According to this seventeenth-century French master, the trunk had to be lowered until it was actually resting on the leading thigh, and practically parallel with the ground. At the same time, the sword-hand and weapon had to be raised as high as was physically possible. The *Estocade de Passe* involved similar contortions, but in this case it was the left leg that was advanced in making the attack.

Estramaçon. The French term for the *stramazone* (q.v.).

Ettenhard Y Abarca, Francisco Antonio De. A late seventeenth-century Spanish master, who like most of his contemporaries remained devotedly loyal to the traditional theories of his country, based on obscure and meaningless geometrical figures.

Exchanged Hits. (See Double Hits.)

Expulsion. (See Froissement.)

Eyes of the Hilt. Andrew Mahon's term for the *pas d'âne* rings; surely a more appropriate description than the 'donkey's footsteps'.

Fabris, Salvator. An illustrious Italian master of the late sixteenth and early seventeenth centuries who, on the invitation of Christian IV, found his way to Denmark where he published a celebrated treatise, *Scienza e Pratica d'Arme* (1606). Its chief significance lay in the fact that it dealt entirely with the technique of swordsmanship and its practical application in the fencing-school, the duel and the brawl, while discarding the pseudo-philosophical ramblings so favoured by his predecessors.

Faible. (See Foible.)

Fairbanks, Douglas (senior) was famous everywhere in the days of the silent screen as the most dashing of Hollywood heroes and swordsmen. He always seemed to be booted and spurred, with sword in hand. He took the name-parts of *Zorro* and *The Son of Zorro* and played d'Artagnan in *The Three Musketeers*. Other great successes were *The Iron Mask*, *The Black Pirate* and *The Private Life of Don Juan*, his last film made in 1934. He was the swashbuckler of swashbucklers. The traditional image, cherished by the older generation, is one of him swinging across a ballroom on the chandeliers with a rapier between his teeth; whether there was ever really such a scene in any of his films is open to question, but there is no doubt that he was a superb athlete, relying on stand-ins only in his later years. His son, Douglas Fairbanks junior, did not quite match his father as one of Hollywood's best swordsmen; it is understood that he often had to make use of stand-ins. Nevertheless, he cut a fine figure in *The Corsican Brothers* and *The Prisoner of Zenda*.

Falchion. A curved sword of the scimitar type, from Latin *falx*, a sickle. (See Fauchion.)

False Attack. Not to be confused with a feint of attack. Whereas in the latter case the feint or feints combine with the genuine attack itself to form a rapid and continuous series of blade movements, the false attack is a quite separate action which is not really intended to be successful, but is merely delivered to distract the opponent's attention, to test his reactions, or to draw his parry and so prepare the way for a counter-riposte or a renewal of the attack.

False Balestra. The jump is performed without gaining any ground at all, generally as part of a second intention phrase with the object of drawing a stop-hit or attack on the preparation from one's opponent.

False Guard. A term used by some masters to describe a situation where a fencer's hand and blade are in a perfectly correct line, but the blades being engaged on the wrong side of each other, he is in fact uncovered and vulnerable to the straight-thrust. Thus we hear of false *quarte*, false *sixte*, etc.

False Return or False Riposte. A riposte delivered with the same intention as the false attack, namely, to draw a reaction from the opponent and exploit it. Generally, it aims at inciting the opponent to parry and counter-riposte, so paving the way for a rapid and well-prepared second counter-riposte.

Falsifying. Sir William Hope's term for feinting.

Falso Dritto, (It.). A cut with the false, or back-edge, from the right.

Falso Manco, (It.). A cut with the false, or back-edge, from the left; i.e., a back-handed cut.

Faubert, Solomon de. A French master and partner in a Parisian academy giving instruction in arms and equitation to the Protestant nobility. The growing persecution of the Huguenots under Louis XIV culminated in the revocation of the Edict of Nantes in 1685, which was foreshadowed by an *Arrêt du Conseil* in 1679 closing all Protestant educational establishments. Fortunately
60

for de Faubert, his influential contacts enabled him to transfer his activities to London where he soon became known as the head of an institution providing education for the sons of noblemen in academic subjects as well as fencing, dancing and riding. Its fame, however, did not prove very enduring and although he was succeeded by his son, Major Henry de Faubert, it had, towards the end of the eighteenth century, dwindled into nothing more than a riding-school.

Fauchion. A short, heavy, slightly curved cutting sword, sometimes used in prize-fights. (cp. Falchion.)

Feather Edge. Hutton's name for the position in which the fencer's trunk is turned so far to his left that only the right shoulder and right hip are visible to the adversary, the chest being entirely effaced. The advantages of this dramatic decrease in exposed target area are obvious; on the other hand, the position is extraordinarily cramped, taxing, and worse still, creates a tendency for the leading foot and knee to follow the chest in its leftward inclination, thus impairing the balance and causing both footwork and lunge to be

directed diagonally across the *piste*. These dangers can only be averted by endless hours of exhausting and monotonous practice which few fencers, at any rate nowadays, are prepared to undergo.

Feather Parade. The term in use at Angelo's academy for the parry of *sixte*. The reason is not clear; it may possibly have been because it protected the feather edge described above.

Feder. German sixteenth-century slang for the rapier.

Fédération Internationale d'Escrime is the International Federation of Fencing, the controlling body of fencing throughout the world. Founded in 1913, it has a membership of sixty countries and organises annual World Championships, except in Olympic years.

Federfechter. A sixteenth-century society of German fencing masters, established under the patronage of the Duke of Mecklenburg, from whom it received its arms – a sable (black) griffin, or lion with the head and wings of an eagle. It was they who imported to Germany the use of

Attack by disengagement with protection from the left hand (from Fabris).

Monsieur Faubert's Academy, 1801 (Crace Collection, British Museum).

the point, from the contemporary Italian and Spanish schools of rapier-play. The great rivals of the Marxbruder (q.v.), the methods of the newer Federfechter fraternity quickly triumphed and the two great guilds thereafter divided the lucrative monopoly of teaching fencing between them. A senior representative of both resided at the Imperial Court; all questions relating to points of honour, the conduct of duels or the technique of swordsmanship, were referred to them.

Feint. A movement of the blade which simulates an attack, the object being to deceive the opponent's parry and deliver the real attack at a very different part of the target. Body feints can also be made, apparently unguarded steps or movements whose purpose is to lure the opponent into some reaction which can be turned to the attacker's advantage. These latter feints are often used in counter-time. (See also Combined, Compound, Passé and Pure Feints.)

Feint and Riposte. Barbasetti's phrase for the compound riposte.

Feint-In-Time or Finta-In-Tempo, (It.). A feint of a stop-hit drawing the parry of the fencer who is himself drawing the stop-hit and thus reacts with a parry; this is deceived and thus a compound stop-hit is executed.

Feinthore. An unusual and archaic name for the bind of *quarte* to *seconde*.

Fencing. The general name, derived from 'defence', for mock combat with blunted weapons. At the present day, fencing in Europe is largely confined to three weapons, the foil, the épée and the sabre. At different times, the recreation has been pursued with others as well, notably the singlestick, the backsword and in the Army, the bayonet, in the form of a spring-mounted, rubber-headed device.

With the heavy swords of the Middle Ages, mostly cutting weapons,

fighting must largely have been a matter of brute force and ignorance, and any practice bout presumably shared the same characteristics. It was not until the sixteenth century, with the appearance of the long, thin rapier, generally provided with at least one cutting edge, but essentially a thrusting weapon, that the way was clear for the development in Italy and Spain of professedly logical and comprehensive schools of swordsmanship. (See Italian and Spanish Schools.) It was the French, however, in the seventeenth century, who carried all before them. The rapier was progressively lightened and shortened, becoming in its final form a perfect instrument for defence as well as attack, obviating all need for a shield, a dagger or a cloak manipulated by the unarmed hand or arm. The practice weapon, the foil, was ideally adapted for a school of swordsmanship reflecting all the precision and logic commonly associated with the Gallic mind. By the nineteenth century, the French school had prevailed even over the indigenous traditions of Italy and Spain, though with some slight adaptions suited to their native genius. It was at this time, while play with the foil was becoming increasingly academic, that the other two weapons, the sabre and the épée, made their appearance, the latter being actually used in the duels still occurring in France and elsewhere. As for the sabre, it was for long considered to be an Italian speciality, but was transplanted to Hungary and for the last sixty or seventy years the Hungarians have been generally acknowledged to be the masters of this art.

There are no native schools of fence in eastern Europe – indeed, duelling was unknown in Imperial Russia – but in recent years the Iron Curtain states have come very much to the

61

fore, to say nothing of such countries as Switzerland and Sweden. The Russians resolved to make their mark on fencing after the conclusion of the Second World War; but having no traditions of their own, realised at once that they could hardly mount a serious challenge in the field of technique to the experts from Italy and France. They therefore determined to rely almost entirely on supreme fitness, opportunism and athleticism, tactics which, while being remarkably successful, inevitably detracted a great deal from the subtlety and artistry of the sport; a development which, as it so chanced, was accentuated by the almost simultaneous introduction of the electrical judging apparatus which necessitated some changes in the construction and balance of the foil.

Britain, which gave practically every ball game to the world, has never excelled at fencing, though this can hardly be ascribed to the circumstance that personalities as distinct in character and times as Edward I and Blackstone alike declared it to be illegal. Nevertheless, there are more fencing clubs in existence today than at any time in the country's history, most of them being registered technically as evening classes, the expenses therefore being a good deal lower than on the open market.

Fencing has never been practised very widely outside Europe and has no indigenous roots elsewhere, though an exception may be made in favour of the Japanese *Aikido* and *Kendo*.

Apart from its obvious connotations, the word 'fencing' has acquired an extended metaphorical significance, particularly in relation to a conversation consisting largely of idle repartees or evasions with no serious purpose involved.

Simultaneous Feints with the sabre — who will gain priority?

Fencing Iron. Slang term for the épée.

Fencing Line. Roughly speaking, what is generally termed the 'line of attack'; but more precisely defined by Imre Vass as the imaginary line drawn through the heels of the adversaries as they stand facing each other on guard. It has nothing to do with markings on the ground.

Fencing Position. Any of the traditional positions in which sword-arm and blade may be placed to protect the various parts of the target. (See Positions.) The Hungarians call these 'invitos'. They also distinguish two other fundamental positions:
1) In line. The arm is extended, with point threatening the opponent's target.

2) On guard. This applies not just to the body position, but to the blade as well, although there appears to be no substantial difference from an invito.

Fencing Time has nothing to do with 'clock' time, or the duration of the bout. It is the time taken to complete a single action of the blade or body and clearly varies considerably according to circumstances and the individual fencer.

Fencing Vision. There is a good deal of dispute as to the exact interpretation of this term, which is certainly not connected with some optimistic view on the future development of the sport. In fact, it relates to the objects on which the fencer's gaze should best be directed during a bout. Some have said it should be on his opponent's hand, others, his blade, many have advocated watching his eyes (very difficult, this, with today's thickly-meshed masks), a few, even, his leading foot. The best opinion appears to be that the head should be kept up, the central vision focussed on the opponent's mask (which at least helps to maintain balance), while the peripheral vision, it is hoped, can observe the movements of the fencer's blade and body and gain some idea of his intentions.

Fendente, (It.). A cut delivered downwards.

Fenton, Sir Nicholas was the hero of John Dickson Carr's *The Devil in Velvet*. The real Sir Nicholas was a seventeenth-century swordsman, but his body became possessed by the mind and character of Professor Fenton, a twentieth-century history don who had dabbled in black magic. Both the original Fenton and the replica were staunch royalists and devoted adherents of Charles II, thus becoming the target of Lord Shaftesbury and Buckingham, Whig leaders of the Green Ribbon Club, an anti-Stuart organisation which held its meetings at the ominously named King's Head tavern.

Cornered by his enemies in an alleyway off the Strand, Fenton had to fight his way out against their hired ruffian 'Long-legs'. The latter was tall, shabby, sneering, well-versed in sword-play and all the shady tricks of the street-brawl. But Fenton was too wily and resourceful and overcame his adversary in a duel which another historian was accustomed to re-enact in the form-room for the edification of those of his pupils supposed to be studying the Restoration. Fenton, by first holding his sword-arm much closer to the body than usual, bluffed his opponent into underestimating his reach. 'Long-legs' only escaped the sudden lightning lunge at full stretch by an acrobatic leap backwards. Fenton avoided the inevitable shower of dirt and pebbles in his eyes by jerking his wig in front of his face at the critical moment. There was a quick exchange of counter-ripostes; then, from Fenton's strong parry of *seconde*, a lethal upward thrust through the blackguard's throat penetrated as far as the brain, filling his eyes, nose and mouth with a gush of blood. For a shocking moment, the doomed wretch staggered and swayed, still remaining upright; then with a crash, he collapsed onto a row of fire-buckets, sending a red tide of blood and water slopping slowly over the mud of the alley.

Meanwhile, at the other end of the alley, Lord George Harwell, Fenton's comrade, was in dire straits, penned in a corner by the second hoodlum, 'Scarface'. Fenton only arrived in the nick of time. 'Scarface', an old Roundhead soldier, was not familiar with the latest refined technique of the French precision school. He was unwise enough to attempt a full-blooded downward cut as though this were a cavalry charge at Marston Moor or Naseby. As his arm went right up and back for that ferocious slash, exposing his whole body, Fenton's point drove deep into his armpit; a salutary reminder to all swordsmen, then and now, of the truth of the old maxim that 'the point is quicker than the edge'.

Ferailleur. An irregular, clumsy fencer, relying on brute force and ignorance.

Ferdinand II of Aragon (1479-1516) and Isabella I (1474-1504) of Castile were known as the 'Catholic Monarchs', a title conferred by Pope Alexander VI in 1494. Medieval Spain, like England under the Saxon Heptarchy, had been divided into a number of separate kingdoms. Apart from Portugal, which was able to retain its independence, there were Galicia, the Asturias, Navarre, Leon, Castile, Aragon and what were to become the latter's dependencies, the Kingdom of Valencia and the County of Catalonia. By the late fifteenth century, if the Moorish kingdom of Granada in the south is excepted, only Castile, having absorbed all its smaller neighbours lying along the southern slopes of the Pyrenees, and the Kingdom of Aragon remained. These last two were themselves united, in practice, if not legally and constitutionally, by the marriage of Ferdinand and Isabella.

Isabella was high-minded, impetuous, public-spirited, a great patroness of scholars and genuinely pious, though unfortunately it was that narrow piety which too often permits or even encourages persecution. Ferdinand was cold, calculating and suspicious, priding himself on being less often deceived than deceiving others and was supposed to have been the model for Machiavelli's *Prince*. In some ways they were typical 'New Monarchy' despots, increasing the powers of the crown at the expense of the nobility and medieval institutions - at any rate, in Castile; but beyond this, they may fairly lay claim to have been the most successful and dedicated rulers of their time, forming a royal and matrimonial partnership unique in history.

The year 1492 saw not only the final overthrow of the Moorish invader by the conquest of Granada, but the first voyage of Columbus which laid the foundations of that mighty empire in the New World, on which, together with the Spanish possessions in the Old, it was truly said, long before the emergence of Great Britain as an imperial power, that 'the sun never set'. It was in this age that the Spanish Infantry became the dread and admiration of Europe and a successful series of wars with France, with Italy as the prize, resulted in the establishment of Spanish dominion over Lombardy and the kingdoms of Naples and Sicily. Intellectual life flourished in the great medieval universities of Salamanca and Valladolid, while in this period seven new ones were founded, including the renowned Alcala. Not all the achievements of these monarchs merit unqualified approval. The lustre of 1492 was dimmed by the expulsion, or forcible conversion, of the Jews, a similar choice being forced on the Moors of Granada ten years later. The infamous Inquisition (established 1478) was at once the support and the tool of the monarchy.

During the latter part of the fifteenth century, two treatises appeared, by Jayme Pona and Pedro de la Torre, which evidently laid the foundations of that great school of Spanish swordsmanship reckoned for a time as the premier in Europe. Despite its manifest absurdities, Spanish swordsmen, like Spanish soldiers, were everywhere feared and respected. Ferdinand and Isabella, like many other monarchs, probably did not regard fencing with unmixed approval, supposing, not without justification, that the schools attracted an undesirable crowd of ne'er-do-wells, roisterers and fire-eaters; and it was in their reign that a decree was first enforced against duelling, at the Cortes of Toledo, in 1480.

Ferire a Piedo Fermo, (It.). To lunge, the rear foot remaining firm, or in

A trade card designed for Figg by William Hogarth.

place, as opposed to the older pass in which it was brought forward in front of the leading foot.

Ferita di Prima, (It.). (See Sbasso.)

Ferite, (It.). An offensive action.

Ferma, (It.). A horizontal thrust.

Fianconata, (It.). (See Flanconnade.)

Fianconata Volante. (See Flying Flanconnade.)

Field Of Play. The *piste*, its extensions and the area immediately round it occupied by the officials and judging apparatus.

Fifth. (See Quinte.)

Figg, James was one of the greatest of the so-called gladiators of the early eighteenth century, who, in addition to teaching the art of the small-sword and backsword, took a leading part in several of the most celebrated prize-fights of the era, spectacles which had, from the sixteenth century onwards, attracted large crowds. Figg received the highest praise from contemporaries, both as swordsman and master, though one pupil (a Captain Godfrey) confessed that he had purchased his skill with the backsword at the expense of many a painful bruise; evidently Figg did not 'pull' his attacks when giving instruction. Figg's great antagonist was Ned Sutton of Kent, with whom he had at least three encounters. One of these, in 1725, preceded by defiances published in the newspapers alternately by both principals, rather in the style of the threats of modern heavy-weight boxers, was described by an eye-witness (Dr John Byron) and was evidently a classic of its kind. Both competitors were wounded, this necessitating several pauses for treatment, both medical and alcoholic; finally, as was customary, once sufficient blood had been shed to satisfy the spectators, the swords were exchanged for quarter-staffs and after further punishment had been sustained by both, the indomitable Figg emerged as the victor.

Figg subsequently began to organise fist-fights as an alternative to the prize-fights with swords, and

himself became recognised as the first British boxing champion. The new development speedily attained such popularity that fencing, for a time, entered into a decline, becoming the diversion of a few men of fashion, or lingered on in the country as the sport of back-swordsmanship (q.v.).

Figure of Eight. (See Moulinets.)

Figure-of-Eight Guard. (See Lunette Guard.)

Fildes, L.V. was a long-standing member and captain of our international and Olympic teams. He was coached by Kirchoffer in Paris. He fought épée in the 1908 Paris Olympics and was runner-up in the Epée Championship of 1913. After the First World War, the claims of business prevented him from fencing until 1925, when he embarked on a remarkable secondary career, winning both the Epée Championship and the Miller-Hallet competition in 1929, at the relatively advanced age of fifty-two.

File. Valdin's name for the foil.

Filo, (It.). 1) The edge of a rapier or sabre. *Filo dritto* was the fore-edge, *filo falso* the back-edge.
2) In Italian terminology, the *coulé*. Similarly, the Hungarians classify it as an engagement followed by a thrust, blade contact being maintained until the moment of the hit.

Final of the Attack. The final blade action, preceded by one or more feints, in a compound attack.

Finda, (It.). A feint, a corruption of *finta*.

Finger-Loop. A small metal ring,

through which one finger of the sword-hand could be passed, set immediately in the angle formed by the blade and the lower edge of one of the *quillons*; a device found in certain sixteenth-century German weapons.

Finger-Play. The classic French method of manipulating the weapon, by means of finger technique employed on the handle. The thumb and forefinger, which play the principal role, are known as the manipulators. The remaining fingers, which play a subsidiary part, are known as the last fingers or aids. The technique of the finger-play at foil and épée is virtually identical; at sabre, there are some differences, as the weapon is held differently and in forming certain parries (notably *prime* and *quinte*) the little finger assumes considerably more importance. Finger-play was never very important in the Italian school, as the handle of the foil was strapped to the wrist and most sabre cuts were delivered with the forearm; now, the contemporary obsession with orthopaedic grips has reduced finger-play to its age of decadence.

Finger-Tip Grip. A method of holding the weapon between forefinger and thumb, the latter not being flat on the handle. Now regarded as erroneous, it was formerly advocated by some masters. Its advantage was that it allowed of very precise point movements, especially with the ultra-light foils of the early twentieth century; its disadvantage was that it contracted and tired the muscles of the hand, so that towards the end of an exhausting bout or competition, efficiency declined.

Fingers, Last. The second, third and little fingers of the sword-hand, otherwise known as the aids.

Finta or Finto, (It.). A feint.

Finta in Tempo. The feint-in-time. (See Time.)

Fiorete or Fioretto, (It.). The *fleuret*, or foil.

First. (See Prime.)

First Intention. An offensive action with which the executant seriously intends to be successful; there is no bluff, or exploratory motive involved in it.

Fitzgerald, George Robert. Nephew of the Bishop of Derry, a see renowned for the eccentricities of its prelates, he was an insatiable duellist and wanton provoker of duels. He favoured the pistol and emerged unscathed from so many encounters that it began to be rumoured that he had stooped to the gross practice of padding, or using some sort of artificial protection beneath his clothes. Be that as it may, one of his intended victims, Major Cunningham, finally managed to insist on the use of swords. Whether Fitzgerald feared that his defensive armour would prove less effective against cold steel than against a bullet, or whether he simply distrusted his own ability as a swordsman (his master, Harry Angelo, who presided over the famous academy in the early nineteenth century, described him as 'rash, lacking caution and coolness'), is uncertain, but with incredible cowardice, he fled London and sought refuge on his Irish estates. There, the forays of his retainers and their depradations on neighbouring property were such as to cause outrage even in that country; when Fitzgerald himself was tried and convicted for kidnapping and murder, there could be no alternative to the capital sentence.

Flanconnade (from Labat).

Fixing. 1) Halting the pupil in the course of a lesson, most commonly at the conclusion of an attack. The pupil is required to remain motionless in order that his position may be thoroughly checked, and he himself realises what, if anything, is wrong.
2) When the point not only arrives cleanly and precisely on the opponent, but remains in place without slipping off, with the blade arching gracefully into the classic curve.

Flamberge. A somewhat imprecise term; originally it indicated any large sword, especially of the two-handed type. Yet the term was used contemporaneously, and for long afterwards, to describe a blade of the wavy, or snakish, variety. Towards the end of the sixteenth century, the word acquired a very different significance. A *flamberge* was understood to be a slender-bladed rapier, with a greatly simplified hilt consisting of cup and *quillons* only, but without rings, knucklebows or other accessories. Finally, in the days of the small-sword, *flamberge*, which in France had once been used as a synonym for almost any type of sword, became an expression of disdain for a clumsy, outmoded weapon.

Flamboyant. A weapon with a wavy,

snakish blade. (See above.)

Flanconado Guard. A position or engagement in *septime*.

Flanconnade. A term of somewhat elastic interpretation, but basically, as the name suggests, is an attack at the opponent's right flank. However, it seems rather to be associated with the small-sword of the late seventeenth and early eighteenth centuries, when masters generally advocated its execution with opposition, than with a sabre attack. Delivered into the *octave* quarter of the target, the hand is fully pronated and kept low, in some cases even below the level of the point.
It may also be noted that Crosnier is a strong advocate, when fencing with the épée, of the riposte to the body by *quarte-croisé*, especially against the left-hander, a stroke by no means dissimilar to the *flanconnade*.

Flanconnade à la Mouche. (See Flying Flanconnade.)

Flash. Castello's term for the *flèche*. His professed intention while teaching in the U.S. was to anglicise the French terminology. Why, therefore, did he not simply refer to the 'arrow' attack? One's suspicions are aroused; did somebody, a secretary or collaborator, transcribe phonetically a misheard or badly pronounced *flèche*?

Flat. (See Plaquer.)

Flèche. The 'running' attack, so-called because when executed at the highest technical level, the fencer's body, legs, arms and weapon together form an almost straight line and by the exercise of some imagination, may be said to bear a certain resemblance to the *flèche* (French 'arrow'). The phrases 'running', or 'to run at the opponent', can, however, be highly misleading. The attack is initiated as usual by the extension of the sword-arm; then the weight is thrown forward, without, however, allowing the head and sword-arm to drop, and finally the rear leg is swung through in front of the original leading foot, the hit being timed to arrive as it is grounded. The *flècheur* should never find himself in the position of doubling frantically up the *piste* after a retreating opponent, who is easily keeping away and probably just awaiting the opportunity to plant a successful stop-hit.

The *flèche* is commonly used at épée and sabre, because of the larger target area and the longer fencing measure. It is probably most effective at sabre, when the prevailing conventions generally give priority to the attacker; rather less so at épée, when an attack *en flèche* is always vulnerable to the counter-attack, resulting in a double hit. The *flèche* is least effective with the foil; simple attacks executed by this method are relatively easy to parry, owing to the restricted target area, while the execution of a successful compound attack necessitates, for the same reason, a very high standard of blade technique, timing, and sense of dis-

tance. Another drawback at all weapons, and more particularly the sabre, is the problem of executing a parry and counter-riposte whilst in full flight. Generally speaking, the *flèche*, if it is to be successful at all, must be successful at the first time of asking.

The most common faults, which masters must be vigilant to correct, are:
1) Failure perfectly to extend the sword-arm before the take-off.
2) Allowing head and sword-arm to drop during the course of the attack.
3) Failure to co-ordinate blade and footwork. The hit should arrive on target simultaneously with the grounding of the rear foot in front of the original leading foot.

It will be observed that the leg-action is reminiscent of the days before the lunge came fully into its own. (See Pass.)

Flèche, The Stepped-On. As a pre-

liminary move, the leading foot is rapidly and aggressively advanced, to encourage an opponent whose predilection for the counter-attack has perhaps been noted, to execute an offensive action. The rear leg, meanwhile, crosses the front leg rather more slowly than is usual, to give the *flècheur* sufficient time to parry and then continue his attack in the normal way.

Fleuret. An old-fashioned term for the foil, introduced in France towards the end of the seventeenth century, when all cutting actions were rapidly becoming obsolete and almost all attacks were executed with the point alone, protected by a small leather cap which might fancifully be supposed to resemble a *fleuret* (flower bud).

Florio, John. An Italian resident in Elizabethan London, he made a spirited translation of Montaigne's

A successful Flèche attack, the sword-arm being perfectly straight.

Essays, which is still obtainable. He also compiled two Anglo-Italian phrase-books, *The First Frutes* (1578) and *The Second Frutes* (1591). True to his Italian ancestry, he was a strong advocate of the rapier against the English broadsword which he describes in the former work as a 'clownish and dastardly weapon, none fit for a gentleman'.

Fluking Iron. Slang for the épée; a highly pejorative term, originating in the days when there was a tendency for the épée to be practised by 'men of a certain age', and when, because of the complete body target and absence of conventions, dedicated foilists affected to regard such contests as being governed by chance rather than skill.

Flute. The groove in the *forte* of the épée; on the *épée de combat*, it allowed the blood to drain away from the hilt.

Fly-Fishing Position. Fencing slang for a guard position adopted by some épéeists. The weapon is held well out to the swordsman's right, with blade elevated, point high and the handle grasped like the butt of a fishing-rod. Such fencers are reduced to relying almost exclusively upon the stop-hit at wrist or arm, delivering it with a throwing action reminiscent of a fisherman casting. As they seldom adopt this method, however, without having acquired a very high degree of accuracy and point control, they often achieve considerable success, the more so as their opponents, baffled by the unfamiliar angles, are generally uncer-

Stephen Paul flèches at Bruniges — note his left foot is still airborne.

tain as to what tactics to adopt.

A remarkably successful exponent of this style, according to Professor Crosnier, was the Frenchman Duchène, who, paradoxically, could exploit the classical method with equal effect, but who preferred the unorthodox approach as likely to afford him more amusement.

Flying Cut-Over. To attack by means of a combined beat and backward glide along the opposing blade, followed instantly by the cut-over.

Flying Double Feint. A two-feint attack initiated from absence of blade, the feints often being accompanied by a *balestra*.

Flying Feint. A feint performed from absence of blade.

Flying Flanconnade. A cut-over finishing with an attack to the flank.

Flying Flèche. A spectacular and exaggerated variety of the *flèche*, in which the executant becomes temporarily air-borne, his head, trunk and leading leg (now extended behind him) forming a perfectly straight line at an angle of about forty degrees to the ground, or, in the finest examples, even less. Such an extreme development of an already difficult technique is unsuitable even for advanced fencers unless they are gifted with exceptional athletic ability.

Flying Lunge. A highly aggressive form of the lunge, attributed originally to the Austrian master Nevalic. In this version the rear foot is not kept firmly on the floor, but as in a jump forward, leaves the ground altogether and is only replaced several inches further on, simultaneously with the landing of the front foot at the full extension of the

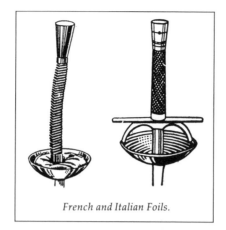
French and Italian Foils.

lunge. Valuable distance can be gained by this method, but it is for advanced fencers only and certainly not to be confused with the deplorable habit of dragging or sliding the rear foot when lunging, which results in a clumsy position much too near the opponent.

Flying Parry and Flying Return. (See Parade de Pointe Volante.)

Flying Thrust. An attack delivered without preliminary contact of the blades.

Flynn, Errol. *Don Juan* (1949) was Flynn's last swashbuckling film. By this time he was not the man he had been, but nevertheless, in the words of Higham and Greenberg (*Hollywood in the Forties*) his swordsmanship was 'very acceptable'. *Don Juan* was superbly screened and the final duel between Don Juan and Leporello (Robert Douglas) was splendidly staged on an immense staircase. As for the scene in the salle with the long double line of King's Cadets attacking, parrying and riposting with consummate style and in exact unison, it was enough to turn most contemporary coaches green with envy and frustration.

Foible. The weak part of the blade, between the centre and the point; seventeenth-century French for *faible*, feeble.

Foil. The practice weapon for the small-sword, evolved in the late seventeenth century, when cutting became an obsolete action, and accordingly, a flat blade was no longer required for training. The word is derived from the French *refouler*, to turn back, and had long been in use in England to describe any rebated weapon (Swetman, in the early seventeenth century, describes practice weapons with flat caps on the points, protected even further by a leather covering as big as a tennis ball, which must seriously have impaired the balance), including lances and the like. Foils in this country were simply blunted weapons. (Cp. the fencing scene in *Hamlet*, Act. V, Sc. ii.)

The original French foil was known as the *fleuret*, from a fancied resemblance between its leather button and a flower bud. The foil of that period was appreciably shorter than its modern counterpart. Liancour, the famous French master, advocated the use of several different types of foil in the salle, including a heavy, guardless weapon for the pupil which was also shorter than that of the master, whose own weapon, for the purpose of avoiding excessive fatigue, was lighter than usual. Within the last decade or so, one prominent London fencing master was known to make his pupils take their lessons with a monstrosity of his own devising, two blades somehow fitted into a single hilt, which occasioned the muscles of the sword-arm the most exquisite agony, the idea probably being that if they could manipulate a weapon of this weight, they could manipulate anything.

Various patterns of guards have found favour at different times. 'Figure-of-eight' guards and narrow, slightly convex, rectangular guards have found favour and given place in turn to the contemporary saucer-shaped guard, a smaller edition of the épée cup-guard.

The foil has been the dominant factor in the development of modern fencing. Even sabre fencing, though involving the cut, and so introducing an entirely different factor, is limited by conventions governing the right to attack, riposte, counter-attack and so forth, identical to those at foil. The sabre target is also restricted. (See Target.) This is, of course, not so at épée, but the fact remains that the terminology and basic concept of sword-play are akin to the foil, although naturally, the tactics and application of the basic system must be greatly modified at this weapon. For long the épée was regarded as the duelling weapon as such – at least one duel has occurred in France since the Second World War – while the sabre, before 1939, was regarded as a speciality of the Hungarians and not practised very widely in England outside the Services. Thirty or forty years ago, the older generation of fencing masters were still reluctant to give sabre or épée lessons except to those about to participate in matches or competitions, of which there were then vastly fewer. For them, the foil reigned supreme – precise, formal and elegant.

Foil Club. According to J.D. Aylward in the *English Master at Arms*, a foil club, drawn largely from theatrical circles, was founded in 1900, with Pinero as its first president. It must have disappeared into oblivion, for C.-L. de Beaumont's *History of British Fencing* informs us that another foil club, the last of those devoted

Fonst (right) against Berger, 1904 (illustration by F.H. Townsend).

specifically to the practice and sponsorship of a particular weapon, was established in 1946. The president on this occasion was Mr P.G. Doyne, the hero of the sensational foil championship of 1912, which he only won after repeated ties, postponements and barrages. Subsequently this club also appears to have languished although an unsuccessful attempt to revive it is reported to have been made in the mid seventies.

Foil, The Electric is the modern weapon which, by means of a spring-loaded head instead of a button on the point of the weapon and a system of wires attached to a recording apparatus (q.v.) enables hits to be signalled by the flashing of light bulbs corresponding to the two fencers. It has now virtually replaced the non-electric weapon and is used at all competitions. The first occasion of importance when the electric foil

was used was at Rome in the World Championship of 1955.

Owing to the wire running up the centre of the blade, and terminating in a socket inside the guard, into which a further wire, ultimately attached to the apparatus itself, can be plugged, the electric foil is sensibly stiffer, thicker and heavier than its predecessor. Phrases, or sequences of blade actions, accordingly tend to be less common and less prolonged than formerly, and much more now depends on continuous footwork, opportunism and extreme rapidity of execution. Such developments, which tend to suit the youthful athlete, have no doubt also favoured the rapid advance of the so-called Iron Curtain states which, with the exception of Hungary and possibly Poland, lacked, even in pre-revolutionary days, any fencing schools or traditions of their own.

Not a few good judges still advocate

that young fencers should begin with the non-electric weapon, because of the superior control and confidence which its comparative lightness allows.

Foil Grip. (See French Grip.)

Foils, Conversation with the. The name given by the old school to an assault, or friendly bout, between two good fencers, each seeking to employ the blade actions best adapted to outwit his adversary whilst at the same time exploiting the utmost subtleties of the foil. Thus, an attack being parried, the defender delivered his riposte which, parried in its turn, allowed

the attacker to counter-riposte. Then, in the next phrase, the rivals would perhaps seek to deceive each other's parries with compound blade actions, which could, if repeated too often, render the executant vulnerable to the stop-hit or *remise*. Thus the offensive passed rapidly back and forth, as in a tennis match, or in a conversation, where the one party makes an observation, only for it to be capped or amplified by the other.

Foin. An Elizabethan term for a thrust with a pointed weapon.

Fonst, R. earned the unique distinction of being the only fencer to win three gold medals at the Olympic

The Full Pass (from de Liancour).

Games for individual events in épée in 1900 and épée and foil in 1904. He was the leading light in the small group of individuals responsible for Cuba's brief but glorious supremacy on the stage of world fencing.

Force, Movements or **Attacks of.** Attacks on the blade; Hutton names the pressure, *coulé*, bind and beat.

Forçonnade. A thrust with a stabbing action, following a withdrawal of the sword-arm; very forceful, but thoroughly bad technique, as, apart from its crudity, a period of fencing time is lost.

Fore-Cut. A cut with the fore-edge of the sabre.

Fore-Edge. The leading edge of the sabre, which is naturally presented towards the opponent when the weapon is correctly held. The fencing sabre is in fact blunted, but in theory the whole of the fore-edge is sharp and valid cuts may be administered with any part of it.

Forked Remise. An angulated *remise*.

Forte. The strong part of the blade, between its approximate centre and the guard.

Forte to Foible. The basic principle of defence at all three weapons. The *forte*, or strong section of the defending blade nearest the guard, is opposed to the *foible*, or weak part nearest the point of the attacker's weapon, thus deflecting the latter by superior strength.

Foul Blow. A hit scored before the president's call of 'play', or after his command to halt.

Four Ancient Masters. In the sixteenth and seventeenth centuries, the title given to the four senior masters of the English corporation of Masters of Defence (q.v.).

Fourth. (See Quarte.)

Fourth Weapon. The name given to the electric foil (not always entirely as a compliment), it having made its appearance long after the traditional three – foil, épée and sabre. It has certainly lent itself to a style of fencing lacking much of the original style and subtlety; it has been more than once suggested that it should be officially recognised as a fourth or additional weapon in its own right, the non-electric foil being retained for use in separate competitions. Certainly, there is enough difference between the two to warrant a clear distinction and the academic possibilities of the older weapon appeal both to the traditionalist and the intellectual fencer.

Fox, Colonel G.M. was inspector of Gymnasia at Aldershot in the final decade of the last century. He issued a handbook of *Infantry Sword Exercises* dealing with sabre fencing only. Largely at his own expense, he brought the famous Italian master, Ferdinando Masiello of Florence, to England, with the result that the Italian school of fencing was for a time predominant in the Army. This incurred the wrath of Captain Hutton, a devoted supporter of the French school and resulted in a prolonged controversy in the correspondence columns of the press and elsewhere.

Foyning. Thrusting, the new method of rapier-play, which in the sixteenth century ousted the crude hacking with the medieval broadsword.

Frecciata, (It.). The *flèche*.

Frederick III, Holy Roman Emperor 1440-93. Despite a Turkish invasion, risings in Bohemia and Hungary, the final establishment of Swiss independence and the loss of Milan, Frederick was in many ways an able, wily and patient ruler who re-united the family domains of the Habsburgs and enabled that house henceforward to regard the imperial title (theoretically elective) as virtually its own possession by hereditary descent. He was a patron of swordsmen and granted the Marxbruder their privileges.

Free Play. Friendly, informal fencing with no jury and no exact time limit or number of hits.

Freezing. To freeze the opponent is to use prolonged footwork with rapid changes of speed and cadence to lure him into a distance suitable for launching an attack; at the same time, so confusing him that he is reduced temporarily to a state of immobility and indecision.

French Foil. The traditional French foil has a handle which, although slightly curved to fit into the palm, is perfectly plain and destitute of the vestigial cross-hilt and *pas d'âne* rings of its Italian counterpart. Hence the distinguishing mark and glory of the French school was its subtle finger-play, not possible with other types of grip, which in turn led to further particularities and tactics. To take but two examples, the French tended to keep the elbow of the sword-arm appreciably bent, it being much harder, with their grip, to parry effectively with an extended arm, in the manner of their Italian rivals. Similarly, the French tended not to commence their attacks until within distance, being much more adept at the *trompement*, or deception of a parry, than the representa-

tives of the other nation, whose fingers were fixed almost rigidly on the handle, which, moreover, was strapped to the wrist.

French Grip. 1) The handle of the French foil.
2) The method of holding the foil in the classical French tradition. The thumb lies flat along the top of the handle; the top sections of the second, third and fourth fingers rest lightly upon its inner surface. By principally using the thumb and forefinger (the manipulators) the circular and semi-circular movements of the point can be controlled very precisely.

French School. The classic technique and theory of small-sword play, on which modern foil-fencing is directly based, was evolved by the great French masters of the late seventeenth and early eighteenth centuries, such as Labat, Besnard, Liancour, Girard and Danet. Their analysis of the subject was at once the most penetrating and comprehensive that had yet appeared. Some of the essential characteristics of the French school, which have never been effaced, were the classic onguard position, the *coupé* (cut-over), the detached parry and immediate riposte and the increasing use of compound attacks, the feints of which deceived the defender's parries. Another hallmark of the tradition was the growing reliance on the circular parry, though in this last case Liancour, for one, raised a dissentient voice. However, the ever-decreasing weight of the small-sword and the appearance towards the end of the eighteenth century of a really light practice foil as well as the mask, permitted the general principles and tactics of the school to be taken to their logical conclusions. The French system eventually obtained virtually universal acceptance. The modern Italian school dating from the nineteenth and early twentieth centuries, is not really indigenous at all, owing little or nothing to the theories of their original sixteenth-century swordsmanship, but is, on the contrary, essentially the system of their French rivals, adapted, with comparatively minor modifications, to the flamboyant and aggressive Italian genius.

Froissé. The *froissé* is a slightly less common term for the *froissement*.

Froissement. One of the three attacks on the blade; the displacement of the opponent's blade by means of a sharp, strong, grazing action, forwards and downwards.

Full Pass. An alternative to the lunge which briefly found favour in seventeenth-century France. The rear leg was advanced in front of the leading leg, as in the normal pass, but to the extreme limit of capability, and bent at the knee, while the rear heel was raised from the ground. The joints protest at the bare sight of de Liancour's illustration.

Fuori Tempo, (It.). Out of time.

Gafflet. A device used in small-sword exhibition bouts and prize-fights in the eighteenth century. It was a cap fitted to the sword-point so that only a trifle of the latter was exposed – sufficient to pink the opponent, but not seriously to wound him.

Gaining on the Lunge. A method of greatly increasing the length and penetration of the lunge. Immediately before lunging, the rear foot is brought forward so that it touches the heel of the leading foot and much distance is thereby gained on the opponent. As an alternative to the *balestra* and step forward, it has a valuable element of surprise.

Some fencers favour gaining on the *reprise* in somewhat similar fashion: in this case, following the initial lunge, the rear foot is carried forward, not to the resumption of the normal on-guard position, but again so that it touches the leading foot. This tactic can be employed very usefully against the perpetually retreating fencer, but is difficult to execute quickly and imposes a severe strain on the thigh muscles. René Paul was seen to exploit it to some effect.

Ganancia. The Spanish term for Guadagnare di Spada.

Garçon de Salle. This figure, familiar enough in private salles before the Second World War, was in effect an apprentice professional. In return for numerous menial duties, he received fencing lessons and as he gained experience and confidence, gave lessons to the younger or less advanced members. In time, he might hope to be taken into partnership, or even to succeed his patron.

The economic and financial pressures of the last thirty or forty years, resulting in the conversion of practically all private fencing clubs into state-subsidised evening classes, have led to the almost total disappearance of the *garçon*.

Gardere, Professor A. was a very well-known French left-handed master. He was second in foil at the Olympics of 1936, and second again in the World Championships of 1937. He gave his name to a type of orthopaedic grip, and was one of the first to adopt this expedient, having lost several fingers of his sword-hand in an accident on the tramlines in Brussels.

Gascony. The most southerly province in France, adjoining the Pyrenees and once forming part of the great medieval dukedom of Aquitaine. Its natives were notorious for their excessive boastfulness and wild exaggerations; hence the term *gasconnade* for an enterprise of this sort. Two of the most famous swordsmen of history and fiction, Cyrano de Bergerac and d'Artagnan, were both Gascons and so was Etienne Gerard, the hero of Conan Doyle's series of short stories set in Napoleonic times.

Gaudin, Lucien. One of the greatest and most graceful fencers of his day, the exponent of a classical style fast becoming a memory; 'poetry in motion' as Professor Bertrand put it. A left-hander and supreme exponent of finger-play, he was World Epée Champion in 1921 and won two Olympic gold medals, for foil and épée, in the same year, 1928; an unprecedented feat which will almost certainly never be repeated. Having been defeated by A. Nadi in 1921, Gaudin excused himself on the plea that he had been carrying an injury. These two, regarded as the leading representatives respectively of the French and Italian schools, therefore met in a special contest in Paris in 1922, (see Nadi) and the superior technique of the former was vindicated in Gaudin's triumph by twenty hits to eleven.

Gautier, Professor A. A renowned épée master who had served in the French Army and who settled in England in 1929 to teach at the London Fencing Club. In allusion to his former rank, he was nicknamed *Le Capitaine*. Charles de Beaumont was among his pupils.

Gautier's Penguins. They were Gautier's Ladies' team and won the Martin Edmunds Cup in 1934, 1937 and 1938, coming second in the intervening years, 1935 and 1936.

Gavigliano, (It.). The cross-bar of the Italian foil.

Gazee, (Arch.). A one-two *en marchant*.

George III. King of Great Britain, 1760-1820. 'George, be a King,' was the famous advice given to him by his mother, Augusta, Princess of Wales. At the start of his reign, George III endeavoured to recover the legitimate royal authority and influence largely dissipated by his two dull-witted Hanoverian predecessors, whilst disclaiming any intention of infringing the spirit or even the letter of the constitution. During the period of successive brief and ineffective Whig administrations (1763-70), George has been accused of 'political ineptitude'; in fact, he was busily engaged in building up a parliamentary following known as the 'King's Friends' whom he was able to install in office with Lord North at their head (1770). George III has received a thoroughly 'bad press' from the nineteenth-century liberal historians for maintaining North in office, often against the latter's inclinations, during the ensuing decade, which saw the American rebellion and the successful assertion of the colonies' independence. The picture of him as a senseless bigot tyrannising over the simple, freedom-loving Americans, is the crudest of distortions; most of the Americans needed little instruction in all the most repellent acts of the bully and the demagogue and a closer study of the period by Professor Lewis Namier has done much to restore the King's reputation. In 1783 he went far to making amends for any previous misjudgement when he invited William Pitt the Younger, then aged twenty-four, to form a government, so launching the great statesman who not only restored the country's pride, prosperity and self-confidence after the American disaster, but successfully steered us through the maelstrom of the French revolutionary wars.

The first of his dynasty to be born in England, to speak English properly, and to regard himself as an Englishman, not a Hanoverian, George 'gloried in the name of Briton' as he himself put it. As time passed, he gained the respect and sympathy of a large part of the nation and above all the support of the new Tory party, which, now that the last Stuart, Cardinal Henry, 'Bonnie Prince Charlie's' brother, had died, could transfer to George without reservation all their traditional loyalty to the crown. He embodied many of the characteristics on which the Englishmen of those times prided themselves: a blunt straightforwardness, loyalty, unshakable resolution and that love of country life which earned him the nickname of 'Farmer George'. On sending his younger sons to Eton he announced that they went to be turned into English gentlemen 'and that includes the floggings too'. His favourite residence being Windsor, his bonds with the famous school nearby could only be strengthened when his own old fencing master, Domenico Angelo, was appointed to instruct the rising generation of Etonians in the art. The King was frequently to be seen in the vicinity of the school, stopping to chat with the boys. Eton's traditional uniform of top-hat, tail-coat and white tie was really only the conventional mourning outfit of the time; assumed as a mark of respect on the King's death in 1820, it was retained permanently.

George III's end was tragic. Having recovered from a temporary bout of mental disorder in 1788-9, he became permanently insane in 1811, the Prince of Wales (later George IV) being declared Regent; mad, blind and deaf, the old King lingered on for another nine years.

George IV. King of Great Britain 1820-30. 'Prinny', as he was almost universally known, was, like all the Hanoverian heirs, on the worst of terms with his father, George III. He accordingly cultivated close relations with the Whig leaders, Fox and Sheridan, rivalling them in their profligacy if not in their intellectual pursuits. He badly let down Fox, solemnly denying that he had secretly gone through a form of marriage with Maria Fitzherbert, a Roman Catholic. Fox repeated this in the House in all good faith, thus undeservedly compromising his own integrity.

Yet H.R.H. was not altogether underserving of the title of 'The First Gentleman of Europe'. Eyewitnesses pay tribute to his easy well-bred informality, and when occasion required, his dignified presence. Assuming the Regency for his insane father in 1811, the name became associated with one of the most brilliant periods of English history, memorable for its sport, its coaching traditions, its elegance and the military glory won by Wellington's Infantry. George IV was the last monarch to proceed from his coronation in the Abbey to the medieval style banquet in Westminster Hall, where for the last time, the hereditary King's Champion, Dymoke, rode in full armour into the assembly, to challenge all or any who dared maintain that the newly-crowned King was not the rightful liege-lord of Britain. George's artistic tastes were at times original – the Brighton Pavilion has been condemned as a monumental exercise in bad taste – but it has intrigued thousands and its interior decoration is a rich example of the then popular *chinoiserie*. He was the possessor of a pleasant singing voice and his virtuosity on the 'cello was such that it was declared, and as no mere empty compliment, that had he not been of royal blood he could have supported himself as a professional musician. His failure to win promotion to high military rank was a sore point. Such were the doubts in high quarters of his competence and reliability that he was obliged to console himself as best he could with the colonelcy of the 10th Hussars. Doubtless it was some form of psychological compensation which led him on to give graphic accounts of the Battle of Waterloo – which, as the years passed, he had apparently won almost single-handed – thereby incurring the ridicule of the Opposition, for he had never seen a shot fired in his life.

With all this, there was something boyishly disarming about him and his gift of rueful humour. He was on the worst of terms with his wife, Caroline of Brunswick, throughout their married life. That choleric and erratic lady, excluded from the coronation ceremony, disgusted even that easy-going age with the edifying spectacle of the Queen of England hammering for admittance on the doors of Westminster Abbey. One sympathises with his pathetic plea to his secretary on his first sight of her. 'Harris, I am not well. Pray fetch me a glass of brandy.' In 1821 Bonaparte died and the news was rushed to George IV, as he had by that time become. 'Sir! Sir! Your greatest enemy is dead!' 'Is she, by God!'

'Prinny's' patronage greatly stimulated interest in fencing and its consequent popularity in the *beau*

Mrs Mary Glen-Haig — sometime president of the Amateur Fencing Association.

monde. In the 1780s, there were several demonstrations at Carlton House, famous not only as the Prince's residence, but as the meeting-place for the wits, gamblers, bucks and fashionable Whig politicians whom he had gathered about him. On one such occasion, all the leading masters were present, the notorious d'Eon acting as president. At the Pavilion, in 1789, H.R.H. was much impressed, as most would have been, by the spectacle of a top-class master, Joseph Roland, giving a lesson to a fellow professional. One does not tip leading fencing masters; so with characteristic delicacy, George asked for a set of weapons, masks and so on to be sent to him, whereupon he felt able to reimburse the pair with his accustomed munificent generosity.

Gerard, Brigadier Etienne. He was the dashing cavalry officer of the Conan Doyle romances, 'the picked horseman and the surest blade in the ten regiments of Hussars'. He was deadly with the sabre; in individual duels he killed both the ex-Jacobin Jean Carabin, or Baron Straubenthal

as he had become, and the brutal Major Sergine of the Russian Dragoons of Kiev. In a brush with a Cossack officer, whom he encountered while carrying despatches to Paris, his point entered the Russian's body just below the fourth tunic button. He had another encounter with the A.D.C. of the Russian Emperor and despatched the two Corsican conspirators sent to assassinate Napoleon; and he emerged unscathed from his legendary conflict with the six regimental fencing masters. Gerard was severe on fencing masters; there was the affair with the Italian master at Milan 'whose widow was pensioned off' as he blandly informs us. On his first night in the mess of the 3rd Hussars he challenged almost all his new comrades, and subsequently had a lively mounted duel with a British officer of the 16th Light Dragoons, known to the reader only as 'Sir Russell, the Bart'. (Like many another foreigner, Gerard found it difficult to understand the use of Christian names by baronets and knights.) Gerard parried *quinte* and cut away half his enemy's plume, deflected the Bart's point and cut away the other half with another riposte. It is clear, as Gerard informs us, that the Bart, like the majority of British officers at that time, was a very poor swordsman.

Never exactly backward in relating his exploits or assessing his own abilities, Gerard hailed, like de Bergerac and d'Artagnan, from Gascony.

Gerevich, A. A sabreur whose achievements were closely linked with those of his contemporary Karpati, both of them figuring in the triumphant Hungarian teams which won at four successive Olympics (1948, 1952, 1956 and 1960). He was Individual Champion at the

Olympics of 1948 and second four years later. He won the World Championships of 1935 and 1951. A most charming man and courteous opponent, as witnessed by anyone who knew him, his fencing repertoire was wide, but if there was one stroke that afforded him especial pleasure it was the *molinello* to chest.

German Gymnastic Society. A London society of the late nineteenth century, which at one time was the only club to hold an open fencing competition.

German Universities. During the eighteenth century, duelling was much practised at the leading German universities, such as Heidelberg, Leipzig, Jena and Halle, the weapon most favoured being the spadroon, a light cut-and-thrust sabre. This was so dangerous and fatalities so common, that towards the end of the century it was abandoned. Instead, a system called the 'Hiebcoment' was introduced, more akin to the English backswording of the same period, from which the thrust was excluded. Various types of sabre used at different times were the *Mensur-sabel* (students' duelling sabre), the *Krummsabel* (curved sabre) and the *Sabeglace*. It was not until well into the nineteenth century that there developed that curious form of sabre duelling with the weapon known as the *Schlaeger*, which was until comparatively recently most widely and commonly associated with German students and universities.

This highly-specialised form of sword-play really bore very little resemblance to any other type of encounter, whether conducted according to pure instinct or the highly-developed principles of a sophisticated system. To begin with, the opponents were placed on guard within a very close measure, and there they had to remain, neither advance nor retreat being permitted. The head and face were the sole objects of attack, and to protect the eyes, metal goggles were worn. The shoulders and sword-arm were likewise padded as a protection against badly aimed cuts, or those deflected away from the target. At such close quarters, speed and nerve were all-important, and feints being clearly hazardous were but seldom employed.

Such encounters were by no means always, or even generally, the result of quarrels which could only be settled by the effusion of blood. On the contrary, regular matches were arranged between the various students' clubs, or corps, within the university. These contests were for a given number of cuts, or lasted for a set period of time, and were not necessarily halted if one or even both of the combatants were wounded; thus arose a strong probability of acquiring one or more of those facial scars so greatly prized by the *Junkers* of a previous era.

Ghersi, Captain F. A Napoleonic officer who, at the end of the wars, settled in London and became fencing master to the Inns of Court. His teaching embodied some strikingly modern principles. In the on-guard position the sword-arm should be bent, the point raised, the elbow a hand's span from the body (exactly as recommended by Professor Crosnier in *Fencing with the Foil*) as opposed to the 'flat' guard taught by his immediate predecessors, including La Boessière. Ghersi was also one of the first to define and advocate the parry of *sixte* in preference to *tierce*.

Giganti, Nicoletto. A famous sixteenth-century Italian master, chiefly notable for having first clearly explained the techniques of the lunge in a publication of an earlier date than that of Capo Ferro. Inexplicably, he appears to have abandoned this seminal development and to have reverted to the fashion of fencing with the left foot in advance. Giganti also did something to simplify the number and theory of the guards; basically, he advocated only two, corresponding to *tierce* and *quarte*.

Gilbert, Sir Humphrey. The author of *Queen Elizabeth's Achademy*, an abortive but grandiose educational project for the use of Elizabethan England. He saw service in the Spanish Netherlands and Ireland where he twice suppressed uprisings and nourished schemes for colonisation. Like many of his contemporaries, he dreamed of discovering the North West Passage. Drowned in 1583, while crossing the Atlantic on a highly ambitious colonising scheme to Canada, his last words, shouted across to a neighbouring vessel in the tumult of the storm were: 'We are as near Heaven on sea as on land.'

Gillray, James. The political and social satire of this most famous of eighteenth-century cartoonists spared no-one, either in the Royal Family, among whom George III was a prime target, or in the highest political circles, Pitt, Fox and Burke all figuring among his victims. Of most interest to fencers is his engraving of the assault between Saint-George and d'Eon at Carlton House, 1787, in the presence of the Prince of Wales and Mrs Fitzherbert, d'Eon pressing the attack home despite his voluminous skirts.

Girard, Le Sieur. A retired French naval officer and master in the early eighteenth century, his system of parries was virtually that of modern times. He also taught the most intricate compound attacks, incorporating not only two, but even three feints.

Giuoco Corto and Lungo, (It.). Fencing at close quarters and at long distance respectively.

Giuoco Perfetto. (It.). A successful attack, the climax of dextrous feints which have all evaded the defender's parries.

Giving the Blade. Offering the blade to the opponent's attack, with some subsequent action in mind.

Glasgow Cuts were the stock-in-trade of those Victorian actors who could not fence. They consisted of wide slashes aimed at the opponent's blade and repeated endlessly until someone had to die.

Glen-Haig, Mrs M., C.B.E. One of the most distinguished of all English lady fencers; she competed in four Olympics, reaching the finals in 1948, and twice won gold medals for ladies' foil in the Commonwealth Games. Betwen 1948 and 1960, she was an automatic member of the Ladies' National Team, captaining it from 1950 to 1957. Mrs Glen-Haig was Ladies' Foil Champion in 1948 and 1950 and her record would certainly have been far more outstanding had she not had the misfortune to be a contemporary of Miss G. Sheen, coming second to her on no less than six consecutive occasions, once after a barrage. Once more, in 1960, she had to be content with the runner's-up position to her great rival. It must have been a great consolation to have beaten her old opponent into second place in the Commonwealth Games at Vancouver (1954).

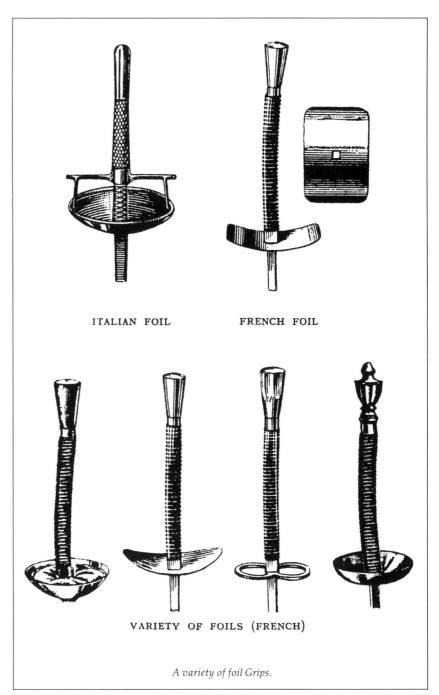

ITALIAN FOIL   FRENCH FOIL

VARIETY OF FOILS (FRENCH)

A variety of foil Grips.

Moreover, in the Desprez Cup the customary result was reversed on three occasions (1946, 1949, 1952) and the same thing happened in the de Beaumont Cup in 1953. Mrs Glen-Haig won the Desprez Cup four times in all (1946, 1947, 1949, 1952), the Jubilee Bowl three times (1951, 1952, 1954) and the de Beaumont Cup twice (1953, 1954).

On abandoning active fencing, Mrs Glen-Haig became equally prominent in administration. Having already been president of the Ladies' Amateur Fencing Union, and served as honorary secretary of the A.F.A., in 1973 she was elected president of the latter body, the first lady to hold that position. She has held a number of other distinguished positions, including those of chairman of the Central Council for Physical Recreation, president of the Sports Association for the Disabled and membership of the International Olympic Committee.

Glide. 1) A smooth, insidious step forward, with a gliding motion. Szabo equates it with a flat, effortless jump, almost akin to the *balestra*. 2) The *coulé*.

Glide-Thrust. A Hungarian term for the *coulé*.

Glise or Glissade. The *coulé*.

Glove. The present A.F.A. rules require competitors at all weapons to wear a glove on the sword-hand, the cuff of which shall extend half-way up the forearm. According to Saviolo, in the days of the rapier and dagger, mailed gloves were worn on both hands at practice, and sometimes mailed shirts and breastplates as well.

Godfrey, Captain John. He was an amateur swordsman who published

his *Treatise on the Useful Art of Defence* in 1735. He emphasises that the weight should be placed equally on both feet, instead of chiefly on the rear foot as required by practically all masters up to that time, and he substitutes a supinated hand position for the normal pronation in *tierce* – i.e., he advocates *sixte* a hundred years before Jean Louis of Montpellier popularised it.

Golpe, (Span.). A hit.

Grand Salute. (See Salute.)

Granger, Stewart was the sleekly good-looking film hero of more than forty comedies, dramas and period romances. He took the lead in the remakes of two famous films, *The Prisoner of Zenda* and *Scaramouche*. *Scaramouche* is a young Frenchman who resolves to learn fencing with the object of challenging and defeating the wicked *aristo* who has just killed his best friend; there is plenty to interest the fencer in these sequences. At the first confrontation of the rivals, Scaramouche seizes a sword and wields it like a battle-axe, his antagonist contemptuously evading the clumsily savage blows with a series of mocking side-steps. There is a scene in which the arch-enemy receives his daily fencing lesson, which terminates with a set of multiple *redoublements* by cut-over to the master's wrist. Then, after Scaramouche has acquired a certain level of proficiency, comes the first serious encounter, the villain loftily defining his attacks as they are delivered and recommending the study and practice of such subtleties as the *triplé*, before cutting the rope securing the huge chandelier which is intended to descend on his luckless victim and literally extinguish him and his pretensions. The final spectacular duel which forms the film's

grand climax lasts ten minutes, which is a very long time in terms of fencing. The combatants perform simultaneous miracles of acrobatics and sword-play, managing in the process to rip the interior of a large theatre to shreds. The irony of all this, which is not likely to be lost on a fencer of any experience, is that the initial clumsy and untutored slashes of Scaramouche would have been far more likely to achieve the desired result than all the dazzling arts of the salle so painfully acquired. (See Scaramouche.)

Granville, Vice-Admiral Earl, K.G., K.C.V.O., C.B., D.S.O. The fourth Earl had a career almost as distinguished as his service in the Royal Navy. Sabre was his great enthusiasm ('the sabre for men', as his oft-repeated belief) and he was Scottish Sabre Champion, five times a finalist in the Amateur Sabre Championship, and fenced in the World Championships in Paris in 1937. From 1946 to 1953 he was president of the A.F.A. He was sometime governor of Northern Ireland and played

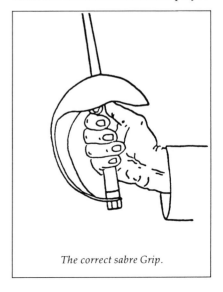

The correct sabre Grip.

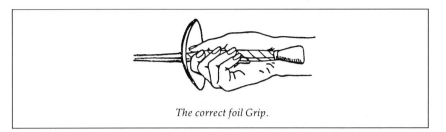

The correct foil Grip.

a great part in the introduction of regular fencing to that province.

Grasp. The grip.

Grassi, Giacomo di. A celebrated Italian master of the sixteenth century. Possibly his chief contribution was his definition and analysis of lines, which still stands today, viz., high and low, inside and outside. A great believer in the use of the dagger – he maintained that, used alone, it afforded a very sure defence – he advocated parrying with it into the opponent's *forte*; any contact nearer the point would, in his opinion, be insufficient to deflect a strong cut.

Graze. The *coulé*.

Graze Feint and Graze Double Feints. A graze feint is made by sliding the blade along that of the opponent, while maintaining contact with it; in other words, a feint of the *coulé*. Graze double feints is the phrase used by Barbasetti for two feints in a compound attack, the first of which is a graze feint.

Great-Sword. The two-hander of the Middle Ages.

Grip. 1) The handle of the weapon. 2) The method of holding the weapon, which can vary according to the type being used and the theories of different schools. The French technique, for instance, is radically different from the Italian.

Grip, The Anatomical. (See Orthopaedic Grip.)

Grosvenor Fencing Club was originally a 'company' club and was founded by Sir George Burt, director of J. Mowlem and Company, Civil Engineers, in 1922, the year he won the British Epée Championship. Its activities were always restricted to épée fencing. Both the Pellings, A.E. and J.A., were members. It won the Savage Shield (Epée Team Championship) or else came second, on occasions too numerous to mention.

Ground, Making and Breaking. Advancing and retreating.

Ground Judges. In the early days of electrical weapons and before the introduction of properly insulated *pistes*, it not seldom happened that a hit was recorded as a result of a fencer's point striking the ground. Two judges were therefore appointed, one at each end, to prevent mistakes arising in this way.

Grypes. Methods of seizing the opponent's arm or hilt and exerting leverage, so that he must either surrender his weapon or suffer a broken wrist. Such expedients were regarded as being of the utmost value in a brawl or sudden encounter and were rehearsed very seriously in the schools of the sixteenth and seventeenth centuries.

Guadagnare di Spada, (It.). Covering oneself on a step forward by an engagement of the adversary's blade.

Guard. 1) (See Coquille.)
2) A fencing position, roughly corresponding to the Hungarian *invito*, more especially adapted to defence, but from which the possibility of offence is not excluded. The term is sometimes also used as a loose synonym for 'on guard', e.g., 'returning to the guard position' instead of 'on-guard position'.

Guard, the French, German, Italian, Portugese, Spanish. (See On guard.)

Guardia, (It.). 1) The guard of the weapon.
2) The fencing position, corresponding roughly to our 'on guard'. According to the Italian theory of the sixteenth and seventeenth centuries, guards were mostly supposed to be adopted in relation to whatever guard was taken by the opponent, though the technical reasons for so doing are now not at all clear to the modern student. Marozzo advocates the master changing his pupil's position from one guard to another, though apart from the fact that the feet were placed alternately in front of each other, so that the exercise could be practised with a series of steps, there seems no real reason why one particular sequence should be preferred.

It should be understood that *guardia* were not positions in the modern sense, i.e., identical with the parry in that particular line. In Marozzo's day, parrying was still performed with a buckler. These *guardia* were supposed to be the best positions from which a time action could be launched on an offensive move by the adversary from any given position.

Half-Circle. 1) The name applied in the late seventeenth and much of the eighteenth century to the modern semi-circular parry terminating in *septime*. In those days this same parry was often alternatively (and most misleadingly) named 'circle' or *cercle*.

2) A semi-circular parry.

Half-Counter Parry. Captain Hutton, writing in the late nineteenth century, gives the same interpretation as the Hungarians today – namely, a parry diagonally crossing the body, from high to low line and vice versa. For the sabre, however, Castello defines the half-counter parries as *quinte* to *prime*, *tierce* to *quinte* and *seconde* to *quarte*.

Half-Disengage. To attack from high to low line or vice versa.

Half-Hangers or Half-Hanging Guards. The eighteenth-century term for certain sabre guards and parries, in which the blade was less vertical than in the 'hanging guards', roughly corresponding to our *prime* and *seconde*.

Half-Parry. At sabre, owing to the large target area to be protected, it is customary, when facing a compound attack, only to half-parry the feints; to execute full parries would render it too difficult to bring the blade back and effectively to parry the final attack. In counter-time, when deliberately inviting stop-cuts, which are usually aimed at the sword-arm, half-parries are generally effective, it being less necessary to parry fully than when protecting the body. Half-*quarte* is the parry most commonly used in this connection in counter-time, though half-*seconde* and half-*tierce* may also be employed. Some authorities have even recommended half-*quinte*, presum-

80

Half-Circle on the right. (From Danet.)

ably against a vertical feint at the forearm delivered over the top of the *coquille*.

Half-Pronation. Pronation is when the sword-hand is held with knuckles uppermost; supination when the palm is uppermost. The midway position, with thumb on top, should therefore logically be styled neutral, or some such term; instead it is usually called half-pronation, though, obviously, just as apt a term would be half-supination.

Half-Stance. Léon Bertrand's term for an on-guard position with as little of the chest exposed as possible.

Half-Supination. Not the midway position between full pronation and full supination, but the intermediate position between 'thumb-on-top' or half-pronation (q.v.) and complete supination is what is generally understood by this term.

Halsted, N. enjoyed notable success at Oxford where he was, of course, an automatic member of the university team besides winning the national Junior Foil Championship (Doyne Cup) in 1963. He was the British Universities Foil Champion that same year and Epée Champion in 1964. In the years that followed he was frequently among the first three in the leading competitions, such as the National Championships at foil and épée, the Coronation Cup and Epée Club Cup, while in 1965 he was runner-up in the Miller-Hallet competition. He represented his country in the World Championships of 1965 and 1971 at both his chosen weapons. He captained the men's foil team from 1974 to 1977 and at the World Championships at Buenos Aires in 1977 he was overall captain. Later he played a prominent part in the administration of the A.F.A. and his contribution was duly rewarded by election to the office of president, which he currently holds.

Hamilton, James Douglas, Fourth Duke of. Originally a Jacobite who opposed the accession of William of Orange and Mary, and was implicated in the rising of 1708, he transferred his loyalties to the moderate Tories who supported Queen Anne. He was on the point of leaving for France to assume the duties of ambassador-extraordinary, for the purpose of negotiating a peace treaty to end the War of the Spanish Succession, when he was killed in a duel with Lord Mohun, the exact causes and details of which have never become entirely clear.

Ostensibly, the challenge was delivered by Mohun in consequence of a disputed law-suit; afterwards, ugly rumours were soon circulating that it was a matter of political assassination, though whether instigated by extreme Whigs who favoured the continuation of the war, or by equally extreme Jacobites, incensed at their leader's supposed defection, must remain forever doubtful. The one generally accepted fact is, that both Hamilton and Mohun, without the slightest pretence of scientific sword-play, charged and ran each other through almost simultaneously. Colonel Hamilton, of the Scots Guards, the Duke's second, rushed to the aid of his principal; then, according to the Colonel's own account, General Macartney, Mohun's second, suddenly leapt upon them and administered a fatal thrust to the wounded Duke.

This testimony, however, has never gained universal credence. The Colonel's version of the affair was not corroborated by the servants who were eyewitnesses. Moreover, his conduct was, at the least, equivocal. He apparently made no attempt to arrest or accuse Macartney on the spot and although, three days later, he swore to the latter's guilt before the Privy Council, years afterwards when Macartney returned to England and stood his trial at the King's Bench, Colonel Hamilton did not repeat his accusation.

Nick Halsted, president of the A.F.A. and a British international.

The Earl of Chesterfield, present at the trial (at which the accused was acquitted) and subsequently, Sir Walter Scott himself, were alike convinced that Macartney did not kill the Duke. It is virtually certain that the real truth of this matter will never now be brought to light; but equally, it is hard to avoid the conclusion, that a dispute which, on the face of it, could have been settled honourably enough at the point of the sword, was in reality stained by deceit and treachery of the blackest description.

In the event, Lord Mohun, who had only been wounded, was also acquitted, despite his reputation as a notorious rakehell and gambler and the fact that he was known to have committed four previous murders, for one of which he had obtained a pardon in advance, an extraordinary circumstance that had led to the suspicion that he was employed as some sort of secret government agent.

On the lighter side, Dean Swift relates an entertaining story of a traveller in Ireland at about the time of these events, who, waylaid by footpads, announced his identity as that of the fugitive Macartney; whereupon, in hope of a reward, he was immediately taken to the nearest jail by his captors, who wereof course themselves promptly arrested.

Hand, To Have a. To parry well.

Hanger. 1) A curved cutting weapon similar to the cutlass, especially as used by members of the armed forces. The name derives from the fact that the weapon was worn hanging perpendicularly. Moreover, as with cutting weapons, the guards of *prime* and *seconde*, in which the hand is high and the blade may be said to be 'hanging' down, were preferred to the *tierce* or *quarte* generally adopted in small-sword play.
2) In the sixteenth and early seventeenth century, a small loop attached to the belt, in which the sword or dagger hung.

Hanging Guard. The name applied in the eighteenth and early nineteenth centuries to those sabre guards in which the point was directed downwards, with the blade almost vertical, or hanging and roughly approximating to the modern *prime* or *seconde*.

Hanisch, Cornelia of West Germany was the most recent of the great trio of lady foilists who all won the World Championships three times. She was victorious in 1979, 1981 and 1985.

Harmer-Brown, Professor W. Sometime British Epée Team Coach, he was a master at Thames F.C. and London F.C. For many years, he taught at Cambridge University with marked success.

Harper, P. is presently one of our

leading foilists. Starting in 1976 as Junior Champion (the Doyne Cup), he then became the National Champion (1978) and winner of both Coronation and Emrys Lloyd Cups, besides being placed second in these competitions on a number of occasions.

Hedgehog Point or Mushroom Head was an early form of point, or head, for the electric épée. A rounded, flattish surface, in shape resembling a very small mushroom, its fix was facilitated by scores of tiny indentations which presumably gave rise to the alternative title.

Heidelberg. Two of the most famous lecturers at this famous University were Reuchlin, the sixteenth-century classical scholar and theologian and Pufendorf, the great historian and jurisprudent, who flourished a century later. It was also the setting for Sigmund Romburg's well-known operetta, *The Student Prince*. (See German Universities.)

Helmet. A solecism for the mask.

Henry III, King of France, 1575-89. The third son of the famous, or infamous, Catherine de Medici, he had, like his immediate predecessor Charles IX, the misfortune to rule over a nation torn by the civil wars between Catholics and Huguenots. At first, one of the Catholic leaders, the contemptuous indifference to monarchical power exhibited by the (Catholic) League and the ever-increasing pretensions of the Guises, induced him to make common cause with the Protestant champion, Henry of Navarre. This provoked his assassination by the Catholic fanatic, Jacques Clément. Henry III has re-ceived scant sympathy from most historians, though it is arguable that his abandonment of the League and liquidation of the third Duke of Guise, 'Le Balafré', were due as much to a statesmanlike desire for balance and moderation as to purely personal reasons. Much given to effeminate habits, such as the habitual use of make-up and other unnatural practices, he was by no means universally unpopular but seems to have attracted a degree of admiration outside the ranks of his *mignons*, for he was a devoted student and practitioner of all forms of swordsmanship and a generous patron of those professing the art, especially the *Compagnie des Maîtres en fait d'Armes*, the famous academy of the Paris masters.

Henry IV, King of France, 1589-1610. Henry *'le Grand'* the best loved and

Military guards, outside and inside (left) and the Hanging Guard, outside and inside (right).

most revered of all France's kings; Henry of Navarre, so-called from the little kingdom in the Pyrenees where he was born and to the crown of which he succeeded in 1562. On his becoming King of France, the sovereign independence of Navarre was neither officially nor in theory extinguished and until the Revolution all French monarchs continued to style themselves 'Kings of France and Navarre'. Historically, Henry's claim to fame rests on his inspired leadership in the long religious wars; his victory at Ivry (1590) forms the subject of one of Macaulay's most spirited ballads. He was not himself a particularly strong religious enthusiast and his statesman-like determination to heal the nation's deep divisions by accepting the crown on the Catholics' condition, namely, that he should embrace their religion, was the occasion of

his most famous epigram – the drily cynical 'Paris is worth a Mass'. It was much that he did not then suffer, at the hands of some Huguenot fanatic, the fate he was ultimately to meet from an obsessed Catholic.

Legends abound; all that he said and did was marked by an incisive vigour. He had about fifty known mistresses and an untraceable number of descendants. He was invariably at his most irrepressively buoyant when his person was in desperate peril and political circumstances at their most forlorn. His many preserved sayings have a terse gusto to them 'like the swish of a sword-blade in the air'. Himself born and bred in the south-west, he had all the characteristic qualities for which the Gascons were famous; a swagger, a gallantry, that quixotic devotion to honour and glory that raised men above all petty mean-

ness, rendering them oblivious of danger and merely contemptuous of treachery.

'Let our enemies fight like jackals; we will fight like lions.'

'What do gentlemen like you and me care about money?'

'You will ever find the white plume of Navarre upon the road to victory and honour.'

And above all, his parting words to the Spanish Catholic troops, the auxiliaries of the Holy League, on their departure from Paris to Spain on the conclusion of the religious wars:

'Good-bye! A safe journey! And – by the way – don't come back again!'

It was during his reign that duelling overstepped all bounds of reason, and degenerated into a fetish. Probably the character of d'Artagnan and the other heroes of Dumas owes something to him; it

Half-Circle Guard and St George's guard (left), and Spanish and Italian guards, (right).

goes without saying that Henry of Navarre was a dashing rider and a spectacular swordsman and he would have personally seconded Duplessis-Mornay, a political theorist of some repute, in a duel, had his position allowed of it. The Duc de Sully, the King's chief minister, was strongly opposed to duelling and prevailed upon the King to issue a whole series of edicts condemning the practice and threatening offenders with the death penalty; but, of course, Henry's sympathies lay in a very different direction and he nullified the whole system by granting no less than 7000 pardons, an average of one a day.

Henry VIII, King of England, 1509-47. That gigantic figure still looms through history to maintain a dominating position in the popular consciousness. The schoolboy is impressed by the number of his executed victims and the frequency of his marriages. For the historian, the Reformation and his leading part in England's breakaway from Rome are Henry's chief titles to fame.

Perhaps it will seem a paradox to most, but it was under Henry VIII that Parliament first played a leading part in affairs of state. The Reformation Parliament (1529-36), co-operating with Henry in every stage of every statute marking the severance

with Rome, established itself once and for all in the forefront of the nation's life; its successors would never again resume the deferential and subordinate place assigned to it by Henry's father, the first Tudor monarch.

Less well known is Henry's great love of sword-play, though the massive suit of tilting armour in the Tower bears sufficient witness to his enthusiasm for jousting. About 1540, Henry granted Letters Patent to the Corporation of Masters of Defence, which conferred on them the lucrative monopoly of teaching fencing throughout the kingdom and the right to bear and display a coat of

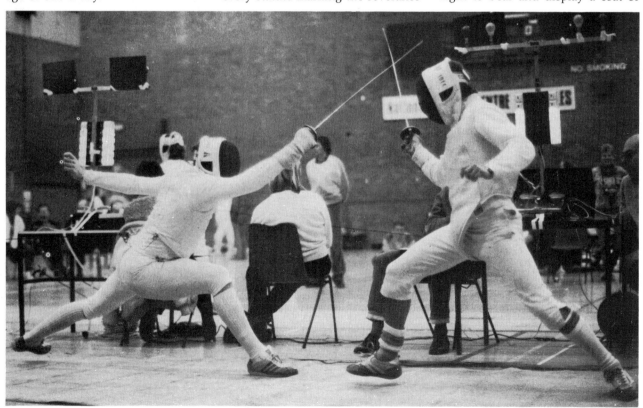

Harper attacks McKenzie in the Welsh Open of 1985.

arms: *gules* a sword *pendant argent*. The British Academy of Fencing, the present association of professional fencing masters, uses a similar heraldic device.

Henry Frederick, Prince of Wales. The eldest son of James I had ample opportunity to perfect himself in swordsmanship and the use of arms in general. The King himself ensured that the boy received instruction in the rapier and dagger, and the Duc de Sully, chief minister of Henry IV, presented the Prince with a gift of weapons and a real live French fencing master, St Anthime, to go along with them.

Prince Henry was good-looking, strongly-built and skilled in horsemanship and all forms of athletics. Not, as his father was, of scholarly tastes, he had a keen brain and the ability to concentrate and make decisions. When in 1612 he was carried off by typhoid fever at the age of eighteen, the whole nation mourned. Much has been made of his undeniable promise ('He was likely, had he been put on, to have proved most royally'), but with his strong military and naval tastes he might have embroiled England in the Thirty Years War which the more pacific James I and Charles I managed to avoid. It is fascinating to speculate on the consequences if Henry had in fact reigned in place of his younger brother Charles. With his personal popularity and an aggressive Protestant foreign policy sure to have appealed to Parliament, the Civil War might well have been averted. That, and the circumstance that presumably neither Charles II nor James II would have ascended the throne would quite possibly have resulted in a left-wing revolution in the nineteenth or twentieth centuries instead of a right-wing revolution in the seventeenth. In any

Henry VIII.

event, it is hardly going too far to assert that the reign of Henry IX would have profoundly altered the constitutional history of England.

Herries, Charles. A city merchant who was instrumental in raising the City of London Light Horse Volunteers in 1794. A pupil of Harry Angelo, Herries earned high praise from his master who described him as 'the finest amateur of his day'. So seriously did Herries take his fencing that he always refused to wear either mask or jacket, believing that such safeguards rendered a man unwary and pre-disposed to accept unnecessary hits. As a consequence, he was once hit in the eye when practising in the Angelo salle, but buttons were much bigger in those days, so fortunately he suffered no serious harm.

Hett, G. V. was a prominent foilist in the last decade before the Second World War. Captain of Cambridge University in 1930, he generally reached the finals of the national Foil Championship and was runner-up in 1934. He figured in the British international team on four occasions, in addition to the Berlin Olympics of 1936. He was the author of a textbook entitled *Fencing*, containing, in addition to the usual sound advice, not a few observations rather more witty and amusing than those generally to be found in coaching manuals.

Hiebcoment. A form of sword-play much favoured by German students in the late eighteenth century and markedly similar to the English 'backswording' of about the same period.

High Lines. The lines protecting the upper part of the fencer's target, *quarte* (on his left-hand side) and *sixte*, or *tierce* (on his right).

Hilt. Strictly, a collective term for all parts of the sword above the *ricasso*, including guard, *quillons*, grip and pommel. The term, however, is often loosely applied to the guard itself, as in cup-hilt, cross-hilt, and the like.

Hit. The A.F.A. rules declare that a hit, whether on or off the target area, must be 'clear, distinct and with an element of penetration', i.e., if sharps were being used, blood would have been drawn; hence, mere contact, without any pressure whatsoever, like the *plaqué* and *passé* hits, is of no avail. Similarly, a cut with the sabre must have some element of springiness or rebound to fulfil the conditions and cannot just be laid on. With this weapon, it must be remembered that hits can be made with any part of the fore-edge and the top third of the back-edge nearest the point, as well as by thrusts with the point itself; the other two weapons have no cutting edges and it is with the point alone that a hit can be made.

At foil and sabre, an off-target hit does not count, but the bout is halted and the fencers are replaced on guard where they were and start afresh. In the case of simultaneous, or nearly simultaneous hits, the president must decide which of the contestants enjoyed priority (q.v.). With the épée there are no conventions or priorities and as the electric apparatus automatically decides whether the two hits arrived within one twenty-fifth of a second of each other, in which case a hit is scored against both fencers – if not, only the first one counts – the president's task is rendered a good deal less onerous.

Until 1986, hits were recorded against, not for, fencers. Hence, at important competitions, where moving scoreboards were in use, the fencer with the higher number of hits against his name was losing, a circumstance which often confused non-fencers in the audience. Since the above-mentioned year, the opposite and perhaps simpler principle, has prevailed.

Most fencing masters allow their pupils to terminate every phrase, however short and simple, with a hit. Could it be a psychological mistake invariably to permit this? It may very well provide a sense of achievement for the beginner, as well as engendering confidence, and instilling accurate point control, but it seems likely to foster in intermediate fencers an impatience which will too easily turn to frustration and recklessness when, in the course of a bout, similar success is not immediately attained.

Hit, Acknowledgement of. It is still the custom honourably to acknowledge all hits received in practice, or informal assaults held without a jury, although there have been cases

86

Alfred Hutton, 'Cold Steel', a cartoon by Jest in Vanity Fair.

in the past when trouble arose through failure to do so. In the late eighteenth century, one Chevalier accused his opponent, McDermott, of his lack of courtesy and the two, who were both pupils of Harry Angelo, repaired to Chelsea to settle the matter in earnest. Their ardour had cooled to such an extent, however, that they were still watching each other hesitantly, sword in hand, without a single thrust having been delivered, when their fencing master arrived and put a summary stop to the proceedings.

It may not be entirely out of place to remind the reader, in passing, that at the 1920 Olympics Captain Dalglish, R.N., who came sixth in the final of the individual sabre, was awarded a special prize for good sportsmanship; indeed, acknowledgement

of hits received was at one time the statutory requirement. The instructions to competitors in the Foil and Sabre Championships of 1898, requested all concerned to comply with the usual custom in this respect. In the 1899 edition of the rules, combatants were categorically instructed that on receiving a hit, they must immediately cease fencing and audibly acknowledge it, at the same time indicating the place; although appeal to the jury was allowed if, for some reason, it was thought that the hit was invalid. New ground was only broken in 1912, when, in the Epée Championship of that year, competitors were not obliged to acknowledge hits; it was not until 1932 that the rule requiring acknowledgement was abolished by a narrow majority, after a card vote by the entire membership of the A.F.A. Perhaps rather surprisingly, the change seems to have been instigated originally by one or two leading members of the Ladies' Amateur Fencing Union.

Hit, Off-Target. A hit which arrives off the restricted target area at foil and sabre. The bout is halted and the fencers replaced on guard where they were, without any alteration to the score. An off-target hit results in the annullment of any subsequent hit in the same phrase, made by either fencer, which would otherwise have been valid.

Hits, Number of. The standard number of hits required to win a bout at all weapons is five. Certain alternatives are, however, permissible. Sometimes in junior competitions the number is reduced to four. In direct elimination at foil, two bouts of four hits each may likewise be arranged. In direct elimination at épée and sabre, one bout of an agreed number of hits may be sub-

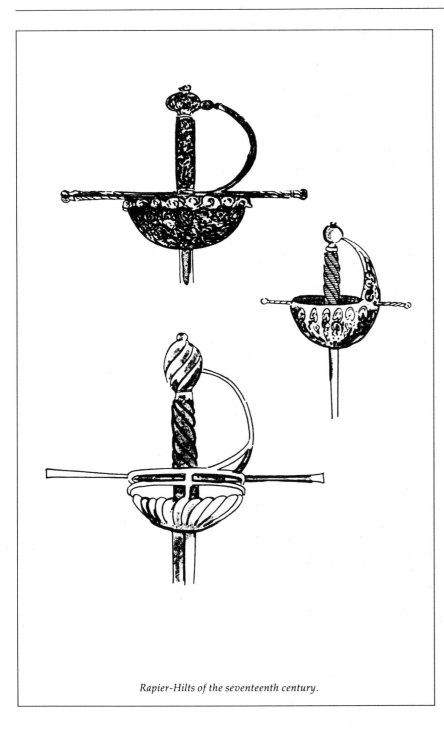

Rapier-Hilts of the seventeenth century.

stituted for two of five hits each. When there is a final of eight competitors to be decided by direct elimination, the winning figure is ten for men and eight for ladies, increasing to twelve and ten respectively when the fencer first reaching the maximum fails to lead by two hits. Similar conditions to this last example apply to bouts by direct elimination in World Championships and Olympics.

These regulations have not always held good; the number of hits has varied widely at different times and for the different weapons. In the late seventeenth century, Hope's regulations allow for the best of five or six hits; in the early nineteenth, Bathurst suggests that the winning number should be as high as twelve. In 1901 and 1902 the number of hits required to win the preliminary rounds of the Foil and Sabre Championships was less than in the final (three and five respectively). Five was the winning number of hits in the National Foil Championship of 1920, but it was not until ten years later that sabre was placed on a similar footing and this arrangement has held good in general ever since.

For a long time, different arrangements prevailed at épée. Supposed to reproduce as closely as possible the conditions of an actual duel, bouts were very logically for one hit only and even today the rules specifically allow a one-hit bout of five minutes. At the international tournament at Ostend in 1904, each bout was for two hits. Bouts for the best of three hits were regularised in the A.F.A. rules of 1932. Finally, in 1956, épée fencing was brought into line with the other two weapons and the winner was the first to reach five, or the best of nine hits.

This standardisation has not met with the unanimous approval of older épée fencers of the classical school. The fact that the swordsman can, in theory, be killed four times over and still win, has, in their view, done much to rob play with this weapon of much of its traditional craft, patience and vigilance.

Ladies' fencing has likewise been assimilated to men's in regard to the number of hits. For years, their winning figure was four; it was increased to five only recently.

Hole in the Parry or Hole in the Hand. A slang phrase denoting an insufficiently formed parry or incorrect position, either because the point has failed to follow the hand in fully closing the line, or because of a hand position faulty in itself. In either case a straight-thrust along the defending blade will not be deflected. The phrase is particularly apposite when a position or parry in *sixte* proves to be unsuccessful, owing to failure to bring the pommel into the inside of the wrist. An angle or hole is then left between hand and shoulder, positively inviting a straight-thrust.

Hope, Sir William. A renowned Scottish fencing master of the late seventeenth century. Although his theory was based largely on the contemporary French school, his system and still more his terminology, were largely individual. His leading particularities may be summarised as follows:

1) *Tierce* and *quarte* were the only guards he taught, referring respectively to the pronation and supination of the hand, but each was also sub-divided into blade positions in which the point was either higher or lower than the hilt. There was obviously a connection there with the *tierce pour le dessus* and *tierce pour le dessous* of the French.

2) Battery was distinguished from a beat by the fact that it was executed with the *foible*, not the *forte*, of the weapon. Beating was to be executed on an attack or beat by the adversary, rather in the fashion recommended by Lukovitch and other modern electric foil masters.

3) 'Caveating', 'falsifying' and 'slipping' were used respectively for disengaging, feinting, and deceiving an opponent's parry.

4) *Contretemps* had nothing to do with counter-time in our technical interpretation of the word, but was the double hit, or *coup fourré* of the French, really used in the familiar non-technical sense, i.e., a disastrous blunder.

5) The 'under-counter' seems to have been a combination of the *flanconnade* (q.v.) plus a species of bind into *tierce*, the blade somehow being slipped under the adversary's in the process.

Hope advocated that the left hand should be kept in readiness to ward off the *contretemps* and was a strong critic of the compound attacks of the French school, because of the ever-present danger of a stop-hit, though, somewhat inconsistently, he gives several examples of such attacks in his *Scots Fencing Master*. He published several books on fencing, his *magnum opus* being *The New Short and Easy Method of Fencing or the Art of the Broad and Small-Sword*.

Horatii and Curatii Cup. This trophy was named after the celebrated Roman legend of the three brothers of the Horatia Gens who encountered the three Curatii brothers of Alba. Two of the Horatii were soon despatched, but all three Curatii were severely wounded. Realising this, the surviving Roman affected to fly, and his three enemies being disabled and incapable of maintaining a united pursuit, he was able to encounter and kill them separately. The bloodshed, however, did not end there. Returning with the spoils, he was met by his sister who recognised a mantle as belonging to one of the victims to whom she had been affianced. Infuriated by her tears, the implacable champion ran her through, deeming this no more than the just punishment for any Roman so weak as to bewail the death of a foe. He just escaped the death penalty himself, but only at the price of undergoing a humiliating penance.

The cup itself was presented by the A.F.A. in 1905 for competition at the Olympics between teams of three épéeists from all countries. It was won by France at the London Olympics of 1908 and by Belgium at Stockholm in 1912. It disappeared during the First World War, but in 1928 was discovered by Sir Theodore Cook in a museum at Lausanne. Re-named the King Edward VII Cup it became the challenge trophy for the annual England-Scotland match.

Hoskyns, H.W.F. One of the really big names of post-war British fencing and one of the élite few who could meet the best foreigners on level terms. This was the more remarkable when it is realised that for the greater part of his career he resided in Somerset, the better to see to his agricultural interests, thus being deprived of the stimulus of top-class opposition in the best London clubs. This disadvantage speaks volumes for his coach during this period, Professor J. Sanders of Yeovil – F.C. Hoskyns's achievements seem endless and speak for themselves. His outstanding triumphs came with the épée: he is the only Englishman ever to have won the World Championship (1958), while in 1962 he won the Challenge Martini, one of only two Englishmen ever to do so. He won two silver medals at the Tokyo Olympics of 1964 and the World Championship of 1965. In the

Commonwealth Games, his record was prodigious. He took the titles at épée and sabre in 1958, in épée again in 1966 and 1970 and came second in the Foil Competition of 1966.

In domestic competition, he was even more of an all-rounder. He was still up at Oxford when in 1952 he won the Junior Championships at foil and épée and came third in the sabre, the nearest anyone has come to 'scooping the pool'. Subsequently, he tended to neglect the sabre, though nevertheless winning the championship in 1966 and the Cole Cup in 1965 and 1967. In épée he naturally, for a time, reigned supreme, registering a hat-trick of championship wins in 1956-7-8, again coming first in 1967 and taking the second place on three occasions (1964, 1968, 1972). He won the Miller-Hallett Competition in 1954 and 1969 and was second in 1966 and 1968. Three times he won the Epée Club Cup (1958, 1964, 1967) and three times he was second (1956, 1957, 1976).

He was hardly less dominating with the foil. He was three times the winner of the British Men's Championship (1959, 1964, 1970) and twice the runner-up (1959, 1963). He won the Coronation Cup in 1959 (he was second in 1960 and 1964) and the Emrys Lloyd Cup no fewer than four times (1961, 1964, 1967, 1968), securing second place in 1959 and 1963. As a major in the North Somerset Yeomanry, he found time to make a clean sweep of the Services Championships, winning at all three weapons in 1964.

At his peak, Hoskyns was almost certainly the finest swordsman in the world. A left-hander, noted for his very late parry and clever variations of speed and distance, his brilliant successes were to be attributed as much to his courage as his skill. At the World Championships in

H.W.F. Hoskyns.

Paris (1965), he turned out in the quarter-finals of the épée team event with a broken rib sustained in a fiery encounter with Kostava of Hungary in the individual championship. Finding it difficult to parry without extreme discomfort, he was constrained to rely solely on attack, producing five lightning *flèches* to win his bout and the match against Hungary and ultimately to gain a silver medal for the team as losing finalists to France. He holds the record for the number of Olympic appearances for great Britain – six, between 1956 and 1976.

Hungarian Principle. In sabre, the now traditional wrist-and-finger technique in the delivery of a cut, which was for long peculiar to the fencers of that country. Highly conducive to fast, light, accurate cuts, especially stop-cuts to the arm, it was infinitely superior to the older method of bending the sword-arm at the elbow, which, up to the last war, was the classical Italian method still in favour in most western European countries. The object in those days was apparently to build up impressively complex and flamboyant cuts, parries and ripostes, rather after the fashion of a stage or screen duel. It is even said that attacks at the

arm were considered to be rather poor form.

Hutton, Captain Alfred, F.S.A. He it was who, at the turn of the century, was largely instrumental in reviving interest in fencing, which had drastically declined since the virtual disappearance of duelling in the early nineteenth century. To this end, Captain Hutton organised displays and lectures all over England and formed a school of arms among the officers and cadets of the London Rifle Brigade. He played a leading part in establishing both the Fencing Branch of the Amateur Gymnastic Association (1895) and after the schism of 1902, the Amateur Fencing Association of which he became the first president. He was a great exponent of the French, as opposed to the Italian school, and therefore a stern critic of Army fencing, then based on the latter system. This controversy generated no little warmth on both sides, and two eminent contemporary medical men actually condemned the Italian methods as being dangerous and exposing their practitioners to great risk; though, somewhat disappointingly, we are not informed of the precise nature of the risk.

I.F.A. and I.W.F.A. The Intercollegiate Fencing Association and the Intercollegiate Women's Fencing Association in the U.S.

Imbracciatura, (It.). A long shield. Shields were still used in combats and duels by the Italian school of the early sixteenth century, but were superseded by the *main-gauche* or dagger when the long Italian rapier came into use.

Imbroccata, (It.). 1) A thrust over the adversary's sword-arm, travelling

downwards; generally executed with a pronated hand and from the right.
2) The *Sports Dictionary in Seven Languages* says: 'A stop-thrust with *croisé.*'
3) One of Barbasetti's 'passive *tempo*' attacks (q.v.). The point is to be directed low, while the executant bends forward sharply.

The one common feature in all the above and the one generally accepted, is that the stroke is delivered downwards in the low line.

Imitational Practice. Szabo's name for the practice, generally for a group, where the pupils work in pairs, one imitating the master's movements and the other making the appropriate response. Sometimes the opposite action must be taken, e.g., when the fencer taking the part of the master steps back, the other must step forward in order to maintain the same relative distance.

Immediate Riposte. A riposte which instantly follows the parry, with no loss of fencing time.

Impetinata, (It.). To strike the ground lightly with the leading foot immediately before the execution of an attack; the same as the *appel.*

Impugnattura, (It.). The guard, handle and pommel.

Imregi, Professor B. A Hungarian who taught before the war at the Military Grammar School; during the conflict, he taught at the Ludovic Academy (the equivalent of Sandhurst). After the war, he became the master at many of the leading clubs, but after the 1956 revolution, political considerations rendered desirable his settlement in this country, where he soon established his reputation at schools and clubs in the capital and elsewhere. He was especially prom-

inent in the training of numerous épéeists and sabreurs at the London Fencing Club. Many leading exponents of these two weapons followed him when he moved to the Polytechnic F.C. in 1967. For some years he coached the British Sabre Team.

Incartata, (It.). (See Inquartata.)

Incontro, (It.). The double hit.

Indicators are mathematical formulae (the ratio between victories and bouts fought) used in major and international competitions where the number of fencers is considerable and a quick decision is needed to decide on the promotion of equally placed teams or individuals to the next round.

Indices. When it is necessary to distinguish between equally placed fencers for the purpose of deciding promotion to the next pool, recourse

is first had to the indices – that is, the difference between the hits scored and received by each of the fencers concerned. Should this be inconclusive, the matter is decided by a barrage, that is to say, a further bout or bouts.

Indirect Attacks. The attacks by disengagement, cut-over, and counter-disengagement. (See Simple Attacks.)

Indirect Initiative. Allowing the opponent to suppose he has seized the initiative and is controlling the phrase, while in reality luring him into a trap, more especially by an adroit use of distance.

Indirect Ripostes. Similarly to the indirect attacks, these are the ripostes by disengagement, cut-over, and counter-disengagement.

Inquarta, Inquartata, Inquarto, (It.). A displacement of the body from the

Sword and Buckler — still in favour with the early Italian School (from Agrippa).

line of attack. The movement is initiated by a pivoting action on the leading heel, while simultaneously the rear leg is thrown backwards and sideways to the fencer's right. Thus he finishes in a position facing directly to the left of the position he originally occupied. Crosnier greatly favours this action combined with a *quarte croisé* against the left-handed *flècheur*. Barbasetti lends support to this recommendation by advising that the *inquartata* should be accompanied with opposition of blade.

Inside Lines. The lines, or blade positions, protecting the fencer's left-hand side, *quarte* (high) and *septime* (low).

Insistence is when the attack is continued in the same line after being parried, or perhaps not quite fully parried. The insistence is frequently either instinctive or accidental; when more or less deliberate, it is often executed with increased opposition, in which case, in a bout, it would almost certainly be phrased as a *remise*.

Insistencia de Corte, (Sp.). The *remise* with a cut.

Insistencia de Punta, (Sp.). The *remise* with the point.

Instance. The term used by Narvaez to describe a step designed to prepare an attack; these instances were based on the most elaborate geometrical system which was very largely irrelevant. Basically, Narvaez regarded it as safer to sidle round the circumference of an imaginary circle than to step along its diameter and so incur the danger of a time attack. The 'first instance' was the initial position taken up at the extremity of the diameter; the 'second instance', the position when one fencer moved

The Inquartata (from de Liancour).

round the circumference, on which his opponent was supposed to take the corresponding step to maintain their relative placings, that is, on the opposite ends of another diameter.

Instinctive Parry. The simple parry.

Insufficient Parry. When contact has been made with the opponent's attacking blade, but, nevertheless the latter is not deflected, but continues straight on its course to reach the target, the parry is said to be insufficient and nowadays is invalid. Until 1951, the rules affirmed that any contact, however light, was deemed to constitute a parry in the conventional sense and conferred on the defender the right to riposte; if he did so successfully, it was his hit which stood, even if he himself received a hit from the original attack. Admittedly, this detracted a good deal from the realism of the encounter; but on the other hand it promoted much skilful bladework and long phrases containing a number of light, rapid, counter-ripostes.

In view of all this, today's president is often faced with the unenviable task of deciding whether the attacker's blade was, or was not, deflected; in the former case, the continuation of the attack resulting in a hit must of course be classed as a *remise*, in which event priority has to be given to the defender's riposte, always assuming that it was immediate.

Intagliata, (It.). A side step to the defender's left, enabling him to

The distinctive guard of the Italian School, right (from Danet).

avoid a thrust into his outside or *tierce* line.

International Federation Guard. A sabre guard with a perfectly smooth surface. Years ago sabre guards were often slightly ornamented, embossed, or patterned with perforations, and this was forbidden because of the risk of catching the point of the opponent's blade and breaking it.

International Fencing Committee. The precursor of the F.I.E., formed in 1905.

Intrecciata, (It.). A favourite action of the old Italian school, facilitated by the somewhat horizontal angle of the blade when on guard. It consisted of the *striccio* (the *froissement*) followed by a disengagement or bind as in the *fianconata*.

Invalid. A hit which arrives on an off-target area; or an on-target hit arriving before the president has ordered the fencers to play, or after he has commanded them to halt.

Invitation. The invitation is a deliberate blade movement which, by exposing some part of the target, encourages the opponent to launch an attack, which can be met either by a counter-attack or a riposte following a parry.

Invito. Although Vass in *Epée Fencing* identifies the *invito* with the invitation, other Hungarian masters define it as the blade position when not in line, i.e., point not threatening target with extended arm. It is virtually synonomous with our on guard. The term arises from the fact that however correct the placing of sword, hand and arm, the major part of the target area must still inevitably remain exposed; hence the

The Italian Foil.

opponent is encouraged or 'invited' to attack or feint towards that area.

Invito Aperto, (It.). Absence of blade.

Irish Amateur Fencing Federation is the body administering and controlling fencing in Eire only; by an F.I.E. ruling of 1950, its jurisdiction does not extend to Northern Ireland.

Irving, Sir Henry was the great Victorian actor-manager who delighted in the most elaborate stage settings, no trouble or expense being spared in producing the most spectacular effects; a long way from today's all-purpose scenery which does duty in all three acts, or the mysterious iron girders so beloved by the conscientiously intellectual playwright. In *Faust*, the intervention of Mephistopheles in the duel between Faust and Valentine was indicated by means of electrified plates on the stage on which the swordsmen stood, a brilliant flash dazzling the audience whenever the swords crossed. Few spectacles delighted the Victorian audience more than the duel between Fabian and de Château-Renaud in *The Corsican Brothers*. The entire stage was used, from the back wall to the footlights and the actors were able to thread their way among separate forest trees. What delighted and baffled the onlooker night after night, was the unbroken expanse of apparent snow, sufficiently thick to be sprayed and scattered by the duellists' feet. The illusion was created by tons of salt, spread and flattened in less than a minute by a horde of stage-hands waiting in the wings until the curtain descended. As for the duel scene between Irving and Bancroft in *The Dead Hand*, that has passed into stage and fencing history.

Realism was the keynote of Irving's productions. In *Romeo and Juliet* the initial affray with swords and cudgels between the adherents of Montague and Capulet was performed with such extraordinary zeal that, as Bram Stoker relates, not a night passed in the entire run without at least one member of the cast receiving hospital treatment.

Italian Foil. The chief difference between the Italian and French weapons lies in the construction of the hilt. The former has a cross-bar, or transverse bar, at right angles to the handle, the vestigial remains of the ancient cross-hilt, a short distance from and just above the cup-hilt. It is known as the *gavigliano* and is joined to the edges of the cup-hilt by two thin curved bars (arches or *archetti*). The thumb and first two fingers are placed on the *ricasso* or flattened section of the blade between the *gavigliano* and the cup-hilt. The last two fingers, on the handle, are separated from the others by the *gavigliano*. The handle itself is shorter than its French counterpart and is strapped to the wrist, which militates against anything much in the way of finger-play, all circular or semi-circular blade actions being controlled by the wrist.

Italian School. The characteristic swordsmanship of Italy developed during the sixteenth and seventeenth centuries under such famous names as Capo Ferro, Senese, Giganti and others. Though never beginning to rival the logical and scientific analysis of the classical French school – most Italian masters of that era professed to know some secret *botta* or infallible parry, the details of which they were prepared to disclose at a price – it far surpassed in practical utility the absurd and complex fantasies of the contemporary Spanish masters. The Italian system was characterised by vigorous and flamboyant footwork which remained a national tradition even when, during the nineteenth century the French methodology was adopted almost in its entirety, Marchionni in 1847 being the first to attempt to reconcile it with the Italian genius. From then on, apart from the retention of a good deal of their own terminology, and certain relatively unimportant variations in the guard position, the only difference of real note was the grip, a singularity still to be encountered even after the Second World War. The fingers were passed through the *pas d'âne* rings and the handle was strapped to the inside of the wrist. Hence those employing this technique were obliged to rely less on the classic French finger-play and far more on preparations, surprise attacks, rapid footwork and renewals of attack executed at great speed.

The spectacular nature of Italian fencing became legendary. John Dickson Carr, in *It Walks by Night*, set in the year 1927, describes the Duc de Savigny as 'possessing a number of startling tricks out of the Italian school'.

Jacob, Jules. A master of the late nineteenth century. At a time when foil play had reached its ultimate stage of elaboration and was, quite rightly, regarded as an art form, his statement that the refined exchanges of the schools bore no relation to reality and stood in need of radical amendment, predictably caused the outrage and stupefied indignation of his more conservative colleagues.

Jacobs, P. An international and sometime Weapon Captain, he won the British Epée Championship in 1962, 1964 and 1970, coming second in 1963. He won the Miller-Hallett competition in 1960 and 1961, taking second place in 1963 and 1967. Twice he came second in the Epée Club Cup (1964, 1967). He was remarkable for a style of fencing which can only be described as arresting – he bounded up and down on both feet from start to finish of a bout, attacking almost solely by means of the *flèche*. This ceaseless activity was justified on the grounds that it masked the start of his attacks, but must have necessitated extreme fitness and in the course of a long competition have imposed a severe physical strain. It is not altogether surprising, therefore, that his career at the top was of shorter duration than that of some others.

James I, King of England, 1603-25. The first of his name to rule England, he was the sixth James of the House of Stuart to succeed to the throne of Scotland which he did in 1567 at the age of twelve months, when his mother, Mary, Queen of Scots, was imprisoned, strongly suspected of complicity in the murder of Henry, Lord Darnley, her second husband and James I's father. James has not found much favour with the majority of historians, and in popular opinion he remains forever the

A.L.N.Jay

goggle-eyed, slobbering, shambling pedant who quarrelled with his Parliaments, persecuted the puritans and prepared the way for the Civil War and the downfall of his son, Charles I. In fact, although tactless in his dealings and unwise in his choice of advisers, he often revealed breadth of view, was a scholar in his own right and, in his earlier days at any rate, one of Scotland's most able rulers, successfully reducing the power of the most turbulent and unprincipled nobility in Europe. In the course of the latter achievement, he became the central figure in the sinister Gowrie conspiracy, a tangled affair of buried treasure, kidnapping, disappearance and assassination, with a nicely flavoured hint of the supernatural. James was seldom for long able to avoid involvement with plots and conspiracies, and quite apart from Guy Fawkes and the Gunpowder Plot – asserted by some authorities to have been a de-

liberate government frame-up – in 1615 the notorious Overbury poisoning scandal came to a head, another highly-spiced mixture of witchcraft and murder, implicating not only the King's favourite, Robert Carr, Earl of Somerset and his Countess, but according to hints dropped in certain quarters, the King himself. Certain it is, that the Earl and Countess, though receiving a free pardon, were permanently banished from Court.

Aside from his well-advertised detestation of tobacco-smoking and compulsive interest in demonology, on which he wrote with considerable learning, James I is of interest to fencers for having in 1605 granted the masters of that day a warrant restoring the privileges originally established under Henry VIII. This is the more remarkable, as he is reputed to have been so cowardly as to be unable to look on a naked sword without flinching. However, as he not only defined the weapons in which his son, Henry, Prince of Wales should be instructed (the 'knightly and honourable rapier-swords and daggers'), but is known to have been present at several exhibition bouts, little credit need be extended to this popular tradition.

James I issued a Proclamation against Private Challenges and Combats in 1613; as usual, it was but half-heartedly enforced and proved ineffectual.

Jarnac, Guy Chabot, Comte de was the victor in the famous duel in 1547 with La Chastaignerai, the finest swordsman and wrestler in France, who had foully slandered the former's mother-in-law. It possessed a number of remarkable features and in many respects, with its trumpets, elaborate ceremonial and pavilions for the principals, resembled rather a medieval trial by combat than a modern affair of honour. De Jarnac,

Jarnac and la Chastaignerai — the famous cut about to come (eighteenth-century engraving).

who, by continental custom, had the choice of weapons, made a long succession of bizarre or frivolous suggestions before finally settling for swords and bucklers, knowing full well that his adversary had recently been wounded in the shield arm. Notions of chivalrous and gentlemanly feeling had not then become quite so finely developed as was the case in later days although, once having overthrown his enemy, de Jarnac exhibited the utmost generosity and forbearance. According to Brantôme, the critical moment came when, after several attacks and trifling wounds on both sides, de Jarnac cut the ham of each of La Chastaignerai's legs, as the latter was making a pass, with that stroke now immortalised as the *coup de Jarnac*. The descriptions of this are never too precise, but it was apparently a stopcut which may have been followed by an immediate *redoublement*. Great speed, accuracy and a perfect sense

of timing were essential, since the swordsman had to approach his enemy very closely and must inevitably have exposed the whole upper part of his body; the slightest error, or less than dexterous use of the buckler and his head must infallibly have been split in two. De Jarnac insisted on sparing La Chastaignerai's life, although the latter obstinately refused to crave mercy as he lay stretched on the ground. However, he had lost so much blood by his refusal to allow the surgeons to attend him, that he died shortly afterwards.

Jay, A.L.N. was the last fencer to win medals at two different weapons in the same year; at the World Championships in Budapest in 1959 he won the Men's Foil and only by a margin of one hit was he kept in second place and prevented from rivalling Gaudin by winning at épée as well. The following year he was

again runner-up at épée in the Rome Olympics. Oddly enough, 'Great Britain's supreme foilist' won the British Foil Championship on only one occasion, 1963. He came second in 1957, 1960, 1964 and 1967. It was perhaps some consolation to him to win the Coronation Cup four times (1957, 1962, 1964, 1965) with four seconds, and the Emrys Lloyd Cup in 1965 with two second placings. He was second in the foil at the Commonwealth Games in 1962 and won outright four years later.

At épée his results were equally outstanding. He won the British Championship on three occasions (1952, 1959, 1960) and was five times second. The Miller-Hallett trophy was his in 1953, then again in a run of three consecutive years (1955-6-7) with second places in 1952, 1958 and 1959. He won the Epée Club Cup in 1959 and 1960, and in the Martini International Epée competition of 1965 was second, the highest position ever reached by an Englishman with the exceptions of the two actual winners, Hoskyns and S. Paul.

In addition, Jay even won the Junior Sabre Championship in 1953, though subsequently laying this weapon aside to concentrate on the other two.

A left-hander, possessing a very fast *flèche*, released with little indication when it was coming, he could also deliver *temps perdu* ripostes with deadly effect. It is difficult to say whether he or Hoskyns was the greatest fencer of that time; certain it is that both were very great, both bridged the gap between the old fencing and the new, and both raised the standard of British fencing to a level which, for a time, earned the respect and admiration of the fencing world.

Jean-Louis, born about 1784, was a coloured swordsman of immense and possibly legendary reputation. Having been subject to repeated insults, he insisted on defending himself with a foil against his enemy's duelling sword. Captain Hutton's account of the proceedings suspiciously resembles the best and most successful duels of fiction. Jean-Louis adopted the familiar tactics of retreating until his opponent was exhausted by his own violence, whereupon he suddenly parried strongly and riposted with a wicked slash across the face. The bully collapsed howling on the ground, having been taught a lesson which of course he would never forget.

During the Napoleonic wars, Jean-Louis became the fencing master of a French regiment involved in a long-standing feud with a unit from Italy. It was agreed that the quarrel should be settled by Jean-Louis fighting it out with his opposite number, one Giacomo Ferrari. The latter having been duly killed, his place was taken by ten of his colleagues, one after the other, all of them being seriously wounded. When only two *prévots* remained, the general who had sanctioned the proceedings called a halt, declaring that honour had been satisfied on both sides.

It is tempting to suppose that, the exuberance of youth behind him, he was identical with the highly respected fencing master of the same name teaching at Montpellier about 1830. Although *sixte* was already known – the term had been established by La Boessière – most masters still taught and advocated the use of *tierce* as well. Jean-Louis wanted to eliminate it entirely.

Jena. All members of German universities, who designated themselves the 'nobility of knowledge', had, from the sixteenth century, assumed the right to wear the rapier, which had at that time superseded

the traditional cutting weapons. During the eighteenth century, however, the rapier was in turn replaced in academic circles by the spadroon, the students of Jena being almost alone in remaining faithful to the older weapon. The traditional reason was that a large proportion of them were theological students who would not have been ordained had their faces been disfigured with duelling scars.

Jena was also noted for its associations with Goethe, Schiller and Fichte, and as the scene of Napoleon Bonaparte's crushing defeat of the Prussians, (1806).

Jeronimo or Hieronimo. One of the several Italian masters who, during the sixteenth century, introduced the new school of rapier-play to this country. The controversy thus aroused, and the furious opposition provoked from the traditionalists and the indigenous masters receives frequent mention in contemporary literature. 'He (i.e. mine host) minds no moderns! Go by, Hieronimo!' (Ben Jonson, *The New Inn*, Act II, Sc. ii.) One of Jeronimo's colleagues was Vincentio. Jeronimo himself was slain by the ruffian Cheese, but no record exists as to whether any proceedings were taken against the latter.

Jeu de Fantaisie. The style, tactics, and strokes beloved of romantic and historically-minded fencers with a taste for old treatises, who delight in experimenting with archaic theories, or in the imitation of the flamboyant play of stage duels; unscientific, obsolete, over-elaborate fencing which could not be risked in a serious encounter.

Jeu de Salle. Play somewhat akin to the *jeu de fantaisie*; formal, stylised fencing lacking aggression and prac-

tical utility and perhaps involving risks acceptable in a friendly bout rather than in the tense conditions of a competition.

Jeu de Soldat. A contemptuous term for the performance of a violent, clumsy fencer. Heavy-handed play was, in the old days, particularly associated with the sabre, the military weapon.

Jeu de Terrain. The sword-play of the real duel, generally fought out-of-doors – 'under the dripping trees at dawn' as Charles de Beaumont used to say. The épée fencing of the late nineteenth century was supposed to reproduce its conditions as far as possible.

Joining. An archaic term for a disarmament.

Jonson, Ben is best known as the most distinguished poet and playwright of the contemporaries of Shakespeare. His experience of the world was possibly wider, for, on leaving Westminster, he served under Maurice of Nassau in the Low Countries before returning to London and going on the stage. In 1598, he killed Gabriel Spence, a fellow-actor, in a duel and although convicted, pleaded Benefit of Clergy and escaped with imprisonment and branding on the thumb. As befitted an old soldier, he was always prepared to introduce fencing or duelling scenes in his plays, notably in *Every Man in his Humour*, (See Bobadil, Captain). Like Shakespeare he was perfectly familiar with the theory and terminology of the rapier- and dagger-play of that era, and all the technical jargon appears again in the companion comedy, *Every Man out of his Humour*, in the scene where Fastidious Brisk describes his duel with one Signior

Luculento; his chief purpose in so doing apparently being to impress on his audience the extreme richness of his foppish and extravagant attire, most of which he reports, item by item, as having been cut to shreds in the desperate encounter. Fastidious apparently had no hesitation in exposing his limitations as a swordsman so long as the creations of his tailor and his own place in the van of fashion received their due recognition.

Incomparably inferior to Shakespeare as a tragedian, Jonson's comedies are at least equal to those of the former and, indeed, considered by not a few critics as much superior in their delineation of character and subtlety of satire. Jonson, moreover, certainly exerted more influence on 'the sons of Ben', the Caroline poets of the next generation and immeasurably surpassed his great rival in correctness of design and depth of scholarship. Yet, with all this, he remains largely unread and there is something stiff and formal in much of his work. It is Shakespeare who carries all before him with his range, his majesty, his universality, above all, his characters, vivid as in a picture-gallery, who, once encountered, never fade from the mind. We would all instantly recognise the moody young prince in black, the monstrously corpulent, purple-nosed old knight, the crazy fugitive king with his attendant jester; but few have ever heard of Volpone, and fewer still of Fallace, Sir Amorous la-Foule, or Zeal-of-the-Land Busy.

Jour. An opening for an attack.

Judges. The four members of the jury, who, in non-electric bouts, assist the president in the awarding of hits.

Junior. Junior competitions, at any rate in the more important categories, have nothing to do with the age of those participating, but are confined to fencers who have never reached the finals of certain leading competitions, been awarded international colours, or previously been a Junior Champion.

Jury. The officials who actually control a bout, composed of a president and four judges, two at either end of the *piste*. The duty of the judges is to detect and signal hits made, on or off target, by the fencer immediately in front of them upon the fencer opposite, who faces them. Only in some altogether unusual situation, as, for example, some bizarre displacement of the target, so that the proper set of judges were totally unsighted, would the other judges be required to decide the validity of hits on the fencer whose back is normally turned towards them. With electric weapons, arm ludges and ground judges may be used.

Jury d'Appel. (See Court of Appeal.)

Jury, The Revolving. When human judges are being used, they frequently move round one place in a clockwise direction for each succeeding bout. It has been found that a change of position is a real help in maintaining interest and concentration.

Kahn, Anton. An eighteenth-century German master, from whose works much can be learned of the history of fencing in the German Universities.

Karpati, I.R. A great Hungarian sabreur, twice World Champion (1954, 1959), twice an Olympic gold medallist (1956, 1960). He came second in the World Championships of 1955 and 1957. Hungary was unbeatable in these years. From 1928 to 1960 their sabre team never once failed to win at the Olympics, Karpati appearing in four winning teams in succession. They were almost equally successful in the World Championships between 1930 and 1958, being victorious on all occasions save four (1938, 1947, 1949 and 1950), when Italy won.

Kean, Edmund. The great Shakespearean actor of the nineteenth century, especially famous in the title role of *Hamlet*. He regularly attended Angelo's establishment when it was in Bond Street. He is said to have given fencing lessons himself when on the provincial stage in his earlier days. Whatever his skill, he probably had little knowledge of the history of swordsmanship, for he was apparently misguided enough to allow the match in *Hamlet* to assume the character, not of a bout with the Elizabethan rapier and dagger as it should have been, but of one with the eighteenth-century small-sword, even to the extent of introducing the proceedings with a contemporary salute.

Keeping Captive. Obliging the opponent to keep his blade in the same line of engagement; both the counter-change of engagement and the counter (circular) parry have this effect.

Kendo. A traditional and highly stylised form of Japanese sword-play, involving the use of long, slightly curved two-handed swords, which, a year or two ago, made some attempt to establish itself in England.

Keresztessy, Joseph was the master at the National Institute of Fencing founded in 1825 at Budapest. Generally regarded as the father of Hungarian sabre fencing, he favoured the use of the wrist rather than the forearm in delivering cuts.

Kershaw, Captain C.A., R.N. British Sabre Champion three times (1920, 1925, 1926), second in 1922 and 1923, he won the Services Sabre Championship four years running (1922-25). He represented his country at three Olympics (1920, 1924 and 1928). This would have been glory enough for most men, but he was the outstanding scrum-half of the period immediately following the First World War, forming a classic half-back partnership with his naval colleague, the almost equally celebrated Davies. The pair distinguished themselves in the William Webb Ellis Centenary Match at Rugby, graphically described by Michael Scott in *A Modern Tom Brown's Schooldays*. Kershaw won sixteen England caps – a great achievement at a time when markedly fewer international matches were played. Described as 'the finest athlete in the world', he excelled also in cricket, hockey and squash racquets in those halcyon days when the amateur could still compete successfully at the highest level in almost any game.

King Edward VII Cup. (See Horatii and Curatii Cup.)

Kirchhoffer. An eminent French master teaching at the Salle Jean-

Edmund Kean (1789–1833).

Louis in Paris at the turn of the century. He was perhaps most renowned for his defeat of the virtuoso Engenio Pini in a celebrated assault in the presence of King Edward VII in London in 1902. The discomfiture of Pini, who had professed to combine all that was best in the French and Italian schools, greatly heightened the reputation and prestige of the pure French method; which was still further enhanced by the subsequent encounters between Mimiague and Tagliapietra, Bergès and Colombetti, Mérignac and Galante from each of which instances the Frenchman, named first, emerged victorious.

Klopffechter. Itinerant German swordsmen who, until the seventeenth century, exhibited their skill in prize-fights at fairs, festivals, or entertainments organised by great lords. They did not, as a rule, profess to offer instruction in the art.

Knitting Needles. Expressive slang for the rapid series of clicks pro-

duced when two fencers are practising a long sequence of changes and counter-changes of engagement, the rapid movements of the points, no less than the sound, being thought to resemble the process of knitting.

Knuckle-bow. A thin curved piece of metal, extending in a bow-shape from the handle, where the latter joins the inside of the guard, to the pommel. In the absence of a basket-hilt, it offered some protection to the hand against a slash. It was frequently still found on a small-sword of the eighteenth century, when, of course, a thrust was the chief danger to be feared.

Konigsmark, Count John Charles von. A member of the celebrated Swedish family, one of whom, Aurora, became the mother of Marshal Saxe by Augustus II of Saxony. His younger brother, Philip Christopher, mysteriously disappeared in 1694 after being accused of adultery with Sophia Dorothea, the Electress of Hanover and wife of George I of Britain. John Charles took service in the French Army under Louis XIV. While visiting London in 1681, he was involved in a murder case. He fell in love with Lady Elizabeth Percy who married Mr Thomas Thynne, a wealthy gentleman, who was shortly afterwards dragged from his coach and murdered in the Haymarket. Certain suspects, when arrested, inculpated Konigsmark, who was put on trial but acquitted. He died at Argos in 1686, serving under the flag of the Venetian republic. A duellist of formidable reputation, the *Colichemarde*, a singular variety of the small-sword, was said to have been invented by him and to be a corruption of his name.

Kovacs, P. Another outstanding Hungarian sabreur, World Champion in 1937 and 1953, Olympic Champion in 1952. He won silver medals at the World Championships of 1951 and 1954.

Kreussler. A well-known dynasty of fencing masters, active for almost two hundred years in the German Universities, from the early seventeenth century onwards. The founder of this long-standing house was Wilhelm, fencing master at the University of Jena for upwards of half a century until his death in 1673. He is generally considered to have been the first to introduce to Germany the rapier-play of the contemporary Italian masters in contradistinction to the broadsword school of the Marxbruder. His eldest son, Gottfried, was almost equally distinguished, while of his grandsons, fencing masters to a man, Heinrich is said to have determined the principles of the characteristic eighteenth-century German school, then regarded as the best in Europe for cut-and-thrust play.

Kulcsar, G. A brilliant Hungarian swordsman of the period when his countrymen threatened to become as pre-eminent with the épée as they already were with the sabre. He won the Challenge Martini in 1967, exhibiting a 'perfect sense of distance and point control'. It seems probable that at his best, he had no need to fear any fencer in the world and would have outclassed most of them. He was Olympic Epée Champion in 1968.

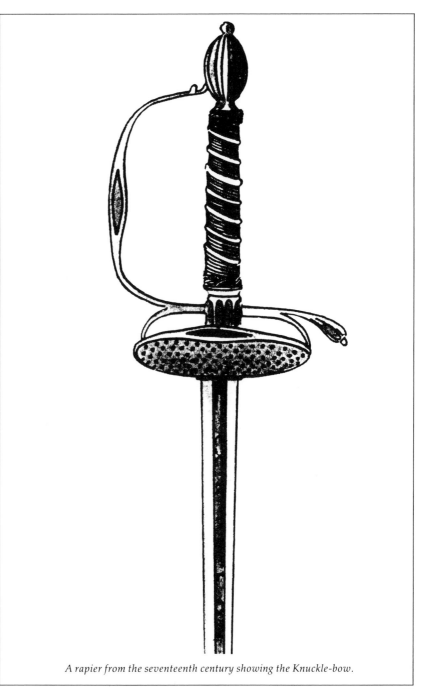

A rapier from the seventeenth century showing the Knuckle-bow.

99

La Boessière. There were two French masters of this name, *père* and *fils*. The elder, who flourished in the mid eighteenth century, is forever famous for having inaugurated the use of the wire mask, which of course permitted much faster and more complicated actions at relatively close range. Unlike his son, he left no written instructions, but La Boessière *fils* was the author of a work entitled *Traité sur l'art de faire les Armes*, addressed principally to fencing masters and even stereotyping the wording of the tuition to be given during lessons. The younger man's career lasted well into the nineteenth century, at a time when foil play ceased to have any real connection with the genuine encounter with the small-swords and could be taught and practised on a purely academic basis. It is accepted that he played a leading part in that group of masters who finally determined the position and terminology of the foil parries of *quinte*, *sixte*, *septime* and *octave*, though it is of course impossible to say how much had been transmitted by his father.

La Frette. (See Chalais.)

La Tousche, Philibert de. A seventeenth-century French master, who enjoyed the privilege of instructing the households of the Queen and 'Monsieur', the Duc d'Orleans, the King's brother, during the reign of Louis XIV. He is now chiefly memorable for his advocacy of an extraordinary exaggeration, if not perversion, of the lunge. The leading foot was placed as far ahead as was physically possible, the trunk was allowed to fall forward until it rested on the thigh, and some sort of balance was maintained by resting the unarmed hand on the ground. That, at least, was the theory, though it may be assumed that no-one but a

Disarming with a heavy parry (from Labat).

professional contortionist could really adopt such an attitude, still less simultaneously control a blade. Other points of interest in La Tousche's instructions (*Les vrayes principes de l'espée seule*, 1670), are that he seems to have been the first to apply the term *dégagement* (disengagement) to the transference of the blade beneath the adversary's weapon from one line to another; secondly, that he expressly forbids the use of circular parries, destined to become so distinctive a feature of the French school. He was also said to have devised the crude and brutal

botte du paysan, a two-handed attack which apparently found some favour in the late seventeenth century.

Labat, Le Sieur. One of a well-known family of French masters, who flourished in the seventeenth century, all connected with the Academy of Toulouse. His *L'Art en fait d'Armes* (1696) was regarded for years as more or less the definitive work on the subject.

Ladies' Amateur Fencing Union was formed in 1929 and recognised by the A.F.A. as an affiliated body hav-

La Tousche — an anatomical curiosity (from Danet).

100

Ladies v gentlemen in Oxford town hall, 1902.

ing the authority to organise competitions restricted to ladies; in 1932, it became an associated body of the A.F.A.

Ladies' Cercle d'Escrime. A well-known club which won the Martin Edmunds Cup in 1922, 1923, 1946 and 1948.

Ladies' Professional Fencing Association was founded in 1936, with Mme S. Perigal as the first president. It was this association which pre-

sented a cup for a schoolgirl's competition, in 1937. The first competition, however, was not held until ten years later.

Lady Fencers. Long before the foundation of the L.A.F.U. (see above), the more active and spirited women of their time eagerly embraced the opportunity to practise the art of the sword. The Princess of Eboli, a great and wealthy lady in sixteenth-century Spain, who was imprisoned by Philip II on

suspicion of being implicated in the notorious Escovedo murder, had lost an eye fencing with a page when she was still a girl. Two centuries later, the Duchess of Queensberry engaged in practice, with less unfortunate results, with a similar opponent, who later became an assistant to Angelo. Then there was Mme Celli, who is depicted in an engraving of Rowlandson, in action, also at Angelo's, during the Regency. Nor were women unknown on the duelling-ground; Robert Baldick in

The Duel records numerous examples of encounters between women with sword or pistol and one or two when the lady called out a faithless lover. An illustration from a painting by Emile Bayard depicts two swordswomen in the heat of combat, encumbered by flowing skirts below, but naked from the waist upwards. In more recent times, Angelo is recorded as having given lessons to actresses and Baptiste Bertrand encouraged the attendance of ladies at his salle. His niece, Hélène, was the first of a distinguished line of lady masters, unforgettable amongst whom are Mesdames Froeschlen and Perigal.

For years, ladies were restricted to use of the foil, the other two weapons being regarded as too heavy or too dangerous; then, in 1975, the A.F.A. officially permitted them to fence competitively at épée and sabre, though not, as yet, against men.

Lafaugère, Louis Justin published an almost inevitable *Traité de l'art de faire des Armes* in 1825. To him is attributed the traditional patter about holding the foil as if it were a small bird, not so tightly as to crush it, but sufficiently firmly to prevent its escape; familiar to countless beginners and handed down by generations of fencing masters.

Laid On. The term applied to a sabre cut devoid of all real penetrative force, which is simply pushed or pressed onto the target, and would therefore, with sharps, inflict little or no injury.

Lama, (It.). The blade.

Lameth, Alexandre-Theodore-Victor, Comte de was one of those well-intentioned nobles who optimistically assumed that the French

Revolution would follow the course of England's 'Glorious Revolution' of 1688 and allow the establishment of a constitutional monarchy. Under this delusion, he forsook the Second Estate and joined the Third, supporting most of the measures in the early, more moderate stages of the Revolution. He fought a well-known duel with Castries, another noble deputy who did not share his opinions, exhibiting his well-bred nonchalance by observing that he hoped he would not kill Castries, as the latter was the only decent orator on the other side, whereas, on his own, there were plenty more. Lameth need not have feared; he himself was wounded, while Castries emerged unscathed. Subsequently, with the fall of the monarchy, the scales fell from Lameth's eyes and he settled in Hamburg, eventually returning to serve in an official capacity under Bonaparte. After the restoration of the Bourbons, he joined the Liberal parliamentary opposition.

Langford was a blind, eighteenth-century master. According to Aylward, he had to be told the length of the pupil's weapon, but then, 'with a guess at his posture', he gave lessons from the *sentiment de fer*. We are not told if he actually fenced bouts, but it is well known that the technique of blindfolded pupils often improves amazingly when they have to rely on the touch of the blades rather than on their sight.

Languette. The tongue of the mask.

Lansdowne F.C. The club, with its fencing section, was founded in 1934. For many years, the senior master was Professor Alfred Parkyns. On his retirement, it was fortunate for the club that he was succeeded by his two sons; thus a fami-

The Comte de Bondy defends desperately against Lafaugère who won 48–3 in this match in 1816 (painting by F. Regamey).

Duel between de Lameth and de Castries, 1790 (contemporary engraving).

ly connection, none too common these days, was in this case maintained. The club team tied with L.F.C. for first place in the Savage Shield in 1947, won it outright in 1949, 1951, 1952, 1954 to 1959, 1961 and came second in 1937 and 1938.

Lansquenette. The sword especially popular in the fifteenth and sixteenth centuries among the German mercenary footsoldiers; hence its name. (Cp. *lansquenet*.) It had several very peculiar features; the blade was short, double-edged and very broad; the guard consisted of two rings, curved so as to form a figure of eight; while the handle, narrowest next the blade, broadened out towards the pommel.

Last Fingers. The second, third and little fingers of the sword-hand; the 'aids'.

Lateral Parry. The parry moving horizontally across the target from *sixte* to *quarte* and vice versa in the high lines, or *septime* to *octave* and vice versa in the low lines; the same as the simple parry.

Laurent-Pagan Apparatus. M Laurent, a French engineer, invented an electric recording apparatus for épée which, shortly afterwards, was improved by M Pagan of Geneva. The first international épée tournament using the apparatus was held in that city in 1931. It was officially adopted by the F.I.E. in 1933 and used at the European Championships in Budapest the same year. In 1938, it made its appearance in this country, both the final pool of the Epée Championship and the entire Miller-Hallett competition being judged by means of the appliance.

Le Perche du Coudray, Jean Baptiste. Generally known as Le Perche, he was one of those seventeenth-century masters who did so much to classify and systematise the art of the small-sword.

Leader. The name originally given to those who had obtained the Leaders' Certificate of the Amateur Fencing Association. Subsequently, they became known as 'coaches', and 'advanced leaders' as 'advanced coaches'.

Leading Attacks, Beats, Feints. Any of these actions when accompanied by a step forward.

Lebrun. A leading Parisian master of the late eighteenth century. While visiting London, it was alleged, probably untruthfully, that he had boasted of possessing such superior skill that he could outfence another French master, Lapière, also resident in the capital, by twelve hits to one. The bout took place at Angelo's salle and according to Aylward in *The House of Angelo*, was remarkable for an early experiment in the use of the Marker Point. Lebrun's button was saturated in liquid black dye, Lapière's in red. Within a very few minutes, Lebrun had made good his words; so extreme was the other's chagrin that he slunk in despair to his lodgings and there, a few days later, callers were greeted by the tragic news that he had committed suicide.

Leckie, A. and G.B. A. 'Sandy' Leckie, an Oxford half-blue, was taught at Merchant Taylors' School by the well-known Professor Nicklen. He must have been one of the very last 'three-weapon' men. He was a member of the Great Britain Epée Team at the World Championships of 1959. He won the British Foil Championships in 1961, 1965 and 1967, and was second in 1962 and 1966. In

104

Le Sieur de Liancour.

the latter year he won the Coronation Cup. He was British Sabre Champion in 1963, 1964 and 1965, again in 1967 and 1968, and came second in 1960 and 1961. He won the Commonwealth Games Men's Foil in 1962, in those of 1966 he won a silver medal at sabre, and four years later improved on this by coming first. His brother, G.B. Leckie, also an ornament of Merchant Taylors', which produced such well-known swordsmen as Jacobs and Higginson, won the Doyne Cup in 1959 and the Junior Sabre Championship the following year.

Left-Hander. The left-hander is the bogey-man of fencing despite the repeated assurances of masters to anxious pupils that, 'There's no difference – it's all just the same really' – encouragement somewhat belied by the fact that half the coaching manuals contain a section on the special tactics to be adopted when fencing a left-hander. There is a universal belief that left-handers are 'weak in *octave*' and this quarter of

their target is indeed nearest and most vulnerable to a right-hander; of course, the converse is equally true and left-handers have far more pratice against right-handers than vice versa. It may be urged that the left-hander will be just as perplexed, and for similar reasons, when facing a fellow left-hander; but this is not entirely the case, the problems in effect being only those which exist between two right-handers. Another difficulty is that the unfamiliar angulation of the left-hander's trunk makes it harder for the right-hander to place his point with confidence and precision. Again, the left-hander can dominate the right-hander's weak, or outside lines, by bearing down on the latter's blade with a strong opposition in *quarte*. To overcome these handicaps, Crosnier is a great believer, with all weapons, in 'drilling' the left-handers's outside lines or his outer arm at sabre, to make him open his *quarte* line, or expose his head and chest. The épéeist is advised to keep his hand and possibly his whole blade too, almost exaggeratedly wide in *sixte*; to make false attacks at the arm or upper target, followed by a sudden *redoublement* to the leg, and to emulate Lepage, the French champion, in the successful use of the time-hit by *croisé* of *septime* against the left-handed *flècheur*.

The fact remains that, despite this wealth of confident advice, left-handers have enjoyed remarkable success of late years. Romankov was World Foil Champion five times (1974, 1977, 1979, 1982, 1983), second in 1978 and second at the 1976 Olympics. Of British foilists and épéeists, Jay, Hoskyns, Jacobs and Bruniges all achieved great things at home and abroad. Cooperman was a left-handed sabreur to be remembered, and our most successful lady fencer of recent years, Mrs Wardell-

Yerburgh, was a left-hander. It is also a most remarkable fact that at the Moscow Olympics of 1980 all the finalists in the men's foil were left-handers.

Legamento, (It.). An engagement of the blades.

Lelio. The foppish braggart in Goldoni's *Venetian Twins*, who encounters Florindo, who unfortunately slips and whom he is about to despatch when Tonino comes to the rescue. This second confrontation ends with the disarming of Lelio, much to the latter's relief. ('What luck! I'm disarmed!') Tonino, the hero of the piece, is of course much too honourable to pursue his advantage. These two duels can be staged with great effect if the actor playing Lelio exhibits an elaborate and flamboyant style of swordsmanship, all too obviously adopted to conceal his inward nervousness.

Lengthened Parry. The name given by Vass to an engagement.

Lepage, Henri. A French Epée Champion and member of the French international team who were World Champions in 1947 and Olympic Champions in 1948. He was well known for his skill in the use of the time-hit by *croisé* of *septime* against the left-handed *flècheur* who attacked into his *sixte* line.

Lessons. The fencing lessons given by masters fall into several different categories:
1) Distance. The primary requirement is for the pupil to maintain a correct distance relative to his opponent, both in attack and defence, to gain ground on his opponent without exposing himself to danger, and in the event of his misjudging the distance, to sense this and to withdraw instantly to a safe position.
2) Mechanical. The mechanical lesson concentrates essentially on the technique of fencing actions as opposed to their application to competitive situations.
3) Mobile. A lesson in which footwork predominates; Szabo, however, emphatically insists that it does not mean that the attacks and parries are merely executed after a rapid series of steps or jumps; in his view, the fact that the pupil's action, after all this, is still executed from a stationary position, does not differentiate the lesson, in principle, from any other type of lesson. The true form of mobile lesson requires that the initiating action, generally performed by the master, must occur while the pupil is still in motion. Only thus will some approximation to the conditions of an actual bout be achieved.
4) Routine or warming-up lesson. This type serves to prepare a fencer for more specialised instruction, informal bouts in the salle, or for competitive play. Starting with the simplest attacks and parries, the lesson proceeds in logical sequence to the more complicated actions, without dwelling unduly on minor points of technique, although any glaring errors must of course be corrected.
5) Silent lesson. One without verbal instructions; instead, the pupil must react correctly to the master's movements and blade actions.
6) Special lesson. One devoted to the practice of one particular stroke or group of strokes; if confined to one only, the latter is rehearsed in as many different situations as possible.
7) Tactical. Here the emphasis is on the application of the sword-play to differing situations or different types of opponent.
8) Technique. Very similar to the mechanical lesson, though attention might in this case be concentrated on the perfecting of one or two strokes in particular.
9) Timing. Here the stress is placed on the seizing of the right moment for an offensive action, its execution in the correct cadence, and the exploitation of any momentary lack of concentration on the part of the adversary.
10) Training. Intensive practice is given on one selected stroke, which must be performed with a high degree of precision under the most diverse conditions and several times over in the course of a pre-arranged phrase.

It will be observed, that the above categories overlap to some extent in certain cases, and that a master may well introduce elements from more than one in the course of a spell with a pupil.

Liancour, Le Sieur Wernesson de. An eminent French master of the late seventeenth century, whose theories, terminology and general system are recognisably modern, although he still discouraged the use of the circular parry. What is perhaps most interesting to the present-day fencer, is his use of several varieties of foil for practice. The foil he himself used in teaching was unusually light, for fairly obvious reasons; the pupil's, on the other hand, was much heavier than that normally used and moreover lacked a guard, so that clean parrying with the *forte* was essential. It was also appreciably shorter than that of the master, thereby instilling patience before the final commitment to an attack and also emphasising the ever-present danger of the stop-hit.

Liberi, Fiore dei was the author of what is believed to be the earliest book on fencing, *Flos Duellatorum*, or *Il Fior di Battaglia* (Italy, 1410). The

A successful parry on the left, a really determined attack gets through on the right (from Liancour).

illustrations demonstrated combats with a number of different weapons.

Liement. 1) An engagement, especially one exerting some control of the opponent's blade. (Cp. the Bind, in the Italo-Hungarian sense.)

2) A *prise-de-fer* from high to low line, or vice versa.

Lifar, Serge. Born at Kiev in the Ukraine, he was a brilliant, athletic dancer and original choreographer with the ballet of the Paris Opera from 1930 to 1955. He held strongly to the opinion that music should be adjusted to the ballet, not take precedence of it. In *Icare* (1935), indeed, he went so far as to exclude the orchestra altogether, with the exception of the percussion section and although he subsequently retreated from this extreme position, he never seriously modified his basic principle. Highly temperamental, like so many connected with the theatre and more

especially the ballet, he fell out with the Marquis de Cuevas over a matter arising from the production of his ballet *Noir et Blanc* and in consequence one of the last recorded duels took place between them in 1958. (See Cuevas.)

Line, Closing the. When the blades are engaged, one, sometimes both fencers, are uncovered and so vulnerable to a straight-thrust. In such a case, a fencer, by a movement of his blade and sword-arm, can pull his opponent's blade laterally across the body to right or left, so increasing his protection by ensuring that his opponent can only attack by disengaging and threatening another part of the target. This action, carrying the opponent's point outside one's target, is called closing the line. The opposite action, when the adversary's point is deliberately allowed to threaten the target, because for tactical reasons, he is to be

encouraged to attack, is called opening the line.

Line, In. To be in line is to hold the sword-arm straight out, with the point threatening the opponent.

Line, Keeping the. Maintaining the blade in line.

Line, Opening the. Moving the blade away from its covered position and so affording the opponent an opening.

Line, Taking the. 1) To assume the in-line position.
2) To engage with, or execute a *prise-de-fer* on the opponent's blade when it is in line.

Line of Attack. An imaginary line roughly parallel with the long sides of the *piste*, along which, broadly speaking, the fencers advance and retire.

Line of Direction. An imaginary line which it should be possible to draw through a fencer's heels parallel to the long sides of the *piste*.

Linea Alta, Bassa, Esterna, Interna, (It.). High, low, outside, inside lines.

Linea Perfetta E Retta, (It.). Keeping the blade in line with point threatening opponent.

Lineas Infinitas, (Span.). In Narvaez' system, the two parallel lines tangent to the theoretical circle and at right angles to its diameter, along which the two swordsmen could move sideways for ever – 'to infinity' – without decreasing the fencing measure.

Lines. The positions, corresponding to the parries, protecting various parts of the target, in which the blade and hand can be held. (See Positions.) Broadly, the lines can be divided into:
1) Inside lines. The lines protecting the left-hand side of a fencer's target, *prime*, *quarte*, *septime* and foil *quinte*.
2) Outside lines. The lines protecting the right-hand side of the fencer's target, *sixte* (or *tierce*) and *octave* (or *seconde*).
3) High lines. The lines protecting the upper part of the target, *quarte* and *sixte* (or *tierce*).
4) Low lines. Those protecting the lower part of the target, *septime* and *octave* (or *seconde*).

Lloyd, J.E., O.B.E. Without doubt, Britain's greatest fencer between the wars. He was seven times Men's Foil Champion (1928, 1930-33, 1937-8), a record approached by no-one else. He was second in 1927, and won the Coronation Cup in the year of its inception, 1937. He was president of the A.F.A. from 1974 to 1978. A classical foilist, he earned the nickname

of 'Wasp-waist' at the 1931 World Championships.

Locking-Nut. A small nut fitting round the tang of the blade and enabling the pommel to be screwed over it.

London Fencing Club. Founded in 1848, it was soon established as one of the leading London clubs. It was first located in Piccadilly, then in Pall Mall, later still in Cleveland Row. Exactly a century after its foundation, it moved yet again, to Tenterden Street, just off Hanover Square. Even this building soon proved too cramped – not only was it shared after the Second World War with Salle Bertrand, but the headquarters of the A.F.A. and the L.A.F.U. were both also located there. Nevertheless, it possessed great atmosphere, though the same could hardly be said of the new surroundings, the de Beaumont Centre in West Kensington, despite the fact that it is spacious and has more up-to-date fittings and modern equipment.

The history of the club indicates only too well the changes that have occurred since its foundation. At one time, a rule of the club was that *remises*, so far from being a matter for exultation, were the occasion for an apology. Lady members, who were not admitted at all until 1946, were subject to restrictions almost as rigid as those operating in an Oxford college before the permissive era, when all manner of ingenious and elaborate subterfuges afforded mirth and satisfaction to their perpetrators. The club merged with Salle Bertrand in 1953 and Thames F.C. in 1977; but its strength was always formidable, counting as it did among its members such famous fencers as J. Emrys Lloyd, Charles de Beaumont, Miss G. Sheen and Mrs M. Glen-Haig. The club won the Magrini Cup (team

sabre) seventeen times; they won the Granville Cup on five occasions, their A and B sides coming first and second in 1964. They won the Savage Shield (team épée) seven times, with one tie, while their ladies' team won the Martin Edmunds Cup on fourteen occasions. It need hardly be said that the club occupied second place in the various competitions on occasions too numerous to mention.

London Ladies Fencing Club was founded in 1901, when fencing as a sport for ladies was fast becoming popular. Captain Hutton, however, was of the opinion that ladies' fencing was merely a temporary craze and that they lacked the patience and application essential to making a success of so exacting an activity.

Long-Sword. The great two-handed sword of the Middle Ages, used on foot, for cutting only.

Loose Play. (See Free Play.)

Louis XIII, King of France, 1610-43. The son of Henry IV and the father of Louis XIV has often been regarded as a mere puppet in the hands of Cardinal Richelieu, but in fact he brought no small degree of application to his reign, and must have approved, at least in broad outline, the policies of his great minister. What cannot be disputed is that this was one of the classic political partnerships of all time. Louis XIII, an enigmatic and introverted personality, had almost spartan habits and a taste for manly and active pursuits. Passionately devoted to the chase, he deliberately wore thin clothes in the severest weather. He had a martial turn, which, doubtless apparent in childhood, resulted in his parents' birthday present of 300 model soldiers in solid silver – a royal gift. He was, too, an enthusiastic swordsman and it was during this period that duelling, which then involved the seconds as well as the principals, became first a fashion, then almost an obsession, and bred such disorder and such serious loss of life, that it had to be banned by royal decree on pain of death, an edict which Richelieu relentlessly enforced whenever he could.

The endless and sanguinary brawls between the two élite regiments, the King's and the Cardinal's Musketeers, have been immortalised in the pages of Dumas, and while vividly portraying the reckless swagger of the contemporary Gascon gentlemen, from amongst whom the former corps was largely recruited, that author minimises, if anything, the alacrity with which the young bloods of that age settled any dispute, however trivial, at the point of the sword.

Louis XIV, King of France, 1643-1715. During his reign, France was the envy and admiration of Europe, the pioneer and the arbiter in the development and perfection of almost every conceivable form of human activity – the art of war and fortification, military and administrative organisation, commerce, colonisation, gardening, the fine arts, literature, architecture, music, diplomacy and cookery – whatever it was, the genius, taste and analytical logic of the French mind reigned supreme. And during the reign of the Sun King, the earlier Hispano-Italian school of sword-play was finally superseded by the classical system of the small-sword, precise, logical and comprehensive, upon which the modern school of foil fencing is still very largely based. The great masters of that era, whose theories and methods of teaching would be recognisable and still largely applicable even today, Le Perche, Besnard,
108

Labat and Liancour, all flourished in this reign.

One throwback to the past was La Tousche, fencing master to the Duc d'Orleans, (the King's brother) and the Queen's household. Among other eccentricities, he advocated an extravagantly elongated lunge, which, as a method of overcompensation, might with advantage be used as a valuable corrective to today's lazy fencers.

King Louis patronised and greatly encouraged fencing by the grant of a coat of arms to the *Compagnie des Maîtres en fait d'Armes*; and even more, by decreeing that the seven senior members of that organisation at any given time should *ex officiis* be enobled. Louis endeavoured to stop the epidemic of duelling which still raged in his reign. He issued no less than ten edicts on the subject. That of 1679, the *Edit des Duels*, imposed the death penalty on all involved, and whipping and branding for any servants concerned; the King, however, like his predecessors, was inconsistent in enforcing it, and it was even rumoured that he was secretly by no means displeased by the high spirit and martial prowess of his aristocracy.

Anecdotes about the King are legion; how, when his coachman was late one morning and he and a large number of courtiers were kept waiting on the palace steps, he silenced all criticism and complaint by remarking: 'Say no more; this poor man is probably far more upset than we are.' Again, on learning that one of the Guards officers, a certain M de Lauzun, had secretly married the King's cousin, 'la grande mademoiselle' contrary to express orders, he deliberately snapped his cane in two and threw the pieces through the window, lest he should so far forget himself as to strike a gentleman. Despite the relative failure of

his foreign policy and the financial, military and religious reverses of his later years, he was a great man, a great king and a great gentleman.

Low Lines. The lines, or positions, protecting the lower part of the fencer's target, *septime*, on his left-hand side, and *octave*, on his right. Older positions and parries, now seldom used, at any rate at foil, were *quinte* and *seconde*, roughly corresponding respectively to the two above-named.

Low Quarte. 1) One of the early names for *septime*.
2) An alternative name for the foil parry of *quinte*.
3) At sabre, this parry guards the left-hand side of the fencer's target, but with the hand low, about level with the left hip, to ward off the lateral cut at belly. The blade is nearly vertical and slants slightly outwards.

Low Sixte. A parry advocated by Crosnier when, after an initial parry of *sixte*, the attack is renewed in the low line. The blade is outside, and on a level with, the thigh. The hand is in much the same position as low *tierce* at sabre.

Low Tierce. The sabre parry guarding the flank or outer arm against a lateral cut. The hand is low, close to the right hip, to prevent the attacking blade whipping up under the guard; the defender's blade is almost vertical, slanting outwards with the cutting edge in the same direction.

Lukovitch, Istvan. An eminent Hungarian master of the present day, who has written with some profundity on the electric foil and has done what he could to eliminate from the use of this weapon some of its grosser crudities.

The Lunge (from La Tousche).

Lunette Guard. The French foil guard of the late nineteenth and early twentieth centuries. It consisted of two narrow oval-shaped rings, one on either side of the handle, which might have been supposed to bear some resemblance to a pair of eyeglasses; hence the name. It has now been replaced by the saucer-shaped *coquille*.

Lunga, (It.). The lunge.

Lunge. The classical movement which replaced the *Passade* or pass, as a means of reaching the opponent and attacking him. Capo Ferro, the great Italian master of the late sixteenth century, is generally given the credit for this vitally significant invention, but Giganti, his compatriot and contemporary, must not be deprived of his share of the credit; at a slightly earlier date he and others

had expounded the advantages of the lunge, albeit in somewhat less detail.

From the on-guard position, the leading foot is raised (toes first) and advanced as far as the individual fencer can conveniently manage. Simultaneously, the rear leg is sharply straightened, the rear foot being kept flat on the ground, so that the whole body is impelled vigorously forward. The rear arm should describe a graceful semi-circle backwards and downwards and terminate, palm opened outwards, parallel to the rear thigh. The trunk is maintained in an almost vertical position at sabre and épée, because at these weapons the head is part of the target. In passing it may be observed, that at the former weapon, some masters permit, or even require, the unarmed hand to remain on the hip, though others object on

the grounds that ease of movement is reduced and the trunk may even be pulled slightly backwards. At foil, the trunk should definitely be inclined further forward, though never so far that the head is in advance of the leading knee; the latter should not project beyond the toes of the leading foot, but should be vertically above them, thigh, knee and shin forming a perfect right angle.

Very few pupils learn this rather complicated action naturally; most, indeed, experience great difficulty in attaining even a moderate degree of efficiency. In particular, most beginners encounter great problems in maintaining the correct trunk posture throughout the lunge; so far from keeping chest and stomach turned slightly towards the adversary, they efface their target almost completely with disastrous effects on the position and balance of the head and placing of the leading leg. One method of correction is to make them do a series of fairly short lunges with the hands loosely linked behind the back, although some masters prefer them to be left dangling at the sides. The former method has the advantage of keeping the shoulders back and the trunk approximately vertical at the start. Both methods promote the placing of head, trunk and leading leg in the correct relationship to each other. When this preliminary technique has been thoroughly acquired, the orthodox use of the arms may be introduced.

Other common faults, which masters are generally alert to check, are:
1) Allowing the rear foot to roll forward instead of keeping it firmly placed and flat on the ground.
2) Failure to straighten the rear knee early enough, or indeed, at all. Pupils should be told to straighten it the moment the leading foot is clear of the floor, in order to obtain maximum forward impulse, and it should remain firmly braced.
3) Failure to carry the leading foot far enough forward. It should be emphasised that on the conclusion of the lunge, the lower leg (ankle to knee) should form a right angle to the thigh, with the foot vertically below the knee, not lagging behind it. Conversely, some fencers carry their leading foot well beyond the knee, thus throwing the trunk, and in consequence the point of the weapon, backwards away from the target.
4) Allowing the sword-hand to drop in the course of the lunge. About shoulder-high when the arm is extended, the hand should be on a level with the face at the conclusion of the lunge – assuming, that is, that the attack is delivered into the high line.
5) Allowing the head and trunk to
110

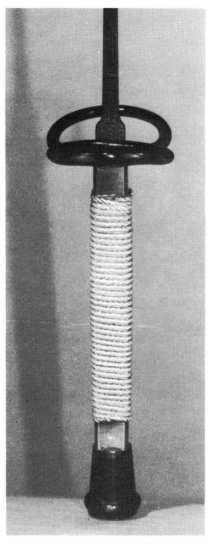

An example of a Lunette Guard.

fall away to the (right-handed) fencer's left. It must be stressed that the head should remain above the leading thigh throughout and the trunk should be in the same *relative* position at the end as at the start of the lunge. It should, indeed, at the termination of the foil lunge be in-

clined somewhat further forward than in the on-guard position, but not at the expense of allowing the head to project beyond the foremost limit of the leading foot.
6) Faulty action of the rear hand and arm. Many novices seem almost incapable of acquiring the correct action. Either they turn the palm of the unarmed hand inwards instead of outwards, or they allow the arm to drop limply at the very outset of the lunge. On the contrary, it should of course be maintained in the raised position until at least half-way through the lunge, when it should be swung back quite vigorously to achieve maximum speed and penetration in the ultimate stages of the attack.
7) Another common fault, among the young and extremely supple, is to allow the trunk to sink down between the legs. Lack of control and difficulty in the execution of subsequent actions result from this. The crutch should never be nearer the ground than the level of the leading thigh.

As a general principle, it is almost impossible to spend too much time and effort on practising the lunge. Years ago, novices were prepared to make anything up to fifty practice lunges a day, armed with an umbrella, walking stick, or poker, in their own rooms; this is less often the case today. The most graceful action in fencing, or probably any other sport, when properly executed, the lunge is likewise quite the safest and most effective method of delivering an attack and registering a hit on one's adversary.

Luxbruder. A medieval German society of fencing masters which apparently made little headway against the more powerful and famous Marxbruder.

Macarthur, John. A purser in the Royal Navy in the eighteenth century, he had a distinguished career on the administrative side, notably as secretary to Admiral Lord Hood, and became well known as an expert on naval law and courts-martial, on which subject he published a book. He also published his own book on fencing, *The Army and Navy Gentleman's Companion*; in this, like many masters of his era and even much later, he advocates *quarte* as the basic guard position as opposed to the modern *sixte*. Like some of his successors, too, he planned a series of lessons for two novices to instruct each other, though like most of those who have cherished this particular illusion, he would probably have been horrified by the enormities that inevitably ensue. MacArthur was also the first, as far as we know, to use the term 'loose play' for the assault, or informal bout.

McBane, Donald. Joining the regular Army in the late seventeenth century, he served in various regiments, tasting active warfare in Ireland and with Marlborough in the Low Countries. He fought more than one duel – generally over women – impartially with N.C.O.s of his own or the (allied) Austrian Army. He established his own school of fencing, first at Limerick and later at Dunkirk when he was posted there. Apparently fencing was not the only attraction available to potential customers at these establishments. On discharge he was found a place at Chelsea Hospital, a position he somehow contrived to combine with that of landlord of a neighbouring tavern and proprietor of yet another

school of fencing. Definitely a fighting rather than an academic master, he addresses himself principally to those likely to become embroiled in armed affrays, ambuscades or brawls, with an enemy unfamiliar with the more delicate shades of honour. In *The Expert Swordsman's Companion* (1728), he warns against 'ruffins' tricks', such as concealing a bag of sand or grit which they would suddenly fling in the face of an adversary. Before, or after an encounter which has proved indecisive, the opponent is never to be trusted behind one's back or anywhere else within reach. J.D. Aylward suggested that McBane was something of a 'ruffin' himself.

McBane favours *reprises* with half-lunges when going for the opponent's arm. He advocates parrying with the unarmed hand, or better

A time-thrust on the disengagement (from McArthur).

still, with a cane or scabbard grasped in the unarmed hand. Like many an old soldier who has seen desperate fighting, McBane was essentially pacific in temperament and strongly recommends the vinous reconciliation promoted by the wares of some convenient tavern as a preferable alternative to the duelling ground at dawn.

McTurk, W. Succeeded Henry Charles, the fourth and last of the Angelos, about 1866. His reputation stood high and with the help of his four sons he kept the famous salle going until 1897.

Magdalen College, Oxford was founded in the fifteenth century by William of Waynflete and from the first was closely associated with royalty. Edward IV lodged there; Richard III held court there; several Princes of Wales, including him who became Edward VIII were undergraduates of the college. In the Civil War, the college, distinguished for its loyalty to the crown in a city and a university which was a hot-bed of royalism, became the military headquarters of Charles I. In Magdalen, Prince Rupert, the 'Mad Cavalier', took up his quarters, and a troop of undergraduates were commanded by a fellow of the college who fell in action against the Roundheads. This was the 'opulent and imposing foundation', so graphically described by Macaulay in *History of England*, which formed the spearhead of the Tory resistance to James II when that obstinate and misguided monarch attempted to impose Roman Catholic Heads, not only on Magdalen, but on at least two other colleges as well, to say nothing of similar enterprises at Cambridge. Rather than submit to these meddlesome threats and the blatant infringement of their sta-
112

A Main-Gauche.

tutes, the fellows suffered ejection and Magdalen was temporarily transformed into a Catholic seminary. However, they returned in triumph in 1688 when the Glorious Revolution restored the *status quo* and heralded the eighteenth-century's Golden Age of constitu-

tional government and established rights.

Magdalen provided the background to a comparatively recent duel in England, the protagonists, Donellan and Poynter, both being members of the college. It would appear that to Poynter was attributed an insulting remark about a young lady who was an acquaintance of both and Donellan, captain of the Assassins (the university second fencing team), demanded satisfaction. It was reported that Poynter received a number of cuts on the arms, but the affair ended amicably enough with a toast in whisky to the fair cause of the embroilment.

Magrini, Professor. A classical Italian sabre master, who, at the start of this century, demonstrated in this country the delicate and subtle play of the light Italian weapon. Previously, the weapon used had approximated to the heavy cavalry sabre and both bouts and lessons could at times be extremely uncomfortable.

Mahon, Andrew. He taught in Dublin and in 1734 translated Labat's famous work. Mahon, like most masters of his day, devotes considerable attention to the subject of parrying with the unarmed hand; he is original insofar as he advocates doing so only after a parry with the blade presumably as a protection against a *remise* while the riposte is delivered. He also informs us, that in the East Indies European fencing masters enjoy excellent opportunities; the fact that at least one familiar figure from the British Academy has established himself in those parts suggests that this is equally true today.

Maindraict. Sainct-Didier's term for the Italian *mandritto*.

Main-Gauche. The dagger held in the left hand for the purpose of defence as well as aggression, in the days when the rapier of the sixteenth and early seventeenth century was too long and cumbersome to be very effective in parrying. Rapier and *main-gauche* were sold as a pair, with their hilts matching. During the later Middle Ages, the buckler (a small round shield) had been carried on the left-arm; indeed, Camillo Agrippa, a sixteenth-century Milanese master, still thought fit to include several illustrated examples of its use for this purpose in his *Treatise on the Science of Arms*, while as late as 1640, Alfieri gives instructions on the use of the cloak in a similar capacity.

Maison Rouge. The barracks of the Musketeers of the French kings; so-called from the colour of their livery, the other Guards regiments wearing blue uniforms.

Maître. In this country (at any rate until quite recently) the generic term 'master' has been used to designate anyone giving instruction in fencing, irrespective of his exact qualifications. Used more precisely – and this applies even more to France and the continent – it denotes a teacher of the highest rank and standing.

Maître en fait d'Armes. The degree conferred in France under the *Ancien Régime*, after six years' study under a master of the Paris Academy and a public trial of skill with three other masters.

Making Ground. Advancing towards the opponent.

Mal Paré. Insufficiently parried; although contact has been made, the attacking blade is not fully deflected from the target.

Malchus. A short, straight, broad-bladed sword; so-called from the somewhat fanciful supposition that it was with a weapon of this type that St Peter sliced off the ear of the High Priest's slave of that name, on the occasion of the arrest of Jesus.

Manchette. 1) A stop-cut to the wrist.
2) The master's thick, padded sleeve, extending from wrist to elbow, donned for épée and sabre lessons.

Mancio, (It.). The handle.

Manciolino. A sixteenth-century Italian master, who, like most of his contemporaries, taught little more than a haphazard collection of actions which he himself personally favoured and who dwelt as much on methods of picking quarrels and fighting duels in a formal and gentlemanly manner as on the technique of swordsmanship itself.

Mandabalo, (It.). An upward cut with the back-edge.

Mandoble, (Span.). A cut delivered from very near the point, by means of a flip of the wrist. (Cp. Italian *strammazone*.)

Mandritto, (It.). A cut delivered from the right, with the fore-edge, at the adversary's left side.

Mangiarotti, D. and E. Eduardo was the son of Professor Giuseppe Mangiarotti of Salle Mangiarotti, where Charles de Beaumont took lessons in the early twenties. Edmund Gray describes him as 'grounded in the classical Italian style' and he was particularly noted for his speed and skill in the *redoublement*. His successes could fill a page or more; Italian Epée Champion in 1951 and 1954, he was World Epée Champion in 1951

and 1954, second in 1938, 1950 and 1958. It is noteworthy that he was runner-up in both his National Championship and the World Championship in years as far apart as 1938 and 1958. At the Olympics, his results were even more impressive. He was the Epée gold medallist in 1952, bronze medallist in 1948 and 1956. He was an automatic member of the Italian Epée team which won in 1936, 1952, 1956 and 1960 and was placed second in 1948. It need hardly be said that the Italians were at this time equally supreme in the World Championships, winning four times in succession between 1953 and 1958.

As for the foil, Mangiarotti was second in the Olympics of 1952 and as a member of his country's team, won a gold medal in 1956 and silvers in 1948, 1952 and 1960. Altogether, he amassed a staggering total of thirteen Olympic medals, six gold, five silver and two bronze, a record likely to remain unapproachable. He never won a World Championship at foil, but came second in 1951, 1953 and 1954, and third in 1947 and 1949.

At his side in the Italian Epée team at the Olympics of 1948 and 1952 was his brother Dario whose own achievements would have loomed larger had he belonged to almost any other family. He was second to Eduardo himself at épée in the Olympics of 1952, second again in the World Championships of 1950, but the preceding year scored a merited and heartening success by himself becoming champion.

Manipulators. The thumb and fore-finger of the sword-hand, since, in the classic French foil technique, they 'manipulated' the blade and the movements of the point, the other fingers ('last fingers' or 'aids') merely lending assistance in the general control. It is to be noted that this paragraph is written in the past tense.

Marcelli, Francesco Antonio. A seventeenth-century Italian master, among whose sterling qualities modesty was not prominent, since in the preface to his *Rules of Fencing*, he asserts that no living man has been able to detect any fault in his system. He is said to have devised the *passata sotto* and the *intrecciata*.

Marchionni, Alberto. A famous Florentine master regarded as the founder of the nineteenth/twentieth century 'neo-classical' Italian school. This system, adapted from that of France, included many of the French practices, especially compound attacks incorporating a large number of feints. This predilection was not shared by the masters of the southern Italian, or Neapolitan school.

Marker Point. As early as the eighteenth century, Sir William Hope advocated the covering of buttons – much larger in those days – with a portion of sponge soaked in vermilion and water, so that there could be no doubt whether a hit had or had not actually arrived. Prior to the invention of the electric apparatus, several similar attempts were subsequently made to discover a reliable method of recording hits. One such experiment was made at the International Tournament held at Earl's Court in 1913. The triple *pointe d'arrêt* of the épées was imbued with some sort of red dye which left an imprint on the opponent's jacket. As there was no agent in the mixture causing the marks to fade, each one had to be crossed out in pencil by a member of the jury to avoid subsequent doubt and confusion. The appearance of those competitors who managed to reach the final can best be imagined.

Marker Point, The Russian was an interesting device invented by the Russian, Tchakirzianov, and demonstrated at the World Championships in Paris in 1957. On an ordinary foil, a spring-head was filled with cotton-wool saturated with various chemicals (including phenolpthalein and ammonia), so that when it was depressed by a hit, a bright red stain appeared temporarily on the body, vanishing completely after a few seconds. The only obvious objection to this invention, which avoided all the paraphernalia of electric wires and boxes, was that it did not register on metallic surfaces, e.g., the wire mesh of a mask.

Marozzo, Achille. A sixteenth-century Italian master, whose terminology is often obscure and none too easy to follow.

Martin, Lieut.-Colonel A. Ridley, O.B.E. fenced for his country at sabre in the Olympics of 1912 and 1920. He was British Sabre Champion in 1910 and 1913. From 1946 to 1948 he was Treasurer of the A.F.A. The present Junior Sabre Championship trophy was named after him.

Martina, Duke of fought the Count of Conversano in a duel at Ostuni in 1664. The affair arose when the Prince of Francavilla, who had been challenged by Conversano in consequence of some long-standing feud, proposed that he should be represented by the Duke on account of his own extreme age. It was agreed that a year should elapse, as the Duke, at that time, was hardly more than a boy. During the intervening period, the crafty Prince managed to insinuate one of his creatures into the Count's household, the gentleman in question affecting to be bitterly resentful of certain alleged wrongs done him in his previous situation. The Count afforded him hospitality, and discovering him to be an expert swordsman, took regular lessons from him. The sequel is not hard to guess. Shortly before the duel, the 'disaffected' master absconded and was able to inform the Prince and Duke of all the strengths and weaknesses of the Count's sword-play, with the expected result. Wounded once, the Count, hurt as much in pride as body, insisted on continuing the fight and shortly afterwards was mortally wounded. It transpired later that the Prince, with that treachery characteristic of the Italian aristocracy and indeed the entire nation at that time, had arranged for the Count to be ambushed and murdered on the way home, in the event of his returning victorious.

Martingale. The leather loop, fixed to the handle just inside the guard and passed round the fencer's fingers in order to prevent the weapon flying out of the hand in the event of a *désarmement*. The general introduction of the electric foil and épée has rendered the martingale obsolescent, since the body-wire now has much the same effect. The sabre has never been equipped with the martingale.

Martini and Rossi were founded in 1834 and since then have done their utmost to slake the thirst of the more discriminating drinker. They have also generously sponsored a wide variety of sports including golf, polo, skiing, tennis and racing. Well to the fore has been their support for fencing, a number of international competitions in different parts of the world having been promoted at their instance. The New York Martini Challenge has been held since 1961, Woyda of Poland, a double gold medallist at the Munich Olympics

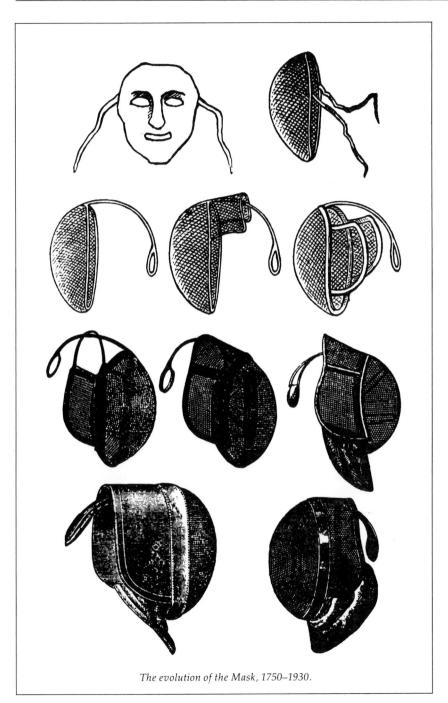

The evolution of the Mask, 1750–1930.

heading the list with five wins in six appearances. Since 1980 the competition has been restricted to sabre, with many of the world's leading exponents of the weapon participating in the finals in a gala setting. The long-standing Paris Martini attracts wide interest in the French press and among the public and an entry from the foremost European foilists. Great names appear in the list of winners: d'Oriola in 1953 and 1954, Hoskyns in 1962, while Closset (1953, 1956, 1959), Magnan (1964, 1965, 1969) and Szabo of Hungary (1966, 1967, 1971) have all achieved the notable feat of winning three times. 1987 was memorable for the triumph of Romankov, doubtless sweet consolation after his repeated Olympic disappointments. On the initiative of Count Lando Rossi, a Ladies' Foil Challenge was organised in Turin from 1966 to 1979. It was coupled to the *Coppa Europa* for club teams and all the leading lady fencers such as Sidorova and Nikonova (Russia), Hanisch (West Germany) and Palm of Sweden took part.

As for the Epée Challenge in London, that has, from its inception in 1961, proved to be one of the season's leading events. P. Boisse of France has won three times (1978, 1984, 1985). Although on home ground, British swordsmen have not often figured in the final pool of eight, let alone emerged victorious. Only twice, in 1962 and 1981, did the National Anthem ring out triumphantly and an enthusiastic crowd have the pleasure of acclaiming Hoskyns and S. Paul as the victors.

Marxbruder. A late medieval society of German 'fighting' masters whose privileges and arms (a golden lion, or lion *or*) were conferred by the Holy Roman Emperor Frederick III and confirmed by several of his successors. Their headquarters were at

115

Frankfurt and their title can be translated as the 'Fraternity of St Mark'.

In the fourteenth century they had maintained a monopoly of their art by the simple expedient of confronting all other instructors with the alternative of fighting them or joining them. For long they remained loyal to the traditional school of broadsword-play, while their chief rivals, the *Federfechter* (q.v.) adopted the point as used in the contemporary Spanish and Italian schools of the sixteenth century. Hence the newcomers challenged their antagonists of the older association to duel 'with cut and thrust'. So inferior did the broadsword prove in these encounters, that by the end of the century, the *Marxbruder* had also adopted the modern techniques and there was no longer any significant difference between the two organisations.

Masiello, Ferdinando. A noted nineteenth-century Florentine master, who, when fencing was officially adopted as a sport in the British Army, was brought to this country at the instance of Colonel Fox, then the officer in charge of physical training at Aldershot. As a result, the Italian system of fencing was adopted throughout the Army, despite the strongest opposition from Captain Hutton, F.S.A., and his supporters, who were whole-hearted adherents of the French school. It is interesting to note, however, that in his own country Masiello was regarded as a leading representative of the northern or mixed Italo-French school.

Mask. Wire masks, tied on with string, are supposed to have been invented by the eminent French master, La Boessière, about the middle of the eighteenth century, but did not become at all common until some thirty or forty years later. It

seems that full masks shaped to fit the features, with open eye-holes, had been tried somewhat earlier, but masks of any sort were discountenanced in the fashionable eighteenth-century salles, as being both conducive to scrappy play and constituting an implied criticism of the skill and style of the fencers. The whole object, in that most mannered and polished of centuries, was to maintain the celebrated 'conversation with the blades'; a measured attack met by parry and riposte, then the counter-riposte, all ripostes, for safety's sake being executed only on the opponent's recovery. For the same reason, counter-attacks were prohibited and the hit had to be very deliberately placed on the adversary's chest. The general acceptance of the mask allowed, of course, a much greater variety of movements – renewals, counter-attacks, *flèches* and the like; but there can be little doubt that there was a corresponding decline in style.

Mask, All-Purpose. The old-fashioned foil mask was a light and rather flimsy affair, the wire and material generally being black. It was certainly inadequate for épée, still less for sabre-play, and stronger masks which covered more of the head came to be used for these weapons. With the rapid increase in popularity of the two last-named after the Second World War and the simultaneous introduction of the heavier and more lethal electric foil, a much larger and stouter mask was manufactured, its wire mesh being silvered and its other parts white. A not unimportant disadvantage, however, is its significantly greater weight.

The use of the mask is obligatory in all competitions and no responsible master will allow a pupil to take a lesson without a mask, still less in-

dulge in free play.

Masks Fencing Club. A subsidiary club of the Army Fencing Union, founded in 1923.

Master. (See Maître.)

Masters of Defence were members of the corporation which received Letters Patent embodying their status from Henry VIII in 1540 and were granted the coat of arms still used by the present British Academy of Fencing. Organised somewhat on the lines of a medieval guild, the members advanced through the grades of Scholar, Free Scholar, Provost, to full Master, being obliged to pass searching examinations in several different weapons at each step. For the scholar's exam, the long-sword and backsword were compulsory. At the more advanced stages there was a choice. Aylward informs us that the free scholars usually opted for sword and buckler in addition to the two foregoing, whilst the provost could add to any two of those already mentioned a pole weapon and rapier and dagger, making four in all. Seven years had to elapse between the examination for the degree of free scholar and that of provost, and another seven before the masters' exam could be attempted. All the subordinate grades were bound to a master rather like the contemporary apprentice. The provost might teach independently only if his master no longer required his services.

In 1603 a warrant from James I conferred on the corporation the monopoly of the right to teach fencing. It was therefore the Monopolies Act of 1624, abolishing such privileges, which brought about the decline of this famous association. Thenceforward, it was open to anyone to teach fencing without being a member of the society. It might have been imagined that its prestige would have been sufficient to ensure that the vast majority of professional swordsmen would have wished to qualify for membership in any case, and that the competence of outsiders would have been suspect; but this did not prove to be the case, probably because the corporation's obstinate attachment to the antiquated and obsolete weapons enumerated above made little appeal to the students and practitioners of the Italian rapier. It would seem, in the absence of any reference in the contemporary records, that the corporation had been entirely dissolved within a decade of the passage of the fatal Act.

Masters, Status of. The status of fencing masters has varied considerably over the years. A statute of Edward I, which forbade the teaching of fencing in the City of London was enforced by the authorities, with varying success, for some hundreds of years. Apparently, in those very early times, it was considered undesirable to allow armed and trained groups to assemble together. In the Tudor period, fencing masters were classified in the successive Vagrancy Acts along with 'sturdy rogues', vagabonds, actors, gypsies and the owners of performing bears. Bacon referred to the fencing master's occupation as an 'ignoble trade'. Joseph Swetnam, the Jacobean master speaks disapprovingly of his colleagues as 'much given to Drunkenness and Ungodliness' and cites the discreditable examples of several who came to bad ends. Thus, one collapsed and died on the spot after gulping a pint of neat spirits; another committed suicide, a third was hanged for murder and yet a fourth died of the pox.

It was the Italian masters, making their appearance in England towards the end of Elizabeth I's reign, who

A fencing Master, P.G. Hamon of the London Fencing Club (portrait by F. Brunary).

A Master of the weapon trade (engraving by N. Bonnard, 1680).

first asserted the claims of the profession to that dignity and social status later so closely associated with it. They were highly conscious of their rank as gentlemen, for in Italy no-one of meaner position was permitted to teach the art of swordsmanship, and they regarded their English counterparts as their inferiors, as much in birth as in skill. Rocco declared the English Masters of Defence to be 'base mechanicals'. Although the prize-fighters of the seventeenth and eighteenth centuries did nothing to enhance the standing of the professional swordsman – in fact, rather the reverse – in the end, the French influence was decisive. In 1656, Louis XIV conferred patents of nobility on the six senior masters of the Paris Academy and the stage was set for the master of the eighteenth and nineteenth centuries, the arbiter of points of honour, punctilious in all matters of courtesy and deportment and everywhere accepted as the equal of the noblemen and gentlemen who formed the bulk of his pupils.

Maupin, Julie de was a popular actress at the Paris Opera in the seventeenth century. The lover and pupil of the great fencing master Serane, she was an accomplished swordswoman and dangerous duellist in an age still greedy for duels. As events revealed, she was more than a match for most men. She called out two fellow-actors whom she accused of insulting her and when they refused to appear, they were publicly humiliated, by being obliged, in the one case, to hand over his personal possessions including his watch; in the other, to make a fulsome apology on his knees. Her most memorable exploit was to challenge all the men at a ball who had defended a lady whom she had insulted. According to the story, she took them outside in turn and killed the lot; though here it may be that history is being somewhat richly embroidered. This formidable lady, whose offences were pardoned by Louis XIV, eventually left France and retired into private life as the mistress of the Elector of Bavaria.

Mayer, Helene. Like Ilona Elek and Cornelia Hanisch, she won three ladies' foil titles at the World Championships of 1929, 1931 and 1937. She won at the Olympics of 1928, but was not, however, quite able to match Elek at those of 1936, having to be content with earning the silver medal for second place.

Measure, The Fencing. The distance between the fencers when on guard. It varies according to the stature of the fencer himself, that of his opponent, and the weapon being used, but in principle it is recognised as the distance at which a lunge is necessary to register a hit on the target area. As the épée and sabre targets include the sword-arm, the measure at these weapons is clearly longer than at foil. The Hungarian master, Lukovitch, recognises no fewer than five variations of the distance, or measure:
1) Close distance – what we should call close quarters.
2) Short distance – riposting distance, i.e. the opponent can be hit by extending the sword-arm alone.
3) Middle distance – lunging distance.
4) Long distance – when the fencer can only reach his opponent by means of a *flèche*, or a movement of the feet in addition to the lunge.
5) Out of distance – this is generally accepted as being the distance at which the fencer can only reach his opponent after a whole series of foot actions.
  Barbasetti's analysis is slightly
118

different:
1) Close distance – riposting distance.
2) Lunging distance.
3) Normal distance – one step before the lunge is needed.
4) Outside of distance – further away yet.

Measure, Out of. At a distance from the opponent, when, to hit him by lunging, it is necessary to take a preliminary step or steps.

Measure, Perfect. At a distance from the opponent when it is possible to hit him by lunging, without any preliminary step.

Measure, Within. At a distance from

the opponent when it is possible to hit or be hit without lunging.

Medina-Sidonia, Alonzo Perez de Guzman, Duke of. The best-known Duke of the great House of Guzman was he who, despite his protests, was put in command of the Armada by Philip II, one of that unperceptive and bureaucratic monarch's least felicitous appointments; for by doing so, he entrusted the naval destinies of Spain to that 'modest gentleman, who on his own admission could hardly distinguish a topmast from an anchor and who confessed that whenever he ventured out in a boat, he was almost always seasick'. The sequel is too well known for repetition; even so, in 1595, as a

A latterday Julie de Maupin.

mark of his unimpaired confidence, Philip did not hesitate to confer on the worsted admiral the grandiloquent title of 'Captain-General of the Ocean' and he remained in command of the Navy under Philip III until he died in 1619.

It was this Duke's descendant who became involved in one of the most extraordinary challenges recorded in history. In 1640 Portugal rose against the dominion of Spain, to which country it had been subjected for eighty years. The Duke of Braganza having headed the rising and assumed the kingly office with the title of John IV, certain details of his plans were intercepted and suppressed by the Marquis of Ayamonte, a sympathiser with the Portuguese and a relation of Medina-Sidonia. Furthermore, these two set in motion a design to establish the Duke on the throne of a separate kingdom of Andalusia. In due course these treasonable projects were detected; Ayamonte was executed, the Duke heavily fined and pardoned only on condition that he challenged the new King of Portugal to a duel. For almost three months he waited on the frontier surrounded by the pomp and pageantry of medieval chivalry, but all in vain. John IV had no mind to put his gains to the hazards and uncertainties of single combat.

Medio Reves, (Span.). A cut from the elbow delivered from one's left.

Medio Taja, (Span.). A cut delivered from the elbow.

Medium Guard. (See Sabre.)

Megga Cavatione, (It.). (See Mezza Cavazione.)

Melfe-Carraccioli, Prince de. He commanded the French forces during Francis I's Italian campaigns of 1545-50. He succeeded in bringing duelling to a temporary stop among the French officers, by insisting that all such encounters took place on the parapet of a bridge, thus condemning at least one, and quite possibly both principals, to almost certain death by drowning.

Mendelenyi, Robert was World Youth Champion at sabre in 1955, sabre silver medallist at the World Championships of 1959 and three times he earned a gold medal as a member of winning Hungarian sabre teams. In 1972 he became Hungarian National Sabre Coach.

Mensur. The German student's duel. (See German Universities.)

Mercutio. A swashbuckling aristocrat and friend of the House of Montague in Shakespeare's *Romeo and Juliet*, he met his death in a duel with Tybalt, rashly undertaken when Romeo, for his own good reasons, refused the challenge. Nor was it surprising that Mercutio felt only disgust at such apparent meanness of spirit; only a few minutes before, he had represented another friend, Benvolio, as quarrelling over such empty pretexts as the amount of hair in a beard, the cracking of nuts, the unguarded cough which had awakened a favourite dog – and duels over such preposterous trifles were by no means unknown in the late sixteenth and early seventeenth centuries. 'O, calm, dishonourable, vile submission!' Mercutio raved. '*Alla stoccata* carries it away! Tybalt, you ratcatcher, will you walk?' (*Stoccata* was Italian for a thrust under the adversary's sword-arm.) Subsequently, realising that he was mortally wounded, Mercutio summed up his feelings with the famous phrase 'A plague o' both your houses!' and lamented that he had met his end at the hands of 'a rogue, a villain, that fights by the book of arithmetic'.

There is altogether a good deal of sword-play in *Romeo and Juliet*. Romeo soon exacts vengeance by despatching Tybalt; and Benvolio, in describing the duel in which Mercutio had met his end, mentions a method of parrying with the unarmed hand still recommended by some of the late seventeenth-century authorities:

'With one hand beats
Cold death aside,
and with the other sends
It back to Tybalt'. (Act III, Sc.i.)

Merignac. (See Kirchhoffer.)

Meyer, Joachim. A German master of the late sixteenth century, who, while maintaining his allegiance to the traditional German weapons, such as the Dusack, and writing copiously upon their practice, is nevertheless credited with having brought the Italian rapier and dagger north of the Alps.

Mezza Cavazione, (It.). An attack from a high into a low line, i.e. it is only a half disengagement. The blade does not travel right round the opponent's, but stops half-way, underneath.

Mezzo Cerchio, (It.). 'Half-circle', the parry from high to low inside line (the modern *septime*). According to some authorities, the term applies also to high *septime*, with the sword-arm extended rather more than usual.

Mezzo-Dritto, (It.). A cut from the executant's right at the inside of the opponent's wrist.

Mezzo-Tempo, (It.). A time-hit, or covered stop-hit, literally 'half-time', i.e. the hit did not arrive *ahead* of the adversary's attack, but simultaneously deflected his blade.

Mignons, Duel des. This duel was one of the most celebrated in the reign of Henry III of France (1575-89) and was fought between two of his *mignons* or favourites, Quelus and d'Entragues, who had fallen out over some lady. It was remarkable for the fact that all four seconds, Riberac and Schomberg for d'Entragues and Mangiron and Livarot for Quelus, fought each other and three were either killed instantly or mortally wounded; Livarot alone survived to die in another duel two years later. Of the principals, d'Entragues was severely wounded, while Quelus, who had been almost cut to pieces, lingered on for several weeks. It is to be hoped that he derived some consolation from his royal master's sympathetic attentions and publicly expressed demand and expectation that all the departed souls would be received into eternal bliss.

Military Salute. (See Salute.)

Miller, Captain James. A noted prize-fighter of the eighteenth century, a term which then signified a professional swordsman who, like the modern boxer, staged public bouts for a purse. The weapon chiefly employed was the backsword. In *The Spectator* of 21 July, 1712, Steele describes his encounter with Timothy Buck (q.v.). Buck sustained 'a large cut on the forehead' while a leg-wound of Miller's was 'exposed to the view of all who could delight in it' and stitched up there and then. Miller, originally an N.C.O., was commissioned by George II and subsequently distinguished himself in the 'Forty-five' rebellion under the command of 'Butcher', the Duke of Cumberland.
120

Misura Larga, (It.). The fencing measure – that distance, basically, at which it is possible to hit the opponent only after advancing a pace or lunging.

Misura Stretta, (It.). Corresponds to our riposting distance, i.e., the distance at which it is possible to hit the opponent merely by extending the sword-arm.

Modern Pentathlon. The five events are swimming, cross-country running and riding – all for prescribed distances, shooting and fencing with the épée. The notion is that the competitor is an agent carrying despatches through enemy-held territory when all the above activities might be necessary. To our ears all this sounds anything but modern; nowadays rally-driving of the Monte Carlo style, flying a helicopter, skill with explosive devices, unarmed combat and accuracy with a sub-machine gun might be considered rather more relevant and of greater utility. However, it must be remembered that the event was first included in the Olympic Games of 1912. Great Britain won the team Gold Medal at the Montreal Olympics in 1976 under the leadership of Capt J. Fox of the Royal Horse Artillery.

At the Olympics held in Montreal in 1976, there was a notorious scandal when a competitor from the U.S.S.R. was detected in the act of using an illicit épée which he had falsified by means of some mechanical contrivance so that hits were being registered without actual contact on the body of his opponent.

Mohun, Lord. (See Hamilton and Multiple Duels.)

Moldovanyi, Professor A. started fencing as a schoolboy. Commissioned into the Hungarian Army in 1939, a wound unluckily restricted his post-war activities to teaching the art. A dramatic feature of his service was the duel between two officers at which he presided. The weapons were sabres, half the cutting edge being sharpened, while use of the point was forbidden. Arriving in this country after the 1956 uprising, he taught at numerous clubs and schools, notably Salle Paul and Merchant Taylors'. An often mentioned feature of his teaching was his anxiously reiterated demand to know if his pupil was feeling tired; a sharp contrast to most of his colleagues who, if they asked the question at all, were merely indulging a taste for heavy sarcasm. The professor's pupils include internationals at all weapons and sabre champions at open and under-twenty level. He holds high office in masters' associations at home and abroad and in 1985 received the Emrys Lloyd trophy for his contribution to British fencing.

Molinello, (It.). A sabre cut to head often following the parry of *prime*. It involves a considerable wrist action for not only must the blade describe the better part of a circle, but it must also be retracted following the parry to allow the point to clear the opponent's blade. Some masters of yesteryear were in the habit, after a long and arduous lesson, of requiring their pupils to finish with twenty or thirty *molinellos*, executed one after the other at high speed. Professor A.T. Simmonds offers a somewhat different interpretation following lengthy discussions with the Hungarian masters, Nagy, Beke and Polgar. He defines it as a circular cut which can be directed to the chest as well as the head, passing through the *prime* position and, to quote his own words, 'both losing and gaining time'. In effect, it can form a broken-

Duel des Mignons, 1578, (nineteenth-century engraving).

time attack, almost invariably causing the opponent to expose his target by a superfluous action. Léon Bertrand classifies any circular cut, be it vertical, diagonal or horizontal, as a *molinello*.

Montant. An Elizabethan term for an upward cut.

Montante, (It.). A vertical cut delivered upwards.

Montante Sotto Mano, (It.). An upward cut with the back-edge.

Montanto, (It.). An early cutting weapon.

Montgomerie, R. was in the habit of carrying all before him in the national foil and épée championships eighty years ago. He was Foil Champion in 1905, 1908, 1909 and 1910; second in 1901, 1904, 1907; and third a cou-

ple of times. The first year that he won at foil, he achieved similar success with the épée, which he was able to repeat on four further occcaions (1907, 1909, 1912, 1914). He was second in 1911. A member of the first British épée team in the International Cup at Paris in 1903, he figured prominently in the team which won silver medals at the Olympics of 1908 and 1912. He was in both foil and épée teams at the games of 1912, 1920 and 1924 and in 1928 appeared in the Individual Epée.

Montgomery Trophy, Field Marshal. The competition was organised in 1946 by the *Union Fraternelle des Anciens Combatants* to commemorate the liberation of Belgium by troops under the command of Montgomery. It was for teams of three fencers (one at each weapon) from British, Belgian and Luxembourg clubs.

Montmorency, François de, Lord of Boutteville. A celebrated duellist during the reign of Louis XIII, he had taken refuge in Brussels to avoid the death sentence incurred by a long series of bloody encounters, and principally that which had resulted in the death of one M de Thorigny; it was a kinsman of the latter, the Marquis de Beuvron, who challenged him with the intention of exacting vengeance. Montmorency was not the man to dream of pleading his predicament and impulsively returned to face his enemy, though there must be strong reservations regarding the propriety of a demand for satisfaction, on French soil, in such circumstances.

Without the slightest attempt at concealment, a dramatic encounter in the Place Royale, in the presence of a thousand or more spectators, ended with the disarming and reconciliation of both the principals, but the Comte de Bussy, one of the seconds – both of whom were themselves fighting, according to the custom of those times – fell dead upon the ground. At this crisis, the watch suddenly appeared, and although Boutteville and the Comte des Chapelles, the other second, made their escape, it proved to be but temporary, for they were arrested while attempting to leave the country; despite widespread appeals to the King and his famous minister, Cardinal Richelieu, both were in due course publicly decapitated.

The fate of de Beuvron is uncertain; it would be strange indeed if the Cardinal, implacably opposed to duelling as he was, had not visited his severest displeasure on the original and deliberate instigator of the entire affray.

Morlaix, M. Quentin de. The fencing master hero of Sabatini's *Marquis de Carabas*. A Frenchman by birth, his salle was in London: 'a long, austerely bare *salle d'armes* on the ground floor . . . the elegant adjacent rooms . . . the little garden where de Morlaix cultivated his roses' – does not this remind some fencers, not in the youngest age-group, of a certain private salle in south-west London years ago? De Morlaix's establishment gradually became a meeting-place, almost a club, for French aristocrats seeking refuge from the Revolution; such was its fame, rivalling even that of Angelo's, that it aroused the jealous hostility of one of de Morlaix's professional rivals, a certain M Rédas, who challenged him to a public bout, in the full expectation of demonstrating his own superiority. So bellicose had been the terms in which Rédas conveyed his challenge, that it was agreed that the contestants should be stripped to the waist and that *pointes d'arrêt* should be used, consisting of caps with three half-inch points fixed over the buttons; evidently highly similar to the *pointes d'arrêt* used on the pre-electric épée.

The bout is described fairly convincingly. We are told that de Morlaix 'ventured no counters, not so much as a riposte'. 'Playing close, forearm well-flexed', he easily tired out his adversary. (If only it were really as simple as this!) A counter parry was at length followed by a direct riposte, de Morlaix was twice successful with low feints and disengagements into the high line, and the ultimate result was that six triple pricks oozing blood made their appearance on the torso of the discomfited Rédas, his young opponent remaining entirely unmarked.

Subsequently de Morlaix discovered himself to be the heir to a title and estate in France and thither he repaired to assert his claim, only to encounter greater danger from the greedy and treacherous members of

his own family than from the revolutionary government whose earlier excesses had now been greatly moderated. In the course of these adventures, he challenged de Boisgelin, leader of the Chouans, the royalist guerilla movement in Brittany, and against him employed much the same tactics as in the earlier encounter. Having tired his frustrated opponent with an impenetrable defence, he finished the affair by deliberately uncovering in the low line to draw the attack, then performing a *volte* and stop-hitting his opponent as the latter lunged.

De Morlaix fought a third successful duel, this time against the treacherous Baron Cormatin who was selling information about the Chouans to feather his own nest, and it was of dramatic brevity. The Baron attacked impetuously, was parried and the riposte was through his forearm in a flash – the shortest possible of phrases!

Mortuary. A type of cavalry sword of the mid seventeenth century, so-called because some were made in memory of Charles I and carried his likeness on the hilt.

Mosley, Sir Oswald. A Member of Parliament as, firstly a Unionist (Conservative), then an Independent and finally a Socialist, he became notorious in the 1930s as the leader of the British Union of Fascists, whose pseudo-uniform of black shirt, flared breeches and military-style belts, no less than their raucous anti-Semitism, was ominously suggestive of the contemporary totalitarian organisations in Germany and Italy under Hitler and Mussolini. Especially provocative were their meetings and marches in East End districts with a large Jewish population, such disorder being bred that the government was obliged to pass

a Public Order Act (1936), entirely forbidding the wearing of unauthorised or unofficial uniforms. The activities of the so-called 'Blackshirts' were somewhat curtailed in consequence, and on the outbreak of the Second World War several of their leaders, including Sir Oswald himself, were detained under Regulation 18B, as being strongly suspected of harbouring sympathies with the enemy. After the release of Sir Oswald, which took place shortly before the final victory over the Axis powers, both he and his movement faded into insignificance, and the Union was able to preserve no more than a vestigial existence. Mosley and his henchmen had never been taken quite seriously by the majority of the British public, and few readers of P.G. Wodehouse are likely to forget his ludicrous caricature of Mosley as Roderick Spode, leader of the 'Blackshorts'.

What is less generally known is that Sir Oswald was an expert swordsman, in 1931 coming equal second with Major Notley in the British épée championship and the following year taking third place in the same event, besides achieving international status. He represented Great Britain at épée in the European Championships of 1935 and the World Championships of 1937. For some years he served on the Committee of the Amateur Fencing Association.

Motet. An eighteenth-century French master, whose chief significance now arises from the fact that Henry Angelo was his pupil, but he was famous in his own time for the strength of his parry. A popular and athletic instructor in the years before the French Revolution, his well-frequented salle stood in the Rue de Seine, but, sadly, no trace of the building now remains.

Moulinet. A slicing sabre cut at chest, followed by a retraction of the sword-arm. One eminent master classified it as a 'bastard *molinello*'.

Moulinets. A sequence of diagonal and horizontal practice cuts designed to improve the suppleness of the wrist and fingers and increase precision and control in the use of the sabre. There are six altogether:
1) Diagonally right to left downwards and vice versa.
2) Diagonally left to right downwards and vice versa.
3) Horizontally right to left and vice versa.
   The so-called 'figure-of-eight' consists in the continuous execution of the two downward diagonal cuts, making an 'X' in the air. When the subsidiary point movements needed to join the arms of the figure are added, an imaginary figure '8', lying on its side, is created.

Mourning Swords. In the eighteenth century, the guards and grips of weapons were sometimes blackened to match the costumes of the bereaved.

Multiple Choice Reaction. Giving the pupil more than two alternatives in response to the actions, offensive or defensive, of the fencing master. Only one choice is correct, and the right solution will depend on each occasion on the varied actions of the master. The stage in the phrase when the pupil must make his decision is sometimes pre-determined; at others, to make matters more difficult still, this too will be varied at the master's discretion.

Multiple Duels. Latterly, the seconds did not play an active part in duels; earlier, however, especially during the seventeenth century, it was quite common for them to do so.

(See Seconds.) For example, in the duel between Lord Cavendish and Mr Power in 1676, the seconds, Lord Mohun and Mr Brummingham engaged each other. Mohun disarmed Brummingham and went to the aid of Cavendish; but the latter and Power were already agreeing to a reconciliation. Subsequently, however, a fresh quarrel broke out between Mohun and Brummingham, as a result of which they again engaged and Mohun died.
   The affair between Coote and French (1698) was a bad example of one of these multiple duels, which apparently only became fashionable in England after the Restoration; it is thought that the habit may have been introduced by gentlemen returning from 'their travels', a euphemism for the enforced exile undertaken, as in the case of Charles II, during the Cromwellian interregnum. Coote and French were supported respectively by the Earl of Warwick and Lord Mohun, and Messrs James and Dockwra. The rumpus started in a bar in the Strand and was temporarily suspended only to be resumed in Leicester Fields. What exactly happened is unknown, but by the time some Sedan chairmen had been summoned, Coote was dead and two of the others wounded. All the survivors had to stand trial, but all were either acquitted or, having been convicted of manslaughter, were released on pleading Benefit of Clergy (q.v.).

Mur, Le. The Military salute. (See Salute.)

Murphy, Arthur. A none-too-reputable actor and man of letters who earned the dubious distinction of being the only man ever to wound the great Domenico Angelo. The incident was, in truth, fortuitous; Murphy drew upon a companion as a

result of some argument in a coffee-house, and Angelo who intervened to separate the couple, was wounded in the general tussle. Providentially, the injury was of the slightest.

Mushroom Head. A name for the head of the early electric foil.

Musketeers. Two of the élite household regiments of France in the seventeenth century, the Grey and Black Musketeers, were so-called from the colour of their horses; their uniforms were scarlet. In the earlier period at least, the entire strength was composed of gentlemen of good family, cadets of noble houses and the like, who provided their own arms and equipment; and the circumstance that a very high proportion of them hailed from Gascony, explains their well-merited reputation for headstrong gallantry and a fiery sense of honour.
   Dumas immortalised them in his *Three Musketeers*; the three comrades were Athos, Porthos and Aramis and d'Artagnan was the young hero. The same characters re-appeared in *Twenty Years After* and *The Vicomte de Bragelonne*. In addition, Rostand's Cyrano de Bergerac, the brilliant and intrepid poet-swordsman with the appalling facial disfigurement, who is the eponymous hero of a play relating to the same period, is also represented as having been an officer of the Musketeers; while in *The Ingoldsby Legends*, Thomas Barham gives us another glimpse of a swashbuckler of the same corps in *The Black Mousquetaire*. Both regiments were finally disbanded in the reign of Louis XVI, during the early stages of the French Revolution.

Mysterious Circle. (See Circle, the Mysterious.)

N.F.C.A.A. The National Fencing Coaches Association of America.

N.I.F.A. The National Intercollegiate Fencing Association of the United States.

Nadi, Aldo. Son of the great Italian master Giuseppe Nadi, he won Olympic gold team medals at all three weapons, but in the individual events had to be content with a silver medal at sabre in 1920, having to give best to his brother Nedo. Nevertheless, for a few years either side of the First World War, he was regarded as the star turn of the contemporary Italian school. All who saw him were enthralled by the speed and brilliance of his footwork. In 1922, a unique foil contest was arranged between him and Lucien Gaudin to settle once and for all the supremacy disputed by the rival Italian and French schools. It must have been a great occasion, with preliminary exhibition bouts by leading European fencers including our own Edgar Seligman and M Paul Anspach who had collaborated in the framing of the rules of 1914. Music was provided by the band of the Garde Républicaine and there was even a brief performance by the *Comédie Française*. Only the devoted adherents of the Italian system could have departed with any sense of disappointment, for Gaudin won by twenty hits to eleven. 'Punch' Bertrand, however, who reported the whole affair in the *Illustrated and Dramatic Sporting News* was of the opinion that Nadi was unlucky. A temporary rule framed immediately prior to the 1920 Olympics allowed hits on the sword-arm above the elbow, even when there was no deliberate shielding of the body. Bertrand reckoned that this cost the Italian at least five hits. But the result would have been the same

124

Nadi, Professor Nedo. A great Italian master of the first half of the twentieth century. He won the individual foil at the Olympics of 1912 and 1920, in which year he also carried off the sabre championship. He also won three gold team medals at each of the three weapons. Later, he taught the immortal 'Punch' Bertrand. In 1925 he met the equally famous French master René Haussy in a match which resulted in a clarification of the rules. Haussy scored with a *remise* on his opponent's favourite riposte by disengagement and both contestants and their supporters claimed the priority. After heated controversy, the International Federation ruled that a riposte by disengagement has 'right of way' over a *remise* provided that it is executed immediately and without any withdrawal of the sword-arm. Charles de Beaumont, who witnessed the bout, avers that Nadi probably did use his arm to clear the left-hander's blade.

Nagy, Dr. Bela. President of the Hungarian Fencing Federation, he chaired the F.I.E. Commission which sat in Paris in June, 1914, and adopted the rules of sabre fencing which are substantially those still in force.

Nagy, P. He defeated Jay 8-6 in the Martini Epée final of 1965. The same year, at the World Championships in Paris, he was involved in a curious dispute arising from his bout with the same fencer. In the épée team event, Nagy claimed to have scored an equalising hit, but it transpired that time had already been called without the president realising it. Eventually, after protracted arguments and discussions, the jury *d'appel* decreed that the hit – about which there was in itself no question – should be annulled and Jay was

duly declared the victor.

Napoleon of the Foil. (See Bertrand, François-Joseph.)

Narvaez, Don Luis Pacheco de. A master who elaborately and verbosely expounded the dignified, but unrealistic principles of the seventeenth-century Spanish school. He based his system of fencing on that imaginary circle which his successor, Thibaust, took to even greater extremes of intricacy. (See Circle, the Mysterious.) Ben Jonson (*The New Inn*, Act II, Sc. ii) ironically refers to him as 'the sole master now, of the world' and Lord Beaufort and Sir Glorious Tipto suggest he should be invited to visit Elysium and there fence with the shade of Euclid, that other great master of geometry.

National Training Scheme was devised by the first National Coach, Professor Roger Crosnier, in the immediate post-war years, when the proliferation of clubs and the influx of novices meant that there were far too many fencers for the readily available masters. The problem was partly solved by Crosnier's scheme, which operated on two levels. On the higher level, a supply of coaches (or 'leaders' as they were originally called), competent to give instruction in basic foil, épée and sabre, was ensured by the requirements of a practical and theoretical examination. These instructors were then in a position to operate the scheme itself, the general conception and details of which were explained in the Professor's *Fencing with the Foil* (and subsequently in other works dealing with the sabre and épée), with a truly Gallic precision, lucidity and logic. Every movement in fencing, both in blade and body, was analysed in admirably systematic fashion, and reduced to a series of

Practising on the mysterious circle — a system developed by Narvaez (from Thibaust).

separate actions, known as 'progressions', which could be practised one at a time, before being gradually joined together to form one complete and unified motion. By this system, every known attack and parry could be learnt and practised in detail, piece being added to piece rather like a Meccano model, and in a period of months the fencer's repertoire would (at all events in theory) be complete.

The group normally worked in two lines, each fencer facing a partner in the opposite line, each entire line constituting the attack and defence in turn. As the instructor called out the numbers – often up to four or five in the first stage of a progression – the fencers performed the appropriate movement. With each stage, the number of movements was reduced from five to four, then to three and so on, until, as already explained, a complete attack, parry, preparation, etc. was executed. The advantage of this system was that the instructor was in complete control of his class, could see each fencer making the same move simultaneously and could correct faults instantly or even go back a stage if necessary. The disadvantage was that fencers tended to become jerky and mechanical.

To obviate this, the system since those days has been greatly modified. The tendency subsequently was to demonstrate a stroke in its entirety and then send the fencers away in pairs to practise it independently, the coach constantly circulating to correct errors or to facilitate progress, and calling all the pupils together again if some widespread fault or basic misapprehension had raised serious difficulties. This development certainly permits the abler fencer to proceed at his own pace and to achieve more independence, but with beginners it can be perilous in the extreme; bad habits abound and are regularly repeated while the coach's eye is elsewhere, while the less competent couples often seem unable to make any headway at all. Inevitably, the conscientious coach tends to concentrate on them and equally inevitably, is obliged to devote less time to those who might profit more. All this tends to reinforce the opinion of a school now passing away, that the one way to learn to fence is on the *piste*, individually, opposite a competent master.

Nelligan, Miss G. was a pupil of Professor Léon ('Punch') Bertrand in the twenties and thirties, when the lady members of his salle enjoyed a prolonged run of dazzling success. It was he who was supposed to have turned her from a very average club fencer into a world-class foilist by allowing her to use the weapon with the Italian handle. Miss Nelligan won the Desprez Cup in 1931, twice won the Alfred Hutton Memorial Cup (1932 and 1934) and was Ladies' Foil Champion in four consecutive years (1934-5-6-7). However, it was at the European Championships at Budapest in 1933 that she earned undying fame, when, by taking the Ladies' Foil Championship she became the first British fencer of either sex to win an international competition at this level. Known as the 'Greta Garbo' of fencing, Miss Nelligan was very tall and strong for a woman. She possessed a classic style and was noted for her attacks *en*
126

marchant; in those days the *flèche* was frowned upon as being not only ungainly, but vulnerable to the riposte or stop-hit in the event of it not being instantly successful.

Nemere, Z. One more of the brilliant succession of swordsmen who brought Hungarian épée to the forefront of the world in the sixties and seventies. He won the World Championship in 1965 and the Challenge Martini the previous year.

Neutral. Fencer's slang for the hand position with 'thumb on top', i.e. half-way between supination and pronation. Sabre text-books refer to it as 'half-pronation', though it might just as logically be termed 'half-supination'. Neutral, therefore, is the most appropriate description.

Ninth Parry or Coward's Parry. Contemptuous terms given to the avoidance of an attack by means of a step back, when, long ago, the whole idea of fencing was to execute a series of blade actions as skilfully and stylishly as possible; to retreat out of distance was felt to militate against this. There were eight recognised foil parries at the peak of the development of the French classical school.

Noailles, Botte de. The illustrious de Noailles family produced, at different times, two Marshals of France, an Admiral, a Cardinal-Archbishop of Paris and a misguided enthusiast who embraced republican principles and was deservedly guillotined during the Terror. The swordsman of the family, in the late sixteenth century, specialised in the *botte* to which his name was attached, a stop-hit between the eyes.

Nobbs, P.E. was a fencer of wide experience and deep reflection whose *Fencing Tactics* (1936) contains

numerous points of interest. There are other suggestions involving elaborate build-ups and complicated compound attacks, which, if attempted today, would probably prove a recipe for disaster. His advice to study the esoteric steps, jumps and turns of old times for their surprise effect is likewise of dubious value. There is a good deal of pure nostalgia: double hits 'verge on crimes'; the salute is 'one of the few inventions of mankind that cannot be improved upon'; to hit with the sabre point on hand or arm is 'bad form'. In Mr Nobbs's eyes, the supreme advantage of fencing is that it is possible to continue to the 'brink of the grave', experience being always likely to discomfit youth. This last was possibly true in his day and his views go far to vindicate the contention of the ancients, that deterioration rather than improvement is the rule of human affairs.

Northern Ireland Amateur Fencing Union. Founded as a 'section' in 1952, it adopted its present superior status in 1963. At the Commonwealth Games of 1974, A. Eames won the gold medal for Men's Foil, while the Men's Foil Team collected the bronze award. The Royal Belfast Academical Institute is easily the leading Irish fencing school and has achieved notable success in the Public Schools' Championships, winning the Graham-Bartlett Cup in 1971; in 1974 S. Carson won both foil and sabre events.

Novice. In the technical sense of A.F.A. regulations, a fencer who has never reached the final or semi-final of certain important competitions, fenced for his country or previously won the Novices' Championship.

Octave. The position and parry protecting the low outside line, or lower right-hand side of the fencer's target, and one of the last to be defined and adopted. In fact, the first recorded use of this term appears to be in a work by Daniel O'Sullivan, *L'Escrime Pratique*, which appeared in 1765. There is some evidence to suggest that, for a short time, the term *quinte* was occasionally used. Previously, *seconde* had been employed. In all these cases, and *octave* is no exception today, the hand is breast-high and the point directed downwards, to about the level of the adversary's knees. The real distinction between *octave* and its predecessor *seconde*, lies in the fact that in the former case, the hand is supinated, not pronated.

Octave, Bind of. Strictly speaking, the bind is the *prise-de-fer* which transports the adversary's blade diagonally across the target from high to low line or vice versa; hence the bind of *octave* should in theory start from the low line and finish in an engagement of *quarte*. However, just as Professor Crosnier speaks of a *croisé* of *octave* which, starting in the high line never results in the executant taking his opponent's blade into a fully covered *quarte* position, so he applies the term 'bind of *octave*' to an almost precisely similar action.

The distinction is, that the *croisé* of *octave* (at any rate, in relation to épée fencing) generally precedes a riposte, or is executed simultaneously with it as part of a time-hitting action. At épée again, binds and envelopments are generally preferred as preparations of attack. So, by a process of association, the term 'bind of *octave*' is used when this specialised action precedes an attack.

Octave, Croisé of. Properly speak-

The parry of Octave — *the hand much higher than today. (From Danet.)*

ing, the *croisé* is that form of *prise-de-fer* whereby the opponent's blade is forced down from high to low line on the same side of the target. The movement that terminates in *octave* starts in *sixte* and is termed the *croisé* of *sixte*. The action is not performed in an upward direction, so strictly speaking there can be no such thing as a *croisé* of *octave*. Professor Crosnier, however, employs the term to describe the action where, when the opponent's stop-hit has been into the *quarte* line, the attacker continues his lunge, but simultaneously brings his blade over his adversary's and takes it down and out into *octave*, placing his point while the blades are still in contact. This might appear to some to resemble the traditional bind; but the blades do not, in this case, travel right out into *quarte* to allow the diagonal movement down and across the target characteristic of the bind proper.

Offensive-Defence is the use of the counter-attack, by means of the stop-hit and time-hit. They are defensive in so far as they can only be executed when the opponent prepares, or in-

itiates, an attack; offensive, since the aim is to register a hit on the opponent.

Offensive-Defensive Position. A blade position when on guard, much favoured by sabreurs. The sword-hand is level with the right breast and in pronation, the arm slightly bent at the elbow. The blade slants slightly forward, cutting edge directed at the opponent's target, with the point about on a level with his mask and on his right-hand side.

Offredy, Miss T.M. A Lady International Foil Champion in 1961 and 1962.

Oldcorn, R. captained the British team at the controversial Moscow Olympics of 1980. He did not appear to enjoy the best of luck in the big competitions, coming second in the Sabre Championship of 1966, second in the Corble Cup in 1967, and was runner-up no fewer than three times in the Cole Cup (1965-6-7).

Olivier. A successful master of the eighteenth century who trained in

Paris but who taught in London, in St Dunstan's Court off Fleet Street. He stressed the value of the circular or counter parry and was closely connected with the fencers of the Inns of Court.

On Guard. The basic position adopted until very recently by almost all modern fencers is essentially the classic attitude devised by the late seventeenth-century school of small-sword play; though, according to the old illustrations, the knees then were considerably less bent than they are (or should be) today. Also, the trunk then was inclined appreciably backwards, as might be expected in an age when the duellist was ever-conscious of the need to keep his face and eyes away from his enemy's blade, and when even in the fencing lesson, the mask had not come into general use. As late as the 1940s, some masters were still insisting that the weight should be kept firmly on the rear foot. Then, in the sixties, there was a tendency to incline the trunk forward from the hips, in order to promote speed and aggression.

For some years there has been fairly general agreement, at least among the followers of Crosnier and the French school, that the chest and stomach should be half-turned towards the adversary, any disadvantage arising from this partial exposure of the target being more than compensated for by the far greater comfort of the posture. In contrast, the modern Italian school for long insisted that the line of the shoulders, instead of being at an angle of approximately forty-five degrees to the *piste*, must be practically parallel to it, so that the target area is almost entirely effaced and the opponent can see little or nothing of it; but this necessitates a very cramped, unnatural position, and in order to keep the

128

leading knee pointing straight ahead, ready for a correct lunge, infinite strain and muscle fatigue is involved.

Many variations of the on-guard position have been recommended over the years:

1) The Italian guard (classical). The sword-arm straight, or almost straight, knees slightly bent, the blade in various positions. Capo Ferro advocated a basic guard in *terza* (*tierce*).

2) The Spanish guard (classical). In the sixteenth and seventeenth centuries, the Spaniards cultivated a very upright position, knees straight, left arm down by the side, sword-arm fully extended. It was in this posture that they gyrated solemnly round the 'Mysterious Circle' of Narvaez and Thibaust.

3) The Portuguese guard. According to McBane, the sword-hand was placed outside the thigh, with the point almost touching the ground. Aylward, however, in *The English Master of Arms*, avers that McBane witnessed this unfamiliar position in the Low Countries, not in Portugal itself.

4) The Spanish guard (eighteenth century). This was after the indigenous Spanish school had really been abandoned in favour of an approximation of the French. The knees were bent, but the feet were brought much closer together than in the French school. The rear upper arm was maintained at shoulder level and at right angles to the line of attack; the rear forearm slanted forward towards the ground at an angle of about forty-five degrees, with the palm facing downwards. The sword-arm was almost straight, the hand in pronation and the blade horizontal.

5) The Italian guard (eighteenth century). The feet closer together than the French, the rear forearm angulated forward, palm downwards.

6) The German guard (eighteenth century). According to Danet's illustration, the weight far more on the front foot than in the rival schools. The sword-hand is pronated and head-high, with the point directed downwards. The rear arm is in a very similar position to that affected by the contemporary Spanish school; apparently the idea was that the unarmed hand might still, in a duel, be of some service in parrying, or warding off a *remise* after a successful parry.

On-Guard Lines. These lines are drawn at right-angles to the *piste*, two metres either side of the centre line. Fencers must remain behind the one on their side until the command 'Play', or 'Allez', is given, when they may advance to cross swords with their opponent.

One-Two. (See Compound Attack.)

One-Two on the Change. (See Compound Attack.)

One-Two and Counter-Disengage. A fairly elaborate compound attack, deceiving the simple and circular parries. The opponent's simple parry is deceived by the feint of one-two; his attempt to find the second feint of disengagement (the 'two') with a circular parry is in turn deceived by a counter-disengagement. This attack could be classified as a feint of disengagement and *doublé*.

One-Two-Three. (See Compound Attack.)

One-Two-Three on the Change. (See Compound Attack.)

Open-Eyes Position. A slang term for the offensive-defensive position at sabre; current mainly in the north of England.

The Spanish guard (right) opposed by the French guard (from Danet).

Opposition. To attack with opposition is to attack while maintaining a contact with the opponent's blade somewhat stronger than a mere engagement. There can be no hard-and-fast rule, but the strength should probably be just enough to carry the defender's blade slightly out of line, without being considerable enough to force it into a new line altogether.

It is possible to parry and riposte with opposition in the same way; but in this case the term is often used to indicate a mere contact or engagement of the blades, in contrast to the detached parry and riposte.

We sometimes hear of an engagement with opposition. This is engaging and holding the opponent's blade rather more firmly than is usual.

D'Oriola, Christian. The leading foilist in the world in the period immediately following the Second World War. A left-hander, he was noted for his immensely long, supple lunge. He won two Olympic gold medals (1952 and 1956) and a silver medal in 1948. He was World Champion in 1947 and 1949, again in 1953 and 1954, and runner-up in 1948 and 1955. In other words, he was effectively World Champion on no fewer than six occasions, a record never previously equalled and almost certainly never to be surpassed.

Orleans, Philippe de France, Duc d' became Regent of France (1715) on the death of his uncle, Louis XIV, on behalf of the latter's great-grandson, Louis XV. Exceptionally gifted, he exhibited talent as a musician, writer, painter, chemist and soldier. Like every aristocrat of the *ancien régime*, he showed courage under fire and particularly distinguished himself with the Life Guards at Neerwinden (1693). From the moment he assumed office, it became abundantly clear that the strait-laced *régime* of Louis XIV's last days was a thing of the past. Not only did he evince scant respect for the niceties of court etiquette and dress, but he had early shown his promise by becoming the father of an illegitimate child at fourteen; and at the age of forty, as regent, he abandoned himself to an unbroken round of debauchery and scandalous nocturnal adventures in the byways of Paris in the style of Haroun-al-Raschid or Prince Florizel. He was very accessible to all, but those who caught him on the morrow of a particularly heavy night, might find themselves grossly insulted. He officially retired at nine in the evening, no matter what the state of public affairs, to his select circle of debauched cronies, where men and women of the highest rank mingled on equal terms with prostitutes, eccentric foreigners and actors, a strong head for drink and a brazen wit being the sole qualifications for admission. Physically gruelling though all this may have been, it was doubtless welcome enough to many of those who remembered the gruesomely formal and refined entertainments relentlessly provided by Louis XIV.

It is hardly surprising that in this lax atmosphere, duelling recovered much of its old popularity and numerous encounters occurred in broad daylight in the centre of Paris, and in one case, the Palace itself. The penalties were either derisory or non-existent, the Court of Honour, as often as not, declining to intervene on one pretext or another; while according to the *Secret Memoirs* of Duclos, the Duke thoroughly approved of the practice and had been overheard to say, that at the end of the previous reign, duelling had gone too much out of fashion.

Orthopaedic Grip. A grip, or handle of a weapon, moulded to fit the user's hand and fingers. It is so-called because, when originally introduced, it was for the benefit of those whose hands were in some way deformed or mutilated. Subsequently, the idea was seized upon with avidity by all who found the French grip and technique complex and troublesome, or who affirmed that they could thus obtain more strength in their parries and attacks on their adversaries' blades. The invention was anathema to the older school of foilists, because, of course, it militated almost entirely against anything in the nature of finger-play. So far, the orthopaedic grip has been confined to the foil and épée, it being impossible to adapt it to the sabre without abandoning altogether the modern wrist-and-finger technique and reverting to the older cut delivered from the elbow.

The chief varieties of the orthopaedic grip at present in use are the Crosse, Contine, Gardère, Dos Santos, Hern, Pistol and *Spada*, or traditional Italian foil grip, which may fairly be said to have been the progenitor of this monstrous brood.

Osric. The 'fantastical courtier' in Shakespeare's *Hamlet*, ever-memorable for his off-handedly confident judgements – 'A hit – a very palpable hit.' He presided at the fencing match between Hamlet and Laertes, in which the latter substituted a poisoned sharp for a foil. Although Hamlet was mortally wounded thereby, the ensuing close-quarter combat resulted in an exchange of weapons so that Laertes, to quote his own words, 'was justly killed by his own treachery'. (Act V, Sc.ii.)

Outside Lines. The lines, or positions, protecting the fencer's right-hand side; *sixte* (*tierce*) high, *octave* (*seconde*) low.

Pallavicini, Morsicato. A seventeenth-century Italian master from whose writings several interesting facts emerge. Firstly, the Spanish masters of that day still enjoyed an absolute monopoly in their country, every one of them having to be recognised by a General Examiner resi-

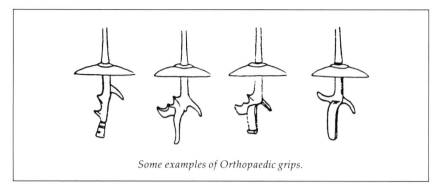

Some examples of Orthopaedic grips.

dent in Madrid. Secondly, he mentions practice weapons with a leather button on the point, about the size of a musket ball, and asserts that some fencers were in the habit of using cardboard *plastrons* to protect themselves during practice. A further deduction that can be made is that the weight of the sword was constantly decreasing during this period. Pallavicini speaks of time-thrusts (i.e., stop-hits) without either opposition or binding of the opponent's weapon.

Parade. The French term for a parry.

Parade de Cercle. Not the same thing as the circular (counter) parry, nor the misleadingly named *cercle* (*quarte* to *septime*), really the semi-circular parry. As described by Danet, it was a sweeping parry going through all lines and guaranteed (so it was hoped) to find the opposing blade on all thrusts or feints, in a style akin to the universal parry. De Liancour termed it the *parade en forme de cercle*, but considered it risky.

Parade en Contre Dégageant. Literally, 'parry in counter-disengagement'; in effect, merely the circular (counter) parry against an attack by disengagement.

Parade de Pointe Volante (from Danet).

Parry of prime *(from Barbasetti).*   *Parry of* seconde *(from Barbasetti).*

Parade de Pointe Volante. A spectacular parry mentioned by Danet and others, though no reference to it is made after the Second World War. The defender's blade was slightly retracted in the act of parrying and simultaneously passed over the opponent's blade for a riposte by cut-over. Others have defined it as a parry composed of a combined beat and backward glide, followed by a cut-over riposte. It was recommended as useful against an opponent who kept his arm and blade pressing, with stiff opposition, on one's own weapon.

Parade au Tac. (See Parry *de Tac*.)

Paradoxes of Defence. (See Silver.)

Parata, (It.). Parry.

Parata Di Pico, (It.). Parry *de tac*.

Pareur. Parryer. A fencer who relies mainly on defence.

Parise, Masaniello. A late nineteenth-century Italian master, he was the mouthpiece of the so-called Neapolitan or south Italian school which deplored the academic approach to fencing, eschewing in particular the multiple-feint attacks favoured by masters in the north of the country, and upholding a down-to-earth system much more closely allied to the conditions of the duelling ground. Neither did he by any means accept all the sabre *maestro* Radaelli's principles, and tried to introduce more wrist-play into this branch of fencing.

Parry. The defensive action whereby the attacker's blade is deflected, or in the case of a sabre cut, is blocked, by the inter-position of the defender's weapon. The principle of defence common to all these weapons is the opposition of the defender's *forte* to the attacker's *foible*.

It was not until well into the seventeenth century that parries were formally differentiated from positions and *bottes* (attacks). The reason is not difficult to find; earlier on, defence had been conducted largely by time-thrusts (covered stop-hits) and even the much lighter transition rapier of the late seventeenth century was best adapted to simple parries, which are identical to the basic positions of the blade (*quarte*, *sixte*, etc). The increasing lightness of the small-sword and the introduction during the course of the eighteenth century of the light practice foil, allowed a much greater use of the semi-circular and the full circular parry.

Parries today are of three types. First, there is the simple or instinctive parry, the blade moving in the most direct path to meet the attack (e.g. from *sixte* to *quarte* or vice versa). Secondly, there is the semi-circular or half-circular parry. Here the point of the weapon describes a semi-circle in the air, generally passing over the adversary's thrust, from high to low line (e.g. *sixte* to *octave*). The semi-circular parry, according to the French school, must always terminate on the same side of the target, that is to say, starting from *quarte*, for example, the blade must finish in *septime*.

Last, but not least in importance, is the circular or counter parry. In this case the defender, dropping his point and blade beneath the adversary's weapon, collects the latter and deflects it safely outside the target. Counter of *sixte* is executed clockwise, counter of *quarte* anti-clockwise. From the low-line positions of *septime* and *octave*, the direction is clockwise and anti-clockwise respectively and naturally, in both these cases, the parry goes over, not under, the attacking blade.

The reason why the slightly misleading term 'counter' parry has for so long been regarded as synonomous with 'circular' parry, apparently stems from the fact that it is executed against (*contre*, or *contra*) the opponent's disengagement.

Although the circular parry was

131

generally considered to be one of the distinctive features of the classical French school, it was supposed by some, using the slightly heavier weapon of the seventeenth century, to involve a high degree of risk, and several prominent masters of that day, notably La Tousche and Liancourt, eschewed its use.

Parry by Distance. To step back out of reach of the attacker's blade, without the use of one's own weapon.

Parry by Giving the Blade. (See Ceding Parry.)

Parry by Half-Counter. The half-circular parry as interpreted by the Italo-Hungarian school; that is to say, it is carried diagonally across the defender's body, from *quarte* to *octave* or *seconde* and vice versa, or from *tierce* or *sixte* to *septime* and vice versa.

Parry by Opposition. To parry and maintain blade contact, as opposed to the parry by detachment. With strong opposition, it is the answer to an attack, a riposte preceded by a *prise-de-fer*.

Parry with the Point. To parry with the point threatening the opponent's target and well in line.

Parry de Tac. A beat parry or parry by detachment, so-called from the sharp, incisive sound produced when properly executed.

Parry by Yielding. (See Ceding Parry.)

Parrying Oneself. Novices or poor fencers are often very slow to parry and accordingly fail to respond to feints. An attacker, therefore, who makes a lightning feint followed by a switch of direction may simply hit

the opponent's blade which has never moved away from its original position. The solution is to reduce the cadence, or better still, resort to well-timed simple attacks when the superiority in sheer speed should be sufficient to ensure success.

Pas d'Ane Rings. Until the eighteenth century, the hilt inside the guard incorporated a metallic construction rather like a pair of spectacles through which the first and second fingers could be passed. In the case of a *désarmement*, the chance of broken fingers must have been great. During the course of the eighteenth century, the orthodox foil grip that we know today was adopted, with the top sections of the first and second fingers closing on the inner surface of the handle; but even so, in many small-swords, two vestigial rings were still included, although they were so minute that it would have been impossible to use them. Translated literally, *pas d'âne* means 'donkey's step'; precisely why such a term should ever have been coined remains a mystery, though some commentators have professed to see a resemblance between the rings and the hoof-marks of a donkey. According to La Tousche, the *pas d'*

ânes are the parts of the butterfly-shaped shell or guard, either side the handle.

Pasada, (Span.). A step of about two feet.

Pasada Doble, (Span.). Two steps, with feet crossed alternately.

Pasada Simple, (Span.). A single step of about the above length.

Pass. 1) A method of advancing and retiring, an alternative to the present fencing step, and also employed, before and long after the invention of the lunge, as a means of shortening the measure so as to deliver the attack. The rear leg was moved forward in front of the leading leg, which, if necessary, was then advanced again, so that the feet resumed, relatively, their original positions. When retiring, the process was, of course, reversed. Rather strangely, the action retained its popularity until well into the eighteenth century, although by that time the modern footwork was perfectly well known.

2) To attack the opponent on the side of his blade opposite to that on which the attacker's blade originally

The Pass (from Labat).

was, generally executed by means of a disengagement. Some authorities distinguish between 'passing' the blade (that is, disengaging from a *quarte* engagement into *sixte*) and 'slipping' the blade (disengaging from a *sixte* engagement into *quarte*). The latter is the easier and faster action, as the opponent's sword-arm does not have to be circumvented.

Passata, (It.). The pass.

Passata Sotto, (It.). A stop-hit in the low line. The whole body is dropped under the opponent's blade and the left leg is thrown diagonally across the line of attack to the executant's right, while he supports himself on the ground with his left hand. Frowned on by severe purists and nerve-ridden utilitarians alike, it would be regrettable if it ever disappeared entirely from the repertoire. The writer has seen it done successfully not so long ago. In the presence of an audience, it brings down the house and the effect on the victim can be imagined.

Passé. A *passé* attack is one in which the blade slides along some part of the opponent's body without the point fixing. No hit can be scored with such an attack, either on or off target and the bout should not be halted, as neither the foil nor the épée is an edged weapon. Even at sabre, either a point attack must fix properly, or a perceptible cut as such is essential; it is not sufficient to push or place the edge on the target.

Passé Feint. A *passé* feint is a blade movement designed to draw a reaction from the opponent, without, however, simulating an attack; as, e.g., an engagement, a pressure, or a light *froissement*.

Passement. A beat.

The Passata Sotto (from Barbasetti).

Passer Dessous. (See Passata Sotto.)

Passere. Described in the *Pallas Armata* as a one-two, from high to low line.

Passive Control is when the opponent is 'stealing distance', i.e., by subtle variations of footwork attempting to come threateningly close without this being realised; the intended victim, however, being well aware of the intention, deliberately allows his opponent to do so, in order to exploit the situation for his own purposes.

Passive Defence or Distance. To defend oneself by stepping back without a parry.

Passo Obliquo, (It.). A step taken diagonally away from the line of attack.

Passo Recto, (It.). A step forward to close the measure.

Patiente, (It.). On the defensive.

Patinando, (It.). A quick step forward, instantly followed by a lunge.

Patrenostrier. A late sixteenth-century Italian master whose influence was, upon the whole, exerted in favour of the greater simplification

already becoming noticeable about that time. For instance, he was in favour of reducing the basic guards to two only – *tierce* and *quarte*. He was also supposed to have been the first master to speak of the *filo* or *coulé*.

Paukerei. The duelling of the German students. 'A disjointed type of fencing suited to all kinds of drunken brawls.' (Barbasetti.)

Paul, B. The son of René Paul, he displayed the inherited ability at foil characteristic of his family. He was Men's Foil Champion in 1975, 1979 and 1980; second in 1971 (to his brother Graham) and second again in 1977. He won the Coronation Cup in 1973 and was second in the Men's Foil at the Commonwealth Games of 1970.

Paul, G. Brother of the above, another outstanding foilist and prolific trophy-winner. He was Men's Foil Champion in 1966, 1968, 1971 and 1973; second to his brother Barry in 1975 (thus exactly reversing the result of 1971) and second again in 1978. He won both the Emrys Lloyd Cup and the Coronation Cup in 1974; in the competitions for the latter, he also won in 1976 and was second on four occasions (1967, 1970, 1972, 1977). With the épée, he was

133

Stephen Paul on his way to victory against Evoquoz of Switzerland in the final of the Challenge Martini.

almost equally formidable. He was British Champion in 1969 and 1971, runner-up in 1966 and 1970 and second in the Epée Club Cup in 1974.

Paul, Raymond. The brother of René and another brilliant member of the Paul dynasty. He won the Men's Foil Championship four times (1953, 1955, 1957, 1958) and was second on five occasions (1951, 1952, 1954, 1956, 1959). The Emrys Lloyd Cup was his five times (1951, 1952, 1954, 1960, 1963), the Coronation Cup three times (1955, 1958, 1960) and he won the gold medal for Men's Foil at the Commonwealth Games of 1958.

Paul, René. The son of 'Papa' Paul, his exploits with the foil were legendary. He was five times Men's Foil Champion (1947, 1949, 1950, 1956, 1962) and second in 1948 and 1961. He won the Coronation Cup three

134

years running (1950-51-52), four times in all (again in 1954), an achievement only equalled by M Breckin. He was the winner of the Emrys Lloyd Cup on four occasions (1955, 1957, 1958, 1959) and second in 1951. He came first in the Men's Foil at the Commonwealth Games of 1954. At épée, he was good enough to take third place once or twice in the major competitions, and was also a successful sabreur at club level for Salle Paul.

Paul, S. The son of Raymond and another younger member of the most dominating family in the history of British fencing. He was British Epée Champion in 1980, won the Miller-Hallet competition in the same year, and in 1981 became only the second Englishman to win the Martini Epée Competition, to the unbounded delight of the fencing fraternity in general and the Paul

family in particular.

Pauleons Ladies. The ladies' team of Salle Paul. They never won the Martin Edmunds Cup, but had five seconds.

Paurnfeindt, Andreas. The German author of the oldest printed book on fencing known to exist (1516). In it he gives earnest and doubtless useful advice on how to mangle one's opponent with a great variety of bladed weapons.

Pelling, A.E. was a very well-known swordsman for a decade or so either side of the Second World War. He was British Epée Champion in 1933, 1934 and 1951, coming second in 1928 and second in the Miller-Hallett Competition of 1933. He held his place in the national Epée Team for the remarkable space of twenty years (1928-48).

Pelling, J.A. The son of the above, he was for a long time coached and taught by his father. Such an arrangement, not always to be recommended, was in this case attended by the happiest results, for John Pelling enjoyed a career as distinguished as that of his father. Twice he was Epée Champion (1961, 1965), second in 1969 and twice he was runner-up in the Miller-Hallet Competition (1961 and 1964). An Epée International from 1957 to 1967, he perhaps gained his greatest fame as a member of the great teams which came second in the Rome Olympics of 1960 and the World Championships at Paris in 1965. In 1962 he took the silver medal for épée in the Commonwealth Games. It was most unfortunate that the claims of his profession compelled his too early retirement from first-class fencing.

Pepys, Samuel. Of all historical characters, Pepys must be the best known to posterity. Never intending his diary for publication, he was disarmingly unselfconscious. The reader is familiar with every quirk of his character, with his greed (the diary is full of menus), his eye for the opposite sex, his matrimonial relations, generally somewhat ruffled, his naive satisfaction at his gradual rise to eminence and accumulation of a modest fortune. Yet we are wrong to suppose him a mere figure of fun; for although the famous diary was his claim to enduring literary fame, it was not in fact the central or vital thing in his life. He discontinued it, to save the strain on his eyes, when only thirty-six and the bulk of his real achievements still lay ahead. His connection with the Earl of Sandwich having gained him a post in the naval administration, he became, in 1673, secretary to the Admiralty and a member of Parlia-

Trade card of Pepys's Sword-cutler.

ment. He was undoubtedly a first-class administrator, typical of our Civil Service in its better days and it is generally agreed that he established the basis for the matchless and professional Royal Navy of the eighteenth and subsequent centuries. However, his official duties so closely associated him with the House of Stuart and in particular its last representative, James II – Pepys was more than once accused of turning Catholic – that at the Glorious Revolution he was obliged to leave the public service and he spent his last years amassing and arranging the great library which bears his name and is housed at his old college, Magdalene, Cambridge.

Pepys, an inveterate theatre-goer, also visited the Bear-Garden more than once to witness the professional prize-fights. On 1 June, 1663, he vividly describes the first contest at which he was present, a gory encounter between Matthews and Westwicke. They fought each other at no less than eight different weapons, three bouts at each; the diarist informs us that as it was no mere exhibition match, but the upshot of some private dispute, 'they did it in good earnest', the swords being almost as sharp as those used in ordinary combat. It is therefore not surprising to learn that West-wicke was 'all over blood' and 'in a sad pickle'. That 'a deal of money was flung to them on the stage between every bout', to quote Pepys's words, may have been some consolation to him; at any rate, Pepys described himself as 'well pleased with the sight'.

On two other occasions, 27 May, 1667 and 9 September of the same year, Pepys describes contests between a butcher and a waterman in the one case and another butcher and a shoemaker in the other, as 'pleasant to see' and 'the sport very good'; though in the second entry, Pepys admits that he was so ashamed to be seen in such surroundings that he kept his face buried in his cloak. Once more, he was tempted back to the Bear-Garden, on 12 April, 1669; but as on this occasion, he could only report that 'a country fellow' had 'soundly beat' a soldier and 'cut him all over the head', it may be that the entertainment provided was less dramatic and bloody than previously. Nevertheless, Pepys declares himself to have been 'mightily pleased'.

Although Pepys was an extremely brave man, remaining in London throughout the Plague to discharge his official business, he was never, so far as is known, involved in a duel; but not surprisingly, the diary contains a number of references to the brawls and duels endemic at the time. The entry of 29 July 1667 refers to a stupid quarrel, arising out of nothing, between Sir Henry Bellassis and Mr Tom Porter, who were, in reality, exceedingly good friends. Both were wounded, Bellassis mortally. Pepys was shocked. 'A fine example! And Bellassis a Parliament-man too!' he writes. It is impossible not to be moved by Bellassis's generous farewell to his opponent; he hoped he would avoid any untoward repercussions and that he would 'make shift to stand on my legs' until the victor had effected a discreet retirement from the scene.

A more famous duel, that between the Duke of Buckingham and the Earl of Shrewsbury, is reported on 17 January of the following year. 'This will make the world think the King hath good councillors about him' comments Pepys sarcastically, adding that the House was talking of nothing else and that he himself hoped that the outcome would be the disgrace of the Duke and his replacement by a worthier member of the government.

Perigal, Mme. A. was well known as one of the very few ladies teaching fencing between the wars. She taught at Salle Gravé and gave lessons, not only at various girls' schools, but privately in her own home.

Perigord. The most illustrious fencing master (entirely fictional) in the famous film *Scaramouche*, set in the early stages of the French Revolution. The character does not appear in Sabatini's book on which the film was based. 'Perigord of Paris', the 'Master of all Masters', was a name uttered in tones of hushed respect; though in the scene actually laid in his salle, his instruction was largely confined to advising his pupils to

136

'fence up here' (indicating his head) 'and not down there' (pointing to his heart). It is not unlikely that many a reputation, not necessarily confined to the realms of fiction, has been similarly based on such oracular generalisations.

Perinat, Don Juan Nicholas. A late eighteenth-century Spanish master. His importance lies in the fact that he was the first of his countrymen to accept that the foil and the sabre are two entirely different weapons – in other words, even in conservative Spain, the rapier had lost its cutting capacity and evolved into the small-sword. Hence, during the nineteenth century, the way was clear for the entire abandonment of the indigenous school dating back to Narvaez and Thibaust, and the adoption, with some slight modifications, of the French and neo-Italian systems.

Peso, (It.). The balance of the weapon.

Philbin, J. A prominent sabreur of the seventies and early eighties. Sabre Champion four times (1976, 1977, 1978 and 1981), he was second in 1974 and 1979. In the Corble Cup, he was victorious three times (1977, 1979, 1981) and was second to R. Cohen three years running (1978-9-80).

Philip IV, King of Spain 1621-1665, had the misfortune to be called on to face problems that might have proved insoluble even by a superman. Massive inflation and an obstinate determination to persevere with the war against the Dutch and the Protestants in Germany led to the ruin and de-population of the ancient Kingdom of Castile where Philip was king and in a position to impose taxation and levy troops. Elsewhere in the peninsula, in the

Kingdoms of Aragon and Portugal and the counties of Catalonia and Valencia, he was entangled in a network of medieval privileges, liberties and constitutional rights which the Cortes were bent on defending, and received but grudging and half-hearted support. Philip, a magnificent horseman and the friend and patron of Velasquez could seldom be persuaded to attend to the details of business. In addition, his chief minister, the Count-Duke Olivares, was careful to keep him immersed in an endless round of bull-fights, cane tourneys, gorgeously disreputable carnivals and extempore comedies at the palace of Buen Retiro, besides accompanying him in the search for nocturnal adventure in the streets of the capital, rather in the style of the Caliph in the *Arabian Nights* or Robert Louis Stevenson's Prince Florizel.

The grandees and all the rest of the nobility imitated the lavish masquerades and prodigal expenditure of their sovereign, if not his periodic fits of remorse and religious melancholia. As well as this, the court and its environs were the centre of endless scandals, intrigues, affrays and duels. In 1635 the Marquis del Aguila insulted and struck Don Juan de Herrera in the theatre of Buen Retiro, the latter drawing his sword in the presence of the King, a capital offence. Both the offenders fled, de Herrera subsequently issuing a public challenge to the Marquis from Switzerland, whither he had made good his escape. Then, shortly afterwards, trouble broke out at a rehearsal, again at Buen Retiro. A mob of spectators erupted onto the ground occupied by the mounted performers, one of whom, Nicholas Spinola, son of the great General, took great exception to being ordered away by one Zapata, Lieutenant of the Guard. Spinola waited outside for his enemy, more high words passed, with the result that Zapata snatched up a sword and set on his opponent, but before a fatality could occur the pair were separated by the bystanders.

It is not surprising that Philip IV, like a later monarch, decided that something must be done. The council recommended much heavier penalties for duelling and the extraordinary suggestion was also made that in future such cases should be referred to the Inquisition. But before either proposal was implemented it was agreed that the opinion of the most senior and respected army officers should be sought. They were considered to be infallible on all points of honour and related matters; but unfortunately, nearly all were then serving with the Cardinal Infante Ferdinand in Flanders. It is by no means certain that the relevant papers even reached them; if they did, no record exists of a reply ever having been received. Characteristically, the whole affair languished and duelling among the stiff-necked grandees and *hidalgos* continued much as before.

Phrase or Phrase d'Armes. A sequence of blade actions, with or without movements of the feet. Ideally, a phrase includes an attack, a riposte and at least one counter-riposte, with perhaps a preparation of the attack and at some stage a *prise-de-fer* as well. However, the long, elaborate phrases at foil, premeditated, executed with technique and style and aiming at a successfully contrived climax, are now largely a thing of the past.

Picking. Making numerous quick, sharp stabs at the forearm and wrist with the épée.

Pied Ferme, A. With feet in place, in the on-guard stance; a phrase generally applied to the bygone technique of compound attacks, when the feint, or feints, were delivered, and the opponent's parry or parries drawn, *before* the leading foot moved into the lunge. Some authorities use the preposition *au* not *à*, apparently the terms are employed indifferently. Larousse, however, gives *de*.

Pilbrow, A.G. An international intimately associated with C.-L. de Beaumont in the British team and at the London Fencing Club. In the mid thirties he was regarded as Britain's leading sabreur. He was four times champion (1932, 1935, 1938 and 1950) and second on as many occasions (1933, 1947, 1948, 1951). He never won the Corble Cup (he was second in 1950) but he gained a gold medal for sabre at the Commonwealth Games of 1950 in Auckland.

Pini, Eugenio. A well-known Italian master, reputed to be a stern perfectionist. On visiting Paris in 1895 for a Masters' Competition, he was the occasion of a duel between two French masters, Vigeant and Rue. He took part in a celebrated match between the leading Italian and French masters in London in 1902, in which the latter had the best of it, though Kirchoffer suffered so severely at Pini's hands that he was ordered 'absolute repose for several days', sustaining injuries to his groin and shoulder, to say nothing of a bruised face and a detached thumb-nail. Pini subsequently taught in the Argentine. He was a great exponent of elaborate compound attacks incorporating triple feints.

Pion. A French firm well known for the excellent quality of their sword-blades. These highly valued articles were obtainable in their shop in the *Place de la Concorde*.

Pirouette. A sudden spin through one hundred and eighty degrees, in which the back was turned on the opponent and the riposte delivered from behind the back or even over the shoulder. Said to have been popularised originally by the Hungarians, it has now been declared illegal.

Piste. The strip of earth, stone, linoleum, cork or rubber on which fencing takes place. The *piste* is always 1.8 to 2 metres wide, but its length varies according to the weapon being used. The foil *piste* is 14 metres long and it is this which is actually used for sabre and épée; but for these two weapons it is increased in theory to 18 metres by allowing the fencer to retreat once to the rear limit without penalty. At épée and sabre he is halted when his back foot reaches the rear limit. He is then replaced on his 'warning line', 2 metres from the end. Only if he then retreats with both feet over the rear limit without first advancing with front foot to the centre line, does he incur a penalty hit at épée; at sabre the warning holds until the next valid hit wherever he goes.

At foil, the warning line is only 1 metre from the rear limit and the fencer is halted and warned immediately he reaches it. As at épée, he concedes a penalty hit if he then crosses the rear limit without first advancing with front foot to the centre line. If he succeeds in doing this, he receives another warning next time he reaches the warning line; otherwise, he must decide for himself exactly where he is and if he is at risk.

Less serious penalties are incurred by crossing the side limits; overstepping these with both feet results in a loss of ground only (2 metres at sabre and épée, 1 metre at foil) unless it was done deliberately to avoid being hit. Following a severe warning for this offence, its repetition in the same bout results in a penalty hit. Should a fencer put one foot only over the line, the bout is halted and the competitors resume play in the same place, but on the central line of the *piste* – no penalty of any sort is imposed.

At each end of the *piste* there should be an extension of at least 1.5 metres for purposes of safety. Important competitions often take place on a raised *piste*, which must not be more than half a metre above the level on which the president stands.

The present measurements of the *piste* have not always obtained. Formerly, the foil *piste* was only 12 metres and the *pistes* for épée and sabre as much as 24 metres. As very few buildings could accommodate so considerable a length, these two weapons were in practice fought on a 14-metre strip. A fencer was allowed to retreat once right over the rear limit – this was called 'once back' – after which the opponents returned to the on-guard lines. If the same fencer then retreated to the warning lines, 2 metres from the end, he was stopped and advised of his position. He was liable to a penalty hit if he then crossed the final limit. This arrangement allowed an effective retreating distance of 10 metres, the same as if the full 24 metres had in fact been used. The greater degree of mobility consequent on the general adoption of the electric foil made the standardisation of the 14-metre *piste* a matter both of sense and convenience.

Pistol Grip. A species of orthopaedic grip, so called because the various knobs and hooks on the handle of the weapon allow it to be held in much the same way as a pistol, the first two fingers fitting round a pro-
138

jection which might be regarded as equivalent to the trigger.

Plain Thrust. A term used by Sir William Hope to describe the practice lunge at a fixed target.

Planche. The same as the *piste*; the narrow, elongated rectangular strip which limits the fencer's movements.

Plane. A line of attack, or guard position, at sabre.

Plaque or Placed On. 1) When a thrust does not arrive properly, that is, roughly at right angles to the target, but is pushed or flipped on from the side, it is said to be *plaqué* or flat. Similarly to the *passé* blade, the judges should not signal a hit either on or off target, and the bout should not be halted, since a sharp point would in such cases inflict no injury. When electrical weapons are in use, there should be no problem, as the apparatus should not register if it is working properly. (Cp. Laid On.)
2) A seventeenth-century term for the guard.

Plastron. A protective pad, originally made of leather, now generally of foam-rubber or similar substance, worn over the chest by masters as protection against the endless hits received when giving lessons. Apart from occasional practice given to an experienced competitive fencer designed to increase his sheer speed, when the master may really try to parry, all movements and phrases, however complex, invariably terminate with the pupil being allowed to score a hit, to ensure accuracy of point and blade control.

Platform. The original name in Captain Hutton's rules for the *piste*. It

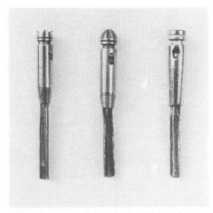

Development of electric épée Points from 1931.

had to be raised at least half an inch from the floor.

Plumet. Hope's term for the pommel.

Point. The tip of the blade, sharp in a duelling weapon. In the pre-electric foil, it was protected by a button. The electric varieties of both foil and épée have a spring-head which, when depressed, makes contact with the recording apparatus. The point of the fencing sabre is merely rebated.

Point of Balance. That part of the *forte* of the blade, some two or three inches below the guard, about which the weapon, when balanced on a finger, maintains its equilibrium.

Point Control. The ability to regulate the movements of the point accurately and place it on the exact part of the target desired. This is of ever-increasing importance, as the use of the electric weapons and recording apparatus allows angulated hits to be made on the flanks, shoulders and so forth, which might not have been seen by human judges.

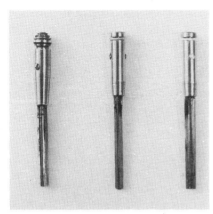

Development of electric foil Points from 1956.

Point, Control the. Nothing to do with point control, but a technical sixteenth-century term signifying the control, or displacement, of the opponent's point.

Pointe d'Arrêt. In the days of non-electric épée, it was often difficult to fix the point on the opponent's arm or wrist, particularly if his cuff was hard and shiny and the blade new and stiff. Accordingly, the *pointe d'arrêt*, a triple-pointed metal cap, was attached to the point instead of the button.

Pointe Volante, Parade de. (See Parade de Pointe Volante.)

Poker. Fencing slang for a weapon with a stiff, heavy blade, which does not bend when fixing on the target; in particular, applied derisively by traditionalists to the early electric foils which were much less flexible than the more refined variety of the weapon now in general use.

Polgar. (See Beke.)

Polytechnic F.C. was founded in 1883. Captain W.C. James, father of Mrs M. Glen-Haig, was a member in the inter-war years. In the 1950s the club was the largest in the country with the most extensive fixture list. There was a long line of distinguished masters – Professor Behmber taught from 1951 until his death, while Imregi attracted the leading sabreurs. Their ladies' team was particularly strong and won the team championships eleven times.

Pommeau, Pomo, (It.). **or Pommel**. The metal cap, in the old days often ornamental, which screws onto and locks in place the 'tang' of the blade, where the latter passes through and projects just beyond the top of the handle. The pommel, by its not inconsiderable weight, also serves to balance the blade.

Pool. Most competitions are based on the pool or group system, and only proceed to direct elimination in the final stages. Each member of a pool fences all the others; the minimum number is five and a minimum of three must be promoted. There must always be at least six in a final pool. Slightly different arrangements obtain in those cases, rare enough nowadays, when an épée competition for one hit only is in progress. For these, the reader is referred to the A.F.A. *Rules for Competitions*, as also for the arrangements for 'mixed' competitions, i.e., those including both pools and direct elimination.

Porthos. A leading character in *The Three Musketeers*, by Dumas.

Portuguese Foil. A name sometimes given to the Spanish foil.

Positions. Refer to the position of hand and blade at any given time and can be analysed on a dual basis:
1) The hand, which may be in pronation, supination, or any intermediate position and
2) The blade, which is generally the primary consideration when reference is made to a position.

The chief blade positions, which also correspond to the parries are:
1) *Quarte* – protecting the upper part of the trunk on the fencer's left-hand side, with the point raised.
2) *Sixte* – protecting the upper part of the trunk on the fencer's right-hand side, with point raised.
3) *Septime* – protecting the lower part of the trunk on the fencer's left-hand side, with point lowered.
4) *Octave* – protecting the lower part of the trunk on the fencer's right-hand side, with point lowered.

In addition, the other positions, once popular, but now used more rarely, at any rate at foil, are:
1) *Prime* – protecting the upper part of the target of the fencer's left, with hand shoulder high and point down.
2) *Seconde* – very similar to *octave*, but the hand is in pronation, not supination.
3) *Tierce* – similar to *sixte*, but again the hand is pronated, not supinated.
4) *Quinte* – a rather low *quarte*, but the hand is pronated and the point angulated outwards. It protects the lower part of the target and is really an instinctive and not entirely effective alternative to *septime*.

All the above applies to foil and épée, though it would indeed be remarkable to see an épéeist parrying *prime*. At sabre, *prime*, *seconde*, *tierce* and *quarte* are very approximately the same, but *quinte* protects the head from the downward cut. The sword-hand is on the fencer's right and the blade, just above the level of the head, is parallel with the ground. *Sixte* has almost vanished from the sabre repertoire, but was used occasionally to serve the same purpose as (sabre) *quinte*; the blade was in the same horizontal position, slightly more than head-high, but the hand, in complete supination, was most awkwardly placed on the fencer's left.

This section gives the contemporary classification; but although the positions in actual practice have always been much the same, it was long before their names were in any way standardised. In the Italo-Spanish schools of the sixteenth and seventeenth centuries, there was a bewildering variety of terminology. To some extent, this was accepted and perpetuated by the French; thus, late in the seventeenth and even into the eighteenth century, we still hear of 'quarte outside' (sixte) and seconde pour le dessus and seconde pour le dessous (tierce and our seconde respectively).

Quinte, septime and octave were the last positions to receive their modern nomenclature.

Postura, (It.). Position of the body.

Prelude, (U.S.). A preparation of attack.

Preparation of Attack. A movement of blade or foot, designed to prepare the way for an attack, either by displacing the opponent's blade from its line, or by obtaining a reaction from him. Preparations involving the use of the feet are normally used to close the fencing measure and come within attacking distance, although occasionally they may succeed in distracting the opponent's attention. Preparations may be classified as follows:
1) With the foot. Steps forward and back, jumps, balestras and so forth are of course included under this heading and a backward movement may well be used in order to tempt the opponent into incautiously advancing within attacking distance.
2) Prises-de-fer or takings of the blade.
140

a) Engagement
b) Change of Engagement
c) Bind
d) Croisé
e) Envelopement
(See under separate headings.)
3) Attacks on the blade.
a) Beat
b) Pressure
c) Froissement
(See under separate headings.)
Preparations of attack are used rather more frequently than used to be the case and some, particularly the beat and somewhat clawing half-pressure, half-engagement, seem to have become almost automatic. This doubtless arises from the fact that the average fencer today is more mobile than formerly and rather than wait and parry an attack, will retreat rapidly; hence the constant need to gain distance upon him and while this is being done, to occupy his attention with some action against his blade. (See also Compound and Double Preparations.)

Preparations of Defence. An ingenious and quite recent suggestion by Professor M. Law, of particular service to the fencer who, for whatever reason, relies mainly on defence. His idea is that the defender should deliberately invite attacks which he is mentally and physically ready to parry and therefore well-placed to execute a successful riposte. Among a wide variety of suggestions, the Professor mentions the beat or the attempted engagement, to draw in the first case, the return-beat and attack and in the second, the simple or compound attack, according to distance. He also advocates a partial or full extension of the sword-arm on the opponent's advance, to encourage the latter's beat or prise-de-fer, such an extension to be designated as the counter-preparation. All this, and the further possibilities arising

from its consideration, will certainly widen the defensive fencer's game and pose problems for his opponents.

Prese di Ferro, (It.). Blade contact, with generally hostile intention, much favoured by the Italian neo-classical school of the late nineteenth and early twentieth centuries.

Presentation of Cutting Edge. An essential preliminary of all sabre attacks is to turn or present the edge towards that part of the opponent's target which is to be attacked. This is done by rolling the handle in the fingers, while the arm is extending, so that the edge is presented at right angles to the target area.

President. The chief member of the jury. He it is who is in general control of every bout, starts and stops the play, enforces the rules and at foil and sabre, analyses each phrase that ends in a hit, and in the event of a double hit awards the priority, if possible, to one or other of the fencers. In the event of disagreement among the judges, or abstention by them, he may also have to decide on the validity or otherwise of a hit.

Press or Pressure. A preparation of attack. Pressure may be exerted on an opponent's blade after an engagement, either to deflect it, or to gain a reaction from it. The usual technique is a simultaneous flexing of the wrist and tightening of the last fingers.

Prévost, Camille. The son of Pierre Prévost, brought up in London, he returned to Paris as a professional master. His Théorie Pratique d'Escrime formed the basis of the section on fencing in the Badminton Library, the set of late nineteenth-century books professing to cover all games when played. Regarded as one of the great masters of his era, he was renowned as an academic purist of the foil.

Prévost, Pierre. A professor at the *Ecole Polytechnique* in Paris, he came to teach at London Fencing Club in 1850. Ten years later, he wrote the *Theory and Practice of Fencing*. He was all for simplicity, reducing the parries to four: *tierce, quarte,* half-circle (*septime*) and *seconde,* or more correctly *octave,* as all actions, both defensive and offensive, were to be performed with the hand in supination. He was an advocate of the pupil-teacher system, sorting his neophytes into four grades for mutual instruction – 'all under the supervision of the master' he adds, a trifle optimistically. Many have tried this and generally found it to be a recipe for pure disaster, as with very rare exceptions the pupil-teacher, though he may put the novice through the motions, cannot correct his mistakes. Meanwhile, the master, rushing headlong from one group to the next, cannot give proper attention to any.

Prima (It.). **or Prime.** The first position and parry, so called because it was supposed to be that which was instinctively assumed when the sword was whipped out of its sheath to meet a surprise attack. It protects the whole of the left-hand side of the body from the shoulder to the knee. The hand, in pronation, is in line with the left shoulder and on the same level; the elbow is no higher. The forearm should not be exactly at right angles to the upper arm, but slightly in advance, the blade slanting forward and downwards, not vertically – this is a beginner's mistake – but with the point directed rather below the level of the opponent's knee.

Castello often postulates its use

against the cut at head; though surely this would only prove effective against a substantially angulated attack, not the normal vertical cut. In reality, the parry of *prime* is the best defence against a sabre-cut directed downwards at the chest or left shoulder, but it does not seem to be used very much today. At foil, it has lately enjoyed something of a renaissance, both as a result of the close-quarter fighting which has become fashionable, and the observations thereon of Lukovitch, the Hungarian master.

Primary Parries. At sabre, *prime, seconde* and *quinte.*

Principle of Defence. At all weapons, the maxim when parrying is to deflect the attacker's blade by the opposition of the defender's *forte* to his *foible.*

Priority. In the event of each fencer hitting the other in the same period of fencing time, the hit is awarded according to a theoretical system of priority. The system is conventional and applies to foil and sabre only. (See Conventions.)

Prise-de-Fer. A preparation of attack, in English a 'taking-of-the-blade' by means of which the opponent's blade is forced away from its existing line and carried into a new one, thus at once controlling his blade and opening his target to an offensive action. The engagement and change of engagement are sometimes, perhaps dubiously, included in this category; the three main examples are the envelopement (circular), the bind (diagonally across the target area) and the *croisé* (from high to low line on the same side of the target). Further information is given under their separate headings.

A *prise-de-fer* can only be effective when the opponent's arm is ex-

tended with blade in line, as without suitable resistance the latter cannot be controlled and transported to a new position by the dominating opposition of *forte* to *foible.* The chances of successful execution are greatest when the opponent has a stiff arm and a strong wrist, or when he is attempting to renew his attack, or force his way through a parry; for the *prise-de-fer* may precede a riposte or counter-riposte just as well as an attack. Tactically, it will be found that the envelopement is most appropriate when the opponent's hand is relatively low; the bind and *croisé* when it is high.

The Hungarian terminology is somewhat different. (See Bind, Filo, Transfer.)

Prize-Fights. Public contests between professional swordsmen, which from the seventeenth century onwards, attracted large crowds. Generally speaking, the weapon employed was the backsword, which could inflict wounds of a satisfactorily grim appearance without being anything like as deadly as the thrusting rapier. There is some dispute as to whether the weapons used were sharp or not. On the whole, the weight of evidence is that they were. Pepys, giving a graphic account of one such contest (1 June, 1663), says that he tested one edge and 'found it to be very little, if at all, blunter on the edge than the common swords are'. M de Sorbière, however, a French visitor to England in the same year, describes the sword-and-buckler fights rather contemptuously; he suspected collusion and opined that the combatants gave up all too readily at the first sign of blood. Their blades, he avers, were blunted, though we learn from another source (M César de Saussure, visiting London in 1728-9) that the top six inches or so were 'razor-sharp'. De Sorbière does admit, however, that the adversaries dealt each other some tremendous blows. M de Rochefort, another French traveller and contemporary of Pepys, sides with de Saussure, recording with deep disapproval one occasion when both contestants were severely wounded. Misson, on the other hand, says in 1698 that the prize-fighters avoided wounding each other dangerously, but had to spill some blood to satisfy the crowd. Von Uffenbach, present in 1710 at the Bear-Garden, Hockley-in-the-Hole (Clerkenwell), where many of these spectacles took place, says that the swords in use were very broad, long, and 'uncommonly sharp'. Several other eyewitnesses give much the same impression; one Maguire was reported to have had his nose hacked clean off by Sutton in 1731. It would appear, however, that only the edge was used, not the far more deadly point, unless the latter was protected by the *gafflet*. The standard procedure seems to have been that when sufficient blood had been shed to satisfy the spectators – whose modern descendants presumably throng the terraces of Chelsea and Millwall – the combatants, having had their wounds dressed, laid aside their broadswords, and assuming they were in a fit state to continue at all, ended the exhibition with a bout at quarter-staff. Other weapons may have been used at times; Randle Holmes gives a list in 1688 which includes the fauchion, the two-handed sword, the halberd, and, most alarmingly, the flail.

During the course of the eighteenth century, these sword-fights were replaced by boxing matches, so that by the time of the Regency, bare-fist boxing had become something of a national cult, while fencing, perhaps partly because of the impossibility of visiting France during the long war,

142

had faded into almost total oblivion. All young men with any pretensions to spirit, professed some degree of expertise in the 'noble art', whilst wealthy young aristocrats in particular patronised the champions of the ring and derived reflected glory from being seen in the company of professional pugilists. (See Figg, Miller, Pepys, Steele.)

Professor. The highest rank in the British Academy of Fencing, the organisation to which most professional fencing masters, whether full-time or part-time, belong. The equivalent title on the continent is generally *maître*.

Progressive Attacks. A method of executing a compound attack, whereby the feint and the final attacking blade action deceiving the opponent's parry are combined into one smooth, flowing movement.

Pronation. The position of the sword-hand when the finger-nails are below and the knuckles on top.

Provost. The second rank in the British Academy of Fencing. Those who have gained the A.F.A. Advanced Coaching Award are considered to hold equivalent status.

Public Schools. Fencing at the public schools goes back a long way. The name of Angelo is indissolubly connected with Eton; his rival, Redman, with whom he was involved in a public *fracas*, and whose invitation to settle the affair in the usual way he astoundingly failed to accept, resorting instead to a civil action for damages, was equally well known at Westminster. A fencing championship for the public schools was first organised by the Army in 1890 as part of the gymnastic and boxing competitions which had been held

since 1878. The very first winner was J. Openshaw of Harrow, and in 1892 the champion was a certain W.S. Churchill from the same school. Foil was the only weapon until 1897, when sabre was added, the épée following in 1933. The Graham-Bartlett Cup was first awarded in 1939 for the school scoring most points in the finals, and there is now hardly a public school in the country which does not include fencing among its activities, at least as a minor sport. The name of Eton appears in the records with the greatest frequency, but Harrow, Westminster, St Paul's, Merchant Taylors' and latterly Brentwood, have all been well to the fore at different times.

Punta, (It.). A point attack.

Punta Dritta, (It.). A point attack delivered from the executant's right, with the hand in pronation.

Punta Reversa, (It.). A thrust delivered from the executant's left to any part of the opponent's body; generally when the anti-clockwise motion of the combatants in the rapier-and-dagger days was suddenly interrupted and the executant took a step in the opposite direction.

Punta Rovescio, (It.). An alternative term for an attack delivered from the executant's left, generally involving the use of the point.

Punta Sopramano, (It.). The lunge, one of the earliest recorded references to which occurs in Angelo Viggiani's book in 1575. His explanation is far from clear as he may have regarded it, at that stage, as a *botta segreta*.

Punto. Our Elizabethan ancestors' name for an attack.

Pure Feints. Feints of the same sort of simple attack, e.g., two feints of disengagement or two feints of counter-disengagement, as opposed to a combination of the two varieties.

Push-Pull. A method of gaining an advantage in distance, by hoodwinking the opponent into matching the wily executant in a series of steps, forward and backward. At the critical moment, the rhythm is unexpectedly broken by a sudden halt, normally as the opponent is advancing. Thus the latter finds himself suddenly stranded in an unfavourable position.

Quadrangular. An annual team encounter between the four home countries; it does not, however, rank as a full international and international colours are not awarded. From a match between England and Scotland alone which started in 1924, it was expanded until by 1950 Northern Ireland and Wales were included. The King Edward VII Cup, however, is still awarded to the winner of the England-Scotland match only.

Quarta, (It.). (See Quarte.)

Quarta Bassa. Low *quarte*, a protection against the sabre cut delivered at the belly. The hand is about on a level with the left hip; the elbow and forearm almost in contact with the stomach.

Quarte. The fourth position and parry, protecting the upper left-hand side of the fencer's trunk. At foil, the hand is breast-high, half-supinated and not too wide, being kept only just outside the line of the left shoulder. The point is slightly elevated. At sabre, the position is that described

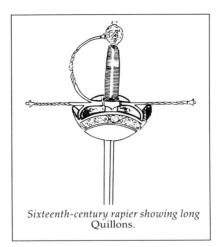

Sixteenth-century rapier showing long Quillons.

immediately above; *quarte* is not widely used at épée.

Quarte over the Arm. A seventeenth-century term for a disengagement following an engagement in *quarte*, which, assuming it was directed into the high line, had of course to be delivered over the adversary's sword-arm.

Quarte, Croisé of. A *prise-de-fer*, executed by forcing the adversary's blade downwards from *quarte* to the *septime* position. Professor Crosnier strongly advocates its use in the form of a time-hit, i.e., the simultaneous taking of the opponent's blade, extension of the sword-arm while maintaining opposition, and delivery of the hit. This *croisé* of *quarte* by time-hit is recommended by him as the most efficacious defence against the left-handed épéeists and the swordsman exploiting the *flèche* attack into *quarte*, particularly when it is combined with the side-step known as the *inquartata* which withdraws the defender's body from the line of attack.

Quarte Medium or Tierce Medium. A central blade position, designated

as either one or the other according to the side on which the blades were engaged.

Quarte Outside. A name given by some masters in the seventeenth and eighteenth century to *sixte*.

Quarte under the Sele. A term appearing in Blackwell's *English Fencing Master* (1705); an attack under the 'shell' or guard. It is conceivable that 'sele' may also be a corruption of 'steel'.

Quarte en Seconde. An attack in *seconde* with the hand in supination; the terminology is that of the seventeenth-century French master, Besnard.

Quarter. The fencer's trunk is theoretically divided into four. The top right (from the fencer's own viewpoint) is *sixte*; the top left, *quarte*; the bottom left, *septime* and the bottom right *octave*. These areas are protected by the parries of the same names.

Quarting or Ecarting. Terms used by Sir William Hope to describe: 1) his favourite defensive posture, body straight and head well back and 2) the *inquartata*.

Quélus, Comte de. A favourite of Henry III of France, Quélus quarrelled with the Sieur de Dunes, a follower of the Duc de Guise. As the great house of Guise was at that time, 1578, the bitter rival of the crown, strong political feeling entered this affair in which the seconds, as was then usual, took part. Three of them were killed and the fourth seriously wounded. Quélus himself was mortally wounded and even de Dunes did not escape entirely unscathed from this bloody affray.

Quevedo, Francisco de. A seventeenth-century Spanish scholar, poet, writer and satirist, one of the earliest exponents of the picaresque novel. He himself killed an opponent in a duel and was obliged for a time to reside in Italy. In his *Vida del Gran Tacano*, he brilliantly ridicules the extravagant theories of the traditional Spanish school of swordsmanship, with an absurd account of how the pompous and long-winded expert is totally worsted by an aggressive and determined novice.

Quill, Company of the. A sixteenth-century German school of fence, which followed the new Italian fashion, using a rapier rather than the two-handed *espadon*.

Quillons. The crossbars of the hilt. On rapiers of the sixteenth century, they often extended beyond the circumference of the guard and were further elaborated with a complicated arrangement of metal rings, designed partly to serve as additional protection for the hand and partly to entangle the adversary's point and facilitate a disarmament. From the seventeenth century onwards, the extremity of one *quillon* was often curved downwards towards the sword-point, while on the opposite side of the grip, the *quillon* and knuckle-bow were combined, thus producing a singularly graceful effect.

Any *quillons* or bars extending beyond the circumference of the guard are prohibited on modern fencing weapons.

Quinta (It.) or Quinte. The fifth position and parry. At sabre, it protects the head; at foil, where it is now seldom used other than instinctively, it is midway between *quarte* and *septime*. (See Positions.) The

Dagger with S-shaped Quillons.

term was finally applied to this position by La Boessière in 1818. Previously, it had been applied to what is now our *septime*, or even *octave*.

Raccoglimento, (It.). The envelopment.

Radaelli, Giuseppe. A famous Milanese master of the nineteenth century, who played a leading part in the development of the light fencing sabre and its academic use under rules and conventions similar to those of foil-play. He advocated control of the weapon with the forearm, with as little use of the wrist as possible, in strong contrast to the technique of later days. Radaelli was regarded as the leader of the northern Italian school which combined elements of French theory and technique with the traditional Italian system. Hence his name was anathema to the exasperated traditionalists of the conservative stronghold in the south.

Raddoppio, (It.). The *reprise*.

Raffine. One of those French courtier-swordsmen who, at the turn

The parry of Quinte (from Danet).

of the sixteenth and seventeenth centuries, made a practice of duelling on the most trivial pretexts. *Raffiner* is to refine. *Raffiner sur le point d'honneur* is to be over-scrupulous on a point of honour.

Rails. The original rules of 1896, recommended to all clubs holding open competitions, required a rail at each end of the *piste* (or platform as it was then called) instead of the present rear limit lines. A fencer could continue the play while in contact with the rail until ordered to stop.

Rapier. The long, narrow thrusting weapon which originated in Italy in the early sixteenth century and was destined entirely to replace the broadsword. It was two-edged, thus combining the advantages of the cut and the thrust, but so long that it was very difficult to use in defence. Some specimens were of extreme, almost absurd length and were regarded as the mark of the bully and the brawler. Holinshed, the author of the *Chronicles* on which Shakespeare based his historical plays, states that the long rapier had become quite the fashion in England – 'longer than the like used in any other country'. Consequently, attacks into the opponent's attack, by a covered extension of the sword-arm, (our time-hit or covered stop-hit) pre-dated the separate parry and riposte, only rendered practicable with the lighter weapons of a later period. For defence as such, either a cloak wrapped round the free arm was used, or a *main-gauche* (dagger) whose guard and hilt exactly resembled its larger companion. More rarely, a combatant employed two rapiers, one in each hand. The etymology of the word is obscure. Some trace it from the Spanish *raspar*, to scrape or scratch; others, from the German *rappen*, to tear out,

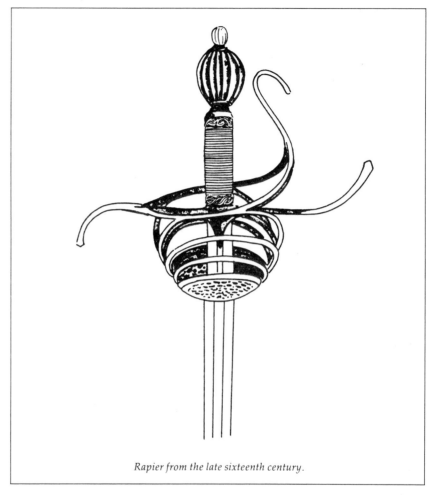

Rapier from the late sixteenth century.

although, as the rapier was a thrusting weapon, this appears to be the less likely of the two.

As time passed, the rapier was progressively shortened and lightened, until it evolved into the eighteenth-century small-sword, sharp on one edge only or neither.

Rapière. A term used contemptuously by the French to signify a sword of unusual length, traditionally the weapon of the blusterer and braggart.

Rassemblement. The withdrawal of the leading foot so that the heels are touching and feet at right angles, an upright position being simultaneously assumed. This action is included in:

1) The salute with which the fencer returns to his normal posture from the on-guard position, at the end of a lesson or bout. At the same time as the foot action, the sword-arm, with weapon, is raised fully above the head and slightly to the right, while the unarmed hand is lowered to the

side. The weapon is then brought down into a vertical position, point uppermost and *coquille* at chin level; finally it is lowered with the point directed at the ground, in front of the fencer and slightly to his right.

2) The stop-hit, and renewal of attack at épée, when the fencer withdraws as much out of reach of his opponent as possible. Standing upright on tip-toe, the leading heel brought back into contact with the rear heel, the executant leans slightly forward from the waist and generally places the hit on his opponent's wrist or forearm.

3) Szabo, the Hungarian master, includes in the term *rassemblement* the closing of the heels by moving the rear foot forward, not back, in preparation for an extra deep lunge.

Rassendyl, Rudolf was the dashing hero of Anthony Hope's Ruritanian novels, *The Prisoner of Zenda* and *Rupert of Hentzau*. Bearing a remarkable resemblance to Rudolf V of Ruritania, he masqueraded as that monarch when the latter was kidnapped by his enemies. On his own admission, he was 'a strong, though hardly a fine, swordsman'. Perhaps this modest estimate of his own ability was confirmed by the fact that when rescuing the King from the Castle of Zenda, and being hardpressed by the villain Gautet, it was only a diversion raised by the manacled royal prisoner that caused Rassendyl's opponent to lose his footing, whereupon he was unceremoniously stabbed as he sprawled on the ground. *Rupert of Hentzau*, one of the very few sequels to equal, if not excel, the original work, records the return of Rudolf Rassendyl to Ruritania and relates how once again he assumed the identity of the King when the latter was assassinated. The climax is reached in his duel with the debonair young villain

146

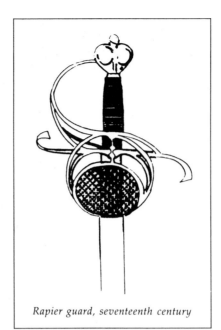

Rapier guard, seventeenth century

whose name gives the book its title. Fortunately, during the three years interval, Rassendyl had 'kept himself in practice and improved his skill' – albeit, according to his friend Fritz von Tarlenheim, this was with regular use of the foil, an uncertain preparation indeed for the *épée de combat* – and his 'slight turns of wrist' served to parry all his opponent's 'fiery attacks and wily feints' and to wear down the latter's resistance. The encounter was finally resolved when Rupert, resorting in desperation to treachery and a hand-to-hand conflict, was shot with his own revolver.

Rathbone, Basil. Educated at Repton, he was a distinguished participator in the Public Schools' Fencing Championships, later serving with distinction in the London Scottish (1915-1918) and being awarded the M.C. on the Western Front. Tall, commanding, good-looking in a faintly sinister way, he was the ideal

sophisticated villain in the richly glamorous and romantic Hollywood films of his day. No mere publicity agent's screen puppet, he had had wide experience of repertory and Shakespearian productions on the English stage. Probably his greatest role, very different from that of his usual swashbuckling swordsman, was the scheming and eccentric Louis XI in *If I were King*, a character he played with relish, adroitness and effect. Of his duelling scenes, the one most widely acclaimed was that with Errol Flynn in *The Adventures of Robin Hood*, Rathbone, naturally assuming the identity of the hero's enemy, Guy of Gisborne. Another spectacular sequence was the duel between the French pirate, Levasseur (Rathbone) and the eponymous hero of *Captain Blood*, again played by Flynn, all along the seashore and over the rocks bordering the Caribbean. Highly impressive was the sabre-play in *The Mark of Zorro*; indeed, many informed critics preferred this to *Robin Hood*, the dramatic exchanges in the latter film being hardly possible with the cumbersome long-swords of the period. Few who saw *Zorro* will forget the famous trick with the candles; brilliant entertainment, which enthralled the audiences and was probably savoured no less by the actors concerned.

Rear Lunge. (See Backward Lunge.)

Rebated. Blunted; until the invention of the *fleuret* in the mid seventeenth century, blunted swords were used in cut-and-thrust rapier practice. The point of the modern fencing sabre is turned back on the blade itself, the edges of which are also blunted.

Recording Apparatus, The Electric. An electric recording apparatus invented by a Mr Little, 'a well-known amateur swordsman', was first demonstrated at Salle Bertrand in 1896 and by all accounts functioned in a fashion very similar to the one familiar to modern fencers. The device was attached by a wire to the combatant's collar and thence down the sleeve to the handle of the foil. The impact of a hit, by pressing the blade into the handle, completed the circuit and caused a bell to ring. The restricted foil target and the need to differentiate between off- and on-target hits caused obvious problems and it was accordingly with the épée that progress was made, with the appearance of the Laurent-Pagan system (q.v.) in the 1930s. It was officially adopted for use in internationals in 1933. In 1938 it was used in the final pool of the British Epée Championship and the whole of the Miller-Hallett competition.

In 1937 the F.I.E. resolved to perfect the foil apparatus, but it was not until the World Championships in Monaco in 1950 that an experimental foil pool was held under these conditions and only in 1955 that it was used at the World Championships of that year. Signor Carmina of Milan was the originator of this machine which was subsequently perfected still further by Dr R. Parfitt, the chairman of the A.F.A. épée sub-committee.

The machine which is used at present is placed opposite the centre of the *piste*, at least one metre away from it, and by means of flashing bulbs, announces the arrival of a hit on one or both of the fencers. Wires connect it to spring-loaded spools at either end of the *piste*, whence further wires lead beneath the backs of the fencers' jackets, inside the sleeves of their sword-arms and finally plug into sockets within the guards of the weapons. An insulated *piste* prevents any reaction when a weapon accidentally strikes the ground; before this last invention, ground judges had to be employed, to signal hits of this sort.

The machine, generally known as the box, and its designer, must alike be regarded as highly ingenious; for at épée, where simultaneous hits alone are permitted, such double hits will be registered only in the event of their being delivered within one twenty-fifth of a second of each other. Should the interval be greater than this, the second bulb remains unlighted and the first hit alone is scored.

For bouts at foil, the foil mechanism is still more artfully contrived. The foil target being confined to the trunk, an over-jacket of silver-threaded *lamé* material, exactly corresponding to the limits, has to be worn over the ordinary jacket. When a thrust is delivered on a non-target area – for example, the leg – a white light flashes. In contrast, a red or green light, corresponding to one or other of the fencers, signals the arrival of the foil-point on the valid area.

As there are no fewer than four lights, a plain and a coloured one for each fencer, it is not at all unusual for all four bulbs to flash at once. This informs the president that both fencers have not only attacked and hit more or less simultaneously, but that each has also struck his opponent, first, on an off-target area, then immediately afterwards on the valid surface, the latter hits of course being annulled by reason of the fact that the non-valid hits occurred first.

Other possible combinations of two or three lights similarly reveal which parts of the body were hit and in what order. In the event of a fencer's valid hit immediately preceding his renewed hit off target, only the appropriate coloured bulb registers,

Rapier and dagger — the true and right gentlemanly weapons (MS Bibliothèque Nationale, Paris).

as of course the valid hit came first and stands.

It must be stressed that the apparatus records only the materiality of hits, and the surface on which they arrived. Questions of priority in the event of double hits, must still be decided by the opinion of the president alone. The box (as yet) cannot think.

This elaborate system is certainly more accurate than the old-fashioned jury with four judges. Whether it is simpler, and whether its effect has been to raise or lower the general standard of fencing, and to increase or diminish the pleasure to be derived from it, are very different matters.

Recovery. The action of recovering to the on-guard position from the lunge. Generally, following the failure of an attack, this is immediate, though in former times fencers frequently remained on the lunge for tactical reasons and continued the phrase from that position.

A combined action of arms, legs and body is required for the recovery, whether this be forward or backward. Should the fencer wish to recover to guard forward for the *reprise*, the left leg is flexed at the knee and brought nearer to the leading leg; meanwhile, the unarmed hand having been raised, he is again in the on-guard position. Should the recovery be backwards, which is more common, the rear knee is again bent, to take the body weight and simultaneously, as the rear arm is raised, the front foot, now freed of its burden, can give a push with the heel that returns the leading leg to its appropriate place.

Redoublement. The renewal of an attacking action which has missed altogether or been parried. Most *redoublements* are executed either by

148

Omnès v Romankov in the final of the Challenge Martini, Paris 1987.

disengagement or cut-over, the attacking blade passing into a different line from the parry. In some cases, there is an intermediate action, such as a beat, or even a mere retraction of the sword-arm, which precedes the renewal. It is possible, also, to execute a *redoublement* with a compound blade action.

Refusing the Blade. Avoiding the opponent's attempts to attack the blade.

Remise. In this renewed attack the blade remains in the line in which it was parried (or missed) and is replaced on the target by a finger action; or else it is left in line for the opponent to lunge onto. In neither case is there any retraction of the sword-arm.

Barbasetti includes *any* form of renewed attack under the general heading of a *remise*. He uses the term 'simple *remise*' not only for the *remise* proper, but for the renewal with

compound blade action which in our view would constitute a *redoublement*. He says that in the former case, it should be accompanied by a tap of the leading foot on the ground; in the latter, the foot should be momentarily withdrawn, presumably to allow the executant more room while making his feint.

Rencontre. Louis XIV's (official) disapproval of duelling and his edicts banning it, led to the *rencontre*, when the opponents arranged a meeting in some remote place under the pretence of an accidental encounter. The survivor would then attempt to exonerate himself by alleging that he had been attacked and acted only in self-defence. However, such unsupervised affairs led to many indignant accusations of foul play; complaints were made that in some cases 'hit-men' had been hired to deal with a specially-feared or dangerous adversary. In consequence, matters were restored to a more regular basis and during the course of the eighteenth century the seconds made their re-appearance, but at this stage took no active part in the proceedings.

The term was also sometimes used for a fresh quarrel arising out of a duel, which necessitated a second meeting or 're-encounter'.

Renewed Attacks. The original attacking action having been parried, or missed, it can be renewed by whatever form of blade action seems most appropriate, provided only that the hit arrives at least one period of fencing time ahead of any riposte or stop-hit. If the opponent executes no offensive action of any sort, the question of fencing time is, of course, irrelevant and does not, in any case, arise at épée. There are three varieties of renewed attack, the *remise, redoublement* and *reprise*. (See separate entries.) Tactically, the value of any renewed attacking action is greatest when premeditated; otherwise, there is a tendency for all technique and common sense to disappear in a flurry of repeated and simultaneous jabs by both fencers.

It is to be noted that at one time the significance of the terms *redoublement* and *reprise* was reversed; Captain Hutton did so in the late nineties, and as late as the 1930s Professor L. Bertrand adopted this interpretation. There are also certain differences in the terminology of the Italian school and their disciples:

1) Redoublement. Castello, writing in the 1930s, increased the confusion by including the *reprise* (the renewal of attack following the recovery to guard) in this category.

2) Raddoppio generally carries the same meaning as our *reprise*.

3) Ripresa d'attacco is not quite the same as a 'reprise of attack'. It includes an extra step forward, or *balestra*, between the recovery to

Rovescio (from Capo Ferro).

guard and the second lunge.

Renewed Ripostes. Ripostes and counter-ripostes may be renewed by exactly the same methods as attacks, that is, by *remise, redoublement* and *reprise*. Should the original riposte have been delivered from the on-guard position, a renewal by means of a lunge, as the opponent effects his recovery, is quite likely to catch him unprepared and off balance. It would appear that such an action cannot strictly be termed a *reprise* as it did not involve a *return* to the on-guard position. When the riposte has been made with a lunge in the first place, then of course the normal reprising action can follow if the opponent continues to retreat. In such circumstances, it is very possible that his vigilance has been relaxed and that he has been lulled into a state of false security.

Renvers. A back-handed cut.

Repechage. A method of ensuring that the losers of bouts by direct elimination are not immediately excluded from any further participation in the competition. Briefly, the principle is that no fencer can be

eliminated until he has been beaten twice, the second time in the *repechage* bouts composed of those who have already been beaten once. In due course, the *repechage* fencers are reduced to two, whereupon they combine with the four semi-finalists of the main stream to form a final pool of six.

Replacement. The *remise*, more especially in the case of foil and épée. The point of the weapon is 'replaced' on target in the line which was closed by the parry, but which is now misguidedly opened while the riposte is delayed.

Reprise. A renewed attack. Following his first attack, the fencer resumes the on-guard position before attacking again, normally by means of another lunge or *flèche*. In most cases, he recovers to guard forwards, but a *reprise* is still executed if the intermediate action is a recovery backwards to his original position before making the second attack. This sometimes occurs when a riposte is anticipated, but, in the event, none is forthcoming. Generally speaking, it is unwise to attack into the low line before a *reprise*; too

149

much of the target is left exposed during the recovery period.

Respost. Sir William Hope's term for the riposte.

Rest. In the World Championships held at Cairo in 1949, the épée final between Dario Mangiarotti and René Bougnol was seriously disrupted by the former's successive attacks of cramp, which occasioned repeated delays. Incredibly, we are informed that the bout lasted several hours. In consequence a rule was introduced entitling an injured or indisposed fencer to a limited period of rest. The president may now allow a fencer ten minutes' rest for an injury sustained during the bout. It would appear that in internationals, at least, the concession has been abused, since a frivolous request confirmed as such by the medical officer in attendance is now penalised by the award of a hit against the offender. Presumably for the same reason, the rule on indisposition was deleted altogether in 1982.

Resting Medium or Resting Guard. The position where the sword-hand was actually lowered until the pommel was supported by the leading thigh; advocated by Hutton when, during a long and exacting bout, the sabreur was temporarily at a safe distance.

Return or Return Thrust. The riposte.

Return to Guard. (See Recovery.)

Revérénce. A seventeenth-century French term for the salute, said to have been first introduced and taught by Besnard.

Reverse. The practice in Elizabethan times was not to advance and retire
150

up and down the narrow rectangle of the *piste*, as is the case today, but to circle cautiously round and round each other, anti-clockwise. It was for this reason that the Spaniards evolved their complex theories of the Mysterious Circle. To reverse, therefore, was to change the direction suddenly and then attack, hoping to take the opponent by surprise. The action was similar to the reverse in an old-fashioned waltz, where the effect on one's partner was often similar.

Reves, (Span.). Reverse; a back-edged cut.

Revolver Grip. Same as the pistol grip, a form of orthopaedic grip.

Ricasso. The flattened part of the tang of the blade, immediately above and within the cup-shaped guard of an Italian foil.

Ricavatione or Ricavazione, (It.). After an initial feint of disengagement, this action deceives the *contra-cavatione* (circular parry) of the opponent with another *contra-cavatione*. In other words, the *ricavatione* is the same thing as the *doublé*. Fabris, the great seventeenth-century Italian master was the first to analyse properly the principles of disengagement and counter-disengagement.

Richelieu, Cardinal Armand Jean Duplessis de. The great object of this famous minister of Louis XIII was to strengthen the monarchy and, by centralising the administration, reduce the particularist and separatist tendencies of the French provinces. His suppression of the Huguenots was due, therefore, less to religious prejudice than to the fear that their federal and military privileges, granted by Henry IV, constituted a

standing danger to the French state. Once they had been defeated by the capture of their great stronghold at La Rochelle and their semi-independent polity gained by the Edict of Nantes had been terminated, he was perfectly prepared to allow them to retain their freedom of worship.

So indifferent was he, in fact, to the religion of the church of which he was a dignitary, that he intervened in the Thirty Years War, (1618-48), on the side of the Protestants against the Catholics, marshalled and incited by the Austrian Habsburgs, whom he regarded as the great external threat to France and a standing obstacle to his long-term plans for strengthening the country's weak frontiers in the north-east and along the Rhine.

In pursuance of his aim of strengthening the authority of the crown, Richelieu systematically endeavoured to undermine the mettlesome spirit and independence of the nobility. With this end in view, he rigorously enforced the royal edicts against duelling, even to the extent of executing the popular and intrepid Boutteville, despite pleas for mercy from every side.

Richelieu and his Capuchin secretary, Father Joseph du Tremblay, were known respectively as 'His Red Eminence' and 'His Grey Eminence', from the colour of their robes. Hence the origin of the phrase *éminence grise*, to symbolise a sinister power behind the scenes.

The great cardinal-statesman has been immortalised in the pages of Dumas, along with the Three Musketeers and their traditional enemies, the bodyguard of the Cardinal, whom the author represents as a highly sinister influence on the King; although, in actual fact, they formed a remarkably successful and stable partnership, which on only one occasion was seriously threatened.

Richelieu, Louis-François Armand de Vignerot Duplessis, Maréchal-Duc de has left a somewhat chequered reputation and is a character none too easy for the historian to assess. He was a colossal snob, wilfully refusing to consent to the marriage of his daughter Septimanie, Comtesse d'Egmont, to the Comte de Gisors, who was not merely of a perfectly good family, but a gallant officer of noble character, solely on the ground that the latter's ancestry was insufficiently distinguished. This was all the more ridiculous insofar as his own great-uncle, the great Cardinal, from whom the family derived its position, had only been of the minor nobility. Richelieu was greedy and corrupt, even allowing for the relaxed standards of the eighteenth century. He had more than one sojourn in the Bastille and in 1718 was involved in the preposterous comic opera plot hatched by the Duchess of Maine and her cronies against the Regent Orléans. As a

Robinson (right) fences Jenkinson in the first Epée Club Cup held at Temple Gardens in 1901 (illustration by F.H. Townsend).

commander in the field, he allowed and perpetrated too much irregularity and extortion in occupied territory; his own troops nicknamed him *Papa la Maraude*. His judgement and sense of responsibility were, to say the least, uncertain; when, more by luck than judgement, he trapped a British Army under the Duke of Cumberland and held the Duke in the hollow of his hand, he let him go, signing the Convention of Klosterseven (1757), which he had no right to do, in exchange for promises of disbandment and inaction which Cumberland had no right to make. Showy and reckless as a general, he possessed little strategic insight, but he did have brilliance, flair and perhaps more important, luck. At Fontenoy (1745) he was the hero of that day of many heroes, bringing up the last available battery of guns and ordering the advance of the *Maison du Roi* (Household Cavalry) when all seemed lost and turning defeat into victory. In 1757, at the beginning of the Seven Years War, he was in command of the invasion of Minorca (then a British possession) and captured the supposedly impregnable Port Mahon. Miss Mitford, in her well-researched book *Madame de Pompadour*, draws the conclusion that the Marshal-Duke had in his time climbed in and out of so many ladies' windows – sometimes by crossing a single plank high above the street – that he found it child's play to lead his men up the most precipitous cliffs.

In keeping with these varied activities, Richelieu was notorious as a duellist. In 1716 the *Parlement* of Paris tried to bring him to trial for this offence, but as a result of the pressure and opposition of his fellow-dukes, the case was dropped. In 1734, during the siege of Philippsburg, he apparently indulged, at supper, in some indiscreet witticisms at the expense of the Prince de Lixin, who in turn taunted the Duke with having married above himself, into the Prince's family; a shaft which so enraged the Duke that an immediate encounter was demanded. The two men met in the trenches, the Duke proving, at the expense of his kinsman's life, that though he might be inferior by birth, he was greatly the superior with sword in hand.

Richelieu lived to a great age, only dying in 1788. *Felix opportunate mortis*; he would not have appreciated the events of the following year.

Right of Way. Fencing slang for priority.

Rimessa, (It.). The *remise*.

Rinverso Tondo, (It.). A reverse horizontal cut in which Tappa, the Milanese master specialised, assuring his grateful pupils that it would certainly remove both eyes from any opponent.

Riporto, (It.). The envelopement.

Riposte. The offensive action following the successful parry of an attack. It may be immediate, or slightly delayed, or delivered in any line. Any type of blade action may be used, simple or compound; the riposte may be executed from the on-guard position, or with a step, *balestra*, lunge or *flèche*.

What beginners often fail to grasp is that simple and compound ripostes correspond exactly in the blade action and in their relation to the opponent's blade position, to simple and compound attacks. Thus simple ripostes (one blade action) may be direct (cp. the straight-thrust), by disengagement, cut-over, or counter-disengagement. The last-named can only take place when the attacker may try to anticipate a direct riposte by dropping his point under the defender's blade and executing, in effect, a circular parry. Such an attempt can readily be deceived by riposting with a counter-disengagement. Similarly, compound ripostes deceive, by one or more feints, the attacker's attempt to parry the riposte, and precisely resemble compound attacks. Indeed, when any sort of riposte is executed with a lunge rather than from the on-guard position, there is no technical difference between it and an attack. The sole distinction is, that it follows a successful parry.

Riposte with Opposition. To riposte while maintaining contact with the opponent's blade, thereby protecting oneself against a *remise* of the attack.

Risposta con Pausa, (It.). A delayed riposte.

Ripresa and Ripresa d'Attaco, (It.). (See Renewed Attacks.)

Robinson, C.N. was very largely responsible for the popularisation of épée fencing in England. In 1900 he invited Professor Anthime Spinnewyn, a well-known French master, to come to London and give lessons at this weapon. Shortly afterwards, the Epée Club was founded. Mr Robinson organised the first official British épée team to go abroad, for the International Cup in Paris in 1904, although they were not very successful. Two years later, he was in the épée team at the Athens Olympics which gained a signal victory over the Germans.

Roland, George. Son of Joseph Roland, a French master who had opened a salle in London in 1773. George, however, followed John

Xavier Tremondo as master at the Royal Academy of Exercises (Edinburgh) in 1820. He published a number of books on fencing in which he makes plain his distaste for the growing popularity of the sabre, stimulated partly by the introduction of the spadroon and partly by the increased general interest in things military fostered by the Napoleonic Wars.

Romankov, A. The brilliant Russian left-hander who in recent years stamped his authority on one World Championship after another. He was victorious with the foil on five occasions (1974, 1977, 1979, 1982, 1983) which is the record number of world titles at any weapon. Only d'Oriola exceeds him in the number of gold medals, but of his six, two were won at Olympics.

Rompre. To break ground.

Rotella, (It.). A small round shield, similar to a buckler.

Round Parry or Round Parade. An old-fashioned name, especially favoured by George Roland, for the circular parry.

Rousseau. Another famous family of French masters, two of whom taught respectively Louis XIV and XV. The third in the dynasty, Augustin, was the last Syndic of the Paris Academy of Arms and was guillotined during the Reign of Terror, solely because he had given lessons to members of the Royal Family. As he was sentenced, a revolutionary judge bawled: *'Pare celle-là*, Rousseau!' ('Parry that one, Rousseau!') a fairly characteristic example of the magnanimity of the breed.

Roversi, (It.). A sixteenth-century Italian term for cuts delivered from the left against the adversary's right-hand side; in other words, a back-handed cut.

Rovescio, (It.). A sixteenth-century term for a point attack delivered from the left with the hand in supination, threatening the same area as the *roversi*.

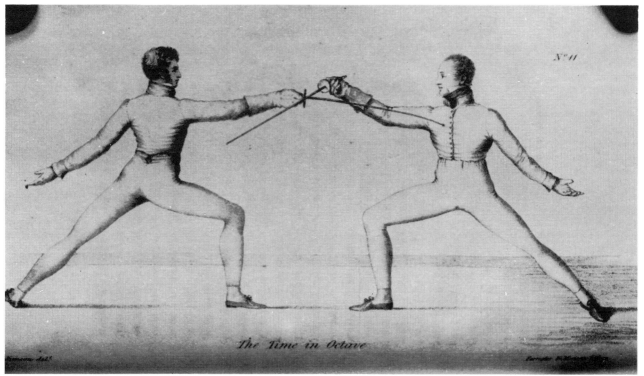

The time in octave — *from George Roland's* Treatise on the Theory and Practice of the Art of Fencing, *1823.*

Royal Air Force Fencing Union. Established in 1921. To start with, there were separate championships for officers and men, but these were combined in 1930.

Royal Edinburgh Academy of Exercises. Founded by John Xavier, brother of Domenico Angelo. He had come to England in 1753 to act as Domenico's assistant. In 1763 he left for Edinburgh, where he assumed the name of Angelo Tremamondo, but was familiarly known to his pupils as 'Mr Ainslie'. His salle and *manège*, on which he conferred the above imposing title, were built at the ratepayers' expense – a departure unusual enough in any case in those days when ratepayers received rather more consideration than they do now – but surely staggering in view of the northern kingdom's reputation in matters financial. Angelo received a basic salary of £200 a year independently of the fees he charged for giving lessons. After his death in 1805, the institution continued under the successive guidance of the two Rolands, another dynasty of French fencing masters to settle in this country.

Royal Naval Amateur Fencing Association. The Royal Navy and Royal Marines Fencing Association was founded in 1919. The title was changed in 1948, but the two branches of the association continued to hold separate championships prior to the Inter-Services Tournament at Olympia.

Rudolph II, Holy Roman Emperor, 1576-1612. An intellectual, but weak and irresolute ruler. He confirmed the privileges of the Marxbruder granted by Frederick III. In 1612, his brother Mathias seized control of affairs and compelled Rudolf to retire to his castle in Prague, where he
154

spent his last few years lost in dreams and shadows, in the company of grooms, astrologers and wizards; events, meanwhile, hurried on to the catastrophe of the Thirty Years War.

Ruffian's Hall. The cant phrase for West Smithfield. According to Howe's *Continuation of Stow's Annals* (1631), 'it was the usual place of Frayes and common fighting during the time that sword and bucklers were in use'. Doubtless the moralists of the period suspected the presence also of fencing masters, generally numbered among the unregenerate members of society until they donned their present mantle of respectability.

Rules. Several ancient sets of rules are extant, including Labat's nineteen, operative in the Academy of Toulouse in the seventeenth century. The target, though not quite the same as today, was nevertheless bounded by the armholes of the waistcoat (as it is today, by the seams of the jacket crossing the shoulders). The lower limit, however, was the top of a belt which must be no more than one foot below the chin. The scoring was radically different – two hits had to be made to score a point, while a double hit was valid if it levelled the scores. As today, a hit occurring simultaneously with a disarmament was valid, and changing hands, or the use of both hands, was forbidden. There was, however, no prohibition of shifting the hand back along the handle in the course of an attack, but this modern rule is to be found in the regulations drawn up by Sir William Hope in 1707.

It was in 1896 that the first official rules for competitions were issued by the Fencing Branch committee of the Amateur Gymnastic Association;

Captain Alfred Hutton having discovered a year or two earlier, on being invited to judge at a competition organised by the German Gymnastic Society, that no such set of regulations existed. There were a number of interesting differences from the rules familiar to modern fencers. To begin with, the target area at foil was much reduced; it was limited on the inside by a vertical line passing through the left nipple and the whole of the back was excluded. Then, if both fencers were hit, but only one was on the lunge, priority was given to the lunger, not the fencer whose arm was first extended with point in line threatening the target; hence, an off-target hit by the lunger invalidated a hit on target by the non-lunger. As for the culprit who persistently attacked into his opponent's attack instead of parrying, he was to be rewarded by summary disqualification. In 1905 there was a very important innovation. It was agreed that the *quality* of the fencing ought to be weighed in the balance and accordingly points were awarded on this basis in addition to the scoring of hits; although it is not explained by what exact system this was done. This version of the rules remained substantially effective until 1925. Only in 1933 were the F.I.E. rules officially adopted for use in this country.

These rules had been codified in 1914 and subsequently adopted by the F.I.E. (*Fédération Internationale d'Escrime*) and accepted by the International Congress of National Olympic Committees held at Paris in the course of the same year. They have been modified, revised and modernised on several occasions since; and an authorised translation from the French, adopted by the Amateur Fencing Association for use in Great Britain, was subsequently kept up to date by Mr C.-L. de Beaumont.

As in most sports, the tendency of late has been for the rules to become even more complicated, a process accelerated by the introduction of the electrical judging equipment. There are now more than 700 rules, though aspiring fencers and presidents may take some heart from the fact that many of them are concerned with the electrical recording apparatus and other purely technical matters, which it is unnecessary and indeed impossible, to memorise. A number of others, however, although appearing separately, are duplicated and apply equally to foil and sabre, or even, in some cases, to all three weapons.

Running Glide. Castello's name for the *flèche*, executed with *coulé* or opposition of blades.

Sabatini, Rafael. A very popular historical novelist of the first half of the twentieth century, the author of literally dozens of somewhat highly coloured romances, of which two, *Captain Blood* and *Scaramouche* became the subject of memorable films. Despite his success, Sabatini's historical accuracy is not exactly beyond reproach. Anachronisms, especially in naval matters, abound; his sloops and frigates are as much out of place in the seventeenth century as Stevenson's *Hispaniola* in *Treasure Island* was in the eighteenth, rigged, it will be remembered, in a style unknown in 1750. Sabatini actually assigns a brig to the Elizabethan period. He also has ships turning to put themselves in line with the enemy fire 'to afford as small a target as possible', in other words, to let themselves be raked fore and aft, the exact thing that a commander in a sea-fight attempted to avoid himself and to inflict on his adversary. Moreover, Sabatini's ships appear to

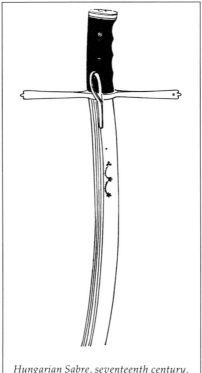

Hungarian Sabre, seventeenth century.

sink very easily. We read of gun-fire blowing great gaping holes in their sides. In point of fact, it was extremely difficult to sink a wooden ship by gunfire. A broadside might inflict fearful damage on the masts and rigging and casualties on the crew, but round-shot tended to lodge in the hull rather than fragment it.

The narratives naturally include numerous sword-fights. Sabatini's terminology is loose in the extreme. When he speaks of a 'counter', it is uncertain whether he means a riposte, a counter-attack, or a counter parry. He also falls into the characteristic trap of ill-informed writers and producers in supposing that the sword-play of the sixteenth century was no different from that 200 years

later. In *The Hounds of God* there is a duel at single rapier between Don Pedro de Mendoza y Luna and young Sir Gervase Crosby. Correctly enough, Crosby resorted to herculean and unscientific slashes in the most approved manner of George Silver, but although his opponent was 'one of those few swordsmen who had made a study of this new art', his style, as represented, is really akin to the eighteenth-century small-sword. He parried *forte* to *foible* – almost impossible with the ultra-long and heavy sixteenth-century weapon and 'kept his arm shortened', whereas the contemporary Spanish school notoriously advocated an extended sword-arm in the guard position. The encounter ended when Don Pedro suddenly shortened the measure and disarmed his opponent by seizing his sword-wrist; this, at least, is authentic enough.

An intriguing aspect of the novels is the archaic or unfamiliar vocabulary. 'Clavecin' for 'clavichord'; 'fulvid' for 'tawny' (the dictionary gives 'fulvous'); 'phlebotomy' for 'bloodshed'; 'jactancy' for 'encouragement' or 'incitement'. 'Mumchance' (masquerader) and 'inquilines' (lodgers) do not appear to be used very appropriately and one wonders if the author occasionally spent a rewarding hour coining these and other mysterious expressions.

Sabre. The first mention of the sabre in print is in Marcelli's manual (1686). Originally the heavy, curved, weapon with which the Household Cavalry is still equipped, it became known to western Europe during the eighteenth century as a result of contact with the Hungarian light horsemen (*Housas* or Hussars) who had themselves adopted the weapon from the Turks, among whom the blade was considerably more curved, forming, in fact, the weapon common to the eastern peoples which among us is generally called the 'scimitar'. Among other Oriental varieties, the Malayan *Kris* and the Gurkha *Kukri* are the most familiar to us in this country.

In the eighteenth and early nineteenth centuries, the cavalry of all nations practised sabre fencing and fighting. Their basic positions were five in number:

1) Inside and outside guard, corresponding respectively to *quarte* and *tierce*.

2) Inside and outside hanging guards, corresponding respectively to *prime* and *seconde*, point down, but blade rather more vertical and the hand somewhat higher than in the modern positions.

3) *Quinte*, with blade in a roughly horizontal position to protect the head. This was also known as St George's Guard.

In addition to the above guards were:

1) Medium guard. The sword-arm was extended in line with the shoulder and the blade was elevated almost vertically.

2) Spadroon guard. The hand was again in line with the shoulder, but was breast high and the sword-arm was slightly bent at the elbow. The hand was in supination and the point was directed downwards. (The spadroon was a light duelling sabre, making its appearance about the turn of the eighteenth and nineteenth centuries.)

In the eighteenth century the small-sword was regarded as essentially the gentleman's weapon and from association with it, the foil enjoyed much the same prestige; the sabre was considered to be a rather crude affair for the military. The Napoleonic Wars aroused a passing enthusiasm for edged weapons, but this quickly faded again. George Ro-
156

The Sabre, German School, nineteenth century.

land poured scorn on the sabre and most traditionally-minded foilists affected to regard it with disdain. Only at the nineteenth century's end did such great Italian masters as Radaelli and Magrini confer respectability on their chosen weapon, since when it has gained steadily in popularity; though British sabreurs have been curiously unsuccessful at international level.

The present-day weapon is extremely light and hits may be scored not only with the fore-edge, but with the top third of the back-edge and the point as well. The contemporary blade is perfectly straight, but within the writer's memory, many still possessed a vestigial curve which, according to the rules, might not deviate more than 4 cm from the straight line. The curved, triangular guard, reminiscent of the old basket-hilt, must now be absolutely smooth; formerly, it was often perforated, grooved, patterned or embossed.

The modern parries are *prime*, *seconde*, *tierce*, *quarte* and *quinte*, although, in regard to *seconde* and *tierce* especially, the positions are far

less precisely defined than is the case at foil, owing to the larger target area and the variety of angles from which cuts can be delivered. At one time, the parry of *sixte* was also used to protect the head; as in *quinte*, the blade was slightly above the head and roughly parallel with the ground, but the hand, in full supination, was placed well to the defender's left. The effect, giving the impression of 'catching' the opponent's cut, was highly spectacular, but the position was awkward in the extreme and this parry is now obsolete. It has been suggested that the one situation in which it might have some genuine value is when a cut at chest has been parried in *quarte* and the riposte is directed to the head. In this case, the orthodox parry of *quinte*, involving the dropping of the point below the riposter's blade, would be very slow and clearly the hand would be in a better position to execute this archaic but dramatic alternative.

Generally speaking, sabreurs today adopt one of two on-guard positions: the defensive position, and the offensive-defensive. (See sepa-

The Sabre salute, first position (from Castello).

The Sabre salute, second position (from Castello).

finger technique regarded as characteristic of that nation and now almost universally copied. Modern sabre fencing has rules and conventions similar to those of foil; they were framed in Paris in 1914 by a committee under the chairmanship of Dr Bela Nagy, president of the Hungarian Fencing Federation, and since then have only been modified in detail.

Sabre Club was founded in 1911. In 1913 the Magrini Cup, named after the celebrated sabre master, was awarded to the winner of an individual competition held among the members. In 1927 the competition was changed to one for teams representing the various clubs.

Sabre, The Electric. For some years now, repeated attempts have been made to perfect an electric sabre which would match developments in the other two weapons. The experiments focussed on two major problems – the restricted area of the sabre target and the difficulty of designing a weapon which would register both cuts and point attacks without fatally altering and impairing its balance.

Electric sabres are now being used at major events.

Sabre versus Epée. In 1905 a match was arranged by the Inns of Court F.C. between teams armed respectively with sabres and épées. A hit could be scored on any part of the body with the point of either weapon or the edge of the sabre. The result was a narrow win for the épéeists, by one hit. Captain Hutton, commenting afterwards, referred to an earlier occasion when, in similar fashion, he had encountered M Thieriet, professor of the London Fencing Club, who had ridiculed the idea that a sabreur could withstand

rate entries.) In the course of a bout, however, sabreurs are in the habit of constantly moving their blades about from one position to another, far more so than at foil. The only other significant differences from the on-guard position at foil, are that the knees are rather less bent, to permit of greater mobility, and the unarmed hand, which constitutes part of the target, is placed on the rear hip, out of harm's way.

The technique of the cut has traditionally been the subject of controversy and has undergone sundry vicissitudes over the years. The military men delivered the cut with a forearm slash from the elbow, or even the shoulder. The great Keresztessy of Budapest, however, preferred the use of the wrist. That was in the 1820s, but when Barbasetti arrived from Italy at the century's end to take charge of fencing in the Austrian Army, he insisted on a return to the forearm method, a retrograde step, but consistent with the contemporary principles of his own country. It was left to Santelli, another Italian expatriate, to introduce in Hungary the classical wrist-

an épéeist. The result had been a victory for the Captain and his sabre, and when the contestants exchanged weapons, the new sabreur was victorious. This, in Captain Hutton's opinion, was largely due to the greater variety of ripostes possible with the sabre. It must be emphasised that the weapon used on this occasion was not the light fencing sabre of the salle, which Hutton ridiculed as 'a silly little toy', but a close approximation to the infantry officer's sword, which must have given the user a considerable advantage in size and weight.

Sabre Grip. The orthodox method of holding the sabre, which allows the cut to be delivered with the Hungarian combination of wrist and finger-play. The thumb and forefinger are placed on the handle with a pincer-like grip just inside the guard; the last fingers, closed on the handle, bringing it to bear against the palm of the hand and very nearly at right angles to it.

Sabre-in-Hand. Another term for sword-in-hand (q.v.).

Sacoon and Sagoone. Archaic terms of uncertain significance; possibly corruptions of *seconde*.

Sainct-Didier, Henri de. A sixteenth-century French master, notable for his lingering fondness for the traditional *estocade*, a weighty edged weapon, and his elaborate system of footwork rendered still less comprehensible by a series of intricate diagrams. Rather surprisingly, he has been hailed as the father of the classical French school and hence, the ultimate originator of modern fencing. Perhaps the explanation lies in his *Traicté sur l'espée seule* (1573); by concentrating on a single weapon, effective in defence as well as attack, the *main-gauche* could be discarded and the long rapier shortened and lightened until it was transformed into the small-sword of the eighteenth century.

Saint-Evremont, Botte de. An allegedly fatal and infallible thrust said to have been devised by the eighteenth-century duellist of that name, but whose exact nature has not, alas, come down to us.

Saint-Foix, Poulain de. The great duelling rival of Saint-Evremont during the reign of Louis XV. He was inconsistent enough to write in eloquent condemnation of duelling, while seldom missing the chance of participating in an affair. His chivalrous spirit was revealed on several occasions when he declined a challenge from an adversary who was clearly his inferior as a swordsman.

Saint-Georges, Chevalier de. The contemporary and great rival in swordsmanship of the Chevalier d'Eon. He was a mulatto, the son of a negress and an official in the French West Indies. Despite this unpromising start in life, his good looks

Sabre v Epée (from Diderot Encyclopaedia).

earned him much popularity with the ladies and the versatility of his talents was such that he might well have become manager of the Paris Opera, had not the racial discrimination of the artistes been expressed with such force that the Queen was prevailed upon to veto the appointment. It was not surprising, therefore, that when the Revolution broke out, he espoused the Republican cause. His skill as a fencer and duellist was such that when a youthful and presumptuous Hussar officer, unaware of his identity, boasted of his own brilliance and was audacious enough to assert that on many occasions he had worsted the celebrated Saint-Georges, the latter suggested a bout with the foils and asked the ladies present to name the order in which he was to touch the young cub's waistcoat buttons, which he promptly proceeded to do. The youth, at once infuriated and humiliated, of course demanded immediate satisfaction, which Saint-Georges quietly refused, dismissing the young braggart with the observation that his day would yet come and that he preferred to let him live to serve his country.

St George's Guard or Parry. The fifth (*quinte*) position and parry at sabre. The name was derived from the traditional position of St George's hand when he slew the dragon. The early sabre masters were most insistent that it should invariably be executed with a step back.

Saint-Martin, J. de. A pupil of Danet and himself a master, he founded a salle in Vienna in the late eighteenth century, where he long remained and established in Austria the classic principles of French small-sword play.

St Matthew, Company of. An organisation of German fencing masters on which Maximilian I (1493-1519) conferred sundry privileges and a coat of arms. The company was under the control of four 'adepts' and a captain; public proof of ability was required before admission. The Company of St Luke was a very similar affair.

St Michele, Confrérie Royale et Chevalière de. A famous confederation of swordsmen founded at Ghent in the seventeenth century. In 1630, in recognition of services at the siege of Ostend, it was awarded the Order of the Golden Fleece, the highest chivalric award of the House of Habsburg. The only parallel in our time was the award of the George Cross to Malta. Originally a society of private gentlemen and citizens, the *Confrérie* became more and more exclusive, until eventually its numbers were reduced to a hundred and none but crowned heads or members of the oldest nobility of the Low Countries could hope for admission.

Salle. Properly speaking, *salle d'armes*, the actual apartment where matches are held, skills are practised and lessons given. In more general use, however, salle has become synonomous with a fencing club as a whole. Members habitually use the term when referring to their club, its organisation, or its premises. It is often linked with the name of the proprietor, or chief master, and there is a convention that the term should not be used officially unless a full master ('professor' in this country) is at its head.

Salle Behmber. Professor 'Reggie' Behmber started teaching under Professor Gravé and on the latter's death continued at Salle Gravé in association with Mme Périgal. In 1951 he established his own salle. There he trained innumerable outstanding fencers, both at international and public school level, and not a few prominent masters as well. A technical purist, he was well known for his endearing mannerisms when giving lessons, in particular, his trick of looking hopefully behind him in search of an invisible fencer when a pupil's attack went wide.

Salle Bertrand. One of the most famous of the London Fencing Clubs, it was founded when Baptiste Bertrand arrived in England in 1857. He was succeeded by his son Félix in 1898 and on the death of the latter in 1930, by the renowned Léon, or 'Punch' as he was always known in the fencing world. The great days of the salle, when it was in the full flood of success, lay between the wars and it was in this period that the Salle Bertrand ladies won the national team championship seven times and the individual title on no fewer than nine occasions. Like too much else, this brilliant epoch was ended by the outbreak of the Second

A Salle d'Armes in the seventeenth century (from La Tousche).

World War, and afterwards, things were never quite the same again. For five years, deprived of its original headquarters, the salle was obliged to share the Tenterden Street building with the London Fencing Club; this was not entirely a success and in 1953, the famous old club ceased to exist. Perhaps, in a sense, this was just as well. The great Salle Bertrand and all it stood for could never have been transplanted with success into the modern egalitarian world.

Salle Boston. Professor Steven Boston had been a noted boxer as well as a fencer, appearing in many films and on television. For years he was the master at Cambridge University, one of his star pupils being the International Sabreur, Richard Cohen. At Brentwood, he laid the foundation of that school's long run of triumphs in the Public Schools' Championships; while from 1960-1980 Salle Boston enjoyed immense success in the club competitions.

Salle Froeschlen and Salle Gravé. The Kensington salle of Professor Félix Gravé, a master of high repute, flourished mightily in the earlier part of this century, and at one time numbered as many as 300 pupils. In 1926, his nephew, Professor Ernest Froeschlen, came from Lorraine to assist with the teaching. In 1931, the depression having affected the prosperity of the senior organisation, the Professor and his wife established their own club. In addition, the Professor taught at many schools, including Harrow, and was the permanent fencing master at R.A.D.A., initiating most of the country's leading actors in the skills of the various weapons. Bombed during the war, the salle found new premises near Olympia, and there it continued, enjoying considerable success, until the Professor's death

160

in 1964. Mme Froeschlen remained in control for some years, but deteriorating eyesight finally compelled her retirement in 1979. One of their best-known fencers in the later years was the Junior Foil Champion of 1956, D. Cawthorne, who also figured briefly on the international scene.

Salle Ganchev. Professor George Ganchev was not only British Sabre Team Coach, but was twice World Professional Sabre Champion. His salle, founded in 1973, was an interesting departure. Sabreurs only were accepted, starting intensive training at the age of eleven. Within a few years the salle had supplied the entire England under-twenty sabre team, the top five under-twenty finalists, several public school champions, and a hat-trick of wins in the Corble Cup. By all accounts, the training was very demanding, the utmost dedication and regularity being required; though it is hard to criticise this, one cannot help but wonder if such rigorous coaching, at so early an age, reminiscent of the Iron Curtain countries, does not dull the keen edge of enjoyment and in the long run stifle enthusiasm. Such has almost certainly been the case at swimming, athletics and lawn tennis.

Salle Goodall. Founded in 1969 by Professor Roy and his wife Professor Angela Goodall, both of whom have had wide experience of coaching at all levels. Professor Goodall himself is an authority on the history of duelling, on which he has published numerous articles, and has also specialised in the teaching and arranging of stage-fighting.

Salle Paul was formed in 1931 by Professor Léon ('Papa') Paul, who had been a fencing master in the

French Army. A great character, like most of the illustrious masters of that era, it is recorded that whenever a pupil's point showed signs of straying, he would emit an anguished cry of 'Eat me! Eat me!' Students of foreign fencing masters' English will no doubt be able to translate.

Salle Paul speedily became one of the most famous of modern London fencing clubs. It has supplied over a quarter of all winners of the national championships and its members have figured in every British team except two between 1947 and 1981. The club has won the Men's Foil team competition twenty-three times, whilst in the team competitions at épée, sabre and ladies' foil, they have on a number of occasions been victorious. The salle has taken the Granville Cup thirteen times and the fact that in 1956 their A and B teams were placed first and second in this competition is sufficient indication of their all-round strength. A.L.N. Jay, at his peak almost the best foilist and swordsman in the world, was at one time a member; while among the masters, Moldovanyi and Lagnado were familiar names. 'Papa's' two sons, Raymond and René, and his two grandsons, Graham and Barry, were all leading internationals with a seemingly endless list of successes to their names.

Salle Zaalov. Zaalov was an ex-Tsarist diplomat, who, after the Revolution, settled in Liverpool where he established a salle of high repute in the 1920s. He also taught fencing for many years at Liverpool University. His greatest enthusiasm was aroused by the sabre, the weapon in which he had been the official instructor of the Imperial Russian Cavalry and the dramatic sweep of his blade, above all in the *molinello*, at which he excelled, held the spectators spellbound. After the Second World War, he stoutly opposed the introduction of Crosnier's national training scheme. This was partly for financial reasons, but he doubtless also dreaded the emergence of a swarm of half-trained amateur instructors and a consequent drop in standards; at all events, he would have none of it. The century was far advanced when he died, and his salle, one of the last private establishments in the country, stayed independent to the end.

Salle Fencer. To describe a fencer thus, is to damn with faint praise. Such a one takes an excellent lesson, his technique is pure, he can execute all the standard strokes with style and confidence; but somehow or other, when it comes to the competitions, he has a depressing record of regular failure. Cricketers will recognise in him the counterpart of the 'net batsman'.

Salles, The Forgotten. Old records and the tarnished silver cups which have found their way into private hands or onto the shelves of antique dealers bear the fascinating names of long-forgotten clubs and salles. Early in the century and even between the wars, they flourished all over London. The name of the Inns of Court School of Arms, once well to the forefront, and winners of the Savage Shield in 1905 and second in 1910, never reappears after 1918; evidence, perhaps, that the sword had finally and in all circumstances been swept from the battlefield by the machine-gun and the hand-grenade. Morel's School of Arms, Stempel's School of Arms, the School of Arms of the McPhersons (W. and F.G.) – one of the leading clubs before 1914 which won the Savage Shield on an impressive number of occasions – and the Sword Club which vanished in

1921, all had their following. Then there were Salle Tassart, Salle Froeschlen, Salle Gravé and Salle Mimiague – all achieved some success in the Savage Shield or other competitions, and all are now but names, nostalgic reminders of an era when taxis were as big as delivery vans, elderly statesmen still wore winged collars, steam locomotives clanked and roared in the main line stations, and now vanished restaurants, such as Frascati's, Quaglino's, Gennaro's and the Trocadero, shed their glare and glitter over night-time London.
Sir Glorious Tiptoe. 'Ay, marry, those had fencing names. What is become of them?'
The Host 'They had their times, and we can say, they were.'
(Ben Jonson, *The New Inn*, Act II, Sc.ii.)

Salto in Dietro, (It.). The jump backwards. Bertrand depicts it as a leap backwards from a full lunge position.

Salute. A courtesy exchanged between fencers and duellists at the start of an encounter. There are many variations, but all, at some stage, require the sword to be brought into a perpendicular position, point uppermost and guard close to and on a level with the chin. The aspirant, however, is to be warned that to kiss the hilt is simply not done. It is usual to conclude a bout or lesson in similar fashion. Besnard, the French master of the late seventeenth century, is said to have been the first to introduce the practice, which he termed the *révérence*.

Salute, The Grand. An incredibly elaborate and complicated form of the salute. Without citing the endless details, the process involved

both pupil and master performing every simple attack and parry in every line, each series culminating in at least one compound attack, the entire sequence being executed with the utmost deliberation, elegance and formality. At certain stages, words were even exchanged. The master signalled the start by intoning sonorously, 'A vous l'honneur' and after the pupil's dutiful response, 'Par obéissance', came the pontifical command, 'Faîtes'.
There were really two forms of the grand salute – the military and the civil. Although the differences between them were not significant, the former was supposed to be performed with the utmost panache and precision, whereas in the latter, the emphasis was on elegance and suppleness of movement.
The grand salute required not only a quite considerable degree of technique, but a high level of concentration, as it was none too easy to retain the exact sequence of movements in the memory. This those ambitious coaches discovered who attempted to include a demonstration of the grand salute at a school or club function; a project normally ending in disaster.

Sanquhar, Lord. A Scots noble of violent temper and unstable personality, he lost an eye while receiving a fencing lesson from John Turner in 1607. After several years of morose brooding, in which the disfigurement evidently became the dominating obsession of his life, he exacted his revenge with shocking suddenness, ordering his men to murder the unfortunate fencing master. On hearing this episode, Henry IV of France is reputed to have said that he was surprised that the victim had remained unscathed for so long. Such a statement from one who, of all men, was least given to malevolence or spite, can only be interpreted as meaning that he was surprised that the vengeance, if it was to be exacted at all, had been so long delayed. However this may be, Sanquhar himself paid the penalty on the gallows.

Santelli, Italo. The great Italian master whose teaching dominated sabre fencing throughout the first half of the twentieth century. He settled in Hungary and these years were the Golden Age of Hungarian sabre.

He was one of the very few masters who nobly refrained from writing a book on fencing. When questioned on the reasons for this heroic self-denial, he would reply: 'Fencing is something that you do, not write!' His son, Gorgio, is said to have begun fencing at the age of six, and having emigrated to the United States, was still teaching there when over eighty.

Sanzi, Don Adelardo played a very important part in the establishment, about the turn of the century, of a modern, yet distinctively Spanish school of sword-play, based on a combination of French and Italian theories and methods.

Savage Shield. Presented by Sir George Savage in 1905, for the winners of the Epée Team Championship.

Saviolo, Vincentio. A popular and widely patronised master in Elizabethan London, one of those who introduced to England the rapier and dagger, the science of which he had studied in Italy and Spain. From 1590 he taught in partnership with Jeronimo, the pair travelling round the country giving lessons. According to Florio, another Italian immigrant and the translator of Montaigne, he was ambidextrous. He wrote a treatise in two parts which was dedicated to Elizabeth I's favourite, the Earl of Essex. This work, the *Practise*, has earned high praise for its excellent literary style and the attractive surroundings of a walled garden in which the master is represented as giving lessons and technical advice to his pupil. Saviolo was a strong supporter of the theory that 'the point is quicker than the edge' and professed to be able to teach his pupils how to thrust two feet further than any possible rival; an indication that he probably favoured the newly-invented lunge to the 'pass'. Shakespeare, whose plays reveal a considerable knowledge of fencing, is said to have taken lessons from him, but nevertheless ridiculed his fashionable theories in *Romeo and Juliet* through the mouth of Mercutio: 'He (Tybalt) fights as you sing prick-song, keeps time, distance and

The Salute, second position (from Angelo).

proportion; rests me his minim rest, one, two and the third in your bosom.' [Act II, Sc.ii.] Like most of his compatriots, Saviolo was none too popular with the English-born masters, and with Jeronimo declined a challenge from the Silver brothers. Despite this, George Silver himself pronounced him to be 'one of the valiantest fencers that ever came from beyond seas'.

Saxe, Maurice, Marshal and Comte de. Maurice de Saxe was the illegitimate son of Augustus II, Elector of Saxony and King of Poland, and of Aurora, Countess of Konigsmark. One of the finest captains of the age, he saw service under many flags in all the wars of the early and mid eighteenth century. His father bought him a German regiment in the French service (there were a number of such) and he attracted attention by the new training method of musketry which he incorporated in his greatly admired military treatise, *Mes Rêveries*. His great triumph, in the War of the Austrian Succession, was at Fontenoy (1745), when, matched against our own Duke of Cumberland, his presence of mind and steadiness of nerve enabled him to snatch a brilliant victory in a battle that had seemed lost. As a consequence, he over-ran practically the whole of the Austrian Netherlands (Belgium) and most students of military history consider that it was only the treaty of Aix-la-Chapelle (1748) which prevented him from adding Holland to the list of his conquests.

The correspondence between the Marshall and the Duke of Cumberland after the battle, couched in the most courteous terms and arranging for the care of the wounded, reveals the civilised relations prevailing in that age between opposing generals and belligerent nations.

Promoted Marshal-General in 1747 (only Turenne and Villars had previously held this rank) he retired to Chambord with his negro guards and favourite German regiment. In his youth, the Marshal had been a keen swordsman, receiving instruction from the celebrated Teillagory, along with the Chevalier d'Eon and the Chevalier de Saint-Georges; on one occasion, he received so many hits in a bout with Domenico Angelo that he swept him up in his arms in a bear-like hug, in a mixture of frustration and admiration. It is hardly surprising, therefore, that after his death it was strongly rumoured that he had been killed in a duel with Louis-François de Bourbon, Prince of Conti. As against this, it must be remembered that the Marshal was suffering from a complication of disorders, yet obstinately refused to modify his rakish and self-indulgent festivities.

Saxon Blade. A small-sword blade of the flat variety, as distinct from one of triangular section.

Sbasso. A low-line stop-hit of the traditional Italian school, executed by ducking under the adversary's blade; an action similar to the *passata sotto*.

Scales, Practising the. Slang used by fencers to describe their routine, independent practice of the basic footwork, lunges, positions and movements of the blade; comparable to the regular practice by musicians of their scales and arpeggios.

Scandaglio, (It.). May be compared, in military terms, to the preliminary reconnaisance. The opponent's technique and ability are probed, by means of feints, false attacks and so on, thus discovering his likely reactions, his favourite forms of defence,

his cadence.

Scannatura, (It.). A form of counter-attack described by Capo Ferro, which involved the use of the left hand to parry, while simultaneously thrusting. (See Mercutio.)

Scaramouche. 1) A stock character of the old Italian farce; a boastful but ingenious liar, and although knavish and cowardly, blessed with such impudent wit and fertility of resource, that he could never present an entirely unsympathetic figure.

2) The eponymous hero of Rafael Sabatini's novel, the illegitimate son of of a noble of whom, ignorant of his parentage, he became the deadly enemy. Obliged to fly from justice for inciting riots on the eve of the French Revolution, Scaramouche, whose real name was André-Louis Moreau, became in turn a strolling player, a fencing master, and a deputy of the Third Estate in the Constituent Assembly whose task was to produce a new constitution for France. Whilst learning the art of swordsmanship at the academy of M des Amis, Scaramouche lighted on the manual of the great Danet and read his passage on double and triple feints, on the basis of which he devised a supposedly infallible system. It consisted of a series of carefully calculated disengagements, the idea that all the time the opponent would be widening his parry, thus leaving himself open to the final triumphant thrust, which could be the fourth, fifth, or even the sixth offensive action. However, in the description of Scaramouche's successful bouts at the academy, the fencing sequences are often difficult to follow, and the terminology is baffling. For instance, Sabatini speaks of a 'low *sixte*' engagement (itself a high-line position) from which Scaramouche lunged in *tierce*,

which is identical to *sixte* apart from the pronated as opposed to the supinated hand position. Nothing is said about advancing or retiring – apparently the combatants were rooted to the spot – and very little about the opponent's reactions. It is not always stated whether the latter riposted or not, and if he did, by what method; evidently his response was invariably such as to ensure the triumph of Scaramouche's ingenious combinations. Most fencers will feel that if they could be provided with equally co-operative opponents, they too would be confident of enjoying success quite as spectacular as that of Rafael Sabatini's hero.

Scelta di Tempo, (It.). Choice of the exact instant to 'time' an attack on the slightest sign of irresolution or inattention on the part of an opponent.

Scherma, (It.). Fencing.

Schiavona. An edged, basket-hilted sword, of the type used by the *schiavoni* – the body-guard of the Doges of Venice. The guard tapered upwards towards the point of its attachment to the pommel, as it does on the modern fencing sabre.

Schlager or Schlaeger. The weapon which, in about the 1830s replaced the rapier and spadroon in the German students' duels or *schlager-mensur*. It had a long, pointless blade sharpened on the first seven or eight inches of the fore-edge and for about a quarter of that distance on the back-edge. The basket-hilt was much larger than usual to afford protection for the hand, the opponents being placed on guard in high *prime* at very close measure, and no retreat being permitted. (See German Universities.)

164

Scholar's Privilege. In the sixteenth-century examinations for English masters, the candidate was obliged to fence a formidable series of bouts at four different weapons against opponents inevitably more experienced than himself. He enjoyed one advantage – the 'privilege' of exemption from attacks deliberately aimed at the face. Among the tough swordsmen of those days, the face was normally a favourite target, even though masks were not used, and the foils, though indeed buttoned on the points and with blunted edges, were the ordinary, quite heavy weapons of the time.

Schutt. (See Flying Lunge.)

Schwerdt. The heavy, edged German weapon of the Middle Ages.

Sciabola di Terreno, (It.). 'Sabre of the terrain', a sabre used in duelling, the counter-part of the *épée de combat*. The contestants adopted a very upright stance and largely confined themselves to light cuts at forearm and wrist, similarly to the tactics of the comparatively recent épée duels.

Sciabola in Mano, (It.). 'Sabre in hand', that is, the sabre gripped correctly and lightly, so that attacks may be made with the full co-ordination of arm, wrist and fingers, Professor Bertrand defines the term as 'the elimination of force and the ability to check the edge on impact with the objective'.

Scimitar. The typical Oriental cutting weapon, with curved blade often broadening towards the point. It was introduced to western Europe by the *housas* or Hungarian light horsemen who became familiar with it in the long-drawn-out Turkish wars, and whose hussar regiments, armed with the sabre, a close imita-

tion of the weapon, set the fashion for every other European army.

Scottish Amateur Fencing Union. The Scottish Fencing Club was founded in 1909. The enthusiasm of its members and the influence of Professor Léon Crosnier at Edinburgh, were alike responsible for the rapid development of fencing north of the border. The S.A.F.U. was formed in 1923, under the presidency of the Duke of Atholl. Six years later, it affiliated to the A.F.A., but retained control of all amateur fencing in Scotland, subject, of course, to the articles of the parent body.

Seax. Very similar to the scimitar, the seax was a broad-bladed, curved Saxon sword, with a semi-circular notch on the back-edge and the point cut off almost square. It is found in the arms of Essex and Middlesex.

Second Intention. 1) According to the purists, counter-time and nothing but counter-time. However, a more liberal and possibly more literal interpretation may surely include a greater diversity of actions, such as, for example, a counter-riposte or renewed attack, the conditions for which have been deliberately induced by the fencer's original action. 2) For Barbasetti, second intention is counter-time as understood by most fencers in this country, i.e., deliberately provoking a stop-hit from an opponent which is met by a parry and riposte. For his interpretation of counter-time, see Contre-Temps.

Second Intention Defence or second intention parries, are parries prepared in advance against an anticipated counter-attack, riposte, or counter-riposte.

Second Tempo. In Italian theory, the second feint in a two-feint attack.

Secondary Parries. At sabre, *tierce*, *quarte* and *sixte*.

Seconde, (Italian *seconda*). The second position and parry protecting the fencer's lower trunk on his right-hand side, similar to *octave*, but the hand is in pronation.

Seconde Pour le Dessus. '*Seconde* above'; La Tousche's name for the parry of *tierce* before the standardisation of terminology.

Seconde Pour le Dessous. '*Seconde* underneath'; La Tousche's name for a semi-circular parry designed to meet any low-line attack.

Seconds. The friends and supporters of the principals in a duel, one or more of whom convey the challenge and arrange the details of the meeting. At one time, notably in the sixteenth and early seventeenth centuries, it was customary for the seconds to engage with each other and there are not a few instances of these fire-eaters, who had no conceivable cause for quarrel, killing or mortally wounding each other. Sometimes they encountered each other in separate pairs; at others, there were no fixed opponents, so that several successful combatants might be in a position to finish off the sole survivor on the opposite side. According to one system, the principals engaged while the leading seconds stood behind each. Should one of the principals fall, his second then faced the disagreeable prospect of encountering, not only the victorious principal, but his second as well.

Secret Attack and Secret Thrust. (See Botta Segreta.)

Section. One of the several geographical areas into which the country is divided by the Amateur Fencing Association, for administrative and competitive purposes.

Walton gets his hit in first against Scott in the Scottish Schools fencing competition.

Securing the Sword. Grasping the opponent's weapon just below the guard, preparatory to disarming him.

Seligman, E. was one of the founding fathers of modern British fencing. He was recognised as the first British Epée Champion, having been the Briton highest placed (seventh) in the annual open tournament held by the Epée Club in 1904. He represented his country with distinction in numerous international matches, including no less than four Olympics, captaining the foil and épée teams at the Antwerp Olympics of 1920. He is the only man ever to have held all three National Championships; foil (1906-7), épée (1904-1906) and sabre (1923-1924).

Semi-Circular Beat. (See Beat.)

Semi-Circular Bind. A term used by Vass to describe a bind (in the Hungarian sense, a fairly strong engagement) following an initial blade action diagonally across the executant's body, from *seconde* to *quarte*, *septime* to *sixte* or vice versa.

Semi-Circular Parry or half-circular parry, is normally employed when on guard in the high line to meet an attack delivered low, the hand remaining breast-high and not being moved, apart from a slight rotation of the wrist. In the French school, this parry must always finish on the same side of the body as it started, i.e., from *sixte* to *octave* (in which case the point, passing over the adversary's blade, describes a capital 'C') or *quarte* to *septime*, in which case it describes the back of a capital 'D'. When parrying *octave* from an initial position in *sixte*, it is most important that the hand is neither dropped nor turned into pronation, while the elbow must not be stuck
166

outwards, but kept beneath the shoulder; otherwise, the covering is inadequate.

A semi-circular parry can be executed equally well from a low-line position, if a high attack threatens, simply by reversing the whole process. It should be remembered, however, that the point still travels inwards.

The nomenclature was late in developing; during the seventeenth and eighteenth century, the action from high line into *septime* was most misleadingly termed *cercle*, and then half-circle, the corresponding parry into *octave* apparently then being seldom if ever employed.

The Hungarians term these parries the 'destruction' or 'destroying' parries; their interpretation of a semi-circular parry is a diagonal movement across the target, from *quarte* to *octave* or *sixte* to *septime*, and vice versa. Such parries have never been taught in this country, although against a wide and heavy-handed opponent, they would seem to have a good deal to recommend them.

Semi-Circular Transfer. Just as the Hungarians describe the parry executed diagonally across the body as semi-circular (see above entry) so the semi-circular transfer, in their parlance, takes the opponent's blade through precisely the same lines; it is in fact, the *prise-de-fer* known in the French school as the 'bind'.

Senese or Senesio, Alessandro. A seventeenth-century master of Bologna. He recommended a guard position similar to ours, with left knee bent and right knee directed straight forward, as being invaluable in street brawls.

Senior. For competitive purposes, a fencer who is debarred from entry to certain junior competitions on the

grounds that he has been awarded international colours or has reached a specified stage in any one of a number of stated events of an important nature.

Sentiment du Fer. 'Sensation of the blade.' In classical foil play, when the blades were normally engaged, it was possible to deduce a great deal from the strength, or lightness, with which the opponent made the contact. Subtle pressures, or exploratory beats, could be returned, or at the crucial moment deceived by disengagements. To encourage this blade-sense, it was no uncommon thing for masters of the old school to give lessons to blindfolded pupils.

Separazione, (It.). To detach one's blade from an engagement.

Septime. The seventh position and parry, protecting the lower part of the fencer's target on the inside (left-hand) line. The hand should be breast-high and the point directed downwards, at about the level of the adversary's knees. When the parry was taken from the high line to ward off a low attack, it was for long misleadingly called *cercle*, and subsequently *demi-cercle*. The contributor to the Badminton Library surprisingly asserts that the point should be breast or shoulder high.

Septime, Croisé of. Just as the *croisé* of *octave* bears some resemblance to the bind from *quarte* to *octave*, so the *croisé* of *septime* might be confused with the bind from *sixte* to *septime*. But, similarly to the example just cited, the executant never moves his blade out to a covered *sixte* position; instead, once contact with and control of the opponent's blade has been secured, the latter is forced down into the *septime* position. When the sword-arm is extended and the point

Singlestick, Somersetshire Gamesters.

placed on target simultaneously with the taking of the blade, the term 'time-hit by *croisé* of *septime*' is used. It is a stroke much recommended at épée against the left-hander's *flèche*, particularly when combined with an *inquartata* side-step.

Septime, Lifted. In this variation of the parry, the hand is lifted considerably above what is usual. Professor Crosnier recommends its use at épée as a protection against the *remise*, or again, as a preparation of attack, when, used as a *prise-de-fer* and combined with a step forward, it ensures that the opponent's blade is deflected away from the executant and even passes behind him. At foil, it has been found to be particularly effective against the 'rusher'; the high hand strongly deflects the attacking blade and it is easier to flip the point up and place it on target than it is to bring it down, avoiding the mask, in a case like this when the distance has been so drastically narrowed.

Sesta, (It.). (See Sixte.)

Seventh Parry. 1) See *septime*.
2) At sabre, a derisive term for the step back; there being six generally recognised parries with the blade.

Sgualembrato, (It.). An oblique cut downwards.

Shakespeare, William. A very considerable amount of sword-play is introduced into his plays and the references scattered through the texts show that the author was at least familiar with the terminology and general principles of the contemporary Italian school of rapier-fighting, introduced into England during the course of his lifetime (1564-1616).

One of the best-known incidents is the challenge to Hamlet conveyed from Laertes by Osric, to the effect that wagers had been laid that Laertes would not exceed Hamlet by three hits in 'a dozen passes'. (Act V, Sc.ii.) A moment's reflection will serve to show that such a result is mathematically impossible. As the King had laid odds of twelve to nine (or four to three) against Laertes accomplishing this feat, it presumably means that, after twenty-one hits, Laertes would have to lead Hamlet by at least twelve to nine if he was to win. It seems likely that all this is one more example of Shakespearian inconsistency and oversight, though, just possibly, the confusion is deliberate, as portraying the vagueness and absent-mindedness of the eccentric Osric. Frank Marshall, the Shakespearian critic and scholar wrote, 'It was impossible that Osric could state anything clearly or simply.'

Shallow, Justice. A character in Shakespeare's *Merry Wives of Windsor* who strongly disapproved of the new rapier school. 'In these times, you stand on distance, your passes, *stoccadoes* (thrusts) and I know not what. 'Tis the heart, Master Page, 'tis here, 'tis here. I have seen the time, with my long sword, I would have made you four tall fellows skip like rats.' (Act II, Sc.i.)

Sharps. The name given to any swords which are to be used in earnest and are not rebated, blunted, equipped with buttons, or otherwise rendered innocuous for practice and fencing.

Shearing Sword. A short-sword, much extolled by Silver.

Sheen, Miss Gillian is famous as the first, and at the time of writing, the last British fencer to win an Olympic gold medal (Melbourne 1956). She won the British Ladies' Foil from 1949 to 1958 inclusive, the one break being in 1950, when the successful competitor was her doughty and longstanding opponent, Mrs M.A. Glen-Haig, Miss Sheen on that occasion having to be content with third place. How close was the rivalry between these two ladies is evinced by the fact that during the period of Miss Sheen's supremacy, Mrs Glen-Haig, who had been the champion in 1948 and 1950, was placed second on no less than six successive occasions, from 1951-1956. Miss Sheen won the championship ten times in all, the last occasion being in 1960, the de Beaumont Cup five times and the Desprez Cup and the Jubilee Cup four times each.

Shell. The *coquille* or guard.

Shell-Guard. The flattish, sea-shell type guard of the sixteenth and seventeenth centuries, sometimes affixed to one side of the hilt only, sometimes to both; an alternative to the much deeper cup-hilt, or the complicated arrangement of bars and rings favoured by some swordsmen with the object of fouling their opponents' blades.

Sheridan, Richard Brinsley was born in Dublin, but settled in London, for like many another born in the provinces of the United Kingdom, he sensed that his talents needed a wider stage. His fame was established with the production of *The Rivals* (1775), its delicious and surprisingly modern humour being nowhere better displayed than in the

168

Slipping the leg (from Alfieri).

scene where Bob Acres and Sir Lucius O'Trigger make their farcical preparations for a duel. (Act V, Sc.iii.) In 1776 Sheridan became manager of Drury Lane Theatre and the same year saw the appearance of his other great masterpiece, *The School for Scandal*, unapproached for its wit, though *The Critic* (1779), an uproarious burlesque of the standard Elizabethan corpse-littered tragedy, must, for sheer rollicking comedy, surely stand alone. Elected to Brooks's, where he met the leading Whig statesmen of the day, he entered the House of Commons in 1780, in due course holding a number of ministerial posts and playing a leading role in the impeachment of Warren Hastings for his alleged malpractices while Governor-General of India. After Drury Lane had been destroyed by fire, Sheridan died in reduced circumstances, but was given a splendid funeral in Westminster Abbey.

Sheridan fought two duels. The first was after he had been accused

of compromising a friend by dissuading him from 'going out'. Sheridan was very reluctant to go through with the affair and endeavoured to maintain an entirely defensive posture, but his reckless antagonist spitted himself on Sheridan's sword and only survived by a miracle.

Then, in 1772, came a two-round encounter. Captain Thomas Matthews of the 54th Foot had cast aspersions on the character of Mrs Sheridan, to whom he had previously been paying his addresses and with whom the playwright had subsequently eloped. In a first meeting by candlelight at the Castle Tavern in London, the Captain was disarmed by the old trick of parrying *prime*, anchoring the captive blade against the flank with the left elbow and simultaneously exerting leverage on the opponent's *forte* with the unarmed hand. Sheridan then put himself hopelessly in the wrong by scornfully snapping his enemy's blade. Inflamed with resentment, the

Captain insisted on another encounter, this time at Kingsdown, near Bath. Sheridan tried his disarming trick again, this time unsuccessfully and the affair degenerated into a brawl. Both men were wounded, Sheridan being reduced to a pitiable state and how he survived, if the description of his multitudinous wounds is even approximately accurate, staggers belief.

Shrewsbury, Francis Talbot, Eleventh Earl of challenged the Duke of Buckingham on learning that his Countess had become the other's mistress. The pair met on 16 January 1668, at Barn-Elms; the Earl was attended by Sir John Talbot, a distant kinsman, and Mr Howard whilst the opposing seconds were Sir Robert Holmes and Captain Jenkins. The usual casualty list of those times ensued. Shrewsbury died two months later of a chest wound, Captain Jenkins was killed on the spot and Sir John's arm was ripped open. What gave particular scandal was the story, never disproved, that Lady Shrewsbury had actually been present at the scene, disguised as a page-boy holding the Duke's horse and had gaily departed with him after witnessing the mortal wounding of her husband.

Side Rings. Protections fixed to one, or sometimes both sides of the hilt on sixteenth-century rapiers, in the days when mailed gauntlets were going out of fashion and some additional protection was needed for the hand.

Silver, George. A swordsman and writer on swordsmanship at the end of Elizabeth I's reign, notable as the eloquent champion of the traditional English school of broadsword-play, against the new methods of rapier and dagger imported from Italy,

An exquisitely mounted Solingen blade.

which he regarded as alien, contemptible and ineffective. He wrote a heated criticism of the use of the point, and an equally vigorous defence of the cutting weapon in a work entitled *The Paradoxes of Silver.* Most of his paradoxes are, in fact, fallacies, but he does make one very significant point, which will be appreciated by all who have taken up the sabre after first accustoming themselves to the foil: namely, that the cut, or blow as he calls it, is much more difficult to parry than the thrust, being delivered from a great variety of angles. He adhered obstinately to the notion that the cut is quicker than the thrust; though, writing as he was with the heavy sixteenth-century rapier in mind, such a statement may well have been rather less untrue then than now, when the opposite theory is generally regarded as axiomatic. He makes no reference to the lunge, so it can only be assumed that he regarded it as one more deplorable foreign innovation. Instead, he advocates attacks with a spring forward, or *balestra.*

George Silver and his brother Toby, in the excess of their indignation against the hated interlopers, challenged the Italian masters Saviolo and Jeronimo at rapier, rapier and dagger, and almost every possible combination and permutation of the weapons then in use, even including the pole weapons. Their bloodthirsty zeal, however, was doomed to disappointment, for in the event, their challenge was declined and no such encounter ever took place.

Silver Jubilee. An annual Ladies' Invitation competition inaugurated in 1935 to commemorate the Silver Jubilee of George V.

Silvie. A sixteenth-century master of Italian extraction, who taught two

169

Kings of France – Charles IX and Henry III.

Simmonds, Professor A.T. started fencing at an early age to escape the punishment inflicted in the boxing ring by his brother (three years younger). His father agreed to pay for two lessons a week under Professor Gravé at his salle in Cleveland Row, but would only advance the fares for one of the journeys, with the result that the future professional sabre champion of Great Britain was obliged to make the round trip of fourteen miles on foot. After distinguished service with the Coldstream Guards in the Western Desert and Italy, he studied under Crosnier and received lessons at different times from every master then teaching in this country, including Anderson and Harmer-Brown. He also studied in Italy and Vincennes under the French master, Couthard, while a visit to Germany resulted in the award of a master's diploma of the academy of that country. The sabre was his great love and to enlarge his experience he regularly travelled to Hungary and practised with the most eminent Hungarian masters. The professor also instigated and organised the remarkable feat of twelve boys at Wandsworth School who took turns in fencing non-stop, night and day for an entire week at Bisham Abbey in 1973. Himself the most forceful of characters, his standards and methods were those to be expected from the youngest-ever R.S.M. of his illustrious regiment.

Simple Attacks. Simple attacks consist of one blade movement only. They are sub-divided into direct and indirect attacks.

1) Direct. There is only one direct attack – the straight-thrust. Whether executed from an initial engagement or not, there is no change in the

relative positions of the blade, the attacker's blade remaining on the same side of his adversary's weapon.

2) Indirect. There are three indirect attacks, in which the attacker's blade passes under or over his adversary's weapon to reach the target.

a) The *disengagement*. The attacking blade normally passes under the adversary's weapon (but over it from the low line).

b) The *cut-over* or *coupé*. Here the blade passes over the defender's weapon.

c) The *counter-disengagement* deceives the defender's attempt to change the line of engagement. As he executes the circular action, designed to engage the attacker's blade in the opposite line, the latter follows the defender's blade round, clockwise or anti-clockwise as the case may be, thus restoring the original relative position of the weapons and allowing an attack to be delivered. It must be stressed to beginners that the defender's blade is *deceived*. They must not try to re-engage, or deflect the other weapon before attacking.

It is to be noted that while a disengagement or cut-over, executed on the opponent's covering (lateral) action, offers the best chance of success, since the attack is delivered into the line away from which the defender's blade is moving, these attacks can be delivered at any time, without any previous action at all by the defender. The technique of the counter-disengagement is indeed identical with the ordinary disengagement – the attack passes under the adversary's blade as he tries to engage in the new line – but, by its very nature, it cannot even be started until the opponent has begun to change his engagement. It is therefore the one attack which, it can be said, is inevitably initiated by the defender.

It may also be added – and this is something that beginners often fail to realise – that simple ripostes and counter-ripostes fall into precisely the same categories as the above simple attacks. The essential distinction is the stage in the phrase at which they are introduced.

Simple Double Feint Attacks. The name given by Vass to such compound attacks as the feint straight-thrust, one-two, or the one-two-three. The attack includes two feints both of a simple as opposed to a circular character, though it is to be observed that he uses the term 'simple' in a sense very different from that of the French school.

Simple Parry. The simple or lateral parry taken horizontally across the target, i.e., *quarte* to *sixte* and vice versa, or *septime* to *octave* and vice versa. When parrying from *sixte* to *quarte*, fencers must beware of a very common tendency to drop the hand, which can impair the effectiveness of the parry.

Simple Remise. A term used by Barbasetti to include not only the *remise* but the *redoublement* as well.

Simple Riposte. A riposte which is either direct or indirect; in the latter case, by disengagement, cut-over, or counter-disengagement.

Simple Single Feint Attacks. The name given by Vass to such compound attacks as the feint straight-thrust, disengage, or the one-two.

Simple Transfer, (Hung.). A *prise-de-fer* taken vertically or diagonally.

Simultaneous Attack. When two fencers attack each other simultaneously, or apparently simultaneously, difficulties can arise at foil and sabre if both should register hits, either on or off target. At foil, if the president is unable to award priority to either side, he must annul both hits and replace the fencers on guard where they were. If only one of the fencers actually scores a hit, there is of course no problem – the hit stands, even though the fencing may have been theoretically incorrect.

At épée where there are no conventions, no problem arises at all – double hits are perfectly valid, one against each fencer, the equivalent of both duellists being killed or wounded.

At sabre, the procedure used to be identical to foil, but is now much more complicated. The decline of classical sabre fencing has plumbed such depths and resulted in such a plethora of simultaneous attacks that the rules have had to be revised and the ludicrous charade at present obtaining has been introduced. After two such attacks, even if no-one was hit, the fencers are warned; if it happens again, the solemn farce of drawing lots is undertaken. The winner is then entitled to the benefit of the hit when next the situation arises; on the subsequent occasion, his adversary scores. And as if this were not enough, the whole laborious performance has to be repeated after the offensive priority has changed twice, and there is yet another simultaneous attack.

In strict theory, there is a distinction between attacks which are literally simultaneous, when no priority can be awarded at the conventional weapons, and attacks resulting in a double hit; in which latter case one party must have been at fault through stop-hitting too late, lunging onto an opponent's straight arm, or some similar blunder.

Single Attack. A simple attack.

Single Guard. A type of knuckle-bow, joining one end of the *quillons* to the pommel in such a way as to form one thin, graceful curve.

Single Rapier. The system of duelling or fencing with one rapier, as opposed to rapier and dagger, or even two rapiers, one in each hand.

Singlestick. 1) Originally, a slightly smaller version of the quarter-staff, approximately 5 feet as against 7 feet in length. Both hands could be used, as with the larger weapon.

2) The practice weapon for the sabre, before the introduction of the light fencing variety. It really was a stick, about the same length as the genuine weapon, and usually had a wicker-work or basket-hilt. It was practised in certain schools and universities during the last century.

3) The most characteristic form of singlestick-play, however, retained the name of 'backswording', for which it had been the original practice weapon and remained popular in country-districts until the third or fourth decade of the nineteenth century. The combatants maintained a very close measure – there was no lunging or passing – but the really distinctive feature was the position of the left arm which was used to protect the left side of the head. The elbow was raised as high as possible and as far forward as a belt passed under the left leg and looped round the hand would allow. Victory was achieved by drawing blood from the opponent's head. The sport was less sanguinary than this would suggest, as the cuts were all delivered with a flip of the wrist, so as to expose the attacker's target as little as possible. Nevertheless, the receipt of a smart crack on the elbow must have occasioned severe discomfort, to say the least. A vivid and enthusiastic description of a rustic comp-

etition of this sort can be read in the second chapter of *Tom Brown's Schooldays*.

Sitting Down. Fencing slang for the bending of the knees in the on-guard position.

Sixte. The sixth position and parry protecting the upper right-hand side of the fencer's trunk. The hand is breast-high, supinated either wholly or partly, and the point slightly elevated. It was one of the last parries to be categorised – indeed, it seems only to have received the name from La Boessière at the turn of the eighteenth and nineteenth centuries. Previously it had been designated as *quarte* outside, or more commonly, *tierce*, when, of course, the hand was in pronation; though fifty years before, Godfrey had in effect recommended it by advocating a supinated hand position in *tierce*. Its tardy development was doubtless due to the need for its execution with the weak, or false edge, of the small-sword and consequently, it could only be really effective with the later, lighter foil. In the early nineteenth century, two French masters, Ghersi and Jean Louis, both favoured *sixte*, the latter contending that *tierce* was superfluous anyway and should be entirely abandoned. Many masters, however, continued to teach its use well into the 1930s.

The term *sixte* was also used for a now obsolete sabre parry, used to protect the head as an alternative to *quinte*; and a very awkward and uncomfortable position it was. (See Sabre.)

Sixte, Lifted. A method of opening the line for a riposte following the parry of *sixte*. The blade is pivoted underneath the opponent's and the hand pushed sharply upwards, thus exposing his target to the thrust.

Sleep, Putting to. (See Freezing.)

Slender. A foolish character in Shakespeare's *Merry Wives of Windsor*, in love with Anne Page, but too irresolute to set about wooing her. Much given to self-pity, as can be seen from his pathetic complaint that he 'had bruised my shin th'other day with playing at sword and dagger with a master of fence'. (Act 1, Sc.i.)

Slinging Parry. (See Tap Parry.)

Slip, To. 1) Hope's term for deceiving the opponent's blade by a *trompement*.
2) To withdraw an advanced part of the target (especially the leg) and simultaneously stop-hit or stop-cut.

Slip Feint. The blades being engaged, to half-extend the arm, maintaining contact, the object being to trick the opponent into a nervous or instinctive covering action, this opening another part of his target.

Small-Sword. The short, light, elegant and beautifully proportioned weapon which superseded the transition rapier at the turn of the seventeenth and eighteenth centuries. The blade, which might be triangular, lozenge (diamond) shaped, hexagonal, or even elliptical in section, was only some thirty inches in length, i.e., less than the modern foil. It was used as a thrusting weapon only, the edge possessed by many specimens being only to facilitate the entry of the blade and to discourage an opponent from deflecting the attack with his hand. J.D. Aylward, in *The Small-Sword in England*, lists the following terms for the different parts of the weapon:
Amande – the centre of the knuckle-bow.
Branche à bouton – one *quillon* with

knob.
Branche à croissant – the rings either side the *ricasso*.
Branche à demi-ellipse – lower part of the knuckle-bow.
Crochet – the part of the knuckle-bow entering the pommel.

Society of Swordmen in Scotland. An association of fencing masters founded in the northern kingdom in 1692, largely at the instigation of Sir William Hope. Subsequently, elaborate plans were afoot to establish, by Act of Parliament, its monopoly right to all teaching, its authority to intervene in all disputes arising from questions of honour (in the pious hope of reducing the frequency of duels) and its power to seize and imprison contumacious persons. However, before any such statutory powers could be obtained, all these ambitious schemes were frustrated by the Union of the Kingdoms (1707) and with the consequent amalgamation of the Scottish parliament with that of England, the whole enterprise languished.

Solingen lies in the Rhineland near Dusseldorf. Sometimes known as the 'German Sheffield' for the excellence of its cutlery, it is even more famous for the quality of its sword-blades which have been renowned since the Middle Ages.

Soubise was the negro servant of the Duchess of Queensberry. In the eighteenth century, a negro, or at any rate a coloured attendant of some sort, was something of a status symbol. His morals, however, were dubious, and he became first a *garçon de salle*, then an assistant master at Angelo's fencing academy. There, his rakish high spirits earned him considerable popularity, but the irregularity of his life and his monstrously excessive expense accounts,

especially on his visits to Eton to give lessons, resulted in his dismissal and exile to India, where he became the proprietor of a highly successful fencing and riding school until a fall from a horse caused his premature end.

Soup-Plate. A very large guard, almost a foot across, fitted to the *schlager*, or German student's duelling sabre.

Souzy were probably the blades most highly regarded of all those forged in France. Their reputation stood so high both before and after the war that it was felt by the traditionalists to be a matter of keen regret when the concern was eventually taken over by Soudet.

Spada, (It.). 1) A sword.
2) Also one of the four suits in the traditional Italo-Spanish pack of cards, the sword symbolising the Nobility, the others, Cups, Money and Batons (Clubs) representing respectively the estates of the priests, merchants and peasants. The names of two of these suits, Spades (*spadas*) and Clubs were early adopted into the English packs, but owing to some misunderstanding, the symbols are respectively those of the *piques* (pikes) and *treflés* (clover leaves) of the French pack. The confusion was increased by the chance resemblance of the spade card to the old-fashioned turfing-spade. Cups and Money were likewise replaced by the French Hearts and *Carreaux* (paving-stones) which might be supposed to represent the townsmen or merchant class. The stylised lozenge shape of the *carreau* is habitually miscalled a 'diamond' in England.

Spada d'Exercisio, (It.). The Italian foil; but it has a much closer resemblance to the *spada* proper than does the French foil to the épée.

Spada Sola, (It.). 'Sword alone' or single rapier, as opposed to rapier and dagger. In many sixteenth-century schools of fencing, it was considered to be the best practical foundation for the novice.

Spadassinicides. A company of re-volutionary swordsmen, fifty strong, formed at an early stage of the Re-volution in France by one Citizen Boyer for the purpose of meeting the aristocratic challenges which flooded in after he had announced that he himself would meet any right-wing member of the National Assembly attempting to force a duel on a repre-sentative of the people. The result was something of an anti-climax; the prospect of encountering this band of fire-eaters apparently proving un-attractive, the host of Boyer's oppo-nents mysteriously faded away, and so far as is known, the Spadassini-cides never found the opportunity to flesh their swords.

Spadone, (It.). Originally, the Italian long-sword. Later, this name, or sometimes *spadrone*, was applied to a very different weapon, the eighteenth-century spadroon.

Spadroon. A light cut-and-thrust weapon, originating in Germany in the eighteenth century. It was hilted like a small-sword and had a flat, pointed blade, sharp on one edge. It must be regarded as the precursor of the modern fencing sabre. It was slightly adapted, by the British Army, for use as the standard infan-try officers' sword, but proving grossly inefficient in the Peninsular War (1808-14), became the subject of many complaints.

Spadroon Guard. A guard position favoured with this weapon. The sword-arm was almost fully ex-tended, the hand was breast-high and in full supination. The point was directed downwards, at about the level of the adversary's thigh.

Spanish Fight. Silver's term for the tactics of the sixteenth-century

Soubise giving instruction to the Duchess of Queensbury.

Spanish rapier-play. The exponents of this school stood very upright and were continually on the move 'as if they were in a dance'; but the distinguishing feature was their habit of maintaining their sword-arm at its full extent, with the point of the weapon directed straight at their adversary's body or face.

Spanish Foil. The distinguishing feature of the Spanish foil, as it evolved at the end of the nineteenth century, lay in the design of the grip, which had two small projecting bars, not quite opposite each other, the vestigial survivors of the traditional cross-hilt. This, so it was claimed, permitted more attacks on the blade and a stronger parry, with a more extended arm than was possible with the French foil.

Spanish School. The illustrious native school of Spanish swordsmanship, in its palmy days from the sixteenth century onwards, was more grandiose and pretentious, and far less practical, than that flourishing in contemporary Italy. Whereas the Italians, without ever becoming thoroughly systematic, did devise a considerable number of *bottas* (attacks), time-thrusts, parries and so forth, the great Spanish masters, notably Carranza and Narvaez, indulged in vain and cloudy speculations depending on geometry, anatomy and even metaphysics. One contribution that they did make, which today is in danger of being over-emphasised, was to lay some stress on the observation of the opponent's psychology and physiology; whether he was tall, short, muscular, or of an obviously nervous or excitable disposition. They then proceeded, however, to make the most extravagant claim that any pupil, who had thoroughly absorbed the intricacies of their system, would

be quite literally invincible against a less privileged opponent – whatever might be the discrepancies in physique or athletic ability.

The basis of these remarkable theories was the 'mysterious circle' adapted and elaborated still more by Thibaust of Antwerp. (See Thibaust.) Much more orthodox was the blade-work, as opposed to the footwork, of this Spanish school. The cuts are familiar enough and the thrusts – the *stoccata* under the arm and the *imbroccata*, over the arm – were perfectly in accordance with standard practice. The on-guard position, however, was strange to modern eyes. The feet were very close, not more than a few inches apart, while the knees were perfectly straight and the unarmed hand dangled very ungracefully by the side. The lunge, it seems, was totally unknown.

The decline of the historic Spanish tradition was not dissimilar to that of Italy, for in the course of the eighteenth and nineteenth centuries it was altogether abandoned, and in its place, apart from a few trifling particulars, a combination of the modern French and Italian systems was adopted.

Spanish Sword. A name used by sixteenth-century Englishmen for the rapier; Spanish influence, at the court of Mary Tudor, preceding the fashionable Italianate cult of the following generation.

Sparizione di Corpo, (It.). A displacement of one's target.

Spigoli, (It.). The edges of the blade.

Spinnewyn, Prof. Anthime. Coming to England in 1900, this French master gave an exhibition with the épée, thus arousing interest and enthusiasm for this weapon, which pre-

viously had been almost unknown in this country. As a result, the Epée Club was formed and English épéeists achieved no little success on the Continent in the years immediately preceding the First World War.

Spratico, (It.) or beginner's assault; a half-way stage between the formal lesson and the bout. It is conducted by the master, who makes attacks on his pupil without pressing them home too aggressively; alternating these with fairly obvious openings and opportunities for the pupil to take the offensive in his turn.

Stance. Strictly speaking, the position of the feet only in the on-guard position. More loosely, the fencer's on-guard position as a whole.

Stealing a March. Gaining distance by bringing the rear foot right up to the leading foot, before taking a step forward or lunging.

Steam Foil. Slang for the traditional, non-electric foil; probably arising from the circumstance that about the time of the introduction of the electric weapon, electric trains were rapidly replacing steam locomotives on the railways of Britain.

Steccata, (It.). The location of a duel; the 'field of play'.

Steele, Sir Richard. Commissioned as a young man into the Coldstream Guards, Steele is remembered for his brilliant contributions to such famous publications of the reign of Queen Anne as *The Tatler*, *The Guardian* and *The Spectator*. Above all else, he achieved immortality by the creation of Sir Roger de Coverley whose club and friends are introduced in the second issue of the last-named paper; also of his account, in *The Englishman*, of the adventures of Alexander Selkirk, traditionally supposed to form the basis of *Robinson Crusoe*. We are also indebted to Steele for a highly detailed account of one of the prize-fights so popular in those times, that between Miller and Buck. (*The Spectator*, No. 436, 21 July, 1712.)

It is of some interest that Steele, who had himself fought a duel when in the Army, strongly condemned the practice in several articles in *The Tatler*, in particular the still surviving custom of the seconds themselves engaging each other. In No. 39, it appears from a conversation between three fictitious characters that duelling was totally prohibited in the Cromwellian Army, but that, as might be expected, the Cavaliers were more inclined to share the views of the Musketeers. In the contemporary eighteenth-century Army, it was, although strongly discouraged, not entirely unknown.

Step Out. To move to one side, away from the centre of the *piste*, towards its edges.

Step-in-Parry. To advance while parrying the opponent's attack. The step-in-parry is performed at the very outset of the forward movement. A very effective manoeuvre against the 'rusher', or the modern competitive fencer who desires above all to get to close quarters, but who, suddenly finding the distance very different from what he had anticipated, feels at a loss and loses confidence.

Stesso Tempo, (It.). To parry and riposte in one action, characteristic of the sixteenth-century Italian rapier-play. The action was what would now be called a 'time-hit', or a 'covered stop-hit', i.e., extending the arm with the point directed at the opponent while simultaneously deflecting his attack. (See Dui Tempi.)

Stirrup-Hilt. The simple hilt, consisting of a straight cross-bar and knuckle-bow, with which the curved sabre of Hungarian origin was equipped when it was first issued to hussar regiments in the eighteenth century.

Stoccada or Stoccata, (It.). A thrust under the adversary's sword-arm; according to Saviolo's classification, from the low right-hand side.

Stock. An English term, derived from the above, or possibly the French *estoc*, for the sixteenth-century Italian rapier; sometimes it denoted merely a thrust by such a weapon. In this sense it is used in *Antonio's Revenge*, by Marston (1602): 'I would pass on him with a mortal stock.' (Act I, Sc.ii.)

Stop-Cut. At sabre, a counter-attack, a cut delivered against the opponent's attack or preparation. As the conventions of foil and sabre are identical, it must, to be valid, arrive one period of fencing time ahead of the last movement of the attack. The great majority of stop-cuts at sabre are directed against the opponent's wrist and forearm. Hence the great importance of covering these parts of the target when taking the offensive.

Castello advocates the execution of the stop-cut with a simultaneous movement of the feet out of line, to the executant's right. The hand and weapon, he argues, should terminate in *quarte*, as protection against an attack which must now come from that side.

Stop-Hit. A form of counter attack, delivered into the opponent's attack or against his preparation. To be valid, it must arrive on the target one movement ahead of the final action of the attack; in other words, gain a period of fencing time on the offensive movement.

Stop-Hit, The Change. A stop-hit by disengagement.

Stop-Hit in Counter-Time. An ambitious form of the counter-attack, virtually confined to épée fencing. A feint is made to draw the stop-hit, but instead of parrying and riposting as in the ordinary form of counter-time, the executant delivers a stop-hit on the stop-hitter. This, at least, is the theory; but so delicately timed an operation can but seldom be attended with success.

Stop-Hit, The Deceiving. Lukovitch's term for a stop-hit by disengagement which entirely avoids the opponent's attempt to engage.

Stop-Hit with Opposition. The more recent name for a time-hit.

Stop-Hit with Three Points. A somewhat unusual name for the *passata sotto*, the fencer's body being supported by the unarmed hand in addition to the legs.

Stop-Point. A stop-hit with the point of the sabre.

Stop Short. A sudden, almost convulsive halt during or after a step forward, either to prepare an attack, to draw an offensive action from the opponent, or to test his reactions.

Stop-Thrust. Another name for the stop-hit. In some illustrations, however, it is depicted as being executed with a lunge. The purist of the Crosnier school would, therefore, insist on its being classified as an 'attack on the preparation'.

Stop-Touch. A stop-hit.

Straight Arm Defence. A tactic especially in favour among épéeists, who keep the sword-arm fully extended, with point permanently threatening the opponent's wrist and forearm.

Straight Lengthening. An Hungarian term for the *remise*; Vass suggests that with épée, it should generally be executed *en flèche*.

Straight Riposte. The direct riposte.

Straight-Thrust or Straight-Attack. The only direct attack; there is but one blade movement and the position of the blades relative to each other does not change. The straight-thrust is generally delivered from absence of blade towards an open part of the target, but it can be executed from an engagement, provided the opponent has left himself uncovered.

Straights, The was the name given to the tortuous maze of narrow alleys and back streets lying in the region between St Martin's Lane and Chandos Street. It is mentioned by more than one seventeenth-century writer and was reputed to be the haunt of 'bullies, knights of the post (i.e., the whipping-post) and fencing masters'. In those days it was not at all unknown for fencing masters to be associated in popular estimation with such objectionable elements of society.

Stramazone or Stramonzello, (It.). A tearing cut, delivered by a wrist-action, using the edge of the blade nearest the point.

Striccio, (It.). The *froissement*.

Stuck. (See Stock.) Shakespeare used the term more than once.

Sir Toby Belch: Why, man, he's a very devil; I have not seen such a firago. I had a pass with him, rapier, scabbard and all and he gives me the stuck in with such a mortal motion that it is inevitable . . . They say he has been fencer to the Sophy. (*Twelfth Night*, Act III, Sc.iv.)

King: I'll have prepared for him
    A chalice for the nonce;
        whereon by sipping
    If he by chance escape your
             venom'd stuck
    Our purpose may hold there
    (*Hamlet*, Act IV, Sc.vii.)

Successive Parries are two or more parries taken in succession and are the defence against compound attacks. The first parry is a reaction to the first feint, but is deceived by a further offensive action, so a second parry becomes necessary to meet the final of the attack. In the old days, this second offensive action might well turn out to be yet another feint, so that, quite commonly, three parries had to be executed before the attacker's blade was finally found.

There are but three parries – simple, semi-circular, or circular – though each may be executed in any line (high, low, inside or outside). Thus – and this is not always appreciated by beginners – successive parries *must* be composed of various permutations and combinations of the above three. The sole limiting factor is that when the defender's blade is in a high line, a feint by the attacker in a low line can hardly be met by anything other than a semi-circular parry; and vice versa.

It has also to be emphasised to the beginner that successive parries must follow each other in immediate succession, with no offensive action in between them; should a defender parry and riposte, be parried in his turn, and then be threatened by a counter-riposte, his parry of the latter most certainly does not constitute a successive parry. Likewise, should the defender, having first parried the attack, then parry a renewal of the attack, this last parry is usually considered to complete a double, not a successive, parry.

Sugaring Strawberries. Control and accuracy tend to suffer when several parries are executed in quick succession against an elaborate compound attack. Beginners especially allow the blade to fly out of line on one side or the other and to alter the height of the hand. This is particularly the case when effecting several rapid parries between *quarte* and *sixte*. There is the greatest danger that the hand will be lowered in *quarte* and raised in *sixte*; when there is a further tendency to pronate the hand as well when moving to the former position and supinate it in the latter, the whole process becomes so exaggerated as to be strongly reminiscent of a diner sprinkling sugar from a cruet over a plate of fruit.

Supination. The position of the sword-hand when the nails are on top and the knuckles below.

Supplementary Parry. The name given by some sabreurs – mostly those trained in the classic Italian school – to low *tierce*.

Swashbuckler. Defined by the Oxford Dictionary as a 'bully' or 'bravo', but colloquially the term is not infrequently used for any dashing, reckless swordsman, given to theatrical gestures. According to Fuller, the seventeenth-century antiquary and historian, the word was derived from the habit of swashing, or making a noise by striking a sword on a buckler.

176

Sweep of the Guard. The curved triangular part of the sabre guard, protecting hand and knuckles, which spreads outwards and downwards from the pommel to the top of the blade.

Swept Hilt. The name given to the interlocking ring guards found on many sixteenth-century rapiers.

Swingebuckler. Similar to Swashbuckler; a reckless, swaggering bully much given to duelling.
Shallow: John Doit of Staffordshire and black George Barnes and Francis Pickbone and Will Squele, a Cotswold man; you had not four such swingebucklers in all the Inns o'Court again! (*Henry IV, Part II*, Act III, Sc.ii.)

Sword. A generic term for any cutting or thrusting weapon palpably larger than a dagger and at the same time neither a hacking weapon like the axe, nor a staff weapon such as the spear or halberd. Latterly, the word has been used in a narrower sense as a literal translation of épée and therefore relating specifically to that particular weapon.

Sword, The. The official journal of the A.F.A., first issued quarterly in 1948.

Sword of Fashion. The small-sword.

Sword-in-Hand. A somewhat misleading term traditionally employed by fencing masters to describe the correct sabre grip which allows the blade movements to be controlled by finger-play; 'sword-in-fingers' might be rather more appropriate.

Sword-and-Lantern. A form of surprise attack delivered by footpads, assassins and other ruffians, the lantern being held in the unarmed hand and used to dazzle the victim. The practice was so common in Naples in the seventeenth and eighteenth centuries, that assaults of this sort were made a capital offence.

Swordsman, The. A book by Captain Hutton, adopted in 1896 by the Fencing Branch Committee of the Amateur Gymnastic and Fencing Association as the standard text on which to examine candidates for the Instructors' Certificate.

The guard of the Sword and Lantern opposed by the guard of the sword and cloak (from Angelo).

Szabo, Laszlo. The Hungarian who wrote *Fencing and the Master*, probably the first and only book addressed specifically to masters. Although his theories were hailed as revolutionary, Szabo is far from being a progressive in the bad sense of that word. He deplores the aggressive but technically incorrect modern style, with its forward rushes at such high speed that presidents are bluffed into allowing priority to them, even though executed with a bent arm; also, he grudgingly permits the use of the orthopaedic grip only to the most advanced fencers. Szabo attaches immense importance to the grip and has evolved all sorts of ingenious exercises with balls, rods and coins. As for those who ignore or condemn the classic rear arm position, he has no time for them at all.

Szabo believes in a combination of group instruction and individual lessons. He places considerable value on the former, but would be the first to admit that beyond a certain level, fencers can develop only by means of the individual lesson, and the individual lesson alone. After the primary stages, group instruction is supplemented by the pupil-master system, when, working in pairs on a pre-arranged exercise, each fencer in turn assumes the duties of the master; though, as has been observed elsewhere, the human material must be unusually reliable to hold the slightest prospect of success.

Szabo's system imposes considerable responsibility on the pupil, who is expected to think for himself and do a good deal of independent training. Shadow-fencing in front of a glass is recommended as useful in correcting faults and devising reactions to the reflections of the aggressive feints and movements. The fencer must impose severe mental discipline on himself. As a psychological stimulus during free play, he must concentrate to the extent of supposing each and every hit to be the decider in an Olympic final. One takes the point, but wonders if the result may not be over caution, tension and the gradual adoption of an altogether negative game. Szabo lays the utmost stress on the observation of the opponent and the prevention of the latter using his powers in this direction. Indeed, he recommends what appears to be almost a complete psycho-analysis of the adversary. This would be difficult enough during the hectic exchange of a modern bout, even were the latter to be of indefinite duration; when it is strictly limited to six minutes of actual fencing, the task must be regarded as beyond what is feasible.

There are several interesting features of Szabo's teaching. In the very early stages, he gives simultaneous instruction in foil and sabre; this develops loose shoulder muscles in the foilists and point control in the sabreurs. Some lessons and practices, under carefully controlled conditions, take place without masks. The eyes reveal much, and much can be learned by the master from facial expressions. Then, by practice in a seated position, the shoulder muscles may be relaxed; the posture of the trunk may be improved by receiving a lesson squatting.

Every imaginable aspect of the individual lesson is explored. The physiology and characteristics of the individual fencer are always to be considered by the master. Szabo is a great believer in regular short pauses for rest in the course of a lesson, which must undoubtedly endear him to the more languid type of pupil. Nor should a particular stroke ever be repeated more than half-a-dozen times – in sharp contrast to the tyrants of old who, so Bertrand assures us, demanded the repetition of the *molinello* with lunge one hundred times in rapid succession, optimistically assuming that the victim's stamina was such as to allow the ordeal to be concluded 'without undue fatigue'.

The pupil and then the assistant of the great Santelli, Szabo has coached an apparently endless succession of Hungarian World and Olympic champions. The honours and acclaim of numerous countries have rewarded this lifetime spent in both the practice and the deepest consideration and analysis of his chosen art. The honest critic, however, is bound to confess that his disquisition, like that of so many of his compatriots, is at times turgid and obscure.

Tableau. A list of competing fencers, for example, those who are in a series of bouts being fought by direct elimination.

Tagli. The term used by Fabris for the cut.

Tagliata, (It.). The cut-over.

Taille. The edge of the blade.

Tajo, (Span.). A cut.

Taken-Over Attack. To take, or recapture, the initiative by attacking an opponent who, by his rapid advance or threatening blade actions or other preparations, obviously has an offensive plan in mind.

Taking the Blade. (See Prise-de-Fer.)

Tang. The thin continuation of the blade which passes up through the *coquille*, inside the handle, and is secured in place by the locking-nut and pommel.

Tap Parry or Slinging Parry. Terms used by Barbasetti for what we should probably describe as the beat parry. From *sixte*, the point is swung across and down to meet an attack in *quarte*, the middle of the blades being the point of contact. The hand is pronated, but otherwise moves but little. Really, it appears to resemble a foil *quinte* parry, though he also recommends its use in *seconde* if the opposing blade is to be deflected downwards and outwards. According to Barbasetti, the tap parry is performed with 'the greatest possible momentum and violence' and is designed most thoroughly to remove the opponent's blade from anywhere near the line.

Target. 1) A small round shield, similar to the buckler.

2) That part of the body on which, in a bout, a valid hit can alone be scored. From quite an early period, the target area was traditionally confined to the trunk; the Tudor Masters of Defence prohibited hits below the waist. In the late seventeenth century, Sir William Hope declares the valid surface to run from beneath the neck to the waistband of the breeches, the sword-arm apparently being excluded. Writing in 1690, Labat specifically excludes the legs and arms; the valid area terminated at the armholes of the waistcoat, strongly reminiscent of the existing rules. At the turn of the eighteenth and nineteenth centuries, the legitimate area seems to have been even more limited. Joseph Roland's target was the right side of the breast only; otherwise, he says 'the art would fall quite into disuse'. That this convention was fairly standard practice is borne out by the circumstance of Domenico Angelo pinning Peg Woffington's roses to that part of his jacket and defying all his opponents at a fencing match to touch a single

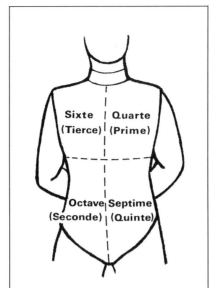

The foil Target and its quartering into lines.

Within the figure:
Sixte (Tierce) | Quarte (Prime)
Octave (Seconde) | Septime (Quinte)

petal. The younger Roland, George, was a little more liberal; he allowed all hits on the right side of the trunk between neck and waistband.

The target area today varies with the weapon concerned:

a) Foil. Broadly speaking, the target is confined to the trunk (including flanks and back), the head, limbs and mask being excluded. In 1912, the modern target, but minus the 'V' formed by the lines of the groins below the waist, was adopted. The 'V' was added a year later, for men only. It was not included for Ladies' Foil until the World Championships of 1955.

b) Epée. The target includes every part of the body and equipment, except, of course, the weapon itself.

c) Sabre. Practically every part of the body except the legs. (For more precise details, see A.F.A. *Rules and Regulations*.)

Target, The Advanced. At épée and sabre, the hand and sword-arm.

Target, Displacement of or Extension of. Ducking, sidestepping and lowering the body are permissible; but if a fencer at foil either deliberately or inadvertently covers a part of the valid target with a non-valid part (most probably, one or other arm, but conceivably the head might be lowered to protect the chest), any hit in such an area is nevertheless awarded. It is to be noted that this rule does not apply to the sword-arm covering the body in an accepted on-guard or parrying position.

Teillagory. A famous eighteenth-century French master and the teacher of both Angelo and d'Eon, he was reputed at one time to be the finest fencer in Europe. Part of his system was to encourage his pupils to fence with all comers, holding that it was essential to gain experience of different styles. Every fencer of correct technique is well aware of the difficulty of coping with the muscular, athletic novice, who charges in at close quarters, clawing at the blade with a heavy hand. With experience, gentry of this kidney can be worsted, but otherwise they can be highly disconcerting and maddeningly and undeservedly successful.

Tempist. A subtle fencer, always ready to take time or counter-time.

Tempo, (It.). (See Time.) Imre Vass defines *tempo* as 'the most suitable moment for the execution of any fencing movement'.

Tempo, Active and Passive. Barbasetti defines active *tempo* as preventing the finish of the opponent's action, e.g., the disengagement into *tempo*. Passive *tempo* consists of counter-attacks on the later stages of the opponent's action and must either forestall or evade the last blade movement of his attack, otherwise

179

a double hit results. Active *tempo* is therefore largely synonomous with an attack on the preparation; passive *tempo* includes the *coup d'arrêt* (stop-hit) and its several variations, such as the *inquartata, passata sotto, imbroccata, appuntata (remise)* and the counter-action or time-hit.

Tempo Comune, (It.). Simultaneous hits.

Tempo Indivisible, (It.). 'Indivisible time'; that is, no pause between parry and riposte.

Tempo Schermistico, (It.). (See Fencing Time.)

Tempo-Stealing, The. Gaining the time and opportunity to attack the opponent by means of patient footwork.

Temps d'Escrime. (See Fencing Time.)

Temps Perdu. 'Time Lost', e.g., a delay between two actions generally continuous, such as a parry and a riposte.

Temps Rompu. (See Broken Time.)

Tension. Bertrand's term for the time-hit.

Tente-Contra-Tente. In Blackwell's terminology, counter-time.

Tenteniac, Marquis de. A tiresome trouble-maker and dedicated duellist of Louis XV's reign. On one occasion, while watching a play from the wings as was still the practice of men of fashion, he edged sufficiently far forward to earn the loud and uncomplimentary rebukes of the audience. Instantly, he usurped the entire stage, haranguing the spectators

A successful attack to the advanced Target.

from the footlights and informing them that he would meet any of them on the morrow, 'in a piece entitled *The Insolence of the Pit Chastised*, of as many acts as may be necessary'. According to the account, no-one saw fit to punish his ill-bred swagger.

Terlin, Maître Jerome was the old fencing master in John Dickson Carr's *It Walks by Night*. His salle was in Paris at the angle of the *Etoile* and *Avenue de la Grande Armée*. It was a long room, the walls covered with weapons and trophies, dusty light stealing down from small windows high up in the roof. The old professor, wrinkled and clad in the master's traditional black, spoke only of swordsmen now ghosts, told anecdotes of Merignac and Conte and how, in the old days, they practised every day 'and they did not use buttons, either'. In these more modern times he himself taught but little; but under the lamplit gate and down the narrow alley still came the great names of the fencing world for gossip, a drink, and spectacular bouts of lightning speed and such skill that few hits were ever recorded.

Terz. The position of *tierce* in German *schlaeger* fencing.

Terza, (It.). *Tierce*.

Terza-Bassa, (It.). Low *tierce*.

Thames F.C. The club was opened in 1952 by Professor W. Harmar-Brown, who was for some time the national Epée Team coach and also enjoyed a long and successful reign as the master at Cambridge University. P. Jacobs was one of his particularly distinguished pupils. The club won the Savage Shield in 1969 and in 1977 amalgamated with London F.C.

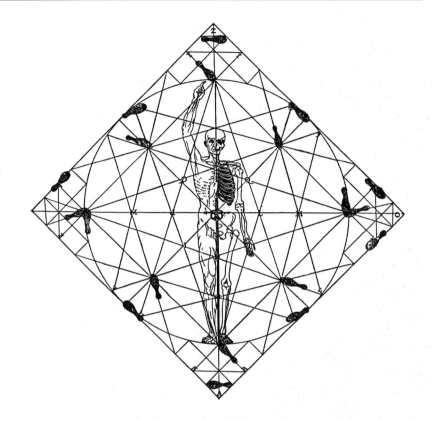

The very mysterious circle of Thibaust.

to form London-Thames.

Thibaust, Girard. A French master of the early seventeenth century when, probably owing to the marriage of Louis XIII to Anne of Austria, Spanish fashions reigned supreme, and there was even some attempt to introduce the elaborately futile and irrelevant theories of the Spanish school. Thibaust sought to develop and still further embellish the Spanish system, particularly those principles recommended by Narvaez. The basis of these was the 'mysterious circle'; Thibaust went even further than his predecessors in entirely arbitrary geometric theories and their supposed relationship to the various proportions of the human body. The general idea, somewhat simplified, was that the duellists faced each other on the diameter of the circle. This was either imaginary, or actually drawn on the ground for practice, and was of such dimensions that when on guard they were just out of reach of each other. If one of them moved round the circumference, the other, by a corresponding movement, could restore their relative position along another diameter. If, on the other hand, one moved into the circle along one of the innumerable chords drawn by the masters, he was within attacking distance of his opponent, but himself vulnerable to the stop-hit or time-hit. It was most dangerous to advance directly along the diameter, for that was tantamount to running onto the opposing point.

The lines, angles and chords in Thibaust's circle are fantastically complicated and he gravely affirms that the proper sequence of steps has only to be taken correctly for the defeat of the opponent to be logically and mathematically inevitable. It is extraordinary, as Egerton Castle has observed, that despite these palpable absurdities, the Spanish swordsmen of that era were universally respected and feared. Probably the explanation he offers is correct – schemes of such bewildering complexity demanded such constant and tenacious practice with a heavy sword that, even though they were never fully mastered, a purely empirical dexterity was attained, which stood its owner in good stead when theory was replaced by practice. Be this as it may, Thibaust's high reputation and his magnificently bound and illustrated book, the *Académie de l'Espée*, published in Leyden in 1628, gave a fresh lease of life to all these erroneous theories.

Third. (See *Tierce*.)

Third Manipulator. At sabre, the name given to the little finger of the sword-hand. In administering the cut, it assists the flexing of the wrist and the squeezing action of thumb and forefinger by an additional pressure on the handle at the moment of impact. A similar pressure also lends valuable strength to the parries, notably those of *prime*, *seconde* and *quinte*.

Thrown Hit. To hit by means of sliding the hand back along the handle in the course of the attack, so,

in effect, lengthening the weapon. The fencer may hold the weapon by any part of the handle, and is even permitted to alter his grip during the course of a bout, but is forbidden to do so once an offensive action has been started.

Thrust in Tempo. To attack the opponent when he pauses on a feint or otherwise hesitates and delays the completion of his own attack.

Thrusting at the Wall. (See Tirer au Mur.)

Thumb-Ring. A ring sometimes found below the *quillons* in German weapons as an additional means of grasping the sword firmly. It was not the same thing as the *anneau*.

Tiefquart. The position of low *quarte* in German *schlaeger* fencing; a parry seldom used, as attacks in the low lines were generally prohibited in these encounters.

Tierce. The third position and parry, protecting the upper right-hand side of the body. During the seventeenth century it passed under a variety of names – *seconde pour le dessus* was not uncommon – and it was Le Perche in *L'Exercice des armes ou le Maniement du fleuret* (1635) who first definitely assigned the name *tierce* to this position. The blade position is identical to *sixte* (hand breast-high, in line with shoulder, point at opponent's eye-level) but the hand is in pronation which supposedly adds strength to the parry. Virtually obsolete at foil, *tierce* and low *tierce* play a very important part in sabre fencing.

Tierce Medium. (See Quarte Medium.)

Tierce en Seconde. Besnard's definition of an attack from the position of

seconde with the hand pronated. If the hand was in supination, he called it *quarte en seconde*.

Tige. The *ricasso*.

Time. A term of somewhat wide and imprecise significance; in England today, generally limited to 'fencing time', i.e., the period of time taken to perform any one action of blade, arm or foot. It has nothing to do with 'clock' time and clearly varies considerably from one individual to another; it will even vary from one moment to another in the same individual, according to the state of his fitness, fatigue and so on. Originally, in the Franco-Italian schools of the seventeenth century, time was used in the sense of 'gaining time', i.e., executing a successful counter-attack which arrested or deflected the opponent's offensive action. In those days, this was very frequently effected by what amounted to a time-hit, or in the latest parlance, a stop-hit with opposition, although in this case a full period of fencing time, in the strict sense defined above, could not be gained.

The term was also used, and still is at times used, to describe the art of attacking an opponent who is preoccupied with some movement of his own, such as a step, a change of line, etc.

Time Attack. Typical of the traditional Italian school, an attack delivered against an opponent who was himself attacking, preparing to do so, or concentrating on some movement of his own. It frequently took the form of a time-hit, but not necessarily so.

Time-Cut. 1) Professor L. Bertrand's term for a stop-cut at sabre.

2) Castello defines it more exactly as a counter-attack at arm, followed by

an immediate step backwards with the parry and in conclusion the riposte. This tactic, he warns, should be used with circumspection, but it is essential against the sabreur who advances with a great many rapid feints which it is not possible to follow.

Time Disengagement Thrust. To attack by a disengagement on the opponent's attempt to take or attack the blade.

Time-Hit. A form of counter-attack; the attacker's blade is intercepted and deflected while the counter-attacker extends his arm and places the point on the target. It is, in fact, a simultaneous parry and riposte. The name is somewhat misleading, as, quite clearly, a period of fencing time is not gained on the attacker. In recent years, the time-hit has been re-christened the 'covered stop-hit' or the 'stop-hit with opposition'; formerly the term was not infrequently used when referring to the stop-hit.

Time-Hit, Offensive. Professor Crosnier's term for offensive counter-time. A feint is executed to draw the opponent's stop-hit, which is then controlled by a combined *prise-de-fer* and straight-thrust.

Time-Thrust or Time-Touch. 1) The same stroke as the time-hit.

2) Lukovitch uses the term for a stop-hit 'with a cadence in hand', i.e., a stop-hit without opposition which arrives before the opponent starts the final action of his attack, which therefore, at least in theory, could never be delivered at all.

3) Others have agreed with Lukovitch; in a word, when these masters speak of the time-thrust or time-hit, they mean what we understand by the stop-hit. There is certainly much

Time-Thrust with a pass under the opponent's blade (from Alfieri).

reason in this; for the stop-hit, to be valid, must gain a period of fencing time on the adversary's attack, whereas the time-hit, or stop-hit with opposition, deflects the opponent's attack in its final stage, and therefore, by definition, cannot gain time on it.

Tin-Tack. Fencer's slang for the single *pointe d'arrêt* on the pre-electric épée. According to Crosnier, it could be extremely dangerous.

Tip-Toe Stance, The. Arises from the habit of many modern fencers of advancing and retiring at great speed, which they seek to increase by moving much more on their toes than with the more flat-footed steps of an earlier era.

Tirailleur. Literally, a sharp-shooter or skirmisher; but in fencing parlance, a term used in days gone by to describe a heavy-handed, unskilful swordsman.

Tirare in Moto, (It.) was the term used by Pallavicini, an Italian master of the seventeenth century, for a thrust delivered on an opponent's feint – in other words, a counter-attack.

Tirer au Mur. Originally a method of practising the lunge, either with a colleague or a master; generally by means of a disengagement at the upper right-hand side of the opponent's trunk, executed slowly and with the most meticulous attention to style and precision of technique. By the twentieth century, the practice lunge was generally made at a padded target fixed to the wall. Sometimes it was adorned with a small red heart, or divided into areas on each of which the point had to be placed in turn. Some traditionally minded masters were said to compel their pupils to concentrate on this alone for periods of anything up to eighteen months, before they received the simplest lesson, let alone attempted free play. Whatever may have been the competitive qualities of the fencers of those days, their technique was clearly far superior to that of most of their modern successors.

Tirer de Pied Ferme. The lunge, in which the rear foot remains in place, not brought forward as in the older 'pass'.

Tocada, (Span.) and **Toccata** (It.). A hit.

Tocchi di Spada, (It.). Blade-sense. (See Sentiment du Fer.)

Tocco, (It.). A touch or hit.

Toledo. The Spanish town famed above all others for the superb quality of its sword-blades. Innumerable literary references bear witness to its pre-eminence.

'I give him three years and a day
    to match my Toledo,
And then we'll fight like dragons.'
(Massinger: *The Maid of Honour*, Act II, Sc.ii.)
'Walk into Moorfields – I dare look on your Toledo.'

(Massinger: *The City Madam*, Act I, Sc.ii.)
This excellence was imputed to some unique property of the local water into which the red-hot blades were plunged.

Tondo, (It.). A horizontal cut.

Tongue. The stout strip of fabric, enclosing a wire frame, which extends from the top of the mask down the back of the fencer's head. All masks are now the same size for adults, but by bending the tongue, a certain amount of adjustment is possible.

Touch or Touché. A rather old-fashioned term for a hit. *Touché* is the cry traditionally given by fencers when they have been hit. To acknowledge a hit, more especially in friendly bouts or during informal practice, is an old and honourable tradition.

Tour du Bretteur, Le. Labat's derisive name for a blade with an exaggerated bend; Mahon's suggested translation was the 'bully's blade'.

Tournament. In the strict sense, a tournament is constituted by more than one fencing competition taking place on the same occasion.

An early but ingenious variation of the Tirer au Mur (from Ficher).

Townsend, F.H. was a member of the British épée teams in the early years of the century, including the first official entry to the International Cup at Paris in 1904. He was also an artist of note and an article introducing his fencing illustrations appears in *The Sword* of April, 1987.

Tramazone, (It.). (See Stramazone.)

Transfer. The Hungarian term for a *prise-de-fer*.

Transition. A movement of the blade from one position to another.

Transition Rapier. The weapon which began to make its appearance about the middle of the seventeenth century, intermediate in the development from the long Italian rapier of the previous century to the small-sword of the eighteenth. It was kept sharp at the edges, less for the purpose of cutting than to prevent its being seized in the disarming routines discussed and recommended by all contemporary fencing masters.

Transport. To take the opponent's blade from one position to another. (Hungarian School.)

Transporto di Ferro, (It.). The transport.

Trattegio, (It.). Finger-play.

Traverse. 1) To move the blade from one guard position to another, especially in connection with the backsword and the spadroon.
2) The *volte* or *inquartata*.
3) According to Hutton, to shift one's feet side-ways; in traversing to the left, the left foot moves first and vice versa.

Tredgold, Dr. R. He was the editor of *The Sword* when the periodical first appeared in 1948. As a foilist and sabreur, he fenced for Britain at foil when still up at Cambridge and represented his country at both weapons in the 1936 Olympics. He was second to René Paul in the Foil Championship of 1947. However, sabre was his strong suit; considering his great height, he was an astonishingly quick mover and in no championship held between 1934 and 1963 did he fail to reach the final, winning in 1937 and 1939 and achieving a hat-trick in the three events from 1947 to 1949. He was to enjoy one more success, in 1955, and the title only just eluded him the following year when he was the runner-up.

Trenck, Baron Franz von. An Austrian nobleman who joined the Army as an ensign in 1727, and soon became notorious as a gambler and a duellist. During the War of the Austrian Succession (1740–48), he organised and commanded some fearsome irregular units, recruited to a great extent in Hungary and known as 'Pandours'. These pandours soon became totally out of hand and inflicted such atrocities on friend and foe alike that they had to be disbanded and their leader arrested and imprisoned. After languishing in gaol for a time, the Baron committed suicide by poison in 1749.

Trial by Combat. In Saxon times, a favourite method of resolving criminal cases was the Ordeal, which might take various forms. There was the 'corsnaed', a chunk of bread and cheese which had to be swallowed whole; if the accused choked, he was guilty. Clearly much depended on whether the official who prepared the morsel was sympathetic or open to corruption. In the water ordeal, the prisoner was tied up and placed on the surface of a pond or river. If he floated, he was guilty; if he proved his innocence by sinking, he was at best half-drowned and quite possibly completely so. After the ordeal of the red-hot iron or boiling water, the hands of the victim were inspected three days later. If they had healed in the interval, he was acquitted. To these, the Normans added a further variation – Ordeal or Trial by Battle, which is of interest as the forerunner of the duel. As time passed, a distinction was drawn between civil and criminal cases; in the former, the parties might be represented by champions, often professionals known as 'pugils', who made it a career of sorts. In cases of felony, a personal appearance was demanded with the exception of women and disabled ex-servicemen. The introduction and gradual development of the jury under Henry II led to the decline of the system and by the late twelfth century it was obsolescent. The last 'Wager of Battle' in a civil action was in 1571; even then, it seems to have been greeted with astonishment. Matters never came to a head, as the *appellant* failed to appear in the lists. Private accusations of treason were by custom transferred to the Court of Chivalry, the weapons which it prescribed for use being both formidable and antiquated – the long-sword, short-sword and battle-axe. The last case of this sort was that of *Rea* v. *Ramsey* (1632). Once again, however, the affair proved abortive, Charles I dissolving the court before the appointed day. The final attempt to demand trial by combat in a criminal case was as late as 1818, when in *Ashford* v. *Thornton* the accusation was one of murder. Nothing came of it in the end, but Lord Ellenborough, the Lord Chancellor, declared the challenge legitimate enough, trial by battle never having been legally abolished, and still in theory, therefore, the law of England. To put the matter beyond doubt, a Parliamentary statute was passed the following year formally declaring the custom to be at an end.

Triangles of Defence. The alternative systems of defence at sabre are, for no very ascertainable reason, known as 'triangles'. The first triangle consists of the parries of *prime*, *seconde* and *quinte*, *prime* and *seconde* protecting respectively the left- and right-hand side of the body against cuts delivered in a vertical plane. The second triangle consists of the parries of *tierce*, *quarte* and *quinte*, the first two protecting respectively the right- and left-hand side of the body against cuts delivered in a lateral plane. *Quinte* is common to both triangles, as the only parry protecting the head, the old sabre parry of *sixte* now being obsolete.

There has recently appeared the practice in some quarters of transposing the title 'first' and 'second'; this makes sense, as beginners nearly always find *tierce* and *quarte* easier to master, and accordingly have for long been taught them initially.

Triangular Tournament. The traditional Anglo-Scottish match became 'triangular' when Ireland became the third country to participate. (See Quadrangular.)

Trinder, O.G. enjoyed a long run of success and was seemingly almost invincible at sabre in the Britain of the early thirties. He was champion four times (1930, 1931, 1933, 1934) second in 1929, 1932 and 1935, and third on three occasions.

Triplé. The *triplé* includes one more feint than the *doublé*, and is thus composed, following the initial feint
186

of disengagement, of two counter-disengagements. Hence this compound attack deceives two successive circular or counter-parries.

Trompement. The evasion of the opponent's parry or parries in the course of executing a compound attack.

Trovare di Spada, (It.). 'To find the blade'; to make contact with, or engage the blades.

Tuck. (See Stock.) Before the farcical duel between those two very reluctant principals, Sir Andrew Aguecheek and Viola (disguised as a youth), Sir Toby Belch encourages the latter thus: 'Dismount thy tuck, be yare in thy preparation, for thy assailant is quick, skilful and deadly.' (Shakespeare: *Twelfth Night*, Act III, Sc.iv.)

Turquet, Dr. P.M. A Cambridge half-blue and sometime captain of Britain's foil and sabre teams, he was Sabre Champion of this country only once (1951), but took the second place on three occasions, 1937, 1939 and 1950. He was second in the Foil Championship of 1939. He participated in three Olympics (1948, 1952, 1956) and each World Championship during that same period. For the A.F.A., he filled several offices, including that of treasurer.

Twiddle. A facetious nickname for the circular parry.

Twist. The *croisé*.

Two-Time. An offensive action executed in two periods of fencing time. Normally it is incorrect, as it incurs the risk of a successful stop-hit before the start of the second movement. Not to be confused with *en deux temps* or *dui tempi*, both of

which were phrases used in the earlier French and Italian schools respectively for a distinctly separate parry and riposte.

Tybalt. A character in Shakespeare's *Romeo and Juliet*, a kinsman of the house of Capulet, eventually killed in a duel with Romeo. According to Mercutio's description of him, which is of interest as including several technical terms of the contemporary school of rapier-play, he was a typical swordsman of the new school, 'keeping time, distance and proportion. One, two, and the third in your bosom.' His point control was evidently admirable – 'the very butcher of a silk button'. The ebullient Mercutio ends his sarcastic eulogy on a climax – 'the immortal *passado*, the *punto reverso*, the HAY!' (Act II, Sc.iv.) The last was the shout of exultation as the point was driven home. Tybalt was subsequently denounced by the dying Mercutio, mortally wounded in an encounter with him, as 'a rogue, a villain, that fights by the book of arithmetic'. (Act III, Sc.i.)

Ulnar Flexion, (U.S.). Bending the wrist so that the little finger of the sword-hand is nearer the forearm, and the point thereby angulated downwards.

Under-Counter. (See Hope, Sir William.)

Under-Plastron. A protective undergarment of hemp or nylon covering the flank, chest and upper arm, formerly used at épée only. Partly because of the stiffer electric foil, and partly, no doubt, because of the shock tactics at close quarters, the under-plastron has, since 1964, been obligatory for all three weapons.

Under Stop-Thrust. The *passata sotto*.

Universal Nut or **Screw**. (See Locking-Nut.)

Universal Parry. Just as the medieval alchemists searched endlessly and unavailingly for the Elixir of Life and the Philosopher's Stone, so the swordsmen of the sixteenth and early seventeenth centuries fondly believed that it was possible to devise an infallible parry, effective against any and every attack. Several of these universal parries are described in the instruction manuals of those days; they all bear a close resemblance to one another, consisting basically of a very wide, sweeping semicircular parry, starting from high *tierce* and describing a gigantic capital 'C' in the air, to terminate in a low *seconde*. Unless the executant is quite blatantly at fault in timing or distance, it must even now be virtually foolproof against any simple attack, particularly one delivered wide, or with a heavy hand. Its weakness is, of course, that it is quite easily deceived by a compound attack. However, with the present-day decline in *finesse*, the universal parry might well come into its own again.

Unnamed Parry. Mentioned in a mysterious passage in Szabo's *Fencing and the Master*. It is described as a combination of *sixte* and high *septime*, to be used against cut-overs in the high lines; an odd combination it must be, as the two parries mentioned are on diametrically opposite sides of the target.

Valdin, M. The French fencing master of the second Duke of Montagu. One innovation in his *Art of Fencing* (1729), was his emphasis on limbering-up exercises and footwork before the novice was ever allowed to handle a weapon.

Valeria, Diego de. A Spanish swordsman of the late fifteenth

The Volte — the left hand is being used as additional protection (from Ficher).

century whose *Treatise on Arms* was one of the earliest works to deal with fencing as both a science and an art.

Varieties of Attack. The highly misleading name which, until quite recently was given to renewed attacks. As Crosnier justly observes, varieties of renewed attack would surely have been more appropriate; but in any case, the term has now been dropped out of use, at any rate in this country.

Vass, Imre. A most distinguished Hungarian épée master, who has published a highly detailed and meticulously analysed scheme of teaching that weapon, *Epée Fencing*. Its one drawback is that owing to differences in terminology and possibly some inaccuracies in translation, the western European finds some passages a little obscure and hard to follow.

Vauclousant or Vouclosant. Obscure and archaic names for the *passata sotto*.

Venie or Veney. A sixteenth-century English term for a hit.

Verdun. A sixteenth-century duelling sword with dagger to match; so called from the town of its origin. So excessively long were these weapons that it is said that not infrequently they were carried behind the owner by his servant.

Vigeant. An eminent Parisian master and fencing bibliographer of the late nineteenth century.

Viggiani, Angelo. A sixteenth-century Italian master, who somewhat cautiously advocated the lunge, in certain circumstances, in preference to the pass.

Volant, (It.). Flying feints. (q.v.)

Volte. A method of effacing the target by swinging the rear leg backwards and sideways to the fencer's right, so that the trunk is brought more or less parallel to the line of attack. (See Inquartata.) As the eighteenth century advanced, it fell into disfavour and by the nineteenth, was absolutely condemned by the French school, all defensive actions being then executed with the blade alone.

Volte-Coupe. Sir William Hope's name for a feint in one line, followed by a thrust in the line directly opposite, e.g., feint high in *quarte*, thrust in *octave/seconde*. The etymology of the term baffles all attempts at elucidation.

Vote. A full jury includes a president and four judges, two at either end of the *piste*, whose duty it is to signal and decide the validity of hits on the fencer facing and opposite to them. Each judge has one vote, the president one and a half. Hence, if both judges are in agreement, they can, if necessary, over-rule the president. If, however, one of them abstains altogether, it is quite clear that with one and a half votes against one, the decision rests with the president. Should the judges differ, their affirmative and negative votes cancel out, so again it is the president who must decide.

Waite, J.M., Corporal-Quartermaster of the Second Life Guards, was well known as a sabre master in the second half of the nineteenth century, at a time when even the fencing sabre was a formidable and heavy weapon compared with the light Italian version shortly afterwards introduced by Magrini to this country.

Waiting Cut. Beke and Polgar advise that, following an attack which is parried, the sabreur should remain with his blade still in position, ready for another action, offensive or defensive, the moment his opponent moves.

Walking Sword. Any type of sword suitable for personal use in the days when it was customary for a gentleman to wear one. The term probably derives not only from the circumstance that it was worn when its owner walked abroad, but in contrast to the much heavier, edged sword in use among the military, and hence associated with the mounted man.

Wall Target. (See Tirer au Mur.) Szabo particularly recommends the use of wall targets for practising close-quarter attacks.

Ward. An archaic term for a parry.

Wardell-Yerburgh, Mrs J. (née Bewley-Cathie) dominated ladies' foil in the sixties much as Miss Sheen and Mrs Glen-Haig had done a decade earlier. She was champion four times in succession (1969-72) and won the championship six times in all, only Miss Sheen with the record ten wins having exceeded this; she was also second in three consecutive years (1962-4). Mrs Wardell-Yerburgh likewise carried off the Silver Jubilee Bowl three times in succession and seven times in all (even Miss Sheen had to be content with winning this trophy five times) and was second on another occasion. All the domestic trophies fell to her repeatedly; the Desprez Cup six times, four between 1964 and 1967, then again in 1969 and 1972. She won the C.-L. de

Beaumont cup thrice and was second once. She won the Ladies' Foil at the Commonwealth Games of 1970 in Edinburgh. Resolute in temperament and showing outstandingly strong and effective bladework, she was supposed to be a little too slow on her feet to match Miss Sheen's triumphs at the highest international level.

Warning Lines. Lines drawn at either end of the *piste* and at right angles to it, one metre from the rear limit for foil, two metres for épée and sabre. When a retreating fencer reaches or crosses the warning line at foil the bout is halted, and he is replaced on guard with his rear foot on the warning line, being advised of his position. (See Piste for épée and sabre.)

Warnings. 1) A warning is given by the president to the fencers one minute before the expiration of the time allotted to their bout.

2) As in most sports, disciplinary problems have multiplied in fencing of late years and it has regrettably been considered necessary to elaborate the system of giving warnings to offending competitors. There are now three separate categories of warning which may be issued by the president.

a) Minor. On the repetition of the offence during the same bout, one hit is deducted from the culprit's score, or alternatively the annulment of an otherwise valid hit made in the course of his impermissible action; should he not yet have scored, his first valid hit thereafter is annulled.

b) Severe. This holds good for the duration of that bout and a repetition of the offence is punished by the award of a penalty hit.

c) Special. This holds for the pool, match, later bouts fought by direct elimination, and the final. On the first repetition, the offender's hit, if any, is annulled as well as a penalty hit being awarded against him. On a second repetition, the punishment is exclusion from the competition.

For the application of the several warnings to the various categories of offence, the A.F.A. *Rules for Competitions* should be consulted.

Waster. A wooden sword used for practice in Elizabethan times.

Waterloo Duels. During the allied occupation of Paris, following Napoleon Bonaparte's downfall in the summer of 1815, numberless challenges were made by the rancorous officers of the disbanded Imperial Army, who were alleged to spend their days practising, and whose fencing masters were accused of sometimes donning uniform so as to lure unwary members of the victorious forces into a probably fatal duel. The British, however, unlike the Austrians and Prussians, not infrequently had the best of it; for the typical British officer of that period, though notoriously ignorant of sword-play, was equally devoid of fear, and generally charged recklessly at his opponent, as often as not spitting him before he could reap the advantage of his superior skill.

Weapon Captain. The individual supervising the training and preparations of those fencers listed as eligible for selection for the Olympics and other important international events at each of the three weapons. The system was inaugurated by the A.F.A. in 1935.

Weapon Control Office. At F.I.E. Championships, all clothing and equipment intended to be used must be checked beforehand by the controlling officials; all items passed are marked as legitimate and no others may be used without incurring penalties of varying degrees of severity.

Welsh Amateur Fencing Union. Established in 1947. Wales won the Quadrangular tournament in 1977 and the Winton Cup in 1980. The Welsh Open Championship has attracted ever greater numbers since its inception in 1972.

Wheel Pommel. A disc-shaped (later fig-shaped) pommel found on certain medieval swords.

Whiffle. Similar to a waster. The attendants, armed in this way, who escorted the Mayor of Norwich on his induction, were known as 'whifflers'.

Whip-Over. A sophisticated version of the *molinello* (parry of *prime*, riposte by cut-over). The action, however, is exaggerated. The trunk is pivoted until the shoulders, hips and elbow are parallel with the line of attack. The weapon, which takes the attacking blade *forte* to *foible* in the usual way, is also parallel to the line of attack, almost horizontal and with the point directed to the rear. The point is then brought over the opposing blade with a very pronounced use of the wrist, the entire action being combined into one very rapid movement rather in the style of the flying cut-over.

Whirl, The. A circular blade action prescribed for sabre practice by Castello. Holding the weapon at arm's length, it is rotated from the elbow in a vertical orbit, either backwards or forwards. The action which terminates in the downward cut would appear to bear a marked similarity to the *molinello*. Also, cuts from left to right can be delivered following a

189

horizontal circling of the blade in either direction.

Wilkinson Swords must be the best-known blades manufactured in this country. The company was founded in 1772 and supplies ceremonial swords to the armed forces, including the Swords of Honour to Sandhurst, Cranwell and the Royal Navy. Swords of Peace are awarded annually to each unit of the three services adjudged to have made the greatest contribution and assistance to society in general. In addition, many special swords have been forged, notably the Stalingrad sword bestowed on that city in recognition of its heroic defence against the Nazi hordes, the Arnhem sword and the Falklands swords presented to the two commanders in that campaign. The company also sponsored invitation foil and sabre championships for under-eighteen fencers, the winners receiving valuable assistance in further coaching and training.

World Fencing Championships are held in years when there are no Olympics. At their inception in 1921, they were known as the European Championships, fencing being practically unknown outside that continent. There were no team events until 1929, when men's foil teams made their appearance. The next year saw team and individual events at all weapons. Ladies' individual foil was introduced at the same time, and ladies' teams in 1933. Ladies' foil teams did not participate in the Olympics until 1960; hence, until then, there was a team championship for ladies even in Olympic years. In 1936, with the steady diffusion of fencing, the present title of the championships was adopted.

Wrapping It Up. Fencing slang for the envelopment.
190

The Zweyhander (from Alfieri).

Wrist Flexion. 1) Pronating or supinating the hand by turning the wrist.
2) Castello restricts the term to the supination of the hand and adds that the point is 'simultaneously angulated to the fencer's left'.

Wrist Hyperextension. Directing the point upwards or downwards by 'breaking' or angulating the wrist. Again Castello's definition differs: the hand is pronated and the point directed outwards.

Wylde, Zachary. In his *English Master of Defence* (1711), he employs several unusual terms not, so far as is known, to be found elsewhere:
Dexter – the outside guard (the fencer's right-hand side).
Sinister – the inside guard (the fencer's left-hand side).
Diameter – St George's guard (sabre *quinte*).
Unicorn – medium guard. It would be fascinating to know the derivation of this; possibly the blade, projecting upwards from the centre of the fencer's body, suggested, to a lively imagination, a unicorn's horn.

Yielding Parry. The ceding parry.

York, Roland. A 'desperado', alleged by Abraham Darcie in *The Annals of Elizabeth* to have introduced the 'wicked and pernicious' Italian rapier to this country.

Zorro or 'The Fox', was the hero of John McCulley's *The Curse of Capistrano*, on which more than one film was based, depicting the adventures of a master swordsman in the California of the early nineteenth century. In the 1938 version, *The Mark of Zorro*, the title role was taken by Tyrone Power, who played it rather in the style of the Red Shadow in *The Desert Song*; a mincing, effeminate fop, who, in disguise after dark, performed incredible feats of agility and heroism, his aim being to liberate Los Angeles from the brutal tyranny of the governor, Don Quintero, and his villainous henchman, Captain Pasquale (Basil Rathbone). The climax of the film was the duel between Diego Vega (Zorro) and Pasquale, a spectacular bout with the sabres. The most effective touch occurred during the preliminaries. After making several impressively elaborate flourishes in the air with his weapon, Pasquale extinguished the flames of half-a-dozen candles with unerring thrusts with the point. Zorro, daunted by nothing, imitated exactly the aerial sword-play, thrust at another candle – and the flame burnt on. The Captain gave a jeering laugh and then his face abruptly turned blank as Zorro calmly removed the tops of the candles, which he had neatly sliced off, without dislodging them from the stumps. All quite impossible, but a brilliant *coup de théâtre* which delighted the audiences.

Zweyhander. The German two-handed sword.

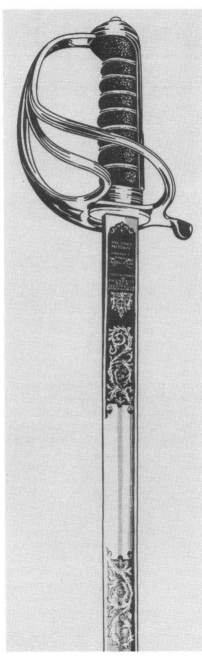

A Wilkinson Sword, Royal Artillery.

A Select Bibliography

Aylward, J.D.	*The House of Angelo*	Batchworth Press, London, 1953.
	The English Master of Arms	Routledge and Kegan Paul, London, 1956.
	The Small-Sword in England	Hutchinson, London 1960.
Ed. 8th Duke of Beaufort	*The Badminton Library of Sports and Pastimes*	Longmans, Green and Co., London, 1897.
Baldick, R.	*The Duel*	Shenval Press, London, 1965.
Barbasetti, L.	*The Art of the Foil*	Hutchinson and Co., London.
de Beaumont, C.-L.	*Modern British Fencing*	Hutchinson's Library of Sports and Pastimes, London, 1949.
	Modern British Fencing, 1948–1956	Edward Hulton, London, 1958.
	Modern British Fencing, 1957–1964	Nicholas Kaye, London, 1966.
	Fencing Techniques in Pictures	Hulton Press, London, 1955.
	Fencing, Ancient Art, Modern Sport	Nicholas Kaye, London, 1960.
Beke and Polgar	*The Methodology of Sabre Fencing*	Corvina Press, Budapest, 1963.
Bertrand, L.	*Cut and Thrust*	Athletic Publications, London, 1927.
	The Fencer's Companion	Gale and Polder, Aldershot, 1934.
Castello, J.M.	*The Theory and Practice of Fencing*	Charles Scribner's Sons, New York and London, 1933.
Castle, Egerton	*Schools and Masters of Fence*	Arms and Armour Press, London, 1969.
Crosnier, Roger	*Fencing with the Foil*	Faber and Faber, London, 1951.
	Fencing with the Sabre	Faber and Faber, London, 1954.
	Fencing with the Epée	Faber and Faber, London, 1958.
	Fencing with the Electric Foil	Faber and Faber, London, 1961.
Encylopaedia Britannica	1912 edition. Article on Fencing.	

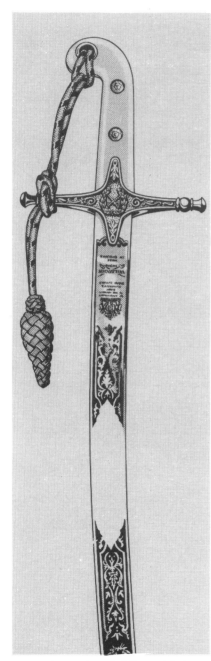

A Wilkinson Sword; Officer's Scimitar

Evered, D.F.	*Sabre Fencing*	Duckworth, London, 1982.
Granger, Stewart	*Sparks Fly Upward*	Granada Publishing, St. Albans and London, 1981.
Gray, Edmund	*Modern British Fencing, 1964–81*	Amateur Fencing Association, London, 1984.
Hepp, Dr. F.	*Sports Dictionary in Seven Languages*	Gyorgy, Budapest, 1960.
Hett, G.V.	*Fencing*	Pitman and Sons, London, 1939.
Higham, C. and Greenberg, J.	*Hollywood in the Forties*	Tantivy Press, London and New York, 1968.
Hutton, Alfred	*Cold Steel*	Clowes and Son, London, 1889.
	The Swordsman	H. Grevel and Co., London, 1891.
	Old Swordplay	Greval and Co., London, 1892.
	The Sword and the Centuries	Grant Richards, London, 1901.
Kobal, John	*Romance of the Cinema*	Studio Vista, 1973.
Lloyd and Robinson	*Movies of the Silent Years*	Orbis, London, 1984.
Lukovitch, Istvan	*Electric Foil Fencing*	Corvina Press, Budapest, 1971.
Mitford, Nancy	*Madame de Pompadour*	Sphere Books Ltd., London, 1970.
Nobbs, P.E.	*Fencing Tactics*	Philip Alan, London, 1936.
Penotti	*Il Fioretto*	Rome, 1966.
Pepys, Samuel	*Diary*	George Bell and Sons, London, 1894.
Stoker, Bram	*Personal Reminiscences of Henry Irving*	2 vols., William Heinemann, London, 1906.
Szabo, Laszlo	*Fencing and the Master*	Corvina Press, Budapest, 1977.
Vass, Imre	*Epée Fencing*	Corvina Press, Budapest, 1965.